ALBERTA

Featured stories by Fred Stenson
"Partners in Progress" by Ron Shewchuk and Sandy Dawson
Produced in cooperation with the Alberta Chamber of Commerce
Windsor Publications (Canada) Ltd., Burlington, Ontario

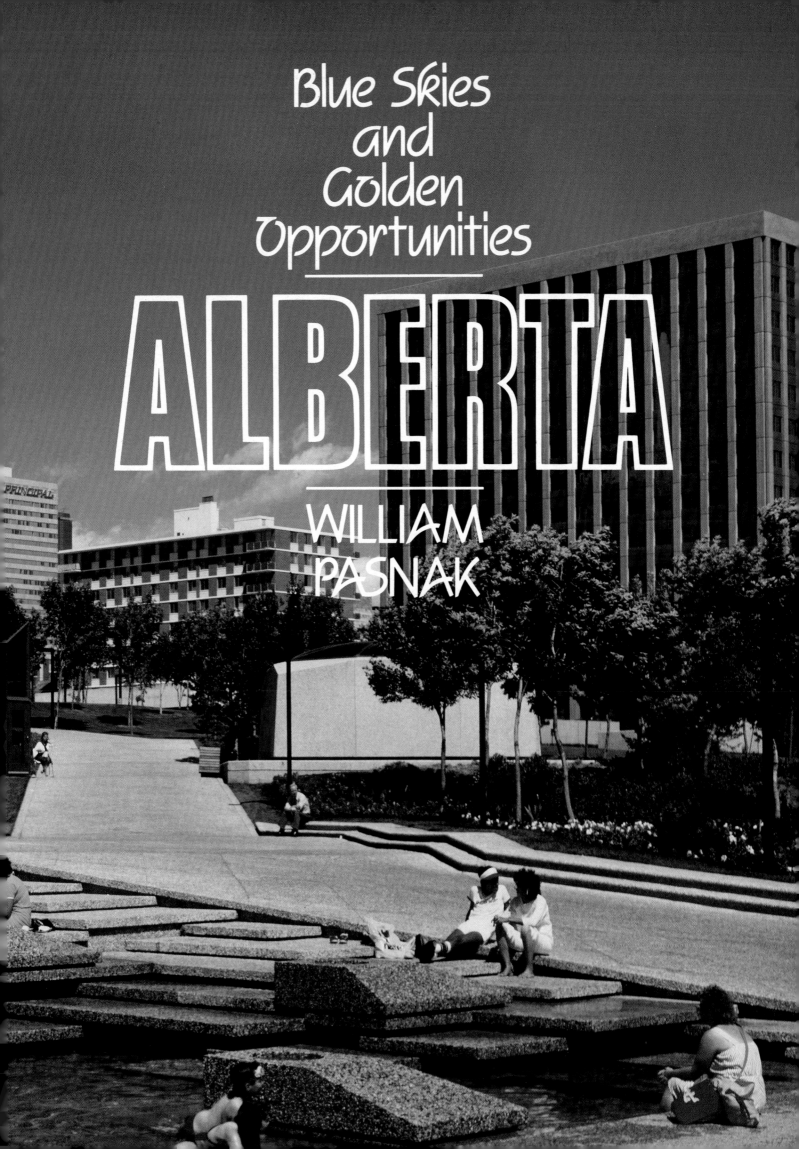

Blue Skies
and
Golden
Opportunities

ALBERTA

WILLIAM PASNAK

Windsor Publications, Inc.—History Books Division
Managing Editor: Karen Story
Design Director: Alexander D'Anca

Staff for *Alberta: Blue Skies and Golden Opportunities*
Manuscript Editor: Amy Adelstein
Photo Editor: Lynne Ferguson Chapman
Assistant Director, Corporate Profiles: Phyllis Gray
Editor, Corporate Profiles: Judith Hunter
Senior Proofreader: Susan J. Muhler
Editorial Assistants: Didier Beauvoir, Thelma Fleischer, Alyson Gould, Kim Kievman,
    Michael Nugwynne, Kathy B. Peyser, Pat Pittman, Theresa Solis
Sales Representatives, Corporate Profiles: Clarence Jeans, Marty Martin, Maria Pender,
    Dun Petch, Eric Sinclair
Designer: Thomas Prager
Layout Artists, Corporate Profiles: Mari Catherine Preimesberger, Michael Burg
Layout Artist, Editorial: Christina Rosepapa

Elliot Martin, Chairman of the Board
James L. Fish, III, Chief Operating Officer
Hal Silverman, Vice-President/Publisher

◀ ◀ *The park in front of the Alberta Legislature Building in Edmonton is a favorite place for adults to relax and children to play on a summer day. Photo by Wes Bergen. Courtesy, Hillstrom Stock Photo*

▶ *Spruce trees covered with snow are lovely features of Alberta's winter landscape. Photo by Chris Bruun. Courtesy, Westfile, Inc.*

Contents

Photo by Dick Dietrich

Preface

Perhaps because they try to do it all the time, writers know better than anyone the impossibility of definitively describing anything. We always leave out more than we put in, and the better we know our subject, the more keenly we feel this lack. A biographer might attempt to do justice to a life in 100,000 words, only to come away shaking his head in frustration. I have tried to do justice to the lives of 2.5 million in less than half that space, and I am, quite frankly, not satisfied.

There have been, first of all, omissions. This book touches on major points about geography, history, business, and culture, but space permits only a general survey, with inevitable oversights. To those people, places, and institutions not recorded here, I offer my apologies. To the reader, I offer this suggestion: if you don't already live in Alberta, spend some time here, and draw your own conclusions.

There is, secondly, the problem of describing that which is alive and unfolding even as it is studied. This is particularly true of recent history. We can speak with some objectivity and perspective about events which took place 50 or 100 years ago; it is more difficult to speak with certainty about that which has happened in the past five years, such as the effects of the worldwide recession on our business climate. One difficulty is in obtaining recent statistics. Although the Alberta Bureau of Statistics may be only a few months behind in some indicators—for example, population estimates—in other areas, the gap may be more than a year. Statistics Canada is a source of much information, but some data are three years out of date by the time they are published.

Nevertheless, against these shortcomings, I must place my profound feeling for the subject. I was born and raised in Alberta, and I think it is a great place. Alberta, in my opinion, bears comparison with any place in the world, and if, in spite of its flaws, this book communicates *that* to its readers, I will have done my job.

◄ *Calgary, located at the edge of the prairies and less than an hour's drive from the Canadian Rockies, is a city known for its hospitality. Photo by Chris Bruun. Courtesy, Westfile, Inc.*

The Land

Begin with the size of it: if you stitched together France, Belgium, Holland, and Denmark, and tried to cover Alberta with your handiwork, you would still have a few square miles peeping out. In U.S. terms, you could quilt together the states of Louisiana, Mississippi, Alabama, Georgia, and Florida, and still need half a dozen Districts of Columbia to finish the job. Alberta is big.

The most westerly of the three prairie provinces, Alberta stretches from the 49th parallel, where it swaps tumbleweed and jackrabbits with Montana, north for more than 1,200 kilometres to the 60th parallel and the Northwest Territories. To the east, it borders Saskatchewan at 110 degrees west longitude. Westward, it goes as far as the 120th meridian where it meets British Columbia. The province would be a perfect rectangle if it were not for the southwest corner, where the border follows the peaks of the Rocky Mountains, the only acknowledgment its boundaries allow of anything as natural as rocks, trees, or water. In all, it adds up to 661.188 square kilometres, or 255,285 square miles, the fourth largest province in Canada.

But size isn't everything. What does Alberta look like?

That depends on where you start. Anthony Henday, the first European known to come here, crossed into what we call Alberta near the present-day town of Chauvin in September of 1754. He wandered westward for weeks through rolling grassland and parkland, across winding river valleys fringed with poplar, willow, and saskatoon, past herds of buffalo, and prairie potholes thick with ducks (and mosquitos!) until, on a height of land near Innisfail, he saw the blue and white fence of the Rocky Mountains in the distance. That is one view of Alberta known to many, although the buffalo no longer toss their heads and graze by Buffalo Lake.

If you start in the extreme southeast, though, you will find that the tawny grasslands are stiff and dry, that there is the scent of sagebrush in the air, and that the flat, heat-faded horizon is cut here and there by the rumpled line of a coulee, refuge for antelope, grouse, and the occasional basking rattlesnake.

In the west, beyond the foothills where the bony knees of the mountains begin to poke through the soil, you could start with the very mountains that Henday glimpsed, scarcely changed in the dozen or so generations since he was here. Folded in the steep-walled valleys, the spruce, pine, and juniper shelter squirrels, elk, black bears, whiskeyjacks, and a few elusive cougar. On the heights above, blinding white snowfields hold summer-awaiting fresh water and a centuries-long meditation on purity.

But if you begin your travels through the north, you will see the vast potential of this province: endless kilometres of spruce forest, broken here and there by muskeg, jack pine, and shallow lake. If you can travel at all here, you will go a long way before meeting another person. More likely acquaintances will be black bear, moose, and beaver. And, regrettably, mosquitos.

Or you could start in one of our cities, where your first impressions might be the tang of a local ale, the blur of neon, and the sound of jazz on a summer's night—or the glare of a laboratory and the concentrated silence of a white-coated researcher peering into a microscope.

In short, this enormous tract of land has many faces, both as an untamed wilderness and as a huge inventory of resources, human and natural. This book will try to offer a few of these for your appreciation.

◄ *The vast sky seems to overwhelm the prairie in this photo taken near Little Fish Lake in Alberta. Photo by Wilfried D. Schurig. Courtesy, Hillstrom Stock Photo*

▲ *The southwest boundary of Alberta is formed by the Rocky Mountains. Shown here is the Valley of Ten Peaks in Banff National Park. Photo by John Elk III*

▲ *The sun sets over the thriving city of Calgary. Photo by Ron Watts. Courtesy, First Light, Toronto*

▲ *A golden-mantled squirrel perches at the Bow Summit in Banff National Park on a morning in June. Photo by Jerg Kroener*

To understand the sprawling piece of real estate known as Alberta, we must first get to know it physically, or topographically. It is landlocked, of course, although rivers flow from Alberta to three sides of the continent. More than half of the province drains north, through the Peace, Athabasca, Slave, and Hay rivers, to Great Slave Lake, the Mackenzie River, and ultimately the Arctic Ocean. The Peace River, which carries the largest flow of all the rivers in Alberta, has carved a valley almost 300 metres deep, and a kilometre and a half wide in places, as it wanders through the fertile Peace River country. Downstream, where it meanders across Wood Buffalo National Park, it and the Athabasca have created a vast alluvial plain. Here, endless mudflats, shallow lakes, and muskeg extend over more than 9,000 square kilometres. Trees are found only on the slightly higher ground bordering the countless stream channels. When water levels are high, much of the area is submerged, but when they are low, impassable mudflats are exposed. Although not inviting to human habitation, this remarkable area is a great sanctuary for wildlife.

South of a northeast-southwest ridge running near Lac La Biche and Westlock, the province is almost completely drained by the Saskatchewan river system, which empties through Lake Winnipeg into Hudson Bay. Major rivers in the system are the Red Deer; the North Saskatchewan, which flows through Edmonton; the Bow, which passes

◀ *The Bow River belongs to the Saskatchewan River system, which empties through Lake Winnipeg into Hudson Bay. Photo by John Elk III*

▲ *Shown here is the confluence of the Peace River and the Smoky River. Photo by Wes Bergen. Courtesy, Hillstrom Stock Photo*

21

through Calgary; and the Oldman, which passes through Lethbridge. When the Oldman and the Bow meet, they become the South Saskatchewan. Most of the water carried in this system is meltwater from glaciers and mountain snowpack. During a wet year, run-off from the prairies may contribute as much as 30 percent of the volume, but in dry times, over 90 percent comes from the mountains. Naturally, this system is an important source of water for drinking, irrigation, and industry.

The final drainage basin is a thin sliver at the bottom of the province, drained by the Milk River. Downstream, this flow joins the Missouri, passes then to the Mississippi, and finally to the Gulf of Mexico. It is curious to throw a chip in the water at Writing on Stone Park, within sight of the hazy Sweet Grass Hills, and imagine that it might someday hit salt water beyond New Orleans. When we look at the geological history of Alberta, however, the evidence begins to fall into place. This part of the world has a long-standing connection with the sea—in all directions. And although we seldom think of the ocean today, it still affects our lives profoundly.

Alberta's geology falls into three easily distinguished regions. Along the southwest lie the folded and faulted strata of the cordillera. In the northeast corner, there is a small portion of the Precambrian or Canadian shield. All the rest is part of the sedimentary western plains region. The story of how these rocks came to their present form is not only interesting, but also helps explain how Alberta came to enjoy the resources it does today.

Although now walled off from the ocean by the Rocky Mountains, Alberta was under the sea's influence through much of its geological history. This area was repeatedly inundated, upthrust, eroded, and recovered with water and fresh deposits. What the deposits laid down—muds, silts, sand, and gravel—varied according to the changing water patterns on the landscape. Roaring cataracts, spreading deltas, pounding seashore—each condition left a different mark on the geological record. Even more important, each set of conditions gave rise to different life forms, and much of present-day Alberta's natural resources depends upon these.

The Precambrian shield in the northeast corner of the province is the oldest of the three physiographic regions. It is apparent east of the Slave River and for a little way south of Lake Athabasca, but the shield does not end here. It dives beneath the overlying plains to form the geological basement, and by the time it reaches the western edge of the province, it is covered by about four miles of assorted sedimentary material.

The rocks in this part of the Precambrian shield, composed primarily of granite, gneiss, and some sandstone, are about 2 billion years old, and contain evidence of even older mountain ranges. Pebbles are included in these formations, which are believed to have been eroded from either a mountain range in the region of Yellowknife or from one in the south, stretching from Ontario to Montana. What we now call Alberta was most likely a deep water channel and a sometimes sub-

▲ *Different ages of sedimentary rock are apparent on the surface of this Alberta mountain. Photo by Joy Spurr. Courtesy, Hillstrom Stock Photo*

▶ ▶ *Early in the Paleozoic Era, the Pacific Ocean flooded into Alberta from the west, putting down layers of sand and then massive layers of limestone. Sandstone underlying limestone can be seen today at Mount Edith Cavell in Jasper National Park. Photo by Dick Dietrich*

merged continental shelf between these two ranges. As time went by, those ranges were worn away, and the sands and muds that resulted eventually hardened into the tough rock that forms our basement today. West of here, there lay but the blue water of the Pacific Ocean, while in the region of Lake Athabasca there was a desert, the sands of which have now hardened to a red quartzite.

By the end of this era, known as the Proterozoic, the Pacific was pushed westward away from Alberta, so that the shore lay near the present-day Cariboo country in British Columbia. Except for minor modifications, the Precambrian rock, our basement, has not changed since that time.

By the early Paleozoic era—about 600 million years ago—life was experimenting with such revolutionary, high-tech forms as the trilobite, a creature with segmented body armour that proved very successful until there evolved fish which could swallow it whole. Already well-established and copiously abundant at the beginning of the Paleozoic were corals, planktons, and algae. The Pacific Ocean returned to Alberta now, and as it flooded in from the west, it first established layers of sand from its beach-building phase, and then began to lay down massive thicknesses of limestone. The sand became sandstone in time, and sandstone underlying limestone can be seen today at Lake Louise in Banff National Park and at Mount Edith Cavell at Jasper National Park.

Through the next 300 million or 400 million years, the oceans retreated and advanced across Alberta many times. At one point, blocked in the west and south by developing highlands, the ocean broke through a low barrier in the Fort Nelson area of northeastern British Columbia and came down from the north. This particular incident created broad salt pans, from which sea water evaporated for several million years. This is the source of two large salt deposits, one stretching south from Fort Smith to Fort Chipewyan and then west some 300 miles to Rainbow Lake, and the other in the region of Cold Lake and St. Paul. This salt is mined commercially today, accounting for over 10 percent of Canada's salt production in 1985.

During this time, judging from the fossil record, the climate in Alberta was much milder than it is today. The shallow seas were warm and swarming with life, perhaps a little like the Caribbean of today. Wherever the depth was right, about 25 to 30 metres, coral reefs formed. Around the reefs, below the turbulence of the surface, fell a slow, silent rain of limy skeletons and organic debris. This continued for thousands and hundreds of thousands of years at a stretch, so that thick deposits of mud and limestone built up. These, along with the loaf-shaped coral reefs, became porous reservoirs for the globules of oil left when the organic material decomposed. At first, of course, the oil globules were mixed with water, but in time they separated. The oil, as well as methane from the decomposition, migrated upwards until it was stopped by later, non-porous deposits. There these hydrocarbons pooled and waited for the geologists and roughnecks of the oilpatch to discover them, millions of years later.

It is difficult to conceive how prolific the sea was. From the first lucky strikes in the last century to 1985, Alberta has produced 1.5 billion cubic metres (bcm) of natural gas and 1.4 bcm of conventional crude. The estimate of marketable reserves that year amounted to 1.7 bcm of gas, and .6 bcm of crude.

Certain pools of gas here are also very rich in hydrogen sulfide. Wells tapping these sour-gas pools require extra caution, since a blowout can be fatal, not to mention distressingly foul, for those further away. However, the sulphur reclaimed from sour-gas wells is worth the effort. In 1985 Alberta accounted for over 95 percent of Canada's 8.3 million tons of sulphur production.

Towards the end of the Paleozoic era, in the Carboniferous period, plants had become well organized enough to colonize the land, although there are no significant coal deposits here from this time. During the Carboniferous, most if not all of Alberta was under water. The extensive coal fields found within our borders were laid down somewhat later.

The next great geological era, the Mesozoic, was also characterized by periodic floodings by the sea, though the climate and the life-forms were changing. Therefore the mineral legacy changed as well. There was volcanic activity to the west, which produced some phosphate deposits. As well, the very salty seas of the middle Triassic produced some excellent gypsum deposits, notably in the Mowitch Creek area north of Jasper.

By the end of the Jurassic period, about 135 million years ago, a broad arm of the Pacific stretched across southern Alberta. Because the land to the east, in the region of the Black Hills, was beginning to lift, this saltwater arm was fringed by delta and freshwater swamp. These produced lush vegetation—and subsequent beds of coal in the Bow Valley and the Crowsnest regions.

At this time the land to the west had also begun to rise, so that the rivers draining into the Pacific could not flow as freely as before. For a while they were able to pass through canyons in the region of Prince George and Quesnel, but much of the sediment they carried was dropped before they reached the sea. Broad gravel flats were left in the foothill regions, from Montana all the way to the Peace River region. When at last the rivers could no longer find their way to the Pacific, they began to flow northward into the Arctic Ocean.

At the beginning of the Cretaceous period, about 120 million years ago, several things happened. The Pacific retreated from Alberta for the last time, and the Coast range began to rise in British Columbia. This sent more rivers to drain northward through Alberta. At the same time, a very deep flow of crustal material toward the Coast range caused Alberta to subside somewhat, and the Arctic Ocean moved inland until it reached the northern part of Alberta. The sand being carried by the rivers was now dropped at the border of this arm, and it is these sands which later were to form the matrix of the Athabasca Tar Sands—a huge deposit of heavy oil. Alberta's conventional crude oil reserves are substantial, but the oil contained in the tar sands, called synthetic crude, amounts to a staggering 48.8 billion cubic metres.

Then, as the Rocky Mountains began to rise up to take their place beside the other ranges west of Alberta, a great flow of mud and gravel spread onto the plains, and much of this area became delta land. On these deltas grew luxuriant vegetation, so that they served as happy playgrounds for dinosaurs. Here frolicked, in their own reptilian ways, the vegetarian Edmontosaurus, the distinctly carnivorous Albertosaurus, the agile, man-sized, predatory Dromeosaurus, and many others. As a result, Alberta is now one of the richest sources of dinosaur fossils in the world, and Dinosaur Provincial Park, on the Red Deer River, has been declared a World Heritage Site by UNESCO.

At the same time, subtropical trees such as magnolias, sycamores, figs, and an ancestor of the giant redwoods, the metasequoia, were laying down thick, black beds of coal. These, and earlier beds, give Alberta an estimated total reserve of close to 800 billion tons of bituminous and sub-bituminous coal.

The end of the Mesozoic era, about 65 million years ago, was also the end of the age of dinosaurs. At the same time, Alberta ceased being a coastal area and became landlocked. The Arctic Ocean drained away to the north, and the Pacific could no longer pass the rocky highlands of British Columbia. The state was now set for the last major event in the formation of the landscape of present-day Alberta.

About one million years ago the polar ice caps began to enlarge,

◀ *This Chasmosaurus skeleton is on display at the Tyrrell Museum of Paleontology at Dinosaur Provincial Park. Photo by Jerg Kroener*

▶ *The Athabaska Glacier is prominent in this photograph of Jasper National Park. Bighorn sheep are in the foreground. Photo by Jerg Kroener*

and the world entered an age of ice. This age was in fact made up of four periods of glaciation, with warm intervals, or interglacials, between them. In North America the main ice sheet was centered on Hudson Bay. Alberta escaped the ice during the first three advances, although the river systems were completely disrupted and the flora and fauna changed dramatically as its climate became Arctic or sub-Arctic. In the fourth advance, however, a massive ice sheet from the northeast met another sheet advancing from the mountains, and the two ground across all of Alberta, with the exception of the Cypress Hills in the southeast.

This ice sheet, which in places was a kilometre and a half thick, had a profound effect on the landscape. It pulverized soft rock and scarred harder formations. It scoured out valleys, ground down hills, and altered the course of rivers. It transported huge boulders hundreds of miles. The debris it left when it retreated formed such features as moraines, drumlins, and eskers; it also became the basic ingredient of our present-day soil. It is now 12,000 years since the ice began to retreat, but that is only the blink of an eye in geological terms. There is some debate among scientists whether the ice is gone for good, or if we are only in the middle of another interglacial period.

To sum up, the geological history of this part of the world has left a wide range of resources. Most notable among these are conventional oil, natural gas, sulphur, coal, and an enormous deposit of tar sands. There are also large deposits of salt, limestone, and sandstone of building quality, gypsum, bentonite, clay suitable for pottery and other uses,

and—although not an exotic resource—large quantities of sand and gravel. In 1985 about a fifth of Canada's sand and gravel production was in Alberta.

The only lack here is of metals. A small amount of gold is panned from the rivers, but there is no gold mining as such; nor is there any production of nickel, copper, zinc, or other such "hard-rock" metals. There are considerable quantities of vanadium, nickel, titanium, and zirconium associated with the tar sands, but these are not presently being exploited. There is also an undeveloped iron formation in the Clear Hills west of Peace River. In the Precambrian basement there may well be valuable deposits, but they are so deeply buried that no one has thought of looking for them, let alone of starting up production.

When a January blizzard blows a foot of snow over the driveway, and it's so cold your car tires stay square all the way to work, you might be tempted to conclude that the ice age is returning. Alberta's climate, though, is not Arctic, nor even sub-Arctic, but cool temperate continental. This means we have cool dry summers, long winters, and moderate precipitation. Depending on latitude, spring begins to stir in March or April, summer takes hold in June, the slide to autumn starts in September, and winter is usually in evidence by the end of October or early November. While we can indulge in statistical generalization, though, it is also true to say that on any given week, we can expect almost anything in the way of weather.

The record high for Alberta is 43.3 degrees Celsius, recorded at Bassano Dam back in 1931. That the record has stood for so long is ample testimony that the summers are usually much cooler here. Typical highs are in the mid-twenties, except in the south, where highs in the low thirties are common. In addition, the range between day and night temperatures on the plains is around 15 degrees Celsius, meaning that the nights are usually cool and comfortable. For most people, the only shortcoming of Alberta summers is their brevity. Cold and snow may come in October and persist until April, with the occasional spring snowstorm in May.

There is great variation in this, though. A white Christmas is not guaranteed, even as far north as Edmonton. As for cold, well, yes, it can be cold here—the record low temperature is -61.1 degrees Celsius, well below the freezing point of mercury, at Fort Vermilion in 1911. Certainly the northern part of the province expects to be below freezing most of the winter, but the cold is tempered somewhat by the dryness. On average the coldest month is February. Total snowfall over most of the province is usually no more than 150 centimetres.

Most of the weather in Alberta comes from frontal systems advancing either from the west or from the north. However, Pacific weather systems leave much of their moisture in the mountains, and the average annual precipitation here ranges from a high of 60, to as little as 30, centimetres.

We are too far inland for the Pacific to have much of a moderating effect on our temperatures. The westerly flow is responsible, though, for a remarkable winter phenomenon, the chinook. Many a

▲ *Snow fences are erected during the winter to prevent the snow from drifting over roads. Photo by Wilfried D. Schurig. Courtesy, Hillstrom Stock Photo*

▶ ▶ *Spring comes to the wide-open prairie country east of Drumheller by April, but snowstorms can occur as late as May. Photo by Wilfried D. Schurig. Courtesy, Hillstrom Stock Photo*

homesteader has reported waking on a midwinter night to find that his breath no longer smoked from the cold, and that the sound of running water outside signalled a thaw. There is also the tale, offered to every easterner in the hopes he will believe it, of a pioneer driving a horse-drawn sleigh, caught from behind by a chinook. He drove his horse to exhaustion just to keep the front of the runners on the snow.

The chinook, that miraculous wind from the southwest, can have remarkable effects. It happens when air pushing east over the mountains drops all its moisture and then, as it plunges out onto the plains, is compressed and therefore warmed. Once the warm, dry wind arrives, heralded by a characteristic arch of clouds across the southwest, the temperature can rise by 20 degrees Celsius or more in as short a span as 10 minutes. The chinook is a regular event in the Lethbridge/ Fort Macleod/Calgary region where it clears pastureland for grazing cattle and allows city dwellers to walk about in shirt sleeves in January. Its benign effects can sometimes be felt as far north as Edmonton and even the Peace River region.

The chinook helped establish cattle ranching here, but from the farmer's point of view, it is probably less significant than the average length of the growing season, also expressed as the frost-free period. This varies considerably through the province, both with latitude and altitude. The shortest season, less than 60 days, is at the northern edge of the province and along the rising land of foothills.

However, there are a few surprises here: Calgary has a shorter growing season than a large portion of the Peace River district, far to the north. Most of the southeast corner of the province has an annual frost-free period of at least 100 days, and in some places over 120 days. These are long-term averages, of course—every Alberta gardener has had to rescue still-green tomatoes from a sudden cold snap, and July is the only month for which there is no recorded snowfall.

In the southern half of the province, there are also a large number of hailstorms each year. These begin as ordinary thunderstorms, but when the cumulo-nimbus clouds boil up high enough, the water vapour circulating through them freezes and hail falls. Light hail is quite common in summer storms, but each year there are a dozen or so severe hailstorms which cut swaths of destruction for 80 kilometres or more. Crops in the path of such storms can be turned into so much chopped salad in seconds, and it is usually too late in the season for them to recover. These storms often begin in the foothills, but do their worst as they drift eastward, becoming most intense east of a line through Lethbridge, Calgary, and Edmonton.

Another intense but rarely seen summer phenomenon is the tornado. Two or three tornadoes are reported each year, but they are not so violent nor so long lived as those of the central United States. In Oklahoma and Texas a tornado may travel for 80 kilometres, destroying everything in its path. In Alberta a tornado seldom lasts for more than a kilometre, though it will still have enough power to uproot trees and shatter buildings.

Both geology and weather contribute to our wall-to-wall carpet,

▶ ▶ *This farm is located in the Cypress Hills, a lush sanctuary of forests, lakes, and streams surrounded by arid plains. Photo by Wes Bergen. Courtesy, Hillstrom Stock Photo*

soil. Soils can be divided between those of the grasslands and those of wooded areas, which have a leached-out layer near the surface. The grasslands of the southeast part of the province are limited in their fertility, partly by centuries of periodic drought and hot dry winds. The grass cover here has never built up a soil with much organic material. This land is best suited to ranching, or if planted, to wheat. Moving northwestward, the soil steadily improves until we reach the aspen parkland and enter the most fertile land in the province. This is a roughly triangular region of black soil, extending in an arc from Lloydminster on the Saskatchewan border to a point southwest of Red Deer, and north to about a hundred kilometres northwest of Edmonton. Here the grasslands have been partly invaded by deciduous forest, and annual precipitation is around 45 centimetres. Soils here are very dark brown to black, abundantly rich, and may be 30 to 35 centimetres in depth. With a growing season in excess of a hundred days, many kinds of crops are possible here.

To the north and west of this zone, the soils are mostly of the wooded varieties, with only limited possibilities for agriculture. There are exceptions in the Peace River region, where much of the soil is technically classified as thin black and the deep Peace valley makes for a longer growing season.

Soil, climate, and terrain work together to shelter characteristic populations of plants and animals, and there is a wide variety of indigenous and introduced species in Alberta. Some are economically significant, but all play their part. If we did not have the forests to visit, the birds to watch, trout to tempt with a dry fly, and loons laughing across a lake at dawn to listen to, there would be little joy in living here.

The province can be divided into several zones: the grasslands, the aspen parkland, the boreal forest, and the mountain and tundra. From a biologist's point of view, a case can also be made for the Cypress Hills as a separate region. This plateau in the southeast—which in fact we share with Saskatchewan—is unique for several reasons. One is its situation. Surrounded by hot, dry plains, Cypress Hills stands above them as a surprising green sanctuary of forests, lakes, and streams. It is also a remarkable window into the past. This area escaped glaciation, and seems to preserve many of the species that were driven away from the rest of the province. Here may be found mountain flora and fauna several hundred kilometres from the Rockies, as well as semitropical species that would seem more at home further south.

In the true grasslands, all of Alberta south and east of Olds except for the plateau of the Cypress Hills, there is enough rain each year to preserve grass cover and keep away the desert, but not enough to grow trees. Technically this is not true prairie but steppe, an area of short grasses, poor soil, and little rainfall. Add to this barrenness the frequent high winds and the extreme range of temperatures, and you have a challenging environment.

Not surprising, then, that the plants growing here are arid and

semi-arid types: sagebrush, buckbrush, prickly pear, and pincushion cacti, and native grasses such as blue grama, June, spear, and wheat grass. Over this cover once drifted herds of buffalo—but these, of course, vanished by the mid-1880s. Other species which once flourished here but now are gone include the plains grizzly and the black bear, the whooping crane and the trumpeter swan, the plains wolf, the moose, the elk, and the kit fox.

One species which has persisted, after near extinction at the beginning of this century, is the pronghorn. This is often called the pronghorn antelope, but in fact is not an antelope. It belongs to a different family, of which it is the only example. When the buffalo disappeared, the pronghorns were hunted heavily by settlers and Indians, and by 1915 had nearly vanished. Now, careful conservation has brought them back. Superbly adapted for their environment, these animals have excellent distance vision, an open-mouthed panting system and enlarged windpipe to dissipate heat and sustain high levels of activity, and hollow hairs to insulate them against the piercing cold of winter. Their only weakness is their inability to deal with deep, crusted snow. Pronghorns feed by sight, and if the snowcover is long lasting and widespread, they do not paw through to their food, but starve. They would seem therefore to be uniquely adapted to the chinook belt.

The pronghorn shares its range with a wide variety of birds and animals, far more than the untrained eye might first observe. White tail and mule deer are found here, drifting silently through the coulees, as are coyotes, bobcats, badgers, rabbits, and a host of small rodents.

In the air you may see sage grouse, rough-legged hawks, prairie falcons, the sweet-voiced meadowlark, and even golden eagles. The reptiles, once represented here by a profusion of dinosaurs, are now reduced to the diminutive horned toad, which is actually a lizard, and snakes—garter, bull, and prairie rattler, the only poisonous snake in the province.

As conditions improve along the north edge of the grasslands, the ecological zone changes to that of the aspen parkland. This is really a transition zone between the grasslands to the south and east, and the boreal forest to the north and west. Here prairie is interspersed with groves of aspen and poplar, and the valleys are cloaked with dense stands of aspen, willow, chokecherry, and saskatoon.

The parkland region has undergone several cycles since the arrival of settlers. The first was toward growth because the settlers tended to check the annual prairie fires that played an important part in the balance between grassland and aspen forest cover. When fire no longer burnt the young saplings, trees began to invade the grassland to the south, and the parkland region expanded. Then, when the human population boomed after the Second World War, and the use of machinery became widespread, fields were cleared, roadways were cut, and much of this woodland was harvested. However, although the parkland has been heavily penetrated by farms, roads, and power, pipe and seismic lines, it seems likely that it is still somewhat more extensive than in pre-settlement times.

The aspen parkland covers only about a tenth of the province, but because it is a meeting point for two other regions, and because it is home for a large portion of the population, it furnishes many of the most beautiful images people conjure when they think "Alberta."

The trembling aspen, which lends its name to the area, is a beautiful tree with smooth, gray-green bark, and small, almost round leaves that respond to the slightest puff of wind. A grove—or bluff, as it is often called in the West—of aspen is almost never silent. And in the fall the leaves turn a clear golden yellow, so that the trees, poised against the blue sky, look like fountains of coins.

Here also you will find Alberta's floral emblem, the wild rose. From early June on, almost any sunny bank will show a profusion of these delicate flowers, ranging in colour from a pale pink to a deep fuschia, with a circle of yellow stamens, like a crown, in the centre. If you can pass the defense of thorns, you will also find the scent delightful.

Just as delightful is the taste of a sun-warmed saskatoon. These delicious purple berries ripen in July, and once were indispensable to Indians and traders. They were pounded together with dried buffalo meat and then mixed with buffalo tallow to make pemmican, a nourishing, sustaining food that kept for years. If you don't want to take the trouble to sun dry a side of buffalo, though, try your berries in a pie, or with just a little cream. There is no finer conclusion to a peaceful afternoon of berry picking.

The aspen parkland is really a collection of different habitats, which adds to its charm. In the stream valleys there are beaver, otter, and muskrat, as well as the ubiquitous jackrabbit, and its equally ubiquitous predator, the coyote. Mink hunt here, too, terrorizing muskrat twice their size. The bird population is exceptionally varied, as this is part of a continental flyway, and many species which nest further north are here in the spring and fall. Warblers, thrushes, and flycatchers can be seen, as can the large goshawk and the provincial emblem, the great horned owl. A favourite year-round resident is the friendly black-capped chickadee, whose cheerful call in February reminds us that winter will not last forever.

Another parkland habitat that deserves mention is the province's collection of lakes, sloughs, and wet meadow lands. Some bodies of water are large enough to be permanent, while others come and go, but all support distinct communities of plants and animals. Some of the larger lakes have developed gravel or sand shores, and now also support communities of boaters, fishermen, and summer cottage residents.

Large or small, these wet areas are incredibly lush in the summer, becoming overgrown with sedges, cattails, grasses, willows, and poplars. Birdlife is also wildly abundant, and a visitor here is sure to hear the song of the red-winged blackbird, or perhaps catch a glimpse of its striking cousin, the yellow-headed blackbird. Ducks, gulls, and shore birds are plentiful and, in fact, these boggy areas are nesting grounds for everything from the tiny wren to the large Canada goose. Underwater, depending on conditions, you might spot pike, perch,

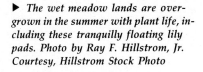

▶ *Saskatoon berries, once used by the Indians in making pemmican, produce the delicate white blossoms shown here. Photo by Joy Spurr. Courtesy, Hillstrom Stock Photo*

▶ *The wet meadow lands are overgrown in the summer with plant life, including these tranquilly floating lily pads. Photo by Ray F. Hillstrom, Jr. Courtesy, Hillstrom Stock Photo*

▶ *The wild rose is the floral emblem of Alberta. Photo by Bill McKeown. Courtesy, Westfile, Inc.*

walleye, or whitefish, while in the many streams there is a happy abundance of trout, char, and arctic grayling. Unfortunately, the smaller ponds and sloughs are also nurseries for millions of mosquitoes and other insects. Although visitors here must be dedicated, they will be amply rewarded.

The boreal or northern forest is by far the largest portion of Alberta, and probably the least known. It has many different faces, depending on the climate and soil available, but typically it is a mixture of aspen, birch, and coniferous trees—spruce, pine, and larch, that beautiful oddity which turns a luminous yellow in the fall. There may be islands of almost pure deciduous, or pure coniferous, but more often there is a mixture. Where the more open canopy of the aspen and birch permits, there is a fairly dense undergrowth of shrubs like the wild rose and the saskatoon. Where the conifers predominate, the traveller's step will be softened by a carpet of needles and feather mosses, with here and there a patch of ground-hugging bearberry.

From 1985 to 1986, Albertans harvested 6.9 million cubic metres of forest products, worth about $65 million. At that time, it was estimated that the usable standing timber in the province amounted to 243 million cubic metres.

Because the boreal forest is little frequented by humans, many of the original species persist here. The wood buffalo, or bison, a little larger than the plains bison, was once common throughout the area, and there is still a large population of them in Wood Buffalo National Park, at the northern edge of the province. Here also you may find, if your woodcraft is good, the much-maligned, much-romanticised timber wolf, as well as moose, elk, deer, lynx, and bear.

▶ *Larch trees display their characteristic shade of yellow on an afternoon in September. Photo by Jerg Kroener*

◀ *The wood buffalo, or bison, was once common in Alberta. Today these animals are found mostly in Wood Buffalo National Park. Photo by Bill McKeown. Courtesy, Westfile, Inc.*

There is no shortage of smaller animals, either. The porcupine may well find you, particularly if you have canoe paddles, or shoelaces, or anything else "flavoured" with sweat. But the fisher, a carnivore like a large weasel, is the equal of the porcupine, which it is able to flip over and kill without being skewered by quills. And, of course, there are beaver everywhere; as we shall see, they were the reason "civilization" came here in the first place.

Another creature sure to find you, especially if you stay in the woods until lunch time, is a bold, gray bird a little bigger than a robin. It is the gray jay, also known as the Canada jay, the whiskey-jack, and the camp robber. It will not wait twice if offered food, though if you do not offer, it will take—whatever it can. Other birds familiar in the area are the ruffed grouse, spruce grouse, goshawk, and peregrine falcon.

Of course, the boreal forest is not homogenous, nor is it even continuous. There are islands of parkland at Grande Prairie, Peace River, and around Fort Vermilion. And for variety, there are patches of black spruce muskeg and larch swamps, and south of Lake Athabasca there are sandplains, where the dry uplands are held by slow-growing jack pine and reindeer lichen.

In all of the boreal forest, fire is periodically a fact of life. It is desirable from an ecological point of view, because it reduces disease and helps to renew mature forest; but from a human point of view, fires must be controlled. If left unchecked, they could destroy valuable timber and wipe out communities. Each summer, therefore, a small army of men and equipment is mobilized to fight fires, and is probably the most visible of our efforts to manage the environment.

The final region to be considered in our tour around the province is the alpine or mountain zone. In some ways this is a conglomeration of all the other zones, since, as we climb in altitude, we reproduce many of the conditions found elsewhere. Certainly, just below treeline, the conditions are quite similar to those in the subarctic boreal forest.

There is a magic here, however, which is not found anywhere else. The mountain zone is no more silent than any other—there are rushing streams here, and wind in the trees, and thunderous avalanches—but there is nevertheless a stillness which restores the soul. Some, raised out on the plain, cannot stay too long here. They feel uneasy and take deep breaths when they come to open country again. But even these would agree that the mountains add a flavour to Alberta that is absolutely essential.

Most of the mountainous region of Alberta is sequestered in national or provincial park, and it was at Banff that Canada's extensive park system got its start, back in 1885. Workers building the Canadian Pacific Railway (CPR) had discovered the hot springs at the Cave and Basin, and the government declared a 10-square-mile sanctuary around them. Visitors to these preserves can encounter a dazzling variety of environments and wildlife.

Notable among the larger animals are the bear, both black and grizzly, although grizzlies are rare now, moose, elk, deer, and bighorn

▲ *Beaver, once highly prized in Alberta for their fur, built this dam in the Rocky Mountain foothills. Photo by Jerg Kroener*

▶ *Bighorn sheep are among the inhabitants of Alberta's mountainous wildlife preserves. Photo by John Elk III*

sheep. Mountain goats may also be glimpsed, but they are shy. The most you may ever see of these might be a few dots of white, making their way at leisure across an impassable cliff face. Of the smaller animals, there are many: red squirrels, marmots, muskrats, beavers, porcupines, ground squirrels, rabbits, and coyotes.

And if you time your visit properly, alpine meadows can be a spectacular carpet of flowers: mountain avens, anemones, and the ankle high snow willow. But if you see a patch of yellow hedysarum, give it a wide berth—the fleshy roots are one of the favourite foods of the grizzly bear.

Plains, parkland, forest, and mountains: these are the faces of Alberta. This is the scenery which feeds us and refreshes us, which shapes our thoughts and our lives. Through it all, there is a flavour and a vitality which add up to a quality found nowhere else in the world. If you are looking for a tangible example, you can see it in the endless blue sky and in the golden promise of the aspens in the fall.

▲ *The harebell (Campanula rotundifolia) is one of the many lovely wildflowers which greet visitors to Alberta. Photo by Joy Spurr. Courtesy, Hillstrom Stock Photo*

◄ *These vivid western wood lilies were found in Jasper National Park. Photo by Kenneth W. Fink. Courtesy, Hillstrom Stock Photo*

▶ *A hoary marmot rests on a rock above Peyto Lake in Banff National Park. Photo by Jerg Kroener*

▶ *A mountain goat nanny pauses for a moment at a mineral lick on the Atha-baska River in Jasper National Park. Photo by Jerg Kroener*

The first white men to reach what is now Alberta were not concerned with understanding the place scientifically. Like the native peoples, they were more interested in meat and fur, and the rivers that would carry them to the best sources of both. Before the fur trade era ended, however, men of more scientific bent made their way to Alberta, and the huge task of precisely mapping the area and interpreting it geologically began.

The forerunner of these men of science was a surveyor, map-maker, and fur trader named David Thompson. Born in England in 1770, and educated in a poor boys' school in West-

Discovering the Lay of the Land

by Fred Stenson

minster, Thompson joined the Hudson's Bay Company as an apprentice in 1784. Perceiving the young man's cleverness, the company allowed him to study under their premier surveyor Philip Turnor, but then neglected to provide Thompson with resources for carrying out his explorations. Fed up, he deserted in 1797 to the rival North West Company, where he was assigned the formidable task of mapping the regions between and around the many "Nor'wester" trading posts.

Perhaps the single most difficult assignment entrusted to Thompson was finding a practical trade route through the Rocky Mountains. In 1807 he succeeded in taking an expedition up the North Saskatchewan River, and across the Rockies into the fur-rich Kootenay Indian territory. Thompson explored the region and, later, led fur brigades down the Athabasca River, past what is now Jasper, to avoid the hostile Piegan Indians to the south.

Thompson returned to Upper Canada in 1812, but was given a three-year retainer by the North West Com-

pany to prepare a map of the fur territories. The accuracy of Thompson's 1813 map has amazed geographers ever since.

Life outside the fur trade proved less successful for Thompson. His eyesight and his business ventures failed; as a last resort, he began writing about his travels. He completely lost his sight, however, before finishing the manuscript. In 1857 Thompson died as he had begun life, in poverty. His manuscript and, with it, his accomplishments went unnoticed for decades.

The first geologist in the territory of present-day Alberta was James Hector, a young Scot assigned to the Palliser Expedition of 1857 to 1860. Captain John Palliser, an Irishman, approached the British Government about making a voyage from Red River to the Rocky Mountains, to which the British responded with a full-blown scientific expedition. James Hector's contributions to history include the discovery that the great plain between Red River and the mountains is not as flat as it appears. It rises, rather, from east to west, in three levels. Hector also noted the presence of coal and collected fossil shells of mollusks.

Sir James Hector was educated as a doctor, and one of the few times he is known to have practised that profession occurred near present-day Calgary. Indian tribes met the expedition there, determined to stop it before it reached the mountains. During this stalemate, dysentery broke out in the Indian camp and James Hector treated the Indians so successfully that they not only agreed to let the expedition continue, but guided it as well.

◄ *David Thompson. Courtesy, Public Archives Canada*

In the mountains near present-day Field, British Columbia, Hector narrowly escaped being buried alive. While trying to force his horse across a raging stream, he was kicked in the chest, and rendered so senseless that his men proceeded to dig his grave. Luckily, he recovered before they were done. The men named the river Kicking-Horse in Hector's honor—or his horse's—and a pass on the Trans-Canada Highway still bears that name.

Scientific exploration of western Canada sped up after 1870 when the new Dominion of Canada acquired territorial rights to the West from the Hudson's Bay Company. In 1873 Her Majesty's North American Boundary Commission was set up in collaboration with the United States to survey and mark the 49th Parallel from Lake of the Woods to the Rocky Mountains. Scientists were sent along with the surveyors to discover which resources the massive new territory might contain.

The official geologist and naturalist on the Canadian side of the expedition was George Mercer Dawson. In southern Saskatchewan, Dawson found the first dinosaur bones ever recorded in western Canada. His second dinosaur find was in the land area of Alberta. He also noted a number of coal deposits and accurately predicted that coal underlay much of Alberta.

Dawson's diaries reveal the conditions under which he worked. In August 1874, the second year of the expedition, Dawson chatted with a whiskey trader named Castillian Joe at his whiskey fort on the St. Mary's River. Joe's stock in trade was buying Indian horses for whiskey in the summer and then selling them back for robes in the winter. He claimed to have traded 14,000 robes the previous winter and to have killed eight

Indians in the last 18 days. Such was the standard of law in the country through which Dawson travelled, often alone.

But the most remarkable thing about Dawson's exploits is that he managed them with a physical deformity. An illness when he was 11 years old, possibly polio, stunted his growth and left him a hunchback. Doctors told his parents that he would never walk, and must have been astounded to see him not only walk, but pursue a career of hiking and riding all over Canada.

In 1875 Dawson joined the Geological Survey of Canada and took on the mapping of Alberta's coal deposits. Given that he helped discover two of Alberta's greatest resources, coal and dinosaur bones, it seems only fitting that Dawson should also have been involved in the discovery of Alberta's petroleum. When natural gas was discovered in a Canadian Pacific Railway water well near Medicine Hat in 1883, Dawson noted that the strata producing the gas were continuous over broad regions of the West. He thus foresaw that much natural gas would be found in the region.

One of George Dawson's assistants on the Geological Survey, Joseph Burr Tyrrell, became a figure almost as legendary as his diminutive boss. Tyrrell is probably best known for the incredible trek he made across the Barren Lands of northern Canada in 1893, one of the epic voyages of all time; but, prior to this, in a single week in June 1884, Tyrrell made two discoveries in Alberta that would have assured him a place in the history books anyway. On June 9 he discovered a dinosaur skeleton sticking up from a bank of the Red Deer River, the first indication of the wealth of dinosaur remains in that valley. On June 13, on the same

river, he located outcroppings of one of Canada's greatest coal deposits, the coal beds that would sustain the future town of Drumheller.

Joseph Tyrrell was not fond of George Dawson when he first worked for him in 1881. He considered Dawson a slave-driver. After Dawson became director of the Geological Survey of Canada in 1895, Tyrrell quit in a dispute over wages and joined the Klondike Gold Rush. Rather than join the fray with shovel and pan, Tyrrell set up shop as a mining consultant, instructing clients on scientific mining methods. He made a fortune this way, though it is doubtful that a single day went by without reminders of his former boss. The town Tyrrell worked in, Dawson City, was named for George Mercer Dawson.

Joseph Tyrrell was quick to enhance his own career, but he also restored the dignity and reputation of one of his predecessors; Tyrrell greatly admired David Thompson and, in the 1890s, he obtained Thompson's unfinished manuscript. Tyrrell edited the work and saw it published in 1914. *David Thompson's Narrative* is now recognized as one of the most important historical documents in North America; David Thompson has become a Canadian hero, even more acclaimed than Joseph Burr Tyrrell.

In the twentieth century, exploitation of Alberta's petroleum and coal wealth began. After 1910, American dinosaur hunters Barnum Brown and Charles H. Sternberg hauled boat and railcar loads of dinosaur skeletons out of the Red Deer River Valley. But it all began with Thompson, Hector, Dawson, and Tyrrell, men of inquiring mind who dared their way into the unsettled wilderness, driven by the desire to discover and the will to understand.

CHAPTER 2

Our Story
So Far

Human occupation of Alberta goes back about 11,000 or 12,000 years. Until recently, it was believed that the North American continent was colonized around the time of the last ice age. There was a phenomenal amount of water locked up in the massive sheets of ice then, which resulted in lower ocean levels. The Bering Strait became a land bridge, and scientists theorized that nomadic hunters came across from Siberia and spread out through the continent.

Recent finds, however, suggest that people may have been here before the last glaciation. It is a fascinating thought that early people may have wandered though this land, hunting mammoth and doing battle with sabre-toothed tigers and gigantic wolves (six feet high at the shoulder); but it may be impossible to know anything of their lives. The huge weight of ice essentially wiped the slate clean. It may someday be proven from other evidence that humans were here that long ago, but we will probably never know where they camped, or how they lived when they walked across this land.

We do have a fairly good picture of native life after the glaciers retreated. The Indian tribes here before the arrival of the Europeans were neolithic, nomadic hunters. They had established territories within which they migrated through the seasons, living primarily on the huge herds of plains and woods buffalo.

Hunting methods included the spear and the highly efficient buffalo jump. In this latter strategy the landscape itself became a tool: simply put, it meant hazing and stampeding buffalo over a cliff or cutbank. The "hunt" might begin with someone on all fours, wearing a robe and impersonating a buffalo calf, because it is the females who lead the herd, and they would naturally try to surround a stray youngster. This deception might be supplemented by others wearing wolf

◀ These Indian artifacts, excavated in Waterton Lakes National Park, are 6,000 years old. Photo by Joy Spurr. Courtesy, Hillstrom Stock Photo

▶ The horse had a profound effect on Indian culture, allowing greater mobility and easier accumulation of material goods. Courtesy, Glenbow Archives, Calgary

skins, apparently threatening the calf. There are a number of known buffalo jumps around the province, drops of 20 feet or more, with the bones of hundreds of thousands of animals lying at the bottom. At Head Smashed In Buffalo Jump, near Fort Macleod, it is estimated that a million buffalo were killed in the thousands of years of use. The bones here lie 10 metres thick.

Cultures such as this change slowly, but at about A.D. 600, projectile points became smaller and finer, which we attribute to the introduction of the bow and arrow. It was to be another thousand years, though, before the pace of change really picked up, catalyzed, of course, by the arrival of Europeans on the continent.

The effect of European civilization was felt in Alberta long before whites actually arrived. Innovations such as iron cooking pots, knives, axes, cloth, and blankets were traded from tribe to tribe, travelling many hundreds of miles inland. Some items, such as guns, did not travel so swiftly, since any tribe obtaining them rightly surmised that firearms would give them a significant advantage over their neighbours. Other things, like smallpox and measles, travelled like the wind; the Indians of the plains were struck down in the thousands before they set eyes on Europeans. But the other great innovation that arrived with the whites was the horse, introduced by the Spaniards in the 1500s. It had a profound effect on the culture as the horse spread northward, allowing a greater mobility and a greater accumulation of material goods; hitherto, the Indians had been limited to what they could pack themselves and whatever their dogs could pull on a travois.

Increased mobility and the destabilizing effect of guns meant that intertribal warfare increased, and some tribes were driven far away from their traditional homes. The Cree of northwestern Ontario, profiting from their association with white traders, extended their range through the parkland and northern forest, forcing the Beaver, Blackfoot, Sarcee, and Slave tribes to move before them. The Kootenay

This totem pole in Jasper is one of the more spectacular artifacts left behind by the Indians. Photo by John Elk III

Indians were pushed right over the mountains to the interior of British Columbia.

By the beginning of the eighteenth century, the Blackfoot nation (composed of the Blackfoot, Blood, and Piegan tribes) had so far acquired neither the gun nor the horse, and they found themselves caught between the armed Cree to the northeast and the mounted Snake, or Shoshoni, to the southwest. Their plight did not last long, however. By the mid-1700s, they had both horses and guns, and in spite of periodic epidemics of European diseases, the confederacy had become a dominant force in the northern plains.

While the buffalo endured, the tribes suffered no need, and so were able to indulge at leisure in such cultural pursuits as horse raiding and long-distance war. David Thompson, the explorer and surveyor, tells of a Piegan raid which began in the vicinity of Edmonton and went south "about thirty two degrees of latitude." It isn't clear how Thompson arrived at the measurement, but the raiders may have travelled as far as present-day Mexico, since they returned with booty taken from the Spanish.

War making was not the only cultural pursuit to flourish; clothes and beadwork that have survived from this time are spectacularly beautiful. If affairs could have stabilized at this point, the Indians of Alberta would no doubt have evolved a very rich culture—but the pressures of the advancing Europeans did not abate. In another century, the Indians would be poor, sick, hungry, and mostly forgotten. It is a reversal from which they have struggled to return for decades, and although there has been progress, there is still far to go. Last to run its course will be the bitterness and mistrust that many natives now hold for whites.

The force that impelled whites to journey into this unknown wilderness was commerce. The fur trade had harvested a great wealth of beaver pelts from Quebec and Ontario, and then, as the streams there were trapped out, traders began to look further afield. The newly formed Company of Adventurers Trading into Hudson's Bay, eventually known as the Hudson's Bay Company (HBC), established York Factory at the mouth of the Nelson River, and in time, Cumberland House, on the Saskatchewan River. Meanwhile, the HBC faced serious competition from independent traders from Montreal who went to the Indians and bought the furs on the spot. The independents were aggressive and unscrupulous; they found that a convenient trade good was brandy—and later rum. Thus to the native acquisition of cloth, guns, horses, and smallpox was added another item: alcohol.

In pursuit of furs, the HBC sent Anthony Henday west from York Factory in 1754. It was an unusual move for the HBC, which preferred to sit tight in centrally located trading posts and persuade the natives to bring the furs to them, but competition was reducing the company's profits.

Henday travelled up the Saskatchewan accompanied by a Cree,

Attickasish, who knew the Blackfoot from trading with them. It was fall when they crossed into what is now Alberta, a little south of present-day Chauvin. Then, at Pine Lake, near present-day Red Deer, they found a small encampment of Blackfoot and were taken on to their main camp.

This was an impressive gathering, consisting of 200 large teepees pitched in two long rows. Henday was brought to the chief's lodge at one end of the camp, which he reported was large enough for 50 people. There he was treated with courtesy, given the place of honour on the chief's right hand, offered several pipes, and then feasted on buffalo tongues. When at last he came to the point, however, asking his hosts if they would travel to Hudson Bay to trade, he received a polite demurral. It was far off, they told him, and they could not paddle.

Shortly thereafter the Blackfoot encampment broke up for the winter, and Henday spent the cold months with a band of Cree. During this time he caught a glimpse of the distant Rocky Mountains, the first white man to do so. The Cree travelled north until they came to a favourite wintering ground on the North Saskatchewan, near the mouth of the Sturgeon River, not far from modern Fort Saskatchewan. There the Indians built canoes and waited for spring. When the ice went out on April 23, flocks of geese and swans were seen flying north, and the travellers spent the night feasting and dancing. Five days later they struck camp and glided downriver.

Henday's reports did not provoke a sudden rush of traders, although the HBC did continue to send a few men west. Henday and Joseph Smith spent the winter of 1759 to 1760 near the site of the present-day town of Rocky Mountain House, and for their troubles brought 61 canoe loads of furs back when they returned.

So far, the traders had mostly concentrated on the Saskatchewan; but in 1778 Peter Pond came across the Methy portage into the fabulously fur-rich Athabasca basin, travelling down the Clearwater and then the Athabasca. About 40 miles from Lake Athabasca, he built a house, by virtue of which he became Alberta's first white resident. Eight years later his associate Archibald McLeod built the second house, where the Clearwater enters the Athabasca, the site of present-day Fort McMurray.

Pond could be found in Alberta off and on for the next 10 years, during which time he heard the Indians tell of a mighty river flowing away to the northwest. He suspected that this would probably lead to the Pacific, though he was never able to follow up on this speculation.

It fell to Alexander Mackenzie, in 1789, to explore the river that now bears his name and to discover that it led not to the Pacific, but to the Arctic. Undeterred, he set out the next year from Fort Chipewyan, travelling up the Peace River. He was not, of course, exploring for the sheer joy of it. Like later Albertans, he was trying to avoid the high cost of shipping through east coast ports. If he could find an easy route to salt water, it would be much more economical. In 1793 he departed from the junction of the Peace and Smoky rivers and succeeded

▲ *York Factory was an early Hudson's Bay Company outpost at the mouth of the Nelson River. Courtesy, Glenbow Archives, Calgary*

59

◄ *In 1793 Alexander Mackenzie succeeded in finding a trade route from Alberta to the Pacific. Courtesy, Glenbow Archives*

at last in reaching the Pacific.

Alberta was now visited fairly regularly by whites working either for the HBC or a rival company, or for themselves. Trying to elbow others aside, they built forts along the Athabasca, Peace, and Saskatchewan rivers, always within sight of the competition. Thus, in 1792, the North West Company built Fort George on the North Saskatchewan, near present-day Elk Point, and the HBC reciprocated with Buckingham House. Fort Augustus was built near the mouth of the Sturgeon in 1795, and the HBC immediately countered with a nearby Fort Edmonton.

These two posts were moved up and down the river over the next 18 years, sometimes within the present city limits, sometimes as far downriver as Smoky Lake. By 1813 they had both returned to Edmonton proper, Fort Edmonton being on the river flats below our present legislature buildings. The site has been in continuous occupation ever since.

Fort is probably too grand a term for most of these structures, which might consist of a couple of log huts in a clearing. Fort Edmonton,

▲ *Fort Edmonton was the grandest structure of its kind when it was built around the end of the eighteenth century by the Hudson's Bay Company. Photo by Grace H. Lanctot. Courtesy, Hillstrom Stock Photo*

▲ *The Reverend and Mrs. Robert Rundle posed for this photograph after his return to England in 1848. Courtesy, Provincial Archives of Alberta, Photograph Collection*

◄ *Father Albert Lacombe was known to the Indians as the "man of good heart." Courtesy, Provincial Archives of Alberta, E. Brown Collection*

however, had palisades—and needed them, because it sat on the boundary between the warring Cree and Blackfoot.

At this time there was also a growing amount of genuine exploration going on. David Thompson, a youth of 17, accompanied James Gaddy to visit the Piegan in 1787. Thompson was later to be trained as a surveyor, and between 1793 and 1812 did such a thorough job on the rivers of Alberta and British Columbia that he was called the Map-Maker. His travels took him along the North Saskatchewan to its headwaters in the mountains, as well as down the Pembina, the Athabasca, the Peace, and the Columbia.

Thompson was not alone in his work, though. Another name worth noting is that of Peter Fidler. In 1794 Fidler, who was also a surveyor, visited the Piegan and accurately charted the Rocky Mountains, as well as the domed peak near the east end of Lake Minnewanka, called the Devil's Head by the whites and Swan's Bill by the Indians. He also charted portions of the Battle, Red Deer, Bow, and Highwood rivers. Near Rosebud Creek he witnessed a buffalo jump in use, and in the valley of the Red Deer, near the mouth of Threehills Creek, he made the first note of coal in Alberta.

Through the first half of the nineteenth century, most of the white exploration, settlement, and trade took place in the northern half of the province. For example, in 1824, a road was cut from Edmonton House to Fort Assiniboine on the Athabasca. Since the Athabasca was part of the overland route to the Pacific, this made Edmonton an important junction. The southern half was still under the sway of the Blackfoot, who guarded their territory with vigour.

In this century the traders were joined on the frontier by the missionaries. The first, the Roman Catholic Fathers Blanchet and Demers, passed through Edmonton in 1838 on their way to open a mission at Fort Vancouver. They stayed with John Rowand, chief factor of Edmonton House, for only five days, but others soon followed. In 1840 the Methodist minister Robert Terrill Rundle came and made Edmonton his base. Two years later, Reverend Father Jean-Baptiste Thibault came as well, and in 1843 he established a mission at Lac Sainte Anne, northwest of Edmonton.

These men of the cloth had dauntingly large parishes. During Rundle's eight-year stay in the territory, he travelled ceaselessly from Lesser Slave Lake to Banff (where the massive mountain southeast of town now bears his name), and from Jasper House out onto the plains as far as Saskatoon. The missionaries were few, and the various churches often competed against each other as shamelessly as the fur traders. However, they did have a certain effect, as the example of Father Albert Lacombe demonstrates.

Father Lacombe came west in 1852 to replace Father Thibault at the Lac Sainte Anne mission. In 1861 he established the St. Albert mission, the beginnings of the town northwest of Edmonton. For more than 60 years he devoted his life to this area, founding missions, homes,

▲ *This painting by talented Edmonton artist Ella May Walker depicts Father Lacombe arriving from St. Albert in 1858 to celebrate Christmas at Fort Edmonton. Courtesy, City of Edmonton Archives, Richard Secord Collection*

and schools, but it was his personal courage as much as his teaching that won respect. To the Indians he was known as "the man of good heart." Once, when Cree were attacking a Blackfoot camp he was visiting, he strode into the middle of the battle, shouting at both sides to stop. The noise of battle was too loud, though, and they could not hear him. When he was wounded by a ricochet, the Blackfoot cried out that "Good Heart" had been killed. The Cree withdrew in dismay, protesting that they had not known he was there.

Not all the peacemakers were clergy, though. Obedient to a vision, the Cree chief Maskepetoon labored to bring harmony between the Cree and Blackfoot. Around 1850 he managed to bring about an uneasy truce, remembered in the name of the Peace Hills, southwest of present-day Wetaskiwin. Sadly, in 1869, he walked into a Blackfoot trap and was killed by Chief Big Swan.

Another civilizing influence that must be mentioned is the father and son Methodist missionary team of George and John McDougall. They came to Edmonton in 1861 and the following year began to build a mission at Victoria, 70 miles downstream. In a rare reversal of the

▶ Captain John Palliser led an 1857 British expedition through Alberta to gather scientific data about the region. Courtesy, Glenbow Archives, Calgary

▲ ◄ *Methodist missionaries George (left) and John McDougall (above) were father and son. They were an important civilizing influence on Alberta in the latter part of the nineteenth century. Courtesy, Glenbow Archives, Calgary*

usual order of things, the Hudson's Bay Company built a post there in 1864, lured by the number of Indian and Metis attracted by the mission. George McDougall continued to work in Alberta until, in 1876, he died suddenly near Nose Creek, north of Fort Calgary. His son soldiered on into the next century, spreading his robust form of Christianity until he passed away in 1917.

The midpoint of the nineteenth century marked a transition for the developing territory, still known only as part of the vast, HBC-governed Rupert's Land. In 1854 John Rowand, rough-and-ready chief trader at Edmonton House, died. The fur trade was less profitable than it had been, and Edmonton House began to suffer losses of thousands of pounds each year. There were still a few whites in the area, but there was a growing population of Metis at Lac Sainte Anne, St. Albert, Victoria, and Lac La Biche. To the east there was mounting friction between the Metis settlers around Red River and the "Canadians" of Ontario and Quebec, while to the south, the Americans were looking at the northern plains with relish. In short, white civilization was pressing forward.

In 1857, aware that more information was needed about the West, the British government sent an expedition, led by Captain John Palliser, to make scientific observations. Palliser and the members of his expedition, which included a botanist and a geologist, presented a generally favourable report. He noted the existence, however, of the dry, short grass prairie, a roughly triangular region of which the base was the American border, and expressed the opinion that it was only a step away from desert. In fact, he overestimated the aridity and barrenness of this area, which now bears his name. Farmers have produced healthy crops off the Palliser Triangle, though it does suffer from wind erosion in dry years. Also in his report, Palliser took it for granted that the herds of buffalo, once uncountable but now shrinking rapidly, would one day disappear, and he wrote with enthusiasm of the fertile parkland. His conclusion: there were millions of acres of land suitable for settlement and agriculture. The major obstacle he foresaw to the expansion of Canada across the western plains was its inaccessibility for Canadians. The land around the north side of Lake Superior was a tangle of underbrush and muskeg, virtually impassable.

But if the West was difficult to reach from Canada, it was wide open to the United States, and a number of Americans took it for granted that this part of the world would one day salute the stars and stripes. This assumption had a major impact on events over the next 30 years.

In 1867 Canada became a nation, a confederation of Ontario, Quebec, New Brunswick, Nova Scotia, and Prince Edward Island. Although there was not a great deal of cohesion among these provinces, there was a general assumption that the West should be annexed. The Metis living at Red River resented this high-handed attitude, and friction eventually erupted in the Red River Rebellion of 1869. The rebellion was short lived, but many of the Metis, dissatisfied with the results and mistrustful of the Canadians, trekked west over a thousand miles, to settle among the Metis at Lac La Biche, Victoria, and St. Albert.

It was also in 1869 that the first American whiskey posts were built in Alberta. Traders from Fort Benton in Montana built the aptly named Fort Whoop-Up near present-day Lethbridge, and two gentlemen named "Dutch Fred" Watcher and "Liver-Eating" Johnson built a post they called Standoff, on the Belly River. A third post in the area had the sly name of Slide-Out.

The presence of these American traders caused a number of problems, and pointed up the insecurity of the "Canadian" west. These were unscrupulous men who wanted to make a lot of money fast, and did not care what happened to the native people with whom they traded. The whiskey was rarely whiskey—more often it was a horrible concoction of substances, from tea to horse liniment, although it contained enough alcohol to make its victims roaring drunk. As the native people had no experience with alcohol, and thus had evolved no social controls to monitor its use, the effect on the Blood, Blackfoot, and Piegan cultures was disastrous.

It was also alarming that the whiskey traders showed no regard for the medicine line, as the Indians called the border. If these traders had been questioned, they could have rightly pointed out that the border was unsurveyed, so that they had no way of knowing whether

they were in American or British territory—but in fact there was no one to question them.

From 1869 to 1870 another smallpox epidemic swept through the area, with the Indians in particular suffering heavy losses. This outbreak, combined with the effects of alcohol, left the Blackfoot in a disastrous state. Not so disastrous, however, that they could not profit by a tactical error made by a large band of Cree and Assiniboine. In October 1870, in the valley of the Oldman, just about where the Canadian Pacific Railway's trestle bridge now stands within the city of Lethbridge, between 600 and 800 Cree and Assiniboine attacked a Blood camp, without knowing that there was a large band of Piegan nearby. The Piegan were armed with repeating rifles, supplied by the Americans, and in the ensuing rout, slaughtered between 200 and 300 of their northern enemy.

▲ *A Beaver Indian traded his furs in the Hudson's Bay Company store at Fort Vermilion, circa 1886. Courtesy, Provincial Archives of Alberta, E. Brown Collection*

▲ *Nicholas Sheran began the first coal mine in Alberta, after realizing that his quest for gold would not bring him much profit. The site of this early mine would become the city of Lethbridge. Courtesy, Glenbow Archives, Calgary*

That year, 1870, also marked the transfer of the HBC's holdings to Canada. The land of the Peace and the Saskatchewan was no longer a vague portion of Rupert's Land, but was now officially recognized as the Northwest Territories. In the exchange, the Hudson's Bay Company gave up its baronial rule of hundreds of thousands of square miles of wilderness, and became instead a simple trading company. It was well compensated, though. Along with $300,000 cash, the HBC retained an average of 3,000 acres around each post and a reserve of 7 million acres, to be allocated as the prairies were surveyed.

As a confirmation that the Age of Furs was drawing to a close, Nicholas Sheran began a mine in 1870, at the junction of the St. Mary and Oldman rivers. Sheran had come north from Montana looking for gold, but had more luck with coal. Two years later he moved his workings downstream to the scene of the Cree massacre. The site was known as Coal Banks until years later when it was renamed Lethbridge.

Gold, incidentally, had already played some part in the opening of Alberta. In 1860 gold prospectors came east from British Columbia to prospect the North Saskatchewan (there is a regular showing of flour gold here, enough to interest small panners, but not enough for commercial operations), and in 1862 a party of 174, known as the Overlanders, came west, heading toward the gold rush in the Cariboo. These had heard reports of the gold in the North Saskatchewan, and some 60 of them stayed on, about doubling the white population at that time.

Canada now became aware that it had a responsibility to the West and, in 1872, sent out a team of surveyors to mark the 49th parallel. The long line of cairns erected every two or three miles was more symbolic than effective, however, and by this time there was a well-beaten trail from Fort Benton in Montana to Fort Whoop-Up.

Along this route came not only the destructive barrels of "whiskey," but also supplies for the American buffalo hunters and wolfers. These men were hunting for hides alone, and left the carcasses of their kills to rot in the sun. Faced with the combined pressure of liquor, disease, and overhunting of the buffalo, the Indians found themselves in a terrible plight. If the situation did not change, they might well face oblivion.

Moved by the entreaties of the missionaries, as well as by fears that the West might be lost to the United States, Canada established the North West Mounted Police (NWMP) in 1873. This was a new adventure for the young country, in that police had been a provincial, not federal, responsibility. It was decided to call the NWMP a police force, however, rather than a militia, so as not to alarm the Americans. To soothe the Indians, red uniforms were chosen so they might see clearly this was not the hated American "blue-coat" cavalry. Thus, by a stroke of the pen were the Mounties born, a force which proved pivotal in the establishment of Alberta.

In July of 1874 the small force of 275 men set out from Dufferin, Manitoba, to make the trek westward. Their first orders were to shut down Fort Whoop-Up. The ride itself was the first gruelling test for

▲ *Red coats were chosen for the North West Mounted Police to distinguish them from the hated American cavalry, dressed in blue. These modern-day mounties can be seen at Fort Macleod. Photo by Wilfried D. Schurig. Courtesy, Hillstrom Stock Photo*

▶ *North West Mounted Police offic- ers posed for this 1906 photograph at Fort Saskatchewan. Courtesy, Provin- cial Archives of Alberta, E. Brown Col- lection*

the young and very green force. Heat, flies, dysentery (probably brought on by drinking from alkali sloughs), and inexperience made the trip slow hell. It was fortunate that they had no other opponent, or they might never have reached their goal.

At last, they came to the Cypress Hills, and while the main force camped here, Commissioner George A. French and his assistant Major James Macleod rode south to Fort Benton in search of supplies. Here the force procured not only flour, tea, and sugar, but also the services of the phenomenal Metis guide, Jerry Potts.

While Commissioner French returned to Swan River for the winter, Potts took a force under Macleod to Fort Whoop-Up, which the Moun- ties approached with due form and proper military caution. They found the fort virtually deserted, however, and the closing of the whis- key post was accomplished without a shot being fired. The force now rode on, at Potts' direction, to a spot overlooking the Oldman River, and began at last to build themselves a home base—Fort Macleod, named for their commander.

The arrival of the NWMP forms a watershed in Alberta history be- tween the wilderness and the beginnings of settlement, and the events of the next five years show this clearly. Early in 1875, the Mounties established Fort Calgary by the confluence of the Elbow and the Bow.

The fort did not start out with this name, however. It was popularly known as Bow Fort until Inspector Ephrem Brisebois issued an order that it be called after him: Fort Brisebois. When word of this got back to headquarters, however, Commissioner A.G. Irvine countermanded the order. Instead, he acceded to the recommendation of (now Colonel) Macleod that the fort be named after a castle on the Isle of Mull, owned

◄ *A telegraph gang raises a pole in the Rocky Mountains, circa 1886. Courtesy, Glenbow Archives, Calgary*

▲ *The Edmonton Hotel, built at the end of the 1870s, was the first hotel west of Winnipeg. Courtesy, City of Edmonton Archives*

by relatives of his by marriage. He declared that the name meant "clear, running water," and although scholars of Gaelic doubt this, it is an appropriate image for this city.

Later in 1875, the 45-metre SS *Northcote* steamed into Edmonton, greatly increasing the freight capacity between Winnipeg and northwestern Canada.

More changes followed. In 1876 the Plains and Woods Cree signed Treaty No. 6; they were followed by the Blood, Blackfoot, Piegan, Sarcee and Stoney, who signed Treaty No. 7 the next year. These agreements were an implicit acknowledgment that the old way of the nomadic hunters had gone, or was quickly going forever. In exchange for the vast territories that had once sustained them, the Indians accepted small parcels of their own choosing to be held in perpetuity, as well as small yearly payments for each man, woman, and child. It was the belief of the government that the natives would now become farmers, and so it was agreed to supply them with tools, cattle, seed, and agricultural training. There was also a provision to provide schools and teachers. Compared to colonial practice in other parts of the world, this was probably a reasonable settlement, though it necessitated a change in livelihood for which the natives were ill prepared.

As the 1870s drew to a close, the telegraph, that miraculous wire

This watercolour illustrates the type of stagecoach that operated between Edmonton and Calgary from 1883 until the arrival of the train in 1891. The stagecoach took a minimum of five days to make a one-way trip. Painting by A.H. Hider. Courtesy, City of Edmonton Archives, Hubert Hollingworth Collection

that made distance vanish, reached Edmonton, and hope ran high in the tiny hamlet that the transcontinental railway was headed that way. Indeed, there was to be such a link—that had been one of the inducements used to lure British Columbia into confederation in 1871. It was widely believed that the prairie portion of the rail line would run northwest from Selkirk, Manitoba, along the old Carlton Trail to Edmonton, and then west through the Yellowhead Pass. And Donald Ross was ready. His Edmonton Hotel was open for business, the first hotel west of Winnipeg.

Meanwhile, in the south of the province, the ranching potential of the area, which had been tested earlier in the decade, was confirmed almost by accident. In 1876 Sergeant Whitney of the NWMP had bought 25 head of cattle from a Montana drover, and then realized he lacked the hay with which to feed them through the winter. Reluctantly, he turned the cattle loose, expecting never to see them again. When spring came, however, he was delighted to find that they had all survived. Alberta's first roundup showed that cattle could do well on the open range. Other men followed suit, some taking an early discharge from the Mounties to set themselves up as ranchers.

When head were counted in 1881, the census showed that there were 263 people at Edmonton, and another 500 in surrounding settlements. Calgary had only 75, clustered around the police post, while Fort Macleod accounted for another 500. This census numbered only white and Metis. The Indian count was much higher—over 11,000 for both Alberta and Saskatchewan. The ratio was changing rapidly, however, as pioneers headed west, lured by the twin promise of land and railroad.

The railroad got under way at last, begun by the newly minted Canadian Pacific Railway Company (CPR) in 1882. The band of steel that the CPR built did as much as anything to open the West and pull Canada into a single country, but it did so with an arrogance born of unassailable monopoly.

In order to attract the private investment necessary, the government gave the company an enormous land grant in the prairies—alternate square mile sections to a depth of 24 miles on either side of the track. This amounted to 25 million acres. Furthermore, because the West was practically empty, the railway was able to choose its route at will. Edmontonians were disappointed, for example, when it was announced that the steel would push more or less straight across the prairies from Winnipeg and cross the Rockies at Kicking Horse Pass. Many land speculators lost their roll when the railway bypassed the site they considered ideal for a siding or station.

That same year, "Alberta" became the official designation for a measured chunk of real estate. The Northwest Territory that year was divided in four: the territories of Alberta, Assiniboia, Athabasca, and Saskatchewan. The last three names of course are renderings of Indian words, but the name of our province came from Princess Louise Alberta, wife of then Governor-General of Canada, the Marquis of Lorne.

▲ *Shown here is a Canadian Pacific Railway heavy grade engine in the Rockies. Courtesy, Provincial Archives of Alberta, E. Brown Collection*

▶ Alberta was named for Princess Louise Alberta, wife of then Governor-General of Canada, the Marquis of Lorne, in 1882. Courtesy, Provincial Archives of Alberta, Public Affairs Collection

The Alberta of 1882 was not as large as the present version. The southern and western borders were the same, but the northern border was about the 55th parallel, beyond which lay the District of Athabasca. This was later divided among the three prairie provinces. As a district, as opposed to a province, Alberta had no government of its own, but could elect members to a Territorial Council whenever there were 1,000 voters living in an area of not more than 1,000 square miles. (Indians did not have the vote, but then, neither did women of any race. A woman could sit upon the throne of the British Empire, but not send a representative to the Territorial Council.) Edmonton attained this political status the following year and elected Frank Oliver, editor of the *Edmonton Bulletin.*

It was the southern part of the territory that was starting to take off, however. It had been shown that ranching worked in the sunny chinook belt; moreover, the railroad was coming and the government had offered to lease huge blocks of crown land for grazing. Would-be ranchers could lease up to 100,000 acres for a penny an acre a year. Within four years almost 3 million acres had been leased.

For a few years the massive ranches created a kind of aristocratic

▲ *The Cochrane Ranche Historic Site is located on the site of the first large-scale ranching venture in Alberta. Photo by Wes Bergen. Courtesy, Hillstrom Stock Photo*

◄ *These branding irons, used by early Alberta cattle ranchers, are on display at Heritage Park in Calgary. Photo by Wilfried D. Schurig. Courtesy, Hillstrom Stock Photo*

ranching community. The hot, dusty work of roundup and branding was tempered by the most elegant of homes and such genteel amusements as polo. Senator H.M. Cochrane's spread, west of Fort Calgary, was not a ranch, but rather a ranche—the Cochrane Ranche Company Ltd., to be exact.

This era of princely ranching was not to last, though it continued in an altered form for some years. There was a growing pressure from the East for open homesteading, a cause supported especially by the Liberal Party. In 1892 the government announced that the lease system was coming to a close, but tenants could purchase up to a tenth of their lease for $1.25 an acre.

However, the baronial ranchers probably did not slow down settlement as much as other factors. In the early 1880s there was a surge of immigration, amounting to about 125,000 settlers spread across the prairies, but after that it slowed to a trickle. This was partly due to a worldwide depression that had begun in 1873 and continued until almost the end of the century. It was also the result of bad press. Reports of drought, grasshoppers, crop failure, and frost came from every farming district, no matter how successful. There were also rumours of unrest among the Metis, and no one was sure whether these might not spread to the Indians. The American cavalry had won its Indian wars, but many settlers had lost their lives in the conflict.

The unrest erupted in 1885 in the Northwest Rebellion. Louis Riel had returned from the United States, and years of rancour over racial and religious discrimination came boiling to the surface. A detachment of Mounties clashed with Metis at Duck Lake, in what is now Saskatchewan, and when the news came stuttering through on the telegraph, all of Alberta held its breath. The Indians still outnumbered the whites.

▼ *The Northwest Rebellion in 1885 was the last serious challenge to white control of the territory. Shown here is the battle of Cutknife Creek. Courtesy, Glenbow Archives, Calgary*

▲ Edmonton artist Harry S. Craig worked from an 1871 black and white photograph taken by pioneer photographer Charles G. Horetzky to create this superb watercolour. Members of the Canadian Pacific Railway survey team are shown resting at their camp on the North Saskatchewan River. Courtesy, City of Edmonton Archives, Hubert Hollingworth Collection

▶ *Chief Crowfoot was a celebrated leader of the Blackfoot confederacy. Courtesy, Provincial Archives of Alberta, H. Pollard Collection*

If they joined in, the settlers could easily be overwhelmed.

Cree under Poundmaker and Big Bear did join the fight, not so much as co-ordinated allies, but in independent retaliation against what they considered encroachment by the whites. In Alberta the question was, would the Blackfoot confederacy attack as well? It would depend upon their celebrated chief, Crowfoot.

Crowfoot had good reason to fight. It was less than 10 years since he had signed Treaty No. 7, but in that time the whites had, in his view, broken their word many times. The Blackfoot had been hard pressed by disease and hunger, and the government's famine relief had been small and slow in coming. Also, the Cree chief Poundmaker was his adopted son. Messengers came frequently from the north, informing him of the Cree victories, and urging him to rise with them.

Then word came of a massacre at Frog Lake, only 130 miles east of Edmonton. Wandering Spirit and a band of Cree killed nine men, and took a man and two women prisoner. The rebellion was spreading. Alarmed and anticipating imminent attack, many settlers moved to the shelter of Edmonton, Fort Saskatchewan, and St. Albert. Troops were rushed westward from Ontario, and at Calgary, Major-General T. Bland Strange threw together the Alberta Field Force, a loose assort-

ment of cowboys and retired soldiers.

Meanwhile, pressure was mounting on Chief Crowfoot. Both whites and Indians came to see him, hoping he would take their side of the dispute. The Cree, however, becoming impatient, and threatened that if Crowfoot did not join them, they would fall upon the Blackfoot after the Europeans had been wiped out. This was bad psychology to use with the proud leader, who, furthermore, knew something of the resources of the white man. Some time before, Indian Commissioner Edgar Dewdney had sent Crowfoot and several other Blackfoot on the train to Winnipeg, and he knew that there was more to the colonists than shacks, tents, and a handful of police. At last, when the chief learned that the neighboring tribes of Blood, Piegan, and Sarcee would not support the rebellion, Crowfoot publicly declared his loyalty to the government.

A month later, at the four-day long Battle of Batoche, the rebel forces were crushed. Riel was taken prisoner and his brilliant general, Gabriel Dumont, fled to the States. This proved to be the last serious challenge to the rapidly developing law and order that would help turn wilderness into a prosperous province.

In the fall of that year, 1885, the two narrow fingers of steel that the CPR had been pushing across the country met in a pass west of Revelstoke, and Alberta was joined with the rest of the country in a transcontinental railroad. This gave a natural advantage to the southern part of the territory. Indeed, Calgary, which was much younger than Edmonton, had been incorporated as a town in 1884, a status Edmonton did not reach for another six years.

Although economic depression still lay upon eastern Canada and Europe, a tide of settlement now began to surge in the West. In June 1887 Charles Ora Card led a party of 40 Mormons north from Utah to the southwest corner of the territory. Camped by Lee Creek, they

This impressive Mormon temple, seen here circa 1940, is located in Cardston. The town was named for Charles Card, who led a party of 40 Mormons there in 1887. Courtesy, Provincial Archives of Alberta, H. Pollard Collection

woke up to find six inches of snow had fallen during the night. The snow did not deter them, however. By 1901 more than 3,000 Mormons had come, and the town of Cardston had a population of 693.

Another group to arrive was a band of German-speaking Galicians, who spent two fruitless years on the dry plains near Medicine Hat before moving north to the lush parkland around Edmonton. Within a few years, several hundred more had come to the area, starting such towns as Bruderheim and Josephsburg.

With gathering speed the map began to fill in as other ethnic groups came, settled, and drew family and friends after. In 1891 Father Morin began to colonize areas around Edmonton with Francophones from Quebec, Michigan, Belgium, and France. Beaumont, Legal, Vegreville, Picardville, and of course Morinville are all fruits of his efforts. In 1892 Anglo-Saxons from the Parry Sound region of Ontario came and settled east of Edmonton. At the same time, Norwegians were settling to the north, Swedes to the south by the Battle River, and Icelanders to the southwest, near present-day Innisfail. Beginning in 1895 there was also a large influx of Ukrainians, brought in largely through the efforts of the philanthropist Dr. Josef Oleskov. Many of the families in the Smoky Lake/Willingdon/Two Hills region came at this time.

Nevertheless, these areas of settlement, small homesteads chopped out of the bush, with perhaps a horse, a cow, and a sod-roofed hut, were only the beginning. The real land rush was about to begin, catalyzed by Clifford Sifton and the new Liberal government.

Clifford Sifton was the federal Minister of the Interior, and he put together a spectacular advertising campaign to bring more settlers into the country. Posters and pamphlets were sent all over the United States and Europe, describing the homestead policy: a quarter section, or 160 acres, free, as long as you lived on it, built on it, and broke a certain portion to crop. Immigration agents went abroad, too, and journalists from Europe and the States were given free trips to the land of golden opportunity.

The propaganda worked. In a few years, thousands of immigrants a year began to fill up the country. Alberta's population in 1895 was about 30,000. By 1901 it was more than double that—just over 73,000. In the next five years it more than doubled again.

This settler rush was aided to some extent by the discovery of gold in the Klondike in 1897. The ensuing gold rush helped shake off the last of the depression that had held the country to a walk, as well as bringing a certain number of gold seekers through Alberta.

Edmonton proudly celebrates Klondike Days every summer, just after Calgary finishes off its Stampede. In fact, Edmonton is 1,500 miles from the Klondike, but some would-be prospectors did pass through here. Of the thousands who swarmed into the Yukon, only a few hundred actually came by way of Edmonton. If you like parades, though, any excuse will do.

With a burgeoning population, it was clear that Alberta would soon need more control over its affairs. In 1905 the Northwest Territories south of 60 degrees north were redivided, and the provinces of Alberta

◄ Edmonton, one of the jumping-off points for the Klondike Gold Rush, celebrates Klondike Days every summer. Photo by Katherine Rodeghier. Courtesy, Hillstrom Stock Photo

and Saskatchewan came into being. George Bulyea was appointed lieutenant-governor, and A.C. Rutherford, a prominent Liberal lawyer from the town of Strathcona, was named as the premier, pending an election.

Calgarians were shocked when the capital was provisionally placed at Edmonton. True, Edmonton was close to the geographic centre, but Calgary was closer to the centre of the population. The real reason for the choice probably had something to do with Edmontonian Frank Oliver, who was now a federal cabinet minister. Calgarian hopes of changing the situation were dashed, however, when the first election returned a Liberal government. Calgary had been Conservative, or at least anti-Grit, since the grazing lease dispute of the early 1890s, while Edmonton had been Liberal.

The new province had a solid base in agriculture—well over 8 percent of its population was rural. Nevertheless, other resources were being developed, as well. Coal was being mined at Coal Bank, now renamed Lethbridge for the president of the North-Western Coal and Navigation Company, as well as in the Crowsnest Pass, west of Cardston. Lumber was being cut from the seemingly limitless forests, and sawn at a number of mills. More intriguing was the needle-in-a-haystack search for gas and oil.

This story of resource development actually begins a couple of hundred years earlier when, in 1718, a Cree named Swan brought samples of the Athabasca tar sands to traders at York Factory on the Hudson Bay. Perhaps he was a visonary, or perhaps he thought the whites were crazy enough to buy anything—we'll never know. In any case, no one really knew what to do with the stiff and sticky stuff, so it remained a curiosity for the time being.

Another hint at the potential of the province was given in 1883, when a CPR crew drilled for water at a siding 40 miles west of Medicine Hat. They found not water but natural gas. In 1890 a commercial gas well was brought in to supply Medicine Hat.

In 1894 the Geological Survey of Canada drilled a well at Athabasca Landing, looking for oil. The hole reached a depth of 1,770 feet by 1896 (drilling being somewhat slower in those days) and showed gas, but no oil. The following year a hole at Pelican Rapids hit an uncontrollable flow of gas at 800 feet and had to be abandoned. The well blew wild for 20 years.

From these and other finds, it was obvious there was *something* under the ground. Alberta had some sort of hydrocarbon future, but the expertise to find it and the know-how to handle it were not in place just yet.

The years immediately following Alberta's rise to the status of a province were boom years. Settlers continued to flood into the countryside, brought by the CPR and the new Canadian Northern line from Winnipeg to Edmonton. Helped by the development of new, earlier-ripening varieties of wheat, homesteaders were also opening up the Peace River district.

An Edmonton Coal Company's mine is pictured, circa 1902. Courtesy, Provincial Archives of Alberta, E. Brown Collection

Lethbridge, Medicine Hat, Wetaskiwin, and Strathcona (the community across the river from Edmonton which had bloomed when the railway reached it in 1891) were all incorpoarted as cities.

In 1908 the University of Alberta was founded, and again the pride of southern Alberta was snubbed. With the capital in Edmonton, it might have been reasonable to situate the campus in Calgary, but instead, Strathcona was chosen. True, the prestigious plum was not given to the capital itself, but Edmonton acquired it anyway, when Strathcona and Edmonton amalgamated in 1912.

Calgary and the south, however, were leading the way in energy development. In 1905 A.W. Dingman hit gas in east Calgary, and by the end of the decade was supplying the Calgary Brewing Company and a number of residences. By 1912 there was a 170-mile pipeline bringing gas to Calgary from the Bow Island region on the Oldman River. Then, in 1914, Dingman struck oil in Turner Valley, about 30 miles southwest of Calgary, setting off an intense flurry of speculation. We know now it was a small, shallow pool, not much compared to the fields found later, but it was enough. Alberta was "well" into the oil business.

Later in the year, the Great War, World War I, broke out, with mixed effect on Alberta. Canada was still very conscious of its British ties, and so there was heavy enlistment. In the course of the war, the province sent over 45,000 men into service, about 10 percent of her total population. Sadly, many of these did not return, leaving gaps in almost every family. The hostilities also slowed immigration to a trickle.

On the other hand, the war created a seller's market for wheat. With increasing mechanization, early ripening varieties, and good weather, the farms did well. In 1915 wheat yielded a record high of 31 bushels to the acre, which might explain why in 1916 there were 2,605,000 acres planted to wheat. Coal was also needed for the war effort. The same year, Alberta produced 4.6 million tons.

When the war concluded, normal life resumed. Major irrigation districts were established through the south of the province, and fields of sugar beets were planted. When these prospered, a sugar factory was built in Raymond. The Edmonton, Dunvegan & British Columbia railway had reached the Peace River district, and the Alberta & Great Waterways line would reach Fort McMurray by 1924. These transportation links not only helped open up the northern part of the province, but also solidified Edmonton's claim to being the Gateway to the North.

It was a claim that took on new meaning in 1920, when oil was discovered at Fort Norman, near Great Bear Lake in the Northwest Territories. The surge of interest in the north combined with the new expertise of a number of demobbed servicemen to produce that unique Canadian phenomenon: the northern bush pilot.

Alberta flyers had won distinction during the war. Perhaps the best-known story was that of "Wop" May and Roy Brown. On his first combat flight, May became the target of the German flying ace von Richtofen, the famous Red Baron. While von Richtofen was pursuing his

▲ *A large crowd gathered to witness the arrival of this Ford motor plane on June 15, 1930. Courtesy, Provincial Archives of Alberta, A. Blyth Collection*

▶ *Lieutenant Wilfred Reid "Wop" May was an Alberta aviator who won fame during World War I because of an encounter with the Red Baron. Courtesy, Glenbow Archives, Calgary*

quarry, Brown shot him down. May was not always the hare, however. By the end of the war, he had hounded 13 enemy craft from the sky.

At first when these aviators returned from battle, there was little for them to do. They made a living around the countryside however they could, offering airplane rides to earthbound farmers and their children. When oil was found in the north, however, the flyers became indispensable. Some were hired outright by oil companies, while others set up companies of their own, ferrying supplies, mail, and people from settlement to settlement.

Courage and resourcefulness were demanded to fly through the unmarked wastes in bone-chilling cold. It became standard practice, for example, upon landing to immediately lean from the cockpit and drain the oil from the engine—into a tin, if there was one, or onto the snow if nothing else would serve. The reason for this maneuver was that the oil would turn almost solid if left in place, and it would then become impossible to crank the motor. Once removed, though, the oil could be warmed over a flame—if the pilot could get one

started—and then poured back into the block just as he was ready to take off.

The courage of the northern pilots was clearly revealed in the flight of "Wop" May and Vic Horner on New Year's Eve, 1928. Diphtheria had broken out near Fort Vermilion, and the two took off with a cargo of antitoxin in an open plane at a temperature of -33 degrees Fahrenheit. When they landed at Edmonton days later, a crowd of 10,000 cheered their return.

The airplane was matched by that other modern invention, the radio. The first Alberta stations went on the air in 1922. The radio proved to be a device that changed Alberta society, not merely because it allowed soap makers to peddle their wares to the masses. In 1925 William Aberhart, a Calgary school principal and evangelist, began broadcasting his two-hour Radio Sunday School program. His Prophetic Bible Institute developed a wide following, but it wasn't until the depths of the Dirty Thirties that the union of minister and microphone had its full, unlooked-for effect.

The Great Depression that began in 1929 devastated Alberta as it did the rest of western Canada. Its effects were exacerbated here by the reversion of the short grass prairie to its fundamental aridity. During the first two decades of this century, rainfalls had been heavier than usual, and farmers were lured onto land that should never have been plowed. By the mid-twenties, crops were failing and farms were being abandoned. When the economy collapsed in 1929, some farmers hung on, each year hoping that the rain would come—but their efforts only worsened the situation. Tilling squandered the last trace of moisture and left the soil a fine, dry powder. Any wind would lift it by the half-inch and the acre, and blow it all the way to Manitoba. To make matters worse, the price of wheat dropped out of sight; any crop that could be raised was hardly worth the effort.

Farms were abandoned to the bank and the wind. Once-sporty Model T Fords, their motors stripped out, were pulled by horses because no one could afford gasoline. In ironic reference to the prime minister R.B. Bennett, a former Albertan, these were called Bennett Buggies. At the worst, an estimated 15 percent of the population was on relief.

In the midst of this gloom, William Aberhart produced a gleam of light. In 1932 he came upon the unusual theories of Major C.H. Douglas, who claimed that there was an inherent flaw in the monetary system. Douglas claimed that the spending power of the consumer could never keep up with potential production, and he thus advocated payments from the government to the citizens, known as social dividends or social credit. To Aberhart it made sense, and he began to preach social credit every Sunday.

It made sense to Albertans, too. In the election of 1935, the Social Credit Party took 56 of the 63 seats, while the incumbent United Farmers of Alberta Party was completely wiped out. "Bible Bill" Aberhart was the new premier.

Although the new government made some attempt to implement

▲ *Evangelist and radio broadcaster William Aberhart was elected premier in 1935 on the strength of his social credit platform. Courtesy, Glenbow Archives, Calgary*

the theories of social credit, such as passing laws to control banking, money, and credit, these were ruled by the courts and the federal government as being out of provincial jurisdiction. In spite of this (or perhaps because of it), the Social Credit Party (Socreds) remained in power in Alberta for another 36 years, always with a sizable majority.

The success of the party probably had more to do with its leaders than with its policies. When Aberhart died in 1943, he was succeeded by Ernest C. Manning, who led the party until 1968. Both men were sincere, hard working, and highly respected.

In 1971 the Social Credit dynasty gave way to the Conservative Party, whose majorities have been even more one-sided, and whose tenure in office may someday rival that of the Socreds. Premier Peter Lougheed resigned in 1985, and was replaced by Don Getty. It is curious to note that while both Aberhart and Manning were preachers, both Lougheed and Getty were once professional football players.

As with the war of 1914 to 1918, the Second World War had a mixed effect on Alberta. Many thousands of men marched away, and for those who stayed behind there was the anxiety of waiting, the bitterness of loss, and the hardship of rationing. There was also welcome employment and even

▶ *The Reverend Ernest C. Manning, successor to "Bible Bill" Aberhart, was sworn into the office of premier on September 16, 1952. Courtesy, Provincial Archives of Alberta, Public Affairs Collection*

prosperity because of the American effort to supply and garrison Alaska.

Even before the Americans entered the war, they had concerns for the security of their northernmost territory and in 1940 arranged for a huge airlift through Edmonton. This concern grew, of course, after the attack on Pearl Harbor, and was further augmented by the transfer of hundreds of lend-lease aircraft to Russia. To accommodate the traffic, a second airport was built in Namao, north of Edmonton, at the time the largest airport in North America.

The Americans were not satisfied with an air link, however, and in 1942 offered to build and maintain an overland route—the Alaska Highway, four-fifths of which would be in Canada. Within days of the agreement, work began. At the height of construction, there were

◄ The Alaska Highway was built through Canada's wilderness by a welcome army of United States soldiers. Courtesy, City of Edmonton Archives

▲ *Enthusiastic crowds gathered for this V-J Day parade on August 15, 1945. Courtesy, Provincial Archives of Alberta, A. Blyth Collection*

◄ *The Imperial Oil Company hit it big with Leduc No. 1 in 1947. Hundreds of people gathered to see the flames, which rose over 200 feet into the air. Courtesy, City of Edmonton Archives*

27,000 men working on the project, which was completed in an astonishing nine months. Needless to say, the tremendous energy electrified northern Alberta, and Edmonton in particular.

When the war ended, Alberta had a population of 803,000, of which more than a quarter lived in the two major cities of Edmonton and Calgary. The rural/urban mix was slowly changing; now only 56 percent of the province lived on the farm.

The move to the city was accelerated in 1947 by the black gusher of Leduc No. 1. There had been a number of successful oil wells since the Turner Valley discovery of 1914, including the revelation of a larger Turner Valley pool in 1934, but the Leduc field was the biggest yet. Even better, it was followed by other finds.

Geologists were getting better at their work, and soon seismic crews were poking into corners of the province no one had ever bothered with before—and finding oil. In the next 25 years, rock sleuths found reserves of 8 billion barrels. Of course, natural gas was also found, and the petrochemical industry became the mainstay of the Alberta economy.

As exploration and production accelerated, so did the establishment of the infrastructures that supported the oil industry. Roads, pipelines, refineries, and airfields were built, as well as necessary secondary industries.

By 1970, production of conventional crude oil had begun to surpass discovery. In other words, reserves, though large, were beginning to shrink. This applied only to conventional crude oil, however. Alberta also has a truly massive supply of oil sand, from which is produced synthetic crude.

The problem with oil sand has always been how to extract the petroleum, and in the mid-sixties Great Canadian Oil Sands began experimenting with a steam extraction process. This proved feasible, and in 1967 oil began to flow from Fort McMurray to Edmonton. Ten years later the Syncrude project came on stream.

Now, millions of cubic metres of oil a year are produced in what is essentially an open pit mining operation. The muskeg is peeled back and huge bucket wheels chew out the oil sand. When the cut is complete, strict environmental guidelines ensure that the land is returned to its original condition.

Alberta continued to expand at a steady pace until 1973, when the formation of the OPEC cartel sent oil prices shooting upward. With them went Alberta's fortunes, or so it seemed. However, these events also brought to the surface the divisions between central and western Canada. The older part of the country had always been the industrial centre, supplying goods to the newer regions, whose contribution to the economy had been the production of cheap raw materials. When the world price of oil rose, however, it became an open question whether the factories in Ontario and Quebec would be sheltered, or whether Alberta would get the market price for its crude.

This led to a classic showdown in Canadian politics: Alberta's Conservative premier Peter Lougheed, whose family had pioneered here,

▲ *Continental Oil Company well number 21 is pictured in 1951. Courtesy, Provincial Archives of Alberta, H. Pollard Collection*

against Liberal prime minister Pierre Trudeau. Both were strong candidates with large majorities, and both had principle on their side. Unfortunately for Alberta, Trudeau won, and a two-price system was implemented.

In spite of this, oil royalties continued to fill the Alberta treasury, and up to 30 percent of this income was diverted into a special account, called the Alberta Heritage Savings Trust Fund. This was a nest egg set up by the government in recognition that oil revenues would one day run out. By 1985, shortly before the government capped the fund, it had reached a total of $12.7 billion.

This rapidly growing fund did not generate sympathy in central Canada, however, and in 1980 the federal government, once again under Trudeau after a brief rule by Albertan Joe Clark and the Conservative Party, brought in the National Energy Program (NEP). Ostensibly, this was meant to ensure that the oil industry would be Canadian owned, and that the oil companies would look for oil in places like the Arctic and offshore (or anywhere besides Alberta). Nevertheless, the NEP put many obstacles in the way of the oil industry here, and when oil prices fell sharply from 1983 to 1984, conventional exploration went into a coma, from which it did not emerge until 1987. Then, when the NEP had been dismantled by a Conservative Ottawa government, and the oil price had begun to rise again, conventional exploration started to recover.

The perceived injustice of the NEP gave rise to a certain separatist sentiment, espoused in particular by the newly formed Western Canada Concept Party, but it is doubtful there is any broad-based support for it. The anger here was more against the Liberal government than it was against the concept of national Canada.

The history of Alberta is in truth the history of Albertans—the people who have built their lives here. Like humans everywhere, we have made mistakes, but the human quality is nevertheless our biggest resource. As the incursion of ancient seas left us geological treasures, so the waves of settlement, beginning thousands of years ago, have given us great riches. It is this endowment, as much as the rocks and trees and soil, which will determine our future.

Albertans of the Lawless Frontier

by Fred Stenson

For many, Alberta was the last frontier. In its lawless state, before the North West Mounted Police arrived in 1874, Alberta spawned and lured a brand of individual the province would have great trouble accommodating within its laws today. Notions of heroism and villainy blur in the life stories of these intrepid and often ferocious early Albertans.

For three difficult decades, 1823 to 1854, the fur trade in the Alberta region was run by one man: John Rowand. Rowand was the proprietor of Fort Edmonton and chief factor of the Saskatchewan fur district. The Indian tribes of the Blackfoot alliance and their bitter enemies, the Cree and Assiniboine, all traded at Fort Edmonton, and John Rowand dealt with the resulting murder and mayhem with a mixture of diplomacy and fury. His men were treated mostly to his fury, physical abuse, and regular tongue lashings in colourful language. They responded by nicknaming him "Twenty-One Shillings" or "One Pound One." Rowand was lame, and "one pound one" was the sound he made stamping about the wooden floors of the fort.

The legend of how Rowand came to have his limp is a rare romantic note in his rugged biography. In his younger years, while riding alone, he fell from his horse and broke a leg. He probably would have perished except that a Metis woman, Louise Umfreville, found and rescued him. Although Louise bore Rowand's children, he never married her, even after the missionaries arrived and gave church blessing to most of the other "country" marriages.

Rowand had a passion for gambling. He raised fine horses and raced them on a track within sight of his fort. He also had a prize fighter who rode along in the spring fur brigades to Hudson Bay. At York Factory, Rowand would pit this bully against the bullies of other brigades, betting heavily on the result.

John Rowand died as he had lived. In 1854 he was riding his last brigade east en route to retirement. At one of the first stops, Fort Pitt, a fight broke out between voyageurs. Rowand knocked the two apart, and had his fist cocked to strike when he himself fell down dead.

One of the men who professed pleasure at the news of Rowand's death was a York boat builder by the name of William Gladstone. Gladstone had suffered at Rowand's hands on several occasions. One spring, Rowand chose Gladstone as an oarsman for the brigade even though Gladstone's trade was carpentry. When Gladstone developed a severe infection in his hand, Rowand refused to take him off his oar. Rowand's reasoning was that, if a man is not dead after three days, he was not really sick to begin with.

The one thing William Gladstone had in common with his old boss was that his life had been saved by a Metis wife; in Gladstone's case, on two occasions. Once, while driving dogs between forts in winter, Gladstone fell through the ice which covered a lake. The dogs raced on, and Gladstone would have been left behind to freeze except that his wife tied a rope around her waist and threw herself off the sled as an anchor. Another time, at a fort whose inhabitants were starving, a man believed Gladstone had cheated him out of food; the man pulled a gun and meant to shoot—but just in time Gladstone's wife knocked the weapon out of his hand with an axe.

After he left the fur trade, William Gladstone applied his carpentry skills to amusingly diverse projects. He built at least two missionary churches and at least one whiskey fort, the notorious Fort Whoop-Up.

The lawless whiskey trade involved several of Alberta's most intriguing figures. Irishman John George "Kootenai" Brown began his experiences in Canada in the mid-nineteenth century as a gold prospector and then a whiskey trader. In an incredible frontier career, Brown also hunted buffalo with the Red River Metis and rode pony express through the Dakotas. He was captured by Sitting Bull and lived to tell about it.

The low point in Brown's life came during his days as a "wolfer." Wolfers poisoned wolves with strychnine and sold the pelts to the fur traders for $1 apiece. Brown got in an

◄ *John George "Kootenai" Brown. Courtesy, Glenbow Archives, Calgary*

argument with a fellow wolfer, stabbed the man to death, and wound up in a Fort Benton jail, awaiting trial for muder. The chances of being lynched first were high. The court, however, set Brown free for lack of evidence, and he promptly took his Metis wife and children north of the 49th parallel, to settle on the shores of Waterton Lakes.

Brown's version of a quieter life was to set up a trading shop at the lakes for the Kootenay Indians. After each trade, Brown and his partner Fred Kanouse gambled with the Indians to try and win their trade goods back. Liquor was involved in the trade, but Brown claimed his customers only drank on the premises and were never sold liquor to take away—a matter of safety rather than ethics.

Before he died in 1916, "Kootenai" Brown had the pleasure of knowing his beloved Waterton Lakes would not change much after he was gone. Largely by his efforts, the area was made a Canadian National Park in 1911.

The whiskey trade also spawned Alberta's first, and perhaps last, double agent. In the middle decades of the nineteenth century, the Hudson's Bay Company was locked in a struggle with the American Fur Company for the trade of the Blackfoot alliance tribes. James Bird, Jr., the Metis son of a Hudson's Bay chief factor, was sent to the prairies to live with the Piegan Indians and to use his influence to bring their trade north to the company.

In the years that followed, "Jimmy Jock" Bird became a war chief of the Piegan. He took money from the Hudson's Bay Company and from the American Fur Company, and was accused of betraying both. The early missionaries also accused him of being a traitor. On two occasions he was hired to escort missionaries onto the prairie and interpret for them. On the first occasion, he took the Wesleyan Robert T. Run-

dle as far as the Bow River and then refused to interpret his words. Later, he brought the Catholic priest Pierre Jean De Smet south and abandoned him there.

In their assessment of Bird as traitor, the traders and missionaries missed the point that he was true to one cause: that of the Piegan Indians amongst whom he lived. By siding with everyone, and therefore with no one, Bird was keeping Piegan territory relatively free of both traders and missionaries.

Bird's ferocity as a Piegan war chief is seen in a story of revenge at Fort Hall in the Montana territory. In 1832 a white trader named Antoine Godin invited a Blackfoot Indian in for a meeting under a truce. Godin shook the Indian's hand and, at the same time, gave the signal for him to be shot. Four years later, Bird brought Piegan braves south to Fort Hall and called for Godin to come across the river to trade. While Godin smoked their pipe of peace, "Jimmy Jock" gave the signal and Godin was shot. Bird scalped Godin himself and carved "N.J.W." on the man's forehead, the initials of N.J. Wyeth, the proprietor of Fort Hall.

A man who was literally born into the violence of the whiskey trade and, in the end, did more than any other to end it on Alberta soil, was the Metis scout Jerry Potts. Jerry's father, Andrew Potts, was a clerk for the American Fur Company, and part of his job was to dispense whiskey out of a wicket on the outside wall of Fort Mackenzie. Wakened in the night by a pounding on the wicket, the clerk Potts went to open it. A flintlock rifle was jammed through the opening and fired. One White Eye, the Piegan Indian who killed Potts, was after a different trader who had thrown him out of the fort the day before.

Jerry Potts was then adopted by Alexander Harvey, probably the most vicious whiskey trader to ever live. Harvey once killed 13 Blackfoot

with a cannon blast. Harvey's tactics were so vile that the other traders hatched a plot to kill him. Harvey escaped and left Potts behind. From then on, Potts was raised by a more benign trader named Dawson.

Most of Jerry Potts' adult life was spent in Alberta. He divided his time between his mother's people, the Blood Indians, and the whiskey forts where he worked as a hunter. In 1870 he was the chief strategist in a bloody victory of the Blackfoot tribes over the Cree and Assiniboine at the present-day site of Lethbridge.

The event that finally disgusted Potts with the liquor trade was the death of his mother and brother in a feud over liquor among Blood Indians. He took his revenge on his mother's murderer and then quit his job at Fort Whoop-Up. He left Alberta and did not return until he was asked to guide the North West Mounted Police upon their arrival in Alberta in 1874.

By the time they reached Alberta, the Mounted Police were exhausted, lost, and largely bootless and unhorsed. Potts took the green troops in hand and circulated among the Blackfoot tribes, convincing the chiefs that these white men were different and really did mean to end the whiskey trade and restore peace.

With Potts' help, the Mounted Police did succeed as peacemakers. After they had established law and order in Alberta, the ranching and settlement eras began. Of the men described here, most lived to see this more peaceful time. Jerry Potts died at Fort Macleod in 1896, of throat cancer aggravated by drinking. William Gladstone and John George Brown lived well into this century, and died within a few miles of each other in the mountains of southwestern Alberta. James Bird, Jr., who had survived smallpox and the desire of so many to see him dead, lived to the ripe old age of 107.

CHAPTER **3**

Living in
the Present

◀ *The average Albertan is young, well off, and well educated. Photo by Bill McKeown. Courtesy, Westfile, Inc.*

It is early morning as the sleek, white and silver jetliner crosses into the air above Alberta. In fact, at 30,000 feet, the sun has just risen, filling the interior of the plane with a warm amber glow. The curious traveller peers out of his porthole, hoping to catch a glimpse of this place he is approaching. Far below, he can see the quilting of green fields and the occasional tuft of trees, but not much more.

Our traveller has never been to Alberta, but he has heard stories: it's all bush, isn't it? Bush, and cattle ranches the size of Montana, peopled by a few grizzled cowpokes and oil patch roughnecks. Small-town, conservative. Our traveller isn't fussy; he doesn't care if it isn't fashionable, just as long as he can do business here. But he is thinking of bringing his family to Alberta, and he knows they may not transplant so easily. The girls, in particular, won't put up with anything less than *cosmopolitan*.

As the plane touches down, the traveller does notice a few cows in neighbouring fields, and a nodding, black oil pump beside the apron, although the airport seems large enough. In fact, when he goes inside to claim his bags, he discovers a busy international terminal, indistinguishable from ones he has passed through in Montreal, Paris, and Amsterdam. Somewhat heartened, he grabs a cab and heads for his hotel in downtown Calgary—but, Calgary—don't they call it *Cowtown*?

It is understandable that Alberta might be seen (from a distance) as rugged and rustic. A hundred years ago, it was exactly that, and growth spurts fueled by agriculture and oil have naturally reinforced the impression. Even now, with about 3.6 people per square kilometre, you might think you would have to comb a lot of real estate to put together a decent dinner party. That figure, however, averages in a lot of unoccupied territory.

In fact, the chances are better than three to one that any given Albertan lives in a town or city. It has been over 30 years since the majority of the population shifted from rural to urban living, and although the rate of change has slowed since the 1950s, the trend continues. In 1981, 77.2 percent of the 2,237,724 residents of Alberta were urbanites.

The largest part of our city-dwelling population lives in either Edmonton (573,982) or Calgary (636,104). If our traveller has a taste for something a little smaller, however, there are over a dozen other cities here with populations between 10,000 and 60,000. A few are satellites of the larger cities, but others, such as Grande Prairie, Lethbridge, and Red Deer, are centres in their own right, supplying trade—and culture—to their surrounding districts.

Travel between centres in Alberta takes place on a scale that would boggle the European or Japanese. Is it possible to go 200 miles for a breakfast meeting? The answer, in Alberta, is yes. Major centres are tied together by frequent passenger flights on several different airlines. In particular, Edmonton and Calgary are served by an efficient airbus system. Weekdays, more than a dozen jet flights each way make the downtown-to-downtown trip possible in less than an hour. In addition, the province is laced with an excellent system of all-weather roads. Even in the white fury of a prairie blizzard, major arteries are rarely closed for more than a few hours.

While the roads and the rails and the airways shuttle their visible cargo of people and freight back and forth across the province, there is another traffic shimmering silently through the air. It is a traffic essential to our traveller's daughters as they track fashions and trends in pop music, just as it is indispensable for their father's business affairs.

◄ Radio station CJCA in Edmonton is one of a total of 63 AM and FM stations covering the province. Photo by Bill McKeown. Courtesy, Westfile, Inc.

► A television camera films an Edmonton Eskimos' football game from a high vantage point. Photo by Bill McKeown. Courtesy, Westfile, Inc.

This traffic is that of radio and television.

There are 46 AM and 17 FM and FM-stereo stations covering the province, offering every kind of format: information and public affairs; pop, country, and classical music; educational, foreign language, and ethno-cultural programming. These are originating stations; there are numerous rebroadcast stations, as well. Television boasts 11 originating stations, all but two affiliated with national networks. In addition, the extensive cable system in place across the province makes it possible to get network programming from across North America in most major centres. Remote centres in the north are fed Canadian Broadcasting Corporation (CBC) radio and television programming via

Anik satellite.

For those who can't live without a telephone in reach, Alberta is amply supplied, with well over a million subscriber lines. There is also a cellular network for those who like to drive and chat, as well as a radio telephone system to reach isolated areas.

Print media are also healthy. Ten daily newspapers have a combined circulation of close to 600,000, reaching about 85 percent of all households. The 160 weeklies in the province, most taking the pulse of smaller communities, have a combined circulation of over one million. There are also a number of news, special interest, and city magazines published here. *Western Report,* started in Edmonton, now spreads weekly news across the four western provinces, while *Roughneck Magazine* finds its way to oil patch offices throughout North America.

But getting up-to-the-minute stock market reports and being able to see the latest rock videos are not the only considerations. If our traveller and his family move here, what will the neighbours be like?

They are apt to find that Albertans are young, well off, and well educated. At the beginning of June 1986, the Alberta Bureau of Statistics estimated that 68.2 percent of the population was under 40. There is, of course, a distinct bulge in the age curve caused by the postwar baby boom, a bulge slumping relentlessly towards middle age. Many of the baby boomers are having late families, though, which produces a smaller bulge in the under-14-year-old category, a kind of demographic echo. Over two-thirds of all the children in Alberta are in fact under 14, and the average family here contains 3.2 people. The net result is that the statistically typical Albertan will stay young for a while to come.

Financially, Alberta has done well in spite of the recession in the first half of this decade. In 1980 the average income for those aged 15 and older in Alberta was $14,691, a substantial 13 percent above the national average. In that year, only residents of the Yukon did better. In 1985 the recession had reduced the margin somewhat, but Alberta was still above the national figure. Our per capita personal income, at $16,839, was 6 percent above the national average, exceeded this time only by Ontario.

Albertans are also well educated. According to the 1981 census, nearly 10 percent of the population here aged 15 or older had a university degree, the highest proportion in the country. On the other hand, the proportion having less than a grade nine education was the lowest across Canada.

Our statistical model of the average Albertan is lifeless, however, unless we know what kind of a world he or she lives in. Every place has a landscape of public and private institutions, associations, and facilities that have a profound effect on the quality of life there. As we shall see, Alberta's version of that landscape is rich, varied, and serviceable.

▶ *A newspaper delivery boy takes a break on his route to count the money he has collected. Photo by Bill McKeown. Courtesy, Westfile, Inc.*

Religio: to tie together. Religion in every age has helped to tie society together, and that is as true of present-day Alberta as it was of ancient Egypt. The difference is that in ancient Egypt the religion was monolithic, whereas in Alberta there is a wide range of faiths.

The first faith here was of course that of the native people. Although it has suffered heavily from the impact of European culture, it persists to this day, giving strength to its followers. The old ways, which emphasized the unity of all life and harmony with nature, are practiced not only on the reserves, but in other places as well. An example is the recently inaugurated sweatlodge program at the Drumheller Penitentiary. Offenders now have the opportunity of taking part in this healing ritual while serving time.

Although the precise details of the sweatlodge vary from tribe to tribe, in some form the ritual is almost universal amongst North American natives. Typically, participants sit in a small lodge made of willows and covered with hides and blankets, pour water on red-hot stones to release steam, and chant holy songs and prayers. Devotees claim that the ritual clears and strengthens both the body and the spirit.

The religious diversity in Alberta is really a reflection of the history of settlement. When Alberta was still just a place where traders could strip mine beaver pelts, missionaries were here, proselytizing and building churches and schools, teaching, and offering what medical care they could. The very first of these were Roman Catholics and Methodists, followed closely by Anglicans and other Protestant churches.

◄ *First Presbyterian Church in Edmonton is located on 105 Street. Photo by Jerg Kroener*

▼ *St. Vladimir's Ukrainian Orthodox Parish in Calgary is representative of Alberta's religious diversity. Photo by Jerg Kroener*

If any one sect thought to secure the territory for itself, however, it was mistaken. As waves of settlers rolled in, they brought with them their own ways of worship. When Germans and Scandinavians came, they founded Lutheran churches, while the Ukrainian settlers built the onion domes and the triple crosses of the Orthodox faith.

Alberta has sometimes been referred to as the bible belt, and it is true that there is no shortage of bible-based evangelical congregations here. The term *bible belt*, though, probably came into currency because Alberta politics were dominated for decades by two strong men— William "Bible Bill" Aberhart and Ernest Manning—who were also ministers. Statistically, however, the largest single denomination in Alberta is Roman Catholic, followed by United Church, Anglican, and Lutheran. These mainstream churches account for two-thirds of the population.

Of course, there is a remarkable variety of beliefs found here now: there are Jews, Moslems, Baha'is, Druzes, Congregationalists, Spiritualists, Chinese Mennonites, Buddhists (Japanese, Vietnamese, and Tibetan), Sikhs, Pentecostals, Hindus, Baptists, Zoroastrians, and Russian, Ukrainian, and Greek Orthodox. This diversity gives newcomers the assurance that no matter what your belief, you are likely to find at least a small band of fellow believers here. It also makes the whole community richer.

The same can be said of the ethnic mix found here. Indeed, the two are difficult to separate, but while the religion of any one group is usually only of interest to the members of that group, their music, dance, dress, food, and customs will reward those outside the group as well. You do not need to be Italian to stroll down Edmonton's 96th Street on a Saturday afternoon in search of some tissue-thin slices of prosciutto, or maybe a light, tart, freshly made limone gelato. You do not have to be Chinese to stop near Calgary's Centre Street and enjoy the clamour and fluid energy of a dragon dance, punctuated by frantic gongs and staccato bursts of firecrackers. Nor do you need to be Japanese to savour the quiet serenity of the Nikka Yuko Japanese Garden in Lethbridge, where water, pine, and stone create pools of silence in the middle of the city.

The multicultural mix also extends to the media. Throughout the province, cable television stations serve as community bulletin boards for third language and cultural groups. In Edmonton, radio station CKER provides exclusively multicultural programming. Also in Edmonton are the French language stations CHFA (radio), CBXFT (television, widely available through the province on cable), and the weekly newspaper, *le Franco-Albertain*.

Not all the ethnic groups that make up Alberta are as visible as this. Some are numerically small, and others, new arrivals, are still working hard just to get a start in life here. Almost everyone is visible, though, on Heritage Day. The first weekend in August has been set aside by the provincial government as a time to celebrate our multicultural origins. At that time, you can see gatherings throughout Alberta, where many groups show off those things that make them

▲ *The Nikka Yuko Japanese Garden, a symbol of Japanese-Canadian friendship, is an ideal place for meditation. The garden contains rocks, shrubs, and water, but no flowers. Courtesy, Westfile, Inc.*

▶ *Chinese immigrants who came to Western Canada to work on the railroads stayed to establish restaurants, groceries, and gift shops in the inner city. Calgary's Chinatown is a 10-minute walk from the Calgary Tower. Photo by Ray F. Hillstrom, Jr. Courtesy, Hillstrom Stock Photo*

special. You may find yourself listening to a Caribbean steel band while you munch a piece of Irish soda bread, or admiring the finer points of a spirited Highland sword dance while savouring a bowl of Korean *bul-go-gi*.

And speaking of food, Alberta has a fine selection of restaurants: not only the familiar and fashionable Greek, French, Italian, Chinese, Japanese, Mexican, Indian, Russian, Swiss, and Spanish, but also more obscure and exotic finds, where you can people-watch to your heart's content while sampling a plate of *nouvelle* something-or-other.

Except for the Native Americans in Alberta, everyone here is an immigrant. Some try to preserve their cultural roots through their language, others through their religion, still others through their food.

In a brightly painted house on a farm near the small hamlet of Markerville, Stephan G. Stephansson preserved his connection with the old ways by writing. Stephansson came to Alberta from his native Iceland, through North Dakota, in 1888. Stephansson was a homesteading farmer, but he was also a community leader and a prolific writer. He wrote some 1,800 pages of poetry in his life, and close to 1,400 pages of prose. Although unknown to English-speaking contemporaries, and only recently acknowledged here, he has long been acclaimed in Iceland as the greatest Icelandic bard since the Middle Ages. In 1975 his

▲ *On Heritage Day, during the first week in August, Alberta celebrates its multicultural origins. Folk dancing, music, and international foods are featured at gatherings held throughout the province. Photo by Richard Siemens. Courtesy, Westfile, Inc.*

▶ On the Yellowhead Highway, outside of Vegreville, stands this enormous aluminum egg, a monument to the thousands of Ukrainians who settled the region. Photo by Jerg Kroener

homestead was proclaimed a Historic Site by the province, and visitors there may now learn something of his life.

We think that the big cities are cosmopolitan, the places where exotic minorities like Patagonians and Ellesmere Islanders can be found; but small towns have their surprises, too. During the tidal wave of immigration at the turn of the century, about 7,000 Arabs came to Canada, mostly from what is now Syria and Lebanon. Some settled in Edmonton (the Al Rashid mosque, built in 1938, was the first mosque in Canada), but others, more adventurous, moved on to Lac La Biche where they became merchants, farmers, fur traders, and mink ranchers. This town of just over 2,000 inhabitants, at the edge of the wild boreal forest, still has a strong Moslem component—and a mosque of its own.

You can learn a lot about Alberta and her ethnic heritage simply by driving around and observing. On the Yellowhead Highway, outside of Vegreville, for example, you will come across a gigantic aluminum egg, sitting high atop a pedestal. The egg represents a Ukrainian *pysanka*, the beautifully decorated Easter eggs that can still be bought in farmer's markets around the province every spring. It appears to be a remarkable monument to the thousands of Ukrainian settlers who came here and helped to build a new country.

If you read the accompanying descriptive plaque, however, you

115

◄ *Costumed interpreters welcome visitors to the Ukrainian Cultural Heritage Village, where numerous historic buildings have been assembled to represent a typical Ukrainian pioneer settlement. Photo by Bill McKeown. Courtesy, Westfile, Inc.*

will find that the monument was intended to commemorate the hundredth anniversary of the Royal Canadian Mounted Police. With a vigorous leap of imagination, you connect the two. The egg is the sign of resurrection, and could presumably include peace as part of its meaning; the mounties brought peace to the prairies, and the Ukrainians derived benefit from that peace . . . It is much better, though, to just appreciate the monument for what it is—a striking union of traditional and modern aesthetics.

But if the giant egg is a tribute to the Ukrainian settlers, what can we make of the centennial project in St. Paul? When Canada turned 100 back in 1967, a lot of grant money was available, and towns across the province built things like parks and curling rinks and swimming pools, all labeled with geometrical maple leaves. The largely francophone population of St. Paul built . . . a flying saucer landing pad.

At first glance, it may seem like a joke. But don't be too quick to shrug it off.

If you stop and inspect the structure, a ceremonial elevated platform, you find that it has a peculiar sort of logic to it. Maybe the citizens of St. Paul do not think a saucer with Antares license plates is going to land on the thing—but as long as it's there, the platform, like a pointer to the sky, or like the spire of a gothic cathedral, seems to be saying, "There's more to the universe. We aren't alone." More than one traveller, stopping, either in bewilderment or amusement, has yet left with a thoughtful look on his or her face.

By the numbers, a little over 87 percent of Albertans claim a single ethnic origin. Of that total, a hair less than half are British. The remainder represents dozens of cultures. After British and German, the largest single group is—did you guess—Ukrainian?

Alberta is a haven for Ukrainians. A quarter of all Ukrainian-Canadians live here. They are far outnumbered, though, by Albertans of German descent. Upwards of 1 in 10 Albertans is of German origin. If they are not as visible as the smaller French population, it is probably because it was better to assimilate during the two world wars. Indeed, there was a camp for German prisoners of war near Canmore during the last war.

Our traveller also needs information about the school system here. Although there may be some differences in the details, he will find that Alberta education is equal to any in Canada.

Public education here is arranged in three stages: primary school, grades 1 through 6; junior high school, grades 7 through 9; and high school, grades 10 through 12. School attendance is mandatory to the completion of grade 8 or age 15, whichever comes first. Education is free to the student, although some school boards, caught in a squeeze between rising costs and tight provincial government budgets, have been forced to implement user fees. These are annual fees, usually less than $100, applied directly to certain programs or facilities.

In most school districts, there are two parallel, equivalent school systems, one known as the public system, and the other as the separate system. This is a historical division, having its roots in the two dominant cultures of early Canada, Protestant English and Catholic French. In most cases, the public system is Protestant, while the separate schools are Catholic, although in areas which are predominantly Catholic, it is the separate system which is Protestant. Students are automatically enrolled in the public system, unless their parents direct their (school) taxes to the separate system.

Graduation from high school with senior matriculation is generally equivalent to university entrance, although this will depend on the university, the faculty, and the standard of the student's achievement. The academic line through high school to university is only one route open to students, however. The school systems are obliged to provide an education for all students, and so there are many options, from business to trades and life skills.

School boards, as the local authorities, are also expected to provide suitable programs for the physically and developmentally handicapped. This integrative approach may place greater demands on teachers and aides, but it encourages students to develop tolerance and a broader understanding of their peers.

The provincial Department of Education oversees the local school boards, setting standards and developing specific programs where needed. There is, for example, a strong language program, and instruction in French, Ukrainian, and native languages is available in a number of school districts, as well as English as a second language, Japanese, Chinese, and Greek. The province has also recently implemented an Integrated Occupational program to support students who have difficulty with traditional academic courses, and maintains a Special Education branch to ensure that exceptional students, both handicapped and gifted, receive proper attention.

Working in collaboration with the Department of Education and the Department of Advanced Education, but separate from them, is the Alberta Educational Communications Corporation, or ACCESS. ACCESS is a crown corporation which produces and broadcasts educational radio and television. The ACCESS network is available province-wide on AM, FM-stereo, and cable, with both formal, curriculum-related material and informal, broad-based cultural and educational programming. The call letters of ACCESS radio—CKUA—indicate the network's ultimate origin as an experiment by the University of Alberta in the early days of broadcasting.

Leaving grade school in Alberta need not be the end of schooling. There is a wide variety of colleges, specialized schools, and universities here, each constantly revising and updating its curriculum to serve the occupational requirements of students and employers. Among these are 3 technical institutes, 11 public colleges, 4 vocational centres, a petroleum industry training centre, 6 hospital-based schools of nursing, 4 universities, and 5 community consortia, in which a number of institutions cooperate to provide post-secondary credit programs in remote areas.

From 1985 to 1986, the Northern Alberta Institute of Technology, in Edmonton, had over 6,000 full-time students in diploma and certificate programs, more than 5,000 apprentices, and close to 29,000 part-time continuing education students. As well as such conventional courses as electrical engineering technology, automotives, food and beverage services, and dental assisting, the institute has planned or implemented courses in state-of-the-art subjects like bio-medical electronics and laser technology. In Calgary the Southern Alberta Institute of Technology has been developing curricula and administrative support for the Daqing Petroleum Institute in northeast China. The project has encouraged the institute to create a Department of International Education, intended to develop further international training opportunities.

The public colleges operate regionally to provide trade and vocational training, as well as academic upgrading and university entrance. Courses vary widely, depending upon local need. A good example is Olds College; located in the middle of Alberta's extensive ranching and farming districts, this college is dedicated to training people involved directly and indirectly in agriculture. Courses are offered in plant and animal sciences, landscape gardening, pest control, and other aspects of agribusiness. By contrast, Red Deer College, located in a rapidly growing city, maintains, among others, a faculty of art and design, and has created a Management Development Centre to provide courses for the regional business community.

Nor do the colleges neglect community needs for artistic development. The Alberta College of Art, in Calgary, is one of only four visual arts colleges in all of Canada. Here students study such subjects as

▶ *Six hundred students per year study drawing, painting, photography, and other subjects at the Alberta College of Art in Calgary. Courtesy, Alberta College of Art*

▲ *The oldest technical institute in Canada, the Southern Alberta Institute of Technology was established in 1916 to retrain World War I veterans. Courtesy, Southern Alberta Institute of Technology*

▲ *Red Deer College features this attractive Arts Centre on its campus. Courtesy, Red Deer College*

drawing and painting, jewelry, textiles, photographic arts, and visual communications. Full-time enrollment is around 600 students per year.

In the mountains to the west, there is another institution which contributes to our cultural development: The Banff Centre for Continuing Education. Built amidst the pines on the rocky slope of Tunnel Mountain, the Banff Centre is not a college, but rather a unique institution composed of three divisions: Conference Services, the School of Management, and the Banff School of Fine Arts. The Banff Centre enjoys an international reputation as a place of study; during the 1985 summer session, less than one student in five came from Alberta. The others came from across Canada and around the world. For recognized artists requiring a period of creative retreat, the school also offers the facilities of the Leighton Artist Colony, in which artists of many disciplines are given food, shelter, a place to work, and, when they tire of their own projects, the company of other artists. Meanwhile, the School of Management offers a variety of programs in such subjects as advanced marketing management, senior health administration, municipal management, and training in arts administration. Private and public organizations wishing to conduct their own programs can also use the facilities of the conference services branch to meet in stunning, secluded surroundings.

The University of Alberta, in Edmonton, is our oldest university. The first three professors (teaching Classics, English, and Modern Languages) were appointed in 1908, when the campus was little more than

▲ *The Banff Centre for Continuing Education enjoys an international reputation as a place of study. Courtesy, Banff Centre for Continuing Education*

▶ *The Tory Building is on the campus of the University of Alberta, the oldest university in the province. Photo by Richard H. Siemens. Courtesy, Westfile, Inc.*

▲ *This impressive indoor speed skating oval was built at the University of Calgary for the 1988 Winter Olympics. Photo by Jerg Kroener*

▲ *Shown here is the 112 Street entrance to the Walter C. Mackenzie Health Sciences Centre. Courtesy, Walter C. Mackenzie Health Sciences Centre*

a clearing in the bush. Now there are more than 1,500 faculty members teaching close to 29,000 full- and part-time students in law, medicine, engineering, science, education, fine arts, and of course, the humanities. The U of A's first suit remains a strong suit, with such programs available as philosophy, Slavic studies, east Asian language, and literature, film, and Canadian studies.

Meanwhile, the slightly smaller University of Calgary has forged ahead, particularly in the realm of business administration. The U of C recently designed a multi-disciplinary New Venture Development program, intended as an incubator for entrepreneurs. At the same time, the university has established a Centre for International Education and Business. Physically, the U of C has benefited greatly from the 1988 Winter Olympics; the campus now has an expanded stadium, an athletes village, and a magnificent indoor speed skating oval.

Athabasca University is Alberta's least-visible university, but it is all the more remarkable for that. Apart from administrative offices in the town of Athabasca, there is no campus. Athabasca U works through tele-courses, correspondence, and telephone tutors to offer undergraduate degrees in the arts, administration, and general studies to students across the province. This concept seems to satisfy a definite need in the community, as Athabasca continues to be the fastest-growing university in Canada. Between the academic years 1980 to 1981 and 1985 to 1986, enrollment increased 137 percent, reaching 9,557 students.

Health care in Alberta is among the best in the world. To begin with, it is covered by a universal health insurance scheme similar to that in other provinces. Except for certain elective procedures and therapies, Alberta health care pays for the medically required services of a doctor, whether general practitioner or specialist. If a stay in hospital is necessary, the plan will pay for that as well, including the cost of medications, nursing, diagnostic tests, and surgery. If your doctor thinks you should be moved to another hospital or nursing home, the plan will also pay for the transportation.

Most Albertans live and work within easy reach of a hospital. There are 125 general hospitals in the province, not to speak of auxiliary hospitals and nursing homes, with over 13,000 active care beds. That works out to a bed for every 181 people. Of course, not all hospitals are the same. At one end of the spectrum is the tiny Cereal Municipal Hospital, with nine beds and bassinets for two newborn babies. At the other is the University of Alberta Hospital, in Edmonton, a virtual self-contained city with room for over 1,200 patients. However, in the event that the facilities at Cereal (or Empress or Westlock or Fairview) are not adequate for the situation, the province operates an emergency air ambulance program for transportation to a more complete centre.

A number of hospitals here operate associated hostels. These provide accommodation for patients who do not need in-patient services, but who need to be close to an acute care facility for diagnosis or treatment. An example of this is at the Foothills General Hospital in Calgary, where the program is operated in co-operation with the Alberta Cancer Board. Patients who stay in these hostels are not charged for their accommodation.

Although the frontiers of medicine continue to expand daily, many of the latest technologies are available here, including, in Edmonton, heart and heart/lung transplants. Since 1985 a team of doctors at the University of Alberta Hospital has been evaluating a project to aid residents of Alberta and other western provinces with this technique. The project so far seems to be successful, the only difficulty being to find sufficient donors.

As the average Albertan hoists a lunch pail off the kitchen counter and heads out to work, he or she is probably not thinking about politics—public opinion, government organization, and legislation, layered like the clouds in the sky that give us the weather. Like the sunshine and rain, however, the politics of a place touches everybody.

In Alberta, as across Canada, there are three layers of government: federal, provincial, and local. The largest power lies with the federal government, but the provincial government is given jurisdiction over a number of important areas. Education and health care are examples already examined in this chapter. In turn, the provincial government delegates certain powers to local authorities. In Alberta, depending upon the local conditions, these authorities may be municipal districts, counties, improvement districts, villages, towns, or cities. Obviously the subtleties of city and county politics are a big, constantly changing subject, varying from place to place; in this book we will concern ourselves only with the provincial aspect.

Briefly, the structure of Alberta government is similar to other provinces: a unicameral legislature, with a lieutenant-governor as the titular head of government. The legislative assembly is divided between the members of the government (usually the members of the party which has won a majority, although it could be a coalition in the event no party wins a majority) and the members of other parties, known as the Loyal Opposition. The assembly meets, with proper ceremony, in the domed and columned, dignified stone Legislative Building in Edmonton, on the bank of the North Saskatchewan River.

Elected representatives are called Members of the Legislative Assembly, or MLAs, and represent the voters in their geographical constituencies. Except in very rare cases, however, MLAs always vote *en bloc* with their party. The consequence is that a majority government is technically able to pass any legislation it wishes. In this case, the power of the government is tempered not so much by the votes of the Opposition as by public pressure. Debate in the legislature is only the tip of the iceberg; if a government senses that a particular piece of legislation is strenuously opposed, or sought, it usually responds.

An example is the recent passing of seatbelt legislation. The Conservative government under Premier Getty was reluctant to enact a law requiring the use of seatbelts. When at last such a bill was intro-

▲ *The Alberta Legislature Building in Edmonton, where the legislative assembly meets, contains exhibits on Alberta's history, art, and technology. The gardens surrounding the building feature beautiful landscaping, a fountain, and a reflecting pool. Photo by Wes Bergen. Courtesy, Hillstrom Stock Photo*

duced, it was not because of debate in the legislative assembly, but because persistent public pressure had convinced the government they must act, or face the consequences later.

Once elected, a government is obliged to hold another election within five years, but not at any specific time. The government, therefore, chooses when to hold the next election, unless in the legislature it is defeated on a vote of no confidence, or on a money bill—which almost never happens.

Party politics in Alberta has, over the years, been characterized by a tendency to large majorities and long tenure. Since Alberta became a province in 1905, only four political parties have governed here. The very first, although it might come as a surprise to oilmen who involuntarily grit their teeth when they remember Pierre Trudeau and his National Energy Policy, was Liberal. In the first election, the Liberals, under Alexander Rutherford, took 23 of 25 seats.

The Liberals held power until 1917, when they were replaced by the United Farmers of Alberta (UFA). In the election of 1921, the UFA had 38 of 59 seats. The UFA did not start as a political party, but became politicized because of a popular perception that power was held by the moneyed classes. It remained in power until a new "popular" party, Social Credit, swept it away in the election of 1935.

That year, Social Credit took 56 of 61 seats, and the UFA won no seats at all. Social Credit then settled down for a phenomenal term of over 35 years.

It was not until 1971 that the Progressive Conservative Party, under Peter Lougheed, finally dislodged Social Credit, winning 69 of 75 seats. After beginning with such a strong majority, one might expect their support to shrink in subsequent elections, but after the 1982 vote, 75 Conservative members of the government faced just four members of the Opposition. As this is written, the Conservatives continue to form the government.

This tendency to stability in provincial politics is balanced by the formation from time to time of political parties somewhat out of the mainstream. The UFA is an example of this, as is the Social Credit Party. The UFA began life as an association to build local schools and recreational facilities, while Social Credit achieved popular success on the strength of monetary policies which were either impossible, or beyond the jurisdiction of the provincial government. Lately there have also been rumblings of separatism, as for example from the short-lived Western Canada Concept Party. Although these reflect the passionate feelings of a few, they are not views that are widely held.

The Alberta government is a large organization, with over 20 departments, and dozens of councils, boards, agencies, and commissions. It does the best it can on everything from highways to international trade, but no system is perfect. From time to time people are mistreated or confused by bureaucratic machinery, and it is to help such people that the position of Alberta Ombudsman was created.

The ombudsman is empowered by the legislature to investigate the case of anyone who thinks he or she has been unfairly dealt with by the province. Each year, thousands of complaints and inquiries are received, though many are about matters not connected with the provincial government. Whenever possible, ombudsman and staff investigate, and, if they feel the complaint is justified, try to remedy the situation. In 1986, after winnowing out the calls and letters merely asking for information, and the complaints about matters outside his jurisdiction, the ombudsman investigated 326 cases, of which 61 were found to be justified. Most of these were resolved to the complainant's satisfaction, and in a number of cases the procedure or policy of a department was subsequently revised at the ombudsman's suggestion.

Another government agency set up to protect the rights of Albertans is the Human Rights Commission. The commission administers the Individual's Rights Protection Act, which prohibits discrimination not only by the provincial government, but also by all employers, individuals, and many organizations. Specifically, the act makes it an offense to discriminate on the grounds of race, ancestry, or place of origin, colour, religious beliefs, physical disability, sex, age, or marital status. These provisions hold with regard to employment, tenancy, public accommodation, signs, and services. In other words, it is not permitted to deny service in a restaurant because of a person's racial origin; a hotel keeper may not refuse accommodation because of religious beliefs; an employer may ask a prospective employee if he or she is available for shiftwork, but not about plans for marriage, family, or child care.

These rights have some far-reaching implications. For example, a manager who makes unwelcome sexual advances towards a secretary can be found in violation of the act: he is discriminating against her on the basis of sex. The same can be said of an employer who dismisses an employee simply because she is pregnant, or who pays female employees less than male employees for substantially the same work.

If anyone feels he has been the victim of discrimination, he may make a complaint to the commission, which will then assign a human rights officer to investigate the case. If the complaint is valid, the commission will try to negotiate a settlement, which may range from an apology to financial compensation. In the unlikely event that a negotiated settlement cannot be reached, the commission may also start legal proceedings.

Figures on average income do not mean too much unless we can make a comparison on the other side of the coin: how fast the money is spent. Cost of living indices cannot be reliably gauged between cities, but they do allow a comparison of relative growth. For example, by June 1987, the all Canada rate had reached 138.2, while in Edmonton it was only 134.4 and in Calgary, 133.4. In Montreal, on the other hand, it was 140.3 and in Toronto, 142.3. In other words, the cost of living has risen more slowly here than in other parts of the country.

It is also possible to make some comparison between tax rates. Alberta does very well in this department. Tax rates vary over time, of course, and also depend on the circumstances of a particular taxpayer. In 1986, though, a family of four with an income of $30,000 would have paid less in taxes in Alberta than anywhere else in Canada. Not only is the basic personal rate lower, but so is the corporate and small business rate. In addition, Albertans pay no tax on their gasoline. Finally, this remains one of the last places in the world with no retail sales tax.

As our traveller walks from the hotel to his waiting cab, he is tired, but satisfied. He slings his bag onto the backseat, climbs in beside it, and settles back for the ride to the airport. His trip has been a success, promising enough that he may have to come back soon. He flips open his pocket diary and studies it for a moment, scanning the weeks to come. He would like to pick a time when his wife could come with him—he knows it is her opinion that will matter to their daughters. He is also convinced that, once she has seen it, her report on Alberta will be favourable.

CHAPTER 4

What Do You Do for a Living?

The short answer is—almost anything. Whereas once upon a time Albertans were mostly farmers, and before that hunters, trappers, and traders, now they may have almost any occupation. Alberta's population is large enough, and her economy diversified enough, that a wide range of trades and professions flourish here, with room for more.

Of course, the primary industry sector is strong. Production of oil, gas, coal, and other primary resources has been a mainstay of the economy here for years, and will continue to play a major part well into the next century. The immediate recovery of these materials, however, is carried on by a relatively small proportion of the Alberta workforce. In 1985 a little over 6 percent of the province's 1.2 million workers were employed in primary industries other than agriculture. And agriculture, once the single most important employer here, accounted for only 7.5 percent of our labour pool. The largest employment field was, in fact, service—a little under 33 percent, or about one in three working Albertans, was employed in a service occupation. This was followed by trade, at 18.3 percent, and transport, communications, and other utilities, at 8.2 percent. Nearly comparable to agriculture and manufacturing was public administration. In other words, it is now equally likely that a given Albertan will be a civil servant or employed in manufacturing as work on a farm.

What follows is a survey, by no means exhaustive, of the major divisions of Alberta industry.

One indicator of an area's growing economic development is its ability to manufacture items locally, rather than import them from other regions of the country or from abroad. In 1985 manufacturing shipments in Alberta were

◀ *Because some cattle ranchers still raise their livestock on the range, the skills of the cowboy are always in demand in Alberta. Courtesy, Westfile, Inc.*

▲ *Just over 8 percent of Albertans are employed in the fields of transportation, communications, and other utilities. This TransAlta Utilities power grid is located in central Alberta. Photo by Chris Bruun. Courtesy, Westfile, Inc.*

▶ *Ipsco Inc. in Calgary produces tubes, pipes, and casings for the petroleum sector. Courtesy, Ipsco Inc.*

worth $16.1 billion, and included everything from paint to plastic sheeting, from portable trailers to fire engines, from 10-gallon hats to thousands of gallons of beer. What's more, that figure is an increase of a billion dollars over the year before.

Somewhat less than a third of the total value of manufacturers' factory shipments in Alberta in 1985 was made up of petroleum products. That proportion has not changed over the last three years, a plateau suggesting that Alberta's dependence on refining crude oil may be levelling off. Closely related to the success of the petroleum industry is a rapid growth in the production of fertilizers and pesticides, organic industrial chemicals, and plastic resins. In the past 10 years, local and international companies have been encouraged by our ample supplies of natural gas and by our wide-reaching, efficient pipeline system to invest $4 billion in plants producing methanol, fertilizers, and ethylene products.

Producing the raw stock is only a beginning, though. Companies here produce not only the plastic resins, but also a wide variety of moulded and extruded products and fiber-reinforced composites. The chemical industry here went from under $8 million to over $2 billion in only six years, and shows no sign of slowing down.

Other industries strongly supported by the petroleum sector are metal fabricating and machinery. These include items such as the range of tube, pipe, and casing produced by Ipsco Inc. of Calgary and other manufacturers, and specialized pieces of equipment, such as dehydrators, gas sweetening units, and the non-explosive heaters manufactured in Calgary by Ruffneck Ltd. for shipment all over the world. There is a natural market here for resource recovery equipment, which allows us to develop innovative products and sell them abroad.

Forest-based industries, not to be confused with logging, include the actual production of wood, paper products, furniture, and printing.

◄ *This Shell Canada chemical plant operates in Scotford, Alberta. Photo by Chris Bruun. Courtesy, Westfile, Inc.*

▶ *Built by Global Thermoelectric Power Systems Ltd., this thermoelectric generator brings power to remote areas. Courtesy, Global Thermoelectric Power Systems Ltd.*

Our huge stands of fine timber ensure a stable supply, while the development of pulp markets in Europe and Asia, as well as the growth of furniture markets in eastern Canada, suggest that these industries will continue to be healthy for years to come.

Our second largest manufacturing industry is food production. The value of food shipments in 1985 was only slightly less than that of petroleum products. Of course, consumer packaging keeps us aware of much of Alberta's activity in this sector. As we cruise the aisles of the supermarket, again and again our eyes are caught by the "Better Buy Alberta" logo, or by the words, "Product of Alberta." Thus packaged are such staples as flour, cereal, and honey, or dairy products ranging from cultured butter to Camembert cheese. You might equally well encounter fresh pasta, tofu, mushrooms, delightfully decadent gourmet chocolates, or succulent lamb. Closely allied is the beverage industry, producing over $300 million worth of soft drinks, spirits, and beer. The brewing industry not only produces vast quantities of standard suds, but also supports such specialty brewing companies as Calgary's Big Rock, where small batches of unpasteurized lager, ale, and stout are bottled. Over the years, several enterprising businesspeople have even started wineries here, although their success remains an open question.

Another area which has recently enjoyed growth is electronics. Typically, local manufacturers have identified a need for specific industrial products, which they have then gone on to develop and market. An example is Caulfield Engineering Ltd. in Sherwood Park, which specializes in such esoteric items as side-scan digital display and analysis systems, and custom microprocessors for navigation systems. Another example is Leaf Electronics Ltd. in St. Albert, which manufactures control modules for artificial limbs.

It is also worth noting that while the manufacturing industry has grown in Alberta, it has not been restricted to the major centres of Edmonton and Calgary. Indeed, while these two metropolitan areas employed 61 percent of the manufacturing labour force in 1976, by 1983, that figure had dropped to 56 percent. This trend toward decentralization is possible because of a healthy transportation network, which helps stimulate the economy of the smaller centres. It isn't surprising, therefore, to discover that Bassano, in the middle of a dry land farming district, is home to Global Thermoelectric Power Systems Ltd., one of only two thermoelectric power companies in the world. Or that College Heights—a small town known for its Bible college—now hosts Canutel Industries Ltd., a maker of specialized printed circuit boards that has just expanded into California and Michigan.

There is no doubt that farming is one of the most important industries in Alberta. In 1985 farm cash receipts totalled more than $3 billion. Since that figure merely notes the money coming in to the farm, and not the money spent by farmers for seed, stock, supplies, machinery, and other necessities of agricultural endeavor, it is clear that agribusiness is responsible for a massive economic turnover. On a per capita basis, our farm output is much higher than most other provinces: with 6 percent of the national population, we generate more than 18 percent of the farm income.

The two largest money earners are wheat and beef, both cattle and calves. Together these account for about half of our farm income, a proportion which has been growing slightly over the last decade. More than any other business, though, agriculture is subject to yearly swings brought on by weather and other market factors. For example, the price of wheat has dropped sharply in the last few years, partly because of the American government's determination to fight European subsidies with subsidies of its own. Wheat farming is therefore no longer as profitable as it once was, and Alberta farmers are looking for other crop possibilities.

One likely candidate is canola, an oil seed derived from the rape plant. (In case you're wondering, rape is a Brassica with yellow flowers,

▶ *Canola is the second most valuable crop in Alberta. This field of canola is located near Red Deer. Photo by Chris Bruun. Courtesy, Westfile, Inc.*

▲ *These grain elevators are a colourful sight on farmland in Carstairs, Alberta. Photo by John Elk III*

related to the cabbage and the turnip.) Canola sales have enjoyed phenomenal growth lately, and this is now our second most valuable crop. In 1985 canola receipts were over $370 million. Canola is a hardy plant, and its acceptance as a high grade salad and cooking oil has garnered for this crop a substantial portion of the agricultural market. Hoping to sustain this momentum, research being conducted here is presently aimed at improving the varieties of canola, and developing new uses for its oil.

Other seed crops grown here include oats, barley, flax, and rye, though their importance has been declining slowly. Barley is still widely grown for feed, and every year some farmers take the gamble and grow two-rowed barley, hoping it will be of high enough quality to merit malting grade. Apart from economics, barley is also a gorgeous-looking crop—a field of barley appears soft and feathery, each head sporting a gleaming beard of awns, which a gust of wind makes toss and tumble like water.

Vegetables have been grown locally since settlers first arrived in Alberta, and decades of research have produced varieties of corn, peas, potatoes, tomatoes, and carrots suited to our climate. At the

▼ *Although the importance of barley has declined in recent years, it is still widely grown for feed. This farmer stands proudly in his field of barley near Boyle. Photo by Chris Bruun. Courtesy, Westfile, Inc.*

▲ *Alberta is beef country. This cattle ranch is located near Hay Lakes. Photo by Bill McKeown. Courtesy, Westfile, Inc.*

commercial level, however, there is strong competition from sources in the United States, notably growers in California. Alberta market gardeners are now making inroads at the supermarket, however, and it is possible to buy locally raised cucumbers, tomatoes, and alfalfa sprouts year round. At Joffre, northeast of Red Deer, an ethylene plant has integrated an industrial-scale greenhouse.

To help foster self-sufficiency, the provincial department of agriculture has co-ordinated a program of local farmer's markets. These may be held as often as once a week, conditional on local supply and demand. Depending on the season, and the part of the province, shoppers may find ears of corn, sacks of new potatoes, bright orange windrows of carrots, beets still sporting their swarthy green tops, firm white cauliflowers, red and green cabbages, peas, beans, garlic, onions, cucumbers in all sizes, raspberries and strawberries, chokecherries and saskatoons, chickens, eggs, cheese, honey—the list is endless. And not only can you select from such a wealth of raw material, but you may also wish to sample the farm wife's handiwork, in the form of breads, pies, pickles, and preserves—or perhaps purchase a homemade quilt or crocheted table runner. The virtue of the farmer's market is largely economic, but there is also the bonus of dealing face to face with the people who nurtured or fashioned whatever you are buying.

Another resource we are developing is that of horticultural and nursery products. Trees, shrubs, houseplants, cut flowers, and turf amounted to a $26 million business in 1985. For the more delicate flowers, commercial greenhouses can benefit from our plentiful heating supplies of natural gas.

As for livestock, there is no doubt that this is beef country. Beef cattle, which have always thrived on Alberta grass and grain, currently

▶ *After cattle, pigs are the second most profitable livestock in Alberta. However, the contribution of pork production to farm income has declined recently. Photo by Chris Bruun. Courtesy, Westfile, Inc.*

account for two-thirds of our livestock receipts. Although most of our beef cattle have been herded into efficient feedlots, some operations still raise their cattle on the range, and the skill of the cowboy is still in demand. There is also a significant export trade in live cattle for breeding.

After beef, our next most profitable livestock animal is the pig. Pork production has been fairly steady over the past five years. In 1985 nearly 1.7 million hogs were slaughtered here. Prices have not been keeping pace, though, and the value of pork production, along with its contribution to farm income—$245 million in 1985—has been declining slowly.

Dairy production, on the other hand, has increased in value, partly because of diversification. As well as milk, butter, yogurt, and ice cream, there is a wide assortment of cheeses made here, all of excellent quality. Quark anyone? Or perhaps a slice of brie? How about some well-aged cheddar?

Poultry and eggs also form a sizable portion of our farm economy, although these have subsided marginally over the last 15 years. In 1985 chicken and egg monies amounted to $131.9 million. Maintaining its position in the market, in spite of strong competition from New Zealand, is Alberta lamb; more than 91,000 sheep and lambs were slaughtered in 1985.

According to the children's story about Dick Whittington and his cat, Whittington journeyed to London because he had heard the streets there were paved with gold. In Alberta, although the ground beneath your feet isn't likely gold, it is valuable all the same. About two-thirds of the value of all mineral production in the entire nation of Canada comes from one province—Alberta.

The most valuable representatives of this huge outpouring are the energy resources—coal, oil, and natural gas. Coal, the black rock that burns, has undergone wide production swings over the years. It declined in the 1950s, for example, but has been growing steadily in the 1980s. In 1986 Alberta produced 27.7 million metric tonnes of coal, of which about 18 million tonnes were consumed here, mostly in power generating stations.

Alberta coal can be classified as thermal (mostly sub-bituminous coal and some lignite in the Plains region), for use in power stations, for example, or as metallurgical coal (low to medium volatile bituminous and some deposits of semi-anthracite, all found in the Foothills and Mountain regions) suitable for steel making. Much of the thermal coal is burned in power stations built there at the mine site, or is shipped to generating stations in Ontario, while the metallurgical coal is mostly sold to steel makers in Japan. The amount of coal underlying Alberta is truly phenomenal. There are coal-bearing formations under more than 45 percent of the province, and the ultimate potential reserves of coal are estimated at 794 billion tonnes.

Mining coal in the Plains region is a relatively simple matter.

▲ Alberta is Canada's major supplier of oil and gas. This Petro Canada refinery operates in Edmonton. Photo by Chris Bruun. Courtesy, Westfile, Inc.

▶ These abandoned coal mine buildings are on the site of the Atlas Mine in the Drumheller area. Coal was the primary economic base here until the late 1940s. Coal production in many regions of Alberta has enjoyed an upsurge in the 1980s. Photo by Jerg Kroener

◀ *Although estimates of known oil reserves indicate that the industry could come to a standstill in 10 years, an active exploration program in pursuit of new sources has been very successful. Photo by Jerg Kroener*

Deposits generally lie flat, beneath an overburden of glacial till, and can be strip mined with a dragline. Reclamation of the mined area is also relatively simple. It is more difficult in the mountains, however, where formations are folded and faulted, and usually overlain by rock. Mine operators must choose between conventional underground mining techniques, which may not be able to follow the seam, and drilling and blasting away the overburden, which necessitates the formidable task of reclamation when mining is complete. The extra cost is somewhat offset, though, by the coal's high quality and low sulfur content.

Rudyard Kipling once said of Medicine Hat that it had all hell for a basement. This, of course, was not a reflection on the moral standards of that Alberta city, but rather a comment on the vast pool of gas that underlies it. Since the first gas well was drilled here in 1880, natural gas has illuminated our homes, fueled our furnaces and our power stations, and gone hissing down pipelines to the east, south, and west. Alberta natural gas burns as far away as Montreal, California, and even Japan, where it arrives by LNG tanker.

In 1985 Alberta produced 90 percent of the natural gas in Canada, a little more than 86.7 million cubic metres. The ultimate potential reserve of natural gas here is estimated at 2.9 trillion cubic metres. Also in 1985 another 1,932 gas wells were drilled here, bringing the total of gas wells capable of production to 30,255.

The natural gas industry is closely allied, of course, with the chemical industry, as well as inextricably linked with oil. Indeed, some of

► *Oil sands recovery will keep Alberta at the forefront of energy production even after the supply of conventional crude has been exhausted. Courtesy, Westfile, Inc.*

the earliest wells here were originally dug in search of oil, but instead brought in gas. Oil was first commercially extracted here in 1925, near Wainwright, where heavy crude was discovered. In 1932 large supplies of light crude were found in Turner Valley, southwest of Calgary; from that time on, Calgary has become a major centre in Canada's oil patch. A similar development followed in Edmonton, when the enormous Leduc field blew in 1947.

Alberta is now Canada's major supplier of oil and gas. In 1985 we produced 69 million cubic metres of crude, or over 80 percent of the national figure. The oil was drawn from only two-thirds of the operable wells in the province, which gives some idea of our reserves. In that year, established reserves were estimated at 648 million cubic metres. In view of our 1985 production, this figure suggests that the oil industry here has only a decade left, but in fact an active exploration program has kept reserves fairly constant for the past few years. In 1985 oil companies spent close to $2 billion on exploration, and Alberta drillers in pursuit of new sources of oil chewed through 2,860 kilometres of rock.

If conventional crude does run out, though, Alberta will still be an energy-rich province. Oil sand deposits here are so large that it is difficult to achieve a reliable estimate. In the north and east of the province, there are oil sands under some 60,000 square kilometres. The three major deposits—Athabasca, Cold Lake, and Peace River—plus other areas capable of being mined, contain about 270 billion cubic metres of bitumen. In addition, bitumen deposits are contained in carbonate rock formations underlying the oil sands. Reserves in the Grosmont formation have been estimated in excess of 50 million cubic metres.

Parts of the Athabasca oil sands are less than 120 metres below the surface, and can thus be surface mined with draglines and bucket wheels. The remainder must either be mined or "recovered" underground. Recovery simply means separating the heavy, viscous bitumen from its matrix of fine sand, and over the years a number of techniques have been proposed. One, now thankfully forgotten, was put forward when the atmospheric testing of nuclear weapons was commonplace—it was suggested that underground atomic explosions would warm the bitumen sufficiently to be pumped from conventional wells.

If and when these deeper deposits are brought into production, it is likely that the technology will be similar to that already in service at Fort McMurray. In this hot-water flotation process developed by the Alberta Research Council, the raw oil sand is exposed to steam to form a slurry, which is then mixed with hot water. Here the oil and sand separate; the bitumen is then upgraded through the removal of sulphur and nitrogen, and the addition of hydrogen or the removal of carbon, to form a high quality synthetic crude. This substance is rich in the aromatics used to produce phenols, polyesters, and other chemical feedstocks.

The oldest and largest oil sands plants are those of Suncor and Syncrude, north of Fort McMurray. Suncor, which began in 1967, has a design capacity of 10,329 cubic metres a day. Syncrude has been in-

▼ *These workers are employed at Syncrude, one of the two oldest and largest oil sands plants in the province. Photo by Bill McKeown. Courtesy, Westfile, Inc.*

▶ *The bucket wheel excavator at Syncrude is shown by night. Photo by Bill McKeown. Courtesy, Westfile, Inc.*

creasing production since it opened in 1978, and presently has a capacity of 22,932 cubic metres a day.

The hot-water flotation process is efficient—you only need to compare the black sticky gunk going into the plant to the fine white sand coming out to see that. However, experiments continue around the province with other methods, including solvent based extraction and in-situ extraction with steam, air, and caustic solutions. In addition, four commercial-scale in-situ operations have received governmental approval, their start up pending improvement in oil prices.

One of the province's major industries, the oil patch is also one of our economy's major driving forces. In 1985 the oil industry spent an estimated $15 billion here. This was an increase of $1.7 billion over the previous year, which reflected the resumption of exploration and drilling in response to stronger oil prices. This figure includes everything from land acquisition to operating costs and royalties. Close to 40,000 people are directly employed in the oil and gas industry, and hundreds of thousands more work in related occupations.

If the amount of real estate concealing oil sands deposits sounds impressive, consider how much forest land we have—360,000 square kilometres, or 55 percent of the province. Not all of that is prime timber, of course, but even when you subtract the muskeg and bushland, and the areas that need to be replanted, there still remain 198,000 square kilometres of forest, almost all of it publicly owned, and managed for the purpose of forestry. About 45 percent is coniferous, 35 percent deciduous, and 20 percent mixed.

◄ *Alberta forests are made up of pop-lar, shown here, as well as spruce, pine, fir, and birch. Over half of the land in the province is covered with forests. Photo by Chris Bruun. Courtesy, Westfile, Inc.*

The dominant species are spruce, pine, fir, poplar, and birch. Of these, the largest in volume is white spruce; 22 percent of the standing timber, or about 527 million cubic metres, is white spruce 25 centimetres or more in diameter.

In order to manage the forests properly, the provincial government retains title to the lands, and grants permission to harvest timber under a Timber Quota, a Timber Permit, or a Forest Management Agreement. At the present rate of timber growth, the total possible cut is over 12 million cubic metres of deciduous timber and 15 million cubic metres of coniferous per year. The amount of timber actually harvested is much less than this—500,000 cubic metres deciduous and 6 million cubic metres coniferous—so there is clearly lots of room for the forest industry here to grow.

Although the past has witnessed production swings between either lumber or pulp, the two are fairly well integrated now. Pulp mills which once demanded roundwood are now happily digesting wood chip residues from lumber production. Presently about 85 percent of the timber being harvested is used for lumber and plywood. Other developments include the contruction or readying for operation of three plants producing oriented strand-and-wafer-board, building material which makes economical use of wood unsuitable for dimensional lumber. In a similar vein is the inauguration of Canada's first medium density fibreboard plant.

The value of this activity to our economy is significant. During the 1985 to 1986 logging season, the value of production on crown land was $656 million. Forest products account for about 7 percent of manufacturing shipments, and in 1986 pulp exports from Alberta were valued at $225 million.

To maintain Alberta's forests, the provincial government has adopted a sustained yield policy, and works with the timber industry to ensure reforestation of logged areas. With funding from the Alberta Heritage Trust Fund, the Pine Ridge Forest Nursery has been established. This nursery will in time provide close to 40 million seedlings a year for reforestation and afforestation, a sufficient supply for at least the next 10 years.

Timber is cut under a number of different administrative arrangements, depending on the scope of the area involved. When the government wishes to open a Timber Development Area, for example, proposals involving the construction of capital facilities are called for and public hearings held before final approval by the Cabinet. Timber quotas, usually for a period of 20 years, tend to be offered at public auction. Local timber permits are issued for a period of one year, and are intended to allow residents to harvest timber for their own use or for small-scale commercial operations.

Since Alberta is landlocked, it might seem surprising that there is a commercial fishing industry here—but there is. There are 225 lakes in which commercial fishing is permitted, and 93 of these were fished during the 1985 to 1986

▲ *Timber is stacked and ready for processing at the St. Regis mill in the Hinton area of west central Alberta. Photo by Chris Bruun. Courtesy, Westfile, Inc.*

◄ *These pine seedlings will help the cause of reforestation in logged areas. Photo by Chris Bruun. Courtesy, Westfile, Inc.*

season. The principal catch is whitefish, mostly taken during the winter, and northern pike. Ten fish-packing plants in the province are licensed by the Freshwater Fish Marketing Corporation in Winnipeg, which buys about 60 percent of the yearly haul. The rest is sold by fishermen directly to the consumer.

The value of fish production in Alberta has varied widely over the years, depending on market conditions and the volume of the catch. In 1985, 3,256 tonnes brought $2,799,000. Since 1983, entry into the fishing industry has been restricted, as the province moves away from open access fisheries. About 2,300 fishermen took part in the 1985 to 1986 season.

In the beginning, Alberta was opened up by the fur trade, and it seems appropriate that trapping still continues. Unlike the early days, however, more than just beaver are trapped—mink, muskrat, marten, fox, and rabbit are also taken, along with a number of other species. The catch depends to some extent on the market as dictated by fashion, and also on the cyclical rise and fall of animal populations. Nevertheless, trapping does not place undue pressure on fur-bearing species. Indeed, in some cases, it is an acceptable means of wildlife management.

In the 1985 to 1986 season there were about 6,900 trappers in the province, some depending exclusively on their traplines for a living. Of that number, about 4,000 trapped on privately owned land, while the rest worked lines on crown land. The catch that season amounted to over 350,000 pelts, valued at $6.6 million.

Tourism is a difficult industry to evaluate quantitatively. There is no doubt that tourists spend money on everything from gasoline to handwoven ties, but determining which portion tourists contribute to the money churning through the economy is problematic. A few indicators, however, are illuminating.

In 1985 close to 110,000 American vehicles travelled across the border into Alberta. The same year, more than 457,000 American visitors came through customs here, as did nearly 74,000 visitors from overseas. The bulk of our tourist trade, though, is home grown. There were 14 million tourist visits in Alberta in 1985—a tourist visit meaning at least one night away from home—and 65 percent of those were Albertans on the move. According to Alberta Tourism, total revenues for resident and non-resident travel in 1985 came to about $2.1 billion. This was a 4.6 percent increase over the previous year, and in fact tourism has been a steady growth industry here for many years.

This should not be surprising, considering the range of Alberta's attractions, everything from spectacular scenery to arts festivals and rodeos. Nor is there a shortage of facilities. More than a thousand hotels are scattered around the province, as well as two world class convention centres, five national parks, and dozens of provincial parks. Within the past decade, Alberta has hosted Canada and the world at numerous

conferences and events, among them the Commonwealth Games in Edmonton in 1978, and the Winter Olympics at Calgary in 1988.

Research and innovation is an essential component in Alberta's economy. Historically, it might even be said that "r&d" built this province, since it was the development of early ripening and rust-resistant strains of wheat that gave grain farmers here an edge over the environment. Now research is carried out in every field, from primary resource industries to high-tech manufacturing, so that we can remain flexible and competitive in world markets, as well as make the most of our natural and human resources.

As a service to business, and to help attract new industry to our borders, the provincial government funds a number of research facilities, among them the Alberta Oil Sands Technology and Research Authority (AOSTRA), the Alberta Research Council, the Coal Research and Technology Office, the Alberta Microelectronic Centre, the Alberta Laser Institute, the Centre for Frontier Engineering Research, and the Food Processing Development Centre. These and other facilities, as well as extensive private research and development, provide avenues for the integration of new tools and technologies into the Alberta economy.

The Alberta Research Council (ARC) is the largest, most broadly

▲ *The Chateau Lake Louise complements the fairy tale setting of Lake Louise in Jasper National Park. Photo by Ray F. Hillstrom, Jr. Courtesy, Hillstrom Stock Photo*

▶ *The 1988 Winter Olympics gave a boost to tourism in Alberta. Here, the Olympic flame burns bright over the opening ceremonies. Photo by Bill McKeown. Courtesy, Westfile, Inc.*

◀ The main laboratories and headquarters of the Alberta Research Council are located at 250 Karl Clark Road in Edmonton. Courtesy, Alberta Research Council

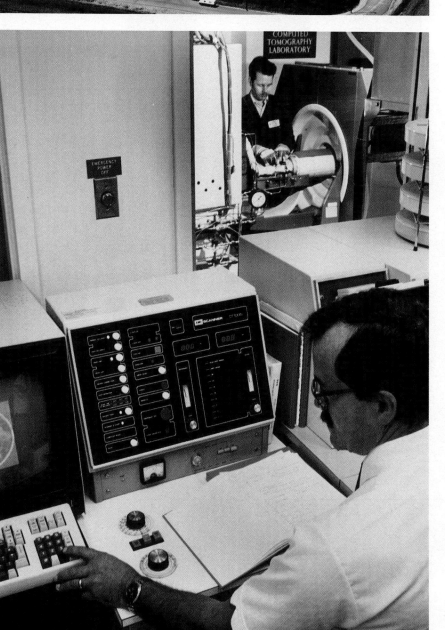

◀ Computed tomography is used by oil sands researchers to examine oil sands core composition and additive reactions. Dr. George Sedgwick sits at the CT console while technologist John Woolley aligns oil sands core in the scanner. Courtesy, Alberta Research Council

based research organization, outside of universities, in Alberta. It is not a government department but a crown corporation, which gives it a certain amount of independence in its operations. The ARC aims to provide technical information and applied research, as well as a scientific infrastructure, responsive to the needs of private industry and supportive of the needs of government. At the moment it maintains seven major research programs: oil sands and hydrocarbon recovery; coal and hydrocarbon processing; biotechnology; industrial technologies including forest products development and testing; computer-based technologies including automation, expert systems, and robotics; service to industry; and natural resources.

Working with private companies and government agencies, the ARC is involved in a number of stimulating, potentially profitable areas. In co-operation with AOSTRA, the Research Council has been investigating the use of steam for in-situ recovery of oil from heavy oil and oil sands deposits for such clients as Texaco Canada Resources. The ARC is also helping Esso Resources Canada and Gulf Canada Corporation to develop processing strategies for their oil sands leases.

Another problem Research Council scientists have been studying is the recovery of bitumen from low-grade ores. The Karl Clark hot-water process works very well on high grade oil sand, but when the oil sand is of lower quality, significant amounts of bitumen end up in the tailings pond instead of in the pipeline. The culprit, it seems, is the interaction of very fine particles, or fines, and salts in the low grade ore. Researchers have now successfully identified conditions necessary to prevent the fines from coagulating.

In biotechnology the Research Council has been active in a number of projects which could have a strong impact on agriculture here and abroad. The Council's biotechnology pilot plant, with a fermentation capacity of more than 20,000 litres, provides excellent scale-up and process development facilities. Among current projects quietly bubbling away in the Council's labs are work on a biological pesticide for Biosis of California, fish vaccines for netpen salmon for Mirotek Research and Development Ltd. of British Columbia, animal vaccines for Vetrepharm Inc. of Ontario, and a biological herbicide for PhilomBios Inc. of Saskatchewan.

Another Council project is the study of ice-nucleating bacteria native to Alberta, with the ultimate hope of minimizing frost damage to Alberta crops. There has been much publicity surrounding the genetic research in California on the bacteria that precipitate the ice crystals which destroy plant tissues during a frost. The hope is that plants inoculated with a non-nucleating form of the bacteria will withstand what would otherwise prove to be a killing frost. It has been found, however, that the bacteria in Alberta are of a different strain. If this high-tech "frost proofing" does work, then, it will have to be adapted for use here.

Also relevant to western farmers is Council research in the east and south of the province, where localized soil salinization is a problem. Council scientists have been studying the specific causes of sa-

◄ *Technologist Peter Taylor holds a sample of "waveboard" developed at the Alberta Research Council's forest products laboratories. Courtesy, Alberta Research Council*

linity, and attempting to devise effective remedies. It has been estimated that saline soils reduce Alberta farm production by $30 to $50 million per year. It now seems that part of the problem may be the discharge of a highly mineralized aquifer.

We are accustomed to using wood in certain standard formats, such as 2x4 studs, for example. However, those formats fall short of maximum use of the full volume of harvested timber. Therefore, to help maximize use of our forests, the ARC has been developing engineered wood composites, notably a corrugated "waveboard" that could be made from our very abundant, low-diameter aspen. Waveboard is a stiff, corrugated panel, produced with technology patented in 1986. If it can be developed to commercial size, waveboard could potentially replace the stud wall system of construction.

One of the Council's more recent and highly successful programs is a series of joint ventures with small and medium-size companies. Since 1983, 11 joint research ventures have been launched, with the ultimate aim of effecting technology transfer and the development of marketable products. The Council and its partners have invested more than $16 million in this program, which has produced such made-in-Alberta products as a map-editing work station, a 3-D vertical seismic profile system, and a well log analysis system.

Although it is impossible to note all the activities of the ARC, one program deserves special mention: the Service to Industry Program. This is a multifaceted program that tries to solve short-term industrial problems by providing companies with information and technical assistance, and by arranging for financing to help commercialize technology. One source of such funding is the Industrial Research Assistance Program (IRAP) run by the federal National Research Council.

One of the 2,000 companies aided this way during 1986 is Brentwood Glass of Calgary. Brentwood Glass manufactures high quality colour base and clear glass bars for the art glass industry. Assistance from IRAP allowed the company to analyze imported glass bars at the University of Calgary, and thus determine that similar glass could be made from chemicals and raw materials found in Alberta.

Another example of such assistance is the case of Commonwealth Seager Group. This company is involved in the cathodic protection of pipelines. Cathodic protection was developed to prevent the corrosion of steel pipe, but in the far north, the Northern Lights set up electric currents in the earth, known as telluric currents, which block such protection and hasten corrosion. In 1985 Commonwealth Seager Group asked for help in developing an instrument to measure the effects of telluric currents. Again, assistance from IRAP was forthcoming, and "tellupol," an instrument which reliably measures the effect of telluric currents on corrosion protection, is now being successfully marketed.

Remarkable as it is, the Alberta Research Council is only part of the scientific community here. There are a number of research bodies working in specific areas, such as the Office of Coal Research and Technology, part of the Alberta Department of Energy, as well as AOSTRA, a crown corporation.

These two organizations support research aimed at two products vital to Alberta. We have enormous deposits of coal and oil sands, and it is important to keep these resources competitive with other sources of energy. Coal has been around for a long time, and current means of production, handling, and combustion await improvement. In open-pit mining, for example, it is important to make the walls of the pit as steep as possible. This reduces the cost of removing overburden per unit of coal mined, yet too steep a wall risks the danger of collapse. A project on the Geotechnical Properties of Overburden allowed the Coal Mining Research Company of Devon to conduct extensive testing, and to compile and publish the Subsidence Handbook. Another line of coal research studies the agglomeration of sub-bituminous coal. Manalta Coal Ltd. in Calgary has been experimenting with a process in which finely ground coal and a liquid hydrocarbon are mixed in a water slurry, so as to form a stable, low-moisture, low-ash, high-heat value product.

The challenges of oil sands are more extensive than coal. It is less than a quarter century since commercial scale extraction began here, and many problems remain to be solved. As noted above, high grade ore can be profitable, but lower grade ore behaves differently. Experiments are also underway on methods of in-situ extraction, including combustion, fracturing, steam injection, and even electrical heating. Other fields of research include the chemistry of bitumen, remote sensing as applied to thermal recovery, and upgrading the use of the coke or pitch residue that comes from turning the raw bitumen into synthetic crude.

Not all the research being carried out here is done by government agencies, however. Private companies also experiment with technologies which they hope will prove profitable; an example is Biotechnica Canada Ltd. of Calgary. As the name implies, this is a company involved in the rapidly developing field of biotechnology. Using sophisticated techniques, the scientists here hope to give farmers in western Canada an edge on the market—and on nature.

Canola is one of the workhorses in the Biotechnica labs, partly because biotechnologists are confident in working with it, but also because Alberta is prime canola country. "And," says Biotechnica president Gordon Wells, "if we can come up with a strain of canola that ripens a few days earlier, or that is resistant to chemicals, that could mean a lot to the farmer." The chemicals he refers to are herbicides used not on canola, but on other crops grown in rotation with it. When traces remain in the soil, they can reduce the yield the following year.

Biotechnica is also working on flax. Wells places two small flasks of oil on his desk: one is a murky amber; the other is clear. "Flax," he says, "was a big crop in the West during the Second World War, when linseed oil was used as a marine oil. And it grows successfully here. It works well in rotation with wheat, doesn't mine the soil. But linseed oil is inedible." He opens the two flasks. From one comes the characteristic smell of linseed, reminiscent of a furniture factory. The other is virtually odorless. "We've developed a linseed oil that is edible," announces Wells.

Canadians spend a lot of money on salad oil, he points out, much of it imported sunflower oil. If even a portion of that market could be won by edible linseed oil, it would not only provide prairie farmers with an alternative crop, but would also help our balance of payments.

Shooting blind in the hopes of finding a marketable product is not Biotechnica's business strategy, and that is why, in the fall of 1987, they formed a joint research venture with RJR Nabisco and Biotechnica International Inc. This venture will involve the cooperation of Nabisco and Del Monte, subsidiaries of RJR Nabisco, to develop products with enhanced consumer appeal and improved agronomic performance. Improvements could include increased nutritional value, better flavour, longer shelf life, and enhanced disease resistance.

It is impossible to mention research in Alberta without also mentioning the electronics industry. There is healthy growth here in applied electronics, particularly in such areas as communications and remote sensing. Dozens of companies specialize in electronic hardware and software, ranging from Novatel Communications Ltd. of Calgary, which installed the first commercially operated cellular telephone system in North America here in Alberta, to SeaScan Technology (Canada) Ltd., designer and manufacturer of low-cost, remotely operated underwater vehicles, used in offshore drilling operations around the world. And although you may not be aware of it, you have most likely profited from the products of Pelorus Aviation Supplies Canada Ltd. This Calgary company makes distance measuring equipment (DME) and automatic weather observation and reporting systems (AWORS), both essential for modern aviation. Their customers include airports from coast to coast.

Because of our extensive experience in pursuit of oil, Alberta has earned international respect in seismology, a field of ongoing interest and development. This is the science of "shaking the earth," either with machines or explosives, and then interpreting the subtle echoes thus gathered from the depths. In the past, seismologists and geologists have had to decode long strips of graph paper covered with tangled, hairline scribbles, as murky to the uninitiated as a black and white television image from 1932. However, Veritas Software Inc., in a joint research venture with the Alberta Research Council, has developed a system which allows the integration of three-dimensional, vertical seismic profiles with the more usual common depth point surface data. Ultimately, the geologist will be able to pilot a path through rock strata thousands of metres underground by means of a computer and joystick, as if guiding a subterranean nautilus.

A defense industry spinoff from the energy sector is Cats Defense Support Systems Inc. of Calgary. This is one of the Atco group of companies, a group that got its start making trailers and portable shelters for drilling crews, and now employs 6,000 people. Using expertise drawn from the group, Cats Defense Support Systems has devised a moving targetry system to be used in training tank gunners. The system comprises a small, remotely controlled vehicle carrying a strong, yet lightweight, realistic superstructure, capable of recording hits electronically. For added realism, the target employs pyrotechnics to simulate return fire. Development and field testing of the target have been completed, and it is now ready to market.

But not all the research conducted here is energy related. Leaf Electronics Ltd. in St. Albert manufactures control modules for powered artificial limbs. Their myoelectric unit, for example, permits the signal from a single muscle group to control more than one function in the prosthesis. The company's product line also includes a biofeedback trainer to help patients learn to use their artificial limbs.

In considering what Albertans do for a living, we have looked mostly at the large divisions of industry, such as agriculture, logging, mining, and manufacturing. Of course, these imply individual occupations: the engineers and truck drivers and receptionists, the accountants and the gas plant operators, and the chemists and the taxi drivers. They also imply a web of cross connections, those personal contacts and contractual agreements and capital and financial resources that we refer to, in shorthand form, as business. We take a closer look at Alberta's business environment in the next chapter.

Get Out and Do Things

by Fred Stenson

The establishment of law and order in Alberta, marked by the coming of the Mounties in 1874 and the signing of the Blackfoot Treaty in 1877, cleared the way for settlers and builders. But fresh territory for investment though it was, Alberta was far from easy pickings for the incoming entrepreneur. The stories of those who built Alberta are often stories of fortunes made, fortunes lost, and fortunes made again.

In the late nineteenth century, the name of the game was cattle. Southern Alberta was attractive to ranchers for two reasons. First, periodically, the warm chinook winds bared the grass in winter. Second, after 1881 the Canadian government began offering leases of up to 100,000 acres, at a penny an acre per year.

Would-be cattle barons from eastern Canada, the United States, and Britain moved to take advantage.

The first major open range outfit in Alberta was started by Senator Matthew Cochrane of Quebec in 1881. That year, Cochrane brought in 3,000 head of cattle from Montana to his grazing lease west of Calgary. Purchases in 1882 expanded the herd to 12,000.

The ranch's beginnings were anything but smooth, however. Rustlers and rough weather badly depleted the Cochrane herd in its first two winters. The third year, the cattle were driven south to winter east of Waterton. As luck would have it, this proved to be an winter of little snow west of Calgary and a winter of smothering blizzards at Waterton. Finally, the Cochrane herd was trapped away from open grass by a solid corral of drifted snow. A Fort Macleod man, Frank Strong, saved the day. Hired by the Cochrane Ranch, Strong gathered a herd of 500 Indian ponies which he drove into the drifts until a path was beaten through to the starving cattle. From these rugged beginnings, the mighty Cochrane Ranch was built.

Pat Burns, another Canadian, left Ontario for the West in 1878. Poor farming prospects drove him off a Manitoba homestead and into cattle dealing. By the time Burns arrived in Calgary to build a slaughterhouse in 1890, he was a full-time cattle buyer.

One of the early coups in Burns' impressive career was his success in bringing live cattle to remote Dawson City during the Klondike gold rush. Beef fetched a pretty penny in Dawson, and Dominic Burns, Pat's brother, was one of the two butchers in town. The first Burns herd went to the Klondike over the treacherous Chilkoot Pass. Part of the trick of get-

◄ *Senator Matthew Henry Cochrane. Courtesy, Glenbow Archives, Calgary*

ting these cattle to their destination was how tame they were; purchased in Oregon, many of them were broke to harness. Once they reached the top of the Pass, the cattle hauled logs for the rafts that carried them the rest of the way to slaughter—and to profit for Pat Burns.

By 1902 Pat Burns was supplying beef to eastern Canada and Britain and was pioneering the shipment of frozen beef to distant ports. Burns had, to use modern terminology, a "fully-integrated" beef business. He supplied beef from his own ranches to his own abatoirs, and marketed through his own stores. In 1928 Burns sold everything but the ranches. He was appointed to the Canadian Senate in 1931, and died in Calgary in 1937.

In the shadow of the glamourous rancher, the farmer is often overlooked. One of Alberta's farmers who stands well outside that shadow is Charles Sherwood Noble. Noble came to Alberta from Iowa in 1903 and, five years later, bought 3,200 acres near Lethbridge. He expanded his operations through the war years, and was noted for being one of the first to fully embrace steam power farming. Dry weather and a collapse in wheat prices caught up with Noble in 1922, forcing foreclosure, but he quickly rebounded. By 1930 he was in business again with 8,000 acres.

Charles Noble was a student of dryland farming, and the dust bowl years of the Depression tested his ingenuity and brought forth invention. In 1936 he built a new kind of cultivator that cut the roots of weeds below ground without disturbing the soil-holding "trash" cover. Topsoil drifting was one of the tragedies of the Alberta Depression, and the Noble Blade was a major step toward its prevention. Noble went into business on his farm, manufacturing these cultivators, and when he died in 1957 the business was still going strong.

The oil and gas industry has long been the engine of Alberta's economy. The first gas was struck in Alberta in 1883, in a Canadian Pacific Railway water well near Medicine Hat. The industry did not leap to life in that moment, however. The first major step was taken by Ontario native Eugene Coste in 1912. Between April and July of that year, Coste built a 170-mile pipeline from the Bow Island gas field to Calgary: one of the great industrial exploits of the time.

Coste's success marked a temporary defeat for another Ontario entrepreneur, Archibald Walter Dingman, who had been competing with Coste to supply Calgary with gas. Dingman was not down for long, however. Shortly afterward, he was approached by William Stewart Herron, a coal hauler who had discovered a gas seep in the Sheep River, southwest of Calgary. Dingman threw in with Herron and, in 1914, their first well blew in: a wet gas discovery that touched off a fever of speculation in Calgary.

The Dingman-Herron strike was the beginning of an era. For the next 22 years, wet gas spewed from dozens of Turner Valley wells, most of it going up in smoke as companies harvested the heavier hydrocarbons and let the methane burn.

In 1936 everyone realized what a mistake this had been. That year, a well originally backed by Calgarians Robert A. Brown, Sr., and George Melrose Bell discovered oil beneath the gas. Most of the gas cap over the oil was spent by then and, without the pressure of the gas to move it, much of the oil was doomed to remain in the rock.

George Bell died before his well came in. Bell had been the owner of the Calgary *Albertan*, a newspaper in deep financial trouble. When he died his son Max Bell inherited a partly drilled well and a newspaper $500,000 in debt. It turned out not to be such a bad deal. The Turner Valley oil strike eventually enabled Bell to buy his father's newspaper back from the bank. He continued to make money in the oil fields, and to use it to buy newspapers until, by 1966, he was a major owner of the largest newspaper chain in Canada.

A close friend and occasional business associate of Max Bell was Frank McMahon. Although McMahon is best known for his tenacious quest to bring north British Columbia gas to southern markets, he made his first fortune in Alberta. Following Max Bell's and Robert A. Brown's lead, Frank and his brother George McMahon struck oil in Turner Valley in 1939. However, during the mid-1940s, the brothers spent $5 million looking for more oil and "didn't find a drop." Then, in 1947, the Imperial Gas Company struck it rich at Leduc, and the McMahons were amongst the first into the bidding for surrounding leases. The first McMahon well at Leduc made world headlines. Atlantic No. 3 blew out and caught fire. It was tremendously wasteful, though it made a fortune for Frank McMahon.

Beyond being famous for making money, Frank McMahon and Max Bell were famous for the ways they spent it. Along with Robert A. Brown's son, "Bobby" Brown, who also used his Turner Valley inheritance to build an oil empire, McMahon and Bell were the jet-set entrepreneurs of their day. Retaining a home base in Calgary, they worked and played all over the continent. Bell, McMahon, and legendary jockey Johnny Longdon co-owned a prestigious breeding stable in California called Alberta Ranches. Four-and-Twenty, one of their best horses, won three $100,000 races in the U.S., but failed in the Kentucky Derby. Max Bell's horses won the Irish Derby in 1962 and the Queen's Plate in 1968. Frank McMahon also backed Broadway plays, and had a string of hits including *Pajama Game, Plain and Fancy,* and *Damn Yankees.* When Max Bell died in 1972, Bing Crosby spoke of him as "an old and dear friend," and Johnny Longdon credited him with all his personal financial success. Frank McMahon died in Bermuda in 1986 at the age of 83.

The men described above are but a small sampling of Alberta's entrepreneurs. If you look for common denominators among them, you will find few. Some were prodigious drinkers; others were teetotallers. Some were formally educated at fine schools; others were drop-outs. Pat Burns, for example, did not learn to read until he was a homesteader in Manitoba.

What they all did have in common is that, although they could have, at one time or another, retired to wealth, they kept active in their business dealings late into life. When asked by a *Time* reporter what drove him, Max Bell said it was the desire "to get out and do things." Likely, all the men described here would have agreed.

CHAPTER **5**

How's Business?

Pretty good, thanks.

After the mid-1970s, Alberta's economy boomed, spurred by the steep rise in oil prices. Lured by jobs, people came from all over the country, increasing our population dramatically. Housing subdivisions appeared overnight, and everyone from hair dressers to investment counsellors thrilled at the throb of crude pumping through the pipeline of the economy.

The economic machinery gained extra torque from the Arab oil embargo and the world's subsequent anxiety over energy. In the early eighties, however, the dilemma created by Canada's national energy policy (NEP), which made it uneconomical for oil companies to explore in Alberta, was compounded by a calamitous drop in oil prices. The price of oil had been headed toward $40 a barrel; suddenly, it plummeted to around $8.

This was our own, particular greased pole to the bottom of the worldwide recession, and many companies trimmed both fat and flesh in an effort to stay alive. Inevitably, the rate of unemployment and business failure went up, and thousands who had migrated here when times were good packed up their cowboy boots and went home again.

The effects of that recession are now fading. The NEP has been dismantled, the price of oil has floated up to around $20 a barrel, double what it fell to in 1985, and unemployment has declined slowly and steadily to around 9 percent. It is not quite the boom we like to remember, but the steady increase does signify healthy growth; in the long run, that may prove more profitable.

One way of measuring the health of the economy is the Gross Domestic Product, or GDP. In current dollars, our GDP has been growing by leaps and bounds, reaching a shade over $62 billion in 1985, an

◀ *During the recession of the early 1980s, unemployment skyrocketed, businesses failed, and the sun seemed to be setting on the oil industry in Alberta. However, the economy's health has improved considerably in the last few years. Photo by Chris Bruun. Courtesy, Westfile, Inc.*

163

◀ *The Stephen Avenue Mall is located in Calgary. Photo by Winston Fraser. Courtesy, Hillstrom Stock Photo*

increase of 7.4 percent over the previous year. It is more accurate to compare years in constant dollars, though, thus removing the illusion of inflation. In 1971 dollars, then, our GDP in 1985 was $14.4 billion, a little less than the peak year of 1981. The total would have been higher had we not spent $6 billion on imports.

Of that GDP amount, over 43 percent came from direct sales, which gives some idea of the power of the consumer. In current dollars that amounts to $26.9 billion being circulated through the economy by ordinary Albertans. The next largest portion, around 21 percent, was contributed by what statisticians call "gross fixed capital formation," or investment in the construction of houses, buildings, factories, and the installation of machinery and equipment. Exports accounted for a hair less than 19 percent of the total. Sales to government came to 12.6 percent of our GDP that year, a respectably small portion in a province dedicated to the principles of free enterprise.

Another key indicator of the health of the Alberta economy is the rate of private and public investment. The forecast figures for 1987 put investment here at about $16 billion, or a per capita rate of $5,473. This compares favourably with the national rate of $4,923, and stands ahead of our provincial neighbours as well. The per capita rate of investment in Saskatchewan for 1987 was $5,308, and in British Columbia, only $4,552.

Analyzing investment industry by industry, we find that the biggest investors in Alberta are still primary industries and construction, accounting for $5.7 billion of the projected outlay in 1987. This is followed by transportation and communications, institutions (such as universities) and government departments, trade, finance and commercial services, housing, and manufacturing.

Especially important to the business climate and to future economic growth are the efforts of government to encourage diversification and decentralization of our industries. Resource industries and agriculture are subject to the cycle of boom and bust, and if we wish to maintain a stable and prosperous society, we must continue to encourage manufacturing and service industries—most profitably in locations outside our two major cities.

One financial flywheel meant to stabilize the surge and slump of Alberta's economy, and to help promote diversity, is the Alberta Heritage Savings Trust Fund. This is a government kitty set up in 1976, when the oil royalties were gladdening the heart of the provincial treasurer. Suddenly there was a lot of extra cash around, and the government then decided that, rather than spend it in an instant rush of consumption, it would be more prudent to stash some of it away. After all, our reserves of conventional oil and gas would run out someday.

The Alberta Heritage Savings Trust Fund siphoned 30 percent of oil and gas revenues until the end of the 1982 to 1983 fiscal year, thus accumulating $11.3 billion. By then, the recession was making it difficult to maintain the same rate of investment, and the transfer rate was reduced to 15 percent for the next three years. In 1986 the drop in oil prices handed the government a large budgetary deficit, and the

▲ *The West Edmonton Mall is the world's largest comprehensive shopping and amusement centre. Photo by Jerg Kroener*

▲ *The biggest investors in Alberta are still primary industries and construction. Photo by Chris Bruun. Courtesy, Westfile, Inc.*

decision was made to put all non-renewable resource income into general revenue. In government parlance, the transfer of money to the Heritage Fund has been "suspended," a term which suggests it might be resumed someday, although no one is holding his breath. In all likelihood, the Heritage Trust Fund has finished its youthful growth spurt. By the time it was capped, the Fund was worth $12.7 billion.

This huge sum has a significant effect on the provincial economy. For one thing, the net income from the Fund's investments is transferred to budgetary revenues. In the 1987 to 1988 fiscal year, this amounted to $1.4 billion, or about one-fifth of all government income. This, of course, helps keep taxes down, and goes a long way toward the government's stated objective of scrubbing out the deficit by fiscal year 1990 to 1991.

The other, widespread effect is that of a lot of money, working in ways not often embraced by private enterprise *or* government. Private enterprise looks for a profitable return from its investments, while government does not usually have surplus funds to apply to economic and social development. Although the administration of the Fund is regularly debated in the legislature, and often criticized by the Opposition, it is undeniable that every Albertan has benefited from its deployment.

The Fund is spread over five investment divisions: the Alberta Investment Division, the Capital Projects Division, the Energy Investment Division, the Canada Investment Division, and the Commercial Investment Division. Money not allocated through these programs is placed in deposits and marketable securities.

The terms of the Canada Investment and Commercial Investment Divisions of the Fund are quite straightforward. These investments must yield a commercial return; categories permitted include, respectively, loans to other provincial governments and shares of Canadian companies. The Canada Investment Division presently holds loans to six provinces or their agencies. The $200-million limit originally imposed on the Commercial Division is now increased quarterly by the amount of net income the division earns. By the end of the 1986 to 1987 fiscal year, the value had risen to $233 million.

There is no set limit on the amount invested in the Alberta and the Energy Divisions of the Fund, although they are required to return a reasonable profit. Investments under the Energy Division are expected to facilitate the development, processing, or transportation of energy resources within Canada, but in fact no investments were made in this division in fiscal year 1986 to 1987. The Alberta Division, on the other hand, was very busy, investing in everything from Alberta Government Telephones to a grain terminal in Prince Rupert. These investments, which may be either debt or equity, are intended to strengthen or diversify the provincial economy. The investment in Ridley Grain Ltd. is a good example. This company operates the Prince Rupert Grain Terminal, and the support of the Heritage Trust Fund has helped to improve the port and increase shipments. About a quarter of all wheat and barley shipped through the west coast now goes through Prince Rupert, and much of it originates in northern Alberta.

The remaining funds are either held as cash and marketable securities, or put into the Capital Projects Division. Capital projects are those with long term social or economic benefits, but they need not yield a direct return. The Capital Projects Division of the Fund is limited to a fifth of the total, including "deemed" assets, or assets which cannot be recovered.

The Capital Projects Division has produced some of the most visible and impressive investments in the short history of the Heritage Trust Fund. Among them are: 1,000 blue and gold rail hopper cars (suitably emblazoned with the Trust Fund logo); the major cost of converting 100,000 rural party lines to individual service; 18 new airport terminals around the province; a number of research facilities, including the Alberta Oil Sands Technology and Research Authority, the Electronics Test Centre, microchip design and fabrication facilities, funding for applied cardiac and cancer research, and a $300-million endowment fund for medical research; the Walter C. Mackenzie Health Sciences Centre in Edmonton and the Tom Baker Cancer Centre and Alberta Children's Hospital in Calgary; a scholarship fund of $100 million; the Pine Ridge Forest Nursery; the reclamation of over 1,100 disturbed sites such as abandoned garbage dumps, sewage lagoons, gravel pits, and mines around the province; and the development of a number of park and recreation areas, including Kananaskis Country, the 4,100-square-kilometre multi-use area which contains Mount Allan, site of the downhill ski events in the 1988 Winter Olympics.

Impressive as this list is, it represents only a selection of the Capital projects. One other investment worth noting is the establishment of Vencap Equities Ltd. In 1983 the government took $200 million of the Trust Fund and set up an arm's-length, venture capital company. By the end of fiscal year 1986 to 1987, Vencap, which is shareholder owned, had invested or committed close to $72 million in 24 companies.

Trying to interpret taxes is like trying to read the channel of a muddy prairie river: a lot of what you need to know is hidden, and changes every year anyway. However, a study by the Provincial Treasurer shows that, as of April 1, 1986, Alberta was one of the least-taxed provinces in the country.

That year our basic rate for personal income tax was 43.5 percent, the lowest in the country. In British Columbia the rate was 47.5 percent; in Ontario it was 50 percent. Some provinces had a high income surtax, in Manitoba as high as 20 percent, but in Alberta there was none. Neither was there a retail sales tax, and our tax on tobacco was the lowest in the land.

Corporate income tax was also favourable. The small business rate was "0/5," meaning that manufacturing and processing firms paid 0 percent, while others paid 5 percent. The general corporate rate was "5/11," or 5 percent for manufacturing and processing, and 11 percent for other types of business. This compares to rates of 14.5 percent to 15.5 percent in Ontario, 16 percent in Manitoba, and 17 percent in

The Capital Projects Division has funded, among other things, the Walter C. Mackenzie Health Sciences Centre (left) and Kananaskis Country, site of the downhill ski events in the 1988 Winter Olympics as well as the 1987 World Cup (below). Courtesy, First Light, Toronto (Photo by Pat Morrow) and the Walter C. Mackenzie Health Sciences Centre

Saskatchewan. Some provinces also have payroll and capital taxes, which do not exist here.

The abundant Alberta farmlands produce far more than Albertans can consume. In fact, our fields and feedlots produce almost a fifth of Canada's agricultural output, with less than a tenth of the population. We have, therefore, a long-standing interest in exporting goods, from grain to breeding stock. Between 1975 and 1984, exports of food, feed, beverages, and live animals increased more than 100 percent, passing the $2 billion mark. In spite of that impressive figure, though, Alberta farmers, like those across North America, face difficult times.

The problem is not with the land. In a good year, it can yield mountains of wheat and beef and barley. The problem is how much it costs the former to raise these crops, and how much can be charged for them.

Between 1976 and 1982, farm capital almost tripled, mostly because of a huge increase in the value of real estate and construction. Since 1982, these values have slowly decreased, but it is still an expensive proposition for a young farmer to get started. At the same time, operating expenses have increased steadily, as has farm debt. In 1985 gross income from farming operations was $3.79 billion, but total farm debt was $5.24 billion. The net income that year was only $450 million. Averaged out over the approximately 57,000 farms in the province, that amounts to less than $8,000 per farm.

▼ *This irrigation system brings water to the surrounding southern Alberta farmland. Photo by David A. McColl. Courtesy, Westfile, Inc.*

▼ *These grain elevators are located in Claresholm. Photo by R. Siemens. Courtesy, Westfile, Inc.*

▲ *Abundant Alberta farmlands, such as these west of Innisfail, produce more than Albertans can consume. However, high operating costs and low farm prices have conspired against farmers here and throughout North America. Photo by Chris Bruun. Courtesy, Westfile, Inc.*

Interest rates have eased considerably since the beginning of the decade, but income from wheat, our largest crop, has fallen badly. This is largely a result of the United States government's decision to strike back at the European Economic Community by subsidizing its own wheat farmers. U.S. grain sales have eaten into traditional Canadian markets in China and the Soviet Union, and Alberta wheat sales fell from $902 million in 1984 to $447 million in 1986.

Along with the rest of the economy, the best recourse for the Alberta farmer is diversification, which is forecast as a steady growth in vegetables, alternative grains, and nursery and horticulture. The provincial government supports this strategy through a number of programs and agencies. Among these are the Agri-Food Development Branch and Agricultural Processing Development Branch, the Food Processing Development Centre, and Farming for the Future, all part of the Alberta Department of Agriculture.

The Agricultural Processing Development Branch, for example, provides technical and financial assistance to the agricultural industry. The Development Branch hopes to improve productivity, increase awareness of new technology, and encourage the development of new products, processes, and packaging methods. If a processor wishes to implement a new process, expand a product line, upgrade a facility or start a whole new one, the Branch can provide both information and financial assistance.

Should the processor need more detailed technical evaluation, or wish to develop an idea that is still in the experimental stage, the Food Processing Development Centre in Leduc may be able to help. This up-to-date facility contains product development and evaluation laboratories, as well as pilot plant processing areas capable of handling everything from meat and dairy to oilseeds and prepared foods. The equipment here allows the controlled variation of processing conditions and the careful monitoring of the product in all stages of processing. Small-scale operators could never afford such a facility, of course, but with access to the Food Processing Development Centre, they have the opportunity to market a product that will bring the consumer back to the store for more—anywhere in the world.

Finally, the province also offers help through the Market Development Division of Alberta Agriculture. Marketing boards have been an agricultural fact of life for decades—these agencies regulate the trade in commodities such as eggs and butter and wheat—but only a few products fall under their care. The rest must be independently marketed, and the Market Development Division stands ready with a wide range of services. These include identification of market opportunities; establishment of contacts with potential marketers and buyers; advice on tariffs, health regulations, labelling requirements, and transportation; arranging for participation in sales missions and trade shows; identification of possible joint venture partners; development of market strategies; and design of market surveys and consumer profiles. In Alberta there is no need for agri-food products to fail because of improper marketing.

► *Alberta has rail links to year-round ports on the Pacific Rim, which is becoming an important area for trade. Photo by Bill McKeown. Courtesy, Westfile, Inc.*

Alberta's economy depends heavily on swapping goods with the rest of the world. Our base of capital and human resources is not yet large enough to form an integrated, self-sustaining industrialized economy, and so we must find markets abroad in order to afford what we do not produce ourselves.

Our performance in this area has been marked by success. In 1985 we exported $13.6 billion worth of goods, well over a tenth of the national total. In 1984 our exports measured 21.1 percent of our provincial gross domestic product. Although this was less than the proportion for Canada as a whole (26.7 percent) it compares favourably with Japan (17.1 percent) and the United States (9.9 percent). It should be noted that these figures reflect a period when oil prices were weak. Since fully two-thirds of our 1985 exports were classified as "Crude Materials, Inedible," mostly oil, natural gas, sulphur, and coal, it seems likely that an even greater part of our GDP goes to exports, now that energy prices have recovered.

Clearly, though, it would be advantageous for us to increase the amount of manufactured goods we export. In order to do so, the province must overcome several hurdles. The first of these is the long-standing accumulation of industrial capital in central Canada, and the natural reluctance of manufacturers to relocate without exceptional inducement. Another difficulty is the dearth of population centres immediately adjacent to Alberta. Saskatchewan, Montana, and Idaho do not offer the sizable markets necessary to support large-scale capital investment. Most of British Columbia's population is concentrated in the lower mainland, with mountain passes and hundreds of miles of highway imposing a geographic barrier.

In the last few decades, however, the Pacific Rim has opened up

▲ Cargo is unloaded from a 767 jet at Edmonton International Airport. Photo by Chris Bruun. Courtesy, Westfile, Inc.

▲ *Novatel, a pioneer in cellular tele-*
phone technology, has exported cellu-
lar telephones to China. Courtesy,
Novatel

as a trading area; with adequate rail links to year-round ports, Alberta can legitimately hope for some of this market. To be able to successfully trade in this area, though, means we must export raw materials—or compete against industrial giants which can draw on sources of very cheap labour. Our best strategy is to concentrate on areas of skill and expertise—as we have successfully done with exports of oil field and communications equipment, and with the "invisible" export of engineering. Novatel, one of the pioneers in cellular telephone technology, for example, is exporting cellular telephones to China, in spite of the advantage traditionally associated with places like Hong Kong, Japan, and Korea in electronics. Novatel made the sale because they know the business—and because they invested in a heavily robotized plant in Lethbridge, which increased their efficiency.

The destination of the largest share of our exports is the United States. In 1985 we sent $10.5 billion worth of goods south of the border, which was better than 77 percent of our total exports. Asia and the Pacific Rim took the next largest share, $1.7 billion, or 12.5 percent. Exports to Europe dropped sharply in 1985, mostly because of decreased grain shipments. The value that year was $624 million, or 4.6 percent.

We noted earlier that the provincial government makes an effort to help develop new markets for the agri-food business; in fact it does the same for any business interested in exporting. To this end it has established an entire department called Economic Development and Trade, of which the Trade Development Division works directly with individual companies or groups of companies to sell Alberta products and services abroad. The staff in this division help businesspeople identify export opportunities, assist with sales missions and trade shows, and provide expert advice for specific export projects.

The Transportation Services Division of the same department helps with the details of ensuring a product's arrival at its intended destination. There is also an office of the Export Development Corporation in Alberta, a service of the federal government, which provides insurance, loans, and guarantees to help develop the export trade. Finally, the Alberta government maintains offices in Europe and the Far East, to help maintain lines of communication with possible markets.

During the late seventies, when some Albertans were earning more money in a day than they could stuff in their lunchpails, new businesses were appearing overnight, like dandelions on a suburban lawn. Not surprisingly, some of these new ventures were financial institutions, trust companies, and even banks with headquarters here in Alberta. (After all, someone had to count all this money.)

When the recession began in 1982, financial institutions began to retrench and consolidate. Prudent managers made certain that they could cover the deposits, and doubtful loans were called in, to the alarm of many a debtor. Even so, some trust companies went under, although given the complete picture this is not so surprising. Trust companies are smaller and not as closely regulated as banks, and brave a greater, inherent risk.

▶ *Downtown Calgary is an important banking center. Photo by Katherine Rodeghier. Courtesy, Hillstrom Stock Photo*

Nevertheless, many were shocked when, in 1985, two Schedule A chartered banks based in Alberta collapsed. The Northlands Bank and the Canadian Commercial Bank constituted the first bank failures in Canada in 60 years, and the closing of their doors raised a dark cloud of accusation and anxiety. It was a theme re-echoed in 1987 when the Alberta-based Principal Group, including Principal Trust and the investment fund companies First Investors Choice and Associated Investors Choice, also had to shut down.

Although the failure in each case probably derived from a variety of causes, it is likely that exposure in the declining real estate market, brought on by the recession, played a major part in both. The consequence, in Alberta at least, was a shift by depositors from trust companies and credit unions to the larger, apparently more secure banks. These events have no doubt led to cases of personal hardship; yet overall, the recession has not made much of a dent in the financial structure here. In 1986 total bank assets were $42.58 billion, down only 2.4 percent from the year before, and only 5 percent off the record high year in 1983. Of those assets, better than 35 percent were in business loans, and another 12 percent were in residential mortgages. Of the $24.3 billion in liabilities, 49 percent, or $12.1 billion, was in the form of personal savings. (You thought your savings account was an asset? It is, for you. Banks tend to see things differently from everyone else.)

Our survey of the financial picture in Alberta would not be complete without a mention of the Alberta Treasury Branches. These were set up by the Social Credit government in the 1930s, as a supplement to the existing banking system. Social Credit's fiscal policies included issuing scrip to citizens so as to stimulate the economy; this scrip was to be issued at Treasury Branch offices. Although most of Social Credit's policies, including the issuance of scrip, fell by the wayside, the Treasury Branches continued, evolving into an institution similar to banks and trust companies. By 1985, Treasury Branch assets exceeded $4 billion.

Not all Alberta businesses are financed through the neighbourhood bank. Some take the plunge and go public, not on the New York exchange or the Toronto Exchange, but on the Alberta Stock Exchange (ASE), located in downtown Calgary.

▶ *The Continental Bank Building is a prominent structure in downtown Edmonton. Courtesy, Westfile, Inc.*

The Alberta exchange is a venerable institution, having got its start in 1913, when it was called the Calgary Stock Exchange. It was in place just in time to catch the flurry of speculation that blew into town with the discovery of oil in Turner Valley in 1914. Like the early days of stock trading in New York, a building was lacking at first; buyers and sellers conducted their business in the open street. The exchange stopped trading in 1917, but resumed in 1924, when fresh discoveries of oil were made. The exchange has operated continuously since then and, for most of its life, has retained its close ties with the energy sector. In the mid-1970s though, a new president and revised government policy led to a broader base on the ASE.

In 1974 the number of shares traded was only 6.3 million—barely enough to keep the four floor traders awake. Now there are 10 times that number of traders, and the volume of shares on a good day comes close to the entire turnover in 1974. Such growth is partly the result of altered regulations, meant to improve the quality of stock, and partly the result of diversification. Issues traded here were once almost exclusively oil and gas stocks; this category now makes up only 25 percent of listings.

Another innovation on the exchange which has stirred up interest is the acceptance of junior capital pools, or, as they are sometimes quite accurately called, blind pools. This was an idea put forward by the provincial government, hoping to provide new sources of venture capital for entrepreneurs. A junior capital pool is a company with a minimum of $30,000 invested by at least 300 shareholders, which goes public on the ASE, usually with shares for a nickel or a dime. What makes these pools "blind" is that they need have no other assets, no history, no prospects, and no business plan. Investors are in fact, then, betting solely on the people involved. As such, the blind pool promises to be an effective mechanism for developing entrepreneurial expertise in the free marketplace, although, of course, it is an investment posing definite risks.

Another innovation which has yet to make much of an impact either on the ASE or on the Alberta economy is the Alberta Stock Savings Plan. The plan offers tax credits of up to $3,000 for investment in eligible Alberta companies. To be eligible, companies must have at least a quarter of their payroll in Alberta, but not many companies have yet taken advantage of the plan. If it does begin to attract companies and investors, the plan will provide another source of funds for Alberta industry.

The Alberta Stock Exchange is not large compared to other markets, but it has been steadily growing in spite of the recession. In 1986, the ASE's best year ever, over 369 million shares were traded, for a dollar volume of $476 million, or about $1.29 per share. About 700 issues were traded on the exchange that year, including some 120 new listings. Obviously the ASE is not suited to every investor nor to every business; nevertheless, it plays an important part in Alberta's economy. For those with the stakes—and the nerve—to play a little frontier poker, the pot can be worth it.

Another essential element in the business environment is attitude. Without the right one, the best business opportunity in the world will fail. With it, however, things happen. What follows is an example.

In an industrial subdivision of southeast Calgary there stands a low, cinder block building. It boasts no distinguishing features, although the persistent can eventually find a door marked with a small sign: Highwood Audio. Inside, Highwood's president, Paul Burton, and a small team of specialists are planning to rewrite a small portion of audio history. "We have designed," says Burton, "a full frequency, non-directional, planar speaker."

This means a speaker that responds to the full audio spectrum and does not "beam" certain frequencies, thus acting as a perfect point source of sound. It also means a speaker that is amazingly light and thin—a full-sized pair can be lifted in one hand, and each measures less than two centimetres thick. Cloth covered, the pair can be discreetly hung, like pictures, on the wall. "There have been planar speakers before," Burton says, "but ours are the first that are non-directional. They are also less than half the price of other planar speakers."

It is too soon in the life of Highwood Audio to tell if this product will succeed—marketing is only just under way—but Burton's comments about the business climate in Alberta are revealing. Burton is not a native Albertan; he has lived in England, in France, and in Switzerland, and has travelled extensively through the United States. Nevertheless, he chose Alberta as the site to build his business. "I don't think Toronto is any better than Calgary for high technology industry," he says. "The cost of doing business here is quite a bit lower—taxes are lower, rents are lower, there's less competition for space. At the same time, there's a lot of venture capital around, and the business community is used to taking risks. They grew up in the oil patch." He concludes: "People have always had big ideas here."

Burton has good reason for his enthusiasm. Armed with two bench models of his speakers, a patent application, and a business plan, he recently acquired half a million dollars in venture capital, and retained control of his company in the bargain. By the time this book is printed, he will have unveiled his product. If his marketing strategy works, five years from now he hopes to be producing 15,000 pairs of speakers a year, 80 percent of which will be exported. If Highwood Audio does achieve full production, it will employ about 50 people full time.

Another venture story worth telling is that of Biotechnica Canada Ltd. We met them in the last chapter, in the context of industrial research and development. What we now ask is: why did Biotechnica decide to settle here?

Biotechnica Canada is the third Biotechnica company to be formed. The first, Biotechnica International Inc., was formed in the United States in 1981. Major investors at that time were Calgary businessmen Jim Gray and John Masters. In 1985 their involvement brought about the potentially dynamic combination of western Canada agribusiness and a Biotechnica company focused on the green end of biotechnology. This means that Biotechnica Canada is interested principally in new

plant varieties, as compared to enzymes and bacterial factories. As such, it fits in well with the Alberta economy and has settled here because of Alberta venture capital.

Here's a scenario every businessman dreads: start a business and before you know it, you're spending more time doing business with your employees than you do with your customers. When labour relations go smoothly, they go almost unnoticed—but when they go wrong, sorting things out can be frustrating and costly.

Labour relations in Alberta are regulated by a number of pieces of legislation, and, depending on the industry, may also involve collective agreements with local, national, or international unions. Federal legislation covers such industries and workplaces as banks, communications, broadcasting, and transportation that crosses provincial borders, but in Alberta this only accounts for a tenth of the workforce. The rest is covered by provincial legislation setting minimum work conditions and wages, as well as the rules under which collective bargaining takes place.

The Employment Standards Act, as the name suggests, sets minimum standards for maximum hours of work per day, overtime, minimum wages and permissible deductions, vacations and vacation pay, general holidays and holiday pay, notification to employees of work schedules, maternity benefits, and termination of employment. The

▲ *Collective bargaining in Alberta generally is governed by the Labour Relations Act, although firefighters, among others, are not covered. Photo by R. Siemens. Courtesy, Westfile, Inc.*

standards set are only the absolute minimum; employers may provide better conditions than the act requires, but they cannot offer worse. There are penalties, of course, for employers who fail to live up to the act.

As well as workers covered by federal legislation, certain other classes of employees are not covered by the Employment Standards Act. The provincial civil service, for example, is covered instead by the Public Service Employee Relations Act, and police are covered by the Police Act. Farm and ranch workers are also generally exempt, as are domestics working in private homes.

Naturally, the specific provisions of the Employment Standards Act change from time to time. Current standards are available from the Employment Standards Branch of the Alberta Department of Labour. The Branch maintains offices at a number of centres around the province.

Generally speaking, collective bargaining in Alberta is governed by the Labour Relations Act, although many of the same exemptions apply. Provincial employees, police, firefighters, farm and ranch hands, domestics, and employees within federal jurisdiction are not covered. Neither are the self-employed, people in managerial positions, and professionally employed doctors, dentists, lawyers, architects, and engineers.

Briefly, the Labour Relations Act sets out the regulations for the certification, registration, and de-certification of both trade unions and employer's organizations. It also governs collective bargaining, and when the bargaining process breaks down, lays down the ground rules for mediation, arbitration, strikes, and lock-outs.

The Labour Relations Act is administered by the quasi-judicial Labour Relations Board, made up of representatives of both labour and management, and chaired by someone acceptable to both sides. The Board holds public hearings on relevant matters, but in exceptional cases it can be superseded by the Minister of Labour. If the provincial cabinet determines that a particular dispute endangers the public, it may, through the Minister of Labour, establish a Public Emergency Tribunal and order the affected employees back to work. This happened in the early eighties, when nurses throughout the province went on strike. The government subsequently altered legislation to prevent a recurrence of the situation, and nurses here are no longer permitted to strike.

It is worth noting that the Labour Relations Act provides for collective bargaining from both sides of the table. That is, not only may employees join together, but so may employers. An employers' organization may negotiate a master agreement with a trade union, which is then binding upon all employers.

This legislation has had particular impact in the construction and building trades. Because construction projects involve large amounts of capital and critical time lines, and because non-striking unions traditionally honor the picket lines of striking workers, contractors have been particularly vulnerable to the threat of a strike. Allowing the

◀ *The Labour Relations Act has had particular impact in the construction and building trades. Photo by Bill McKeown. Courtesy, Westfile, Inc.*

▲ *Cement workers combine efforts on a job in Edmonton. Photo by Chris Bruun. Courtesy, Westfile, Inc.*

negotiation of master agreements has given builders and contractors some protection, as well as more leverage at the bargaining table. It also has reduced the possibility of "whipsawing," in which unions or employers play one group against another, as, for example, the union that says: "X employer is offering us this. You must provide at least as much." In a way, the arrangement has upped the ante, since a disagreement can lead to an industry-wide shutdown. Ultimately, however, it has also meant less time and money lost in work stoppages.

The amount of time actually lost in labour disputes is difficult to gauge. In fact, it is difficult to gauge the proportion of Albertans covered by collective agreements. The federal Department of Labour keeps statistics on agreements applying to 500 employees or more, and based on that information, it claims that, across Canada, about two-fifths of paid, non-agricultural workers are union members. The department freely admits, though, that if smaller contracts were tallied as well, their estimate could be wide of the mark by a million or more. That said, it is still worth noting that in 1986 the amount of time lost in work stoppages (nation-wide, still involving 500 workers or more) was only 0.22 percent of estimated working time. In Alberta, for the first quarter of 1987, no time was lost in labour disputes.

Through the first half of this decade, wages overall in Alberta continued to rise. The industrial aggregate weekly earnings rose from $429.34 in 1983 to $448.82 in 1986. It was an advance that barely covered inflation, but we *were* slogging through a recession.

In some trades, however, wages actually fell. The weekly average wage in construction fell from $539.20 in 1983 to less than $500 in 1986. In the first five months of 1987, the average was $487.64. Small wonder, then, that in the fall of 1984, construction and building trades workers formed an informal self-help group known as the Dandelions.

The Dandelions—a grass-roots movement if there ever was one— formally organized in 1985 under the title, The Association of Political Action Committee. The hardy flower that represents the group is virtually unkillable, and this is how the members of the Dandelions see themselves. In spite of the group's name, though, their action is less political than lobbyist in nature. They have concentrated their efforts on presenting the labour point of view to MLAs and other politicians. Since the economy has improved, however, they have been less visible.

Businesspeople are no different from other mortals in that they always prefer what they know best. With that in mind, you could probably make out a case for a great business environment anywhere in the world, if you happened to be familiar with the place. Patagonia might be a hot property, for example, or North Greenland. But there is also an international language of business, a syntax of exchange, agreement, and organization that lets the banker from Hong Kong and the oilman from Abu Dhabi sit down with the Swiss chemical magnate and cut a deal. Alberta understands that language—and there is no shortage of opportunities here.

▲ *Construction of the health sciences centre at the University of Alberta in Edmonton is shown. Courtesy, West-file, Inc.*

CHAPTER **6**

What Do You Do for Fun?

In the preceding chapters we have looked closely at the physical shape of Alberta, at how we make money, and at how we take care of ourselves as far as things like education and health care are concerned. All properly sober and serious stuff. But if that were all there was to life—in Alberta or anywhere—then we might as well let the mortgage lapse and give the whole show back to the trilobites. Humans like to amuse themselves and each other in a delightfully rich assortment of ways, and that is as true here as it is in Toronto, Paris, or New Orleans.

If we want to cover the subject from the ground up, so to speak, then the first item on the list must be the tremendous recreational opportunities offered by the Alberta landscape. Alberta is strikingly beautiful and contains a rich mixture of mountains, plains, forests, and bodies of water. It is no accident that when the young country of Canada established its first national park, it did so here. We also have more square kilometres thus enshrined than any other province.

These parks certainly make a worthwhile beginning to the exploration of our outdoors. There are three mountain parks: Banff, Jasper, and Waterton Lakes. The vast wilderness of Wood Buffalo National Park, and the relatively small, often overlooked Elk Island Park, lie just east of Edmonton. Each one has a distinct personality and offers a range of recreational possibilities, from the simple pleasure of breathing fresh air beside a sun-dappled stream in the spring to the adrenaline cocktail of climbing ice falls in the winter.

Banff National Park is the oldest, most developed and best known of the parks. When the steel of the CPR was being pushed up the valley of the Bow and on towards the Kicking Horse pass in the winter of 1883, workers saw steam rising across the valley, from the flank of Sulphur Mountain. Upon investigation, they found the warm springs and grotto now called the Cave and Basin, and then, elsewhere on the mountain, the Middle and Upper Hot Springs. In 1885 the government declared a 25.9-square-kilometre area around the springs a preserve, and called it Rocky Mountains Park. Renamed and enlarged, Banff Park now covers 6,641 square kilometres.

Millions of people visit Banff every year, and if you stop on Banff Avenue in the middle of August, you may think they are all there at once. Their sunglasses glinting, herds of sunburned tourists, often loosely grouped in families, move slowly down the street, buying film and t-shirts, and standing in line for ice cream. They haven't come for the ice cream, though; a glance at the delicate tracery of Cascade Mountain or the majestic slab of Mount Rundle makes that clear. And though the street may seem crowded, the silence of the forest is only moments away. For hikers and mountain bikers, an extensive network of trails snakes through the valleys and over the passes, offering day hikes and extended back country trips through spectacular wilderness. Those accustomed to the saddle may prefer a trail ride, while others might choose the dip and splash of a canoe gliding across the Vermilion Lakes. Whichever way you enjoy the park, there are always the healing waters of the Upper Hot Springs to soothe tired muscles when your journey is done.

In winter Banff is ski country, as is Jasper Park. Slopes and cross-country trails, both groomed and ungroomed, create a crisp white

◄ During the summer Banff Avenue is usually crowded with tourists who have made the pilgrimage to see some of the world's most breathtaking mountain scenery. Photo by John Elk III

▲ *In winter Banff National Park is ski country. Deer Lodge on Lake Louise is pictured here. Photo by Kenneth W. Fink. Courtesy, Hillstrom Stock Photo*

playground for thousands. If your timing is right, you may be in the park for a world-class downhill race at Sunshine or Lake Louise. Others, more sedate or more solitary, may prefer snowshoes as a means of exploring the snow-filled valleys.

The facilities in Banff Park are extensive, including campgrounds, motels, youth hostels, and luxury hotels. For the mountaineering enthusiast, the Canadian Alpine Club maintains huts in certain remote, strategic locations. Wherever you stay, your trip will not be complete without a visit to the "castle." The Banff Springs Hotel, surveying Bow Falls, is a grand old pile of stone from another era. Built when luxury meant a lower berth in a pullman car and a porter to haul your trunks, its grand arches, unexpected stairways, and replicas of Spanish medieval furniture are a great delight to children and incurable romantics of all ages.

Another must-see in Banff Park is Lake Louise. Not only is the lake extraordinarily beautiful, but it offers a lesson of a sort, as well. The clear, extravagant turquoise of the water and the brilliantly white, snow-covered peaks beyond the lake form one of the most frequently reproduced images anywhere in the world—and yet the actual, first-hand experience of Lake Louise is ever dazzling, ever new. Nature, it seems, is still somewhat advanced of our technical skills.

Waterton Lakes and Jasper, the other two mountain parks, are less commercialized and less heavily travelled, but offer a similar range of accommodation and recreation. Waterton adjoins the American Glacier National Park, across the border, to form the Waterton-Glacier International Peace Park. Waterton is also one of our most dramatic parks, as the landscape changes abruptly, in less than a kilometre, from

▲ *The impressive Prince of Wales Hotel is in Waterton Lakes National Park. Photo by Kenneth W. Fink. Courtesy, Hillstrom Stock Photo*

▶ *This view from the park at Chateau Lake Louise in Banff National Park includes Mount Victoria in the background. Photo by Jerg Kroener*

rolling prairie to snow-covered peaks nearly 3,000 metres high. When the Blackfoot Indians ruled here, this was one of their strongholds. Thus there are many sacred spots, such as the sites of vision quests, in this area.

Like Banff, Jasper also has excellent downhill skiing, at Marmot and Whistler, and extensive trails for cross-country skiing in winter and hiking in summer. Rugged back-country trails, as, for example, along the Snake Indian River, give the adventurous some idea of what the first explorers encountered when the fur trade opened this area up over 150 years ago—except that David Thompson and Jasper Hawkes and their like had to forge their own trails.

Imagine their delight, then, at the waters of Miette Hot Springs. Just inside the park gate, and a short drive south of the highway as you approach from Edmonton, these springs are very hot indeed. The developed pool is kept somewhere around 37 degrees Celsius, a moderate temperature—the hottest of the several sources in the area has been measured at 56 degrees.

At the town of Jasper the highway divides, one road running west to the Yellowhead Pass into British Columbia and the valley of the Fraser, the other curling away southeast toward Lake Louise and Banff. Before it reaches these, however, it passes through some of the most beautiful scenery in the province. Called the Columbia Icefields

◄ ◄ *The red rock at Red Rock Canyon, Waterton Lakes National Park, is the result of rusting iron deposits. Photo by Wes Bergen. Courtesy, Hillstrom Stock Photo*

◄ *A moose takes a refreshing dip in Maligne Lake, Jasper National Park. Photo by Dick Dietrich*

▲ *The Icefield Centre Lodge is located in a beautiful setting in Jasper National Park. Photo by Jerg Kroener*

Parkway, the route offers tremendous views of mountaintops and glaciers, but only when the weather permits. The Columbia Icefield itself covers nearly 400 square kilometres and, because it sits on the continental divide, sends meltwater to the Arctic Ocean, Hudson Bay, and the Pacific.

All the parks are rich in wildlife. In the mountains you may encounter herds of elk, flocks of mountain sheep and mountain goats, marmots, elusive coyotes, even shyer cougars, black bears, an occasional moose, and, very rarely, grizzlies. It should hardly be necessary to point out that all these creatures are wild, and their wildness should be respected. Bears in particular can be dangerous if fed, but even feeding sheep can be risky. In this case the danger is not to the humans, but to the sheep. When hooked on human "junk food," their condition suffers, and they have trouble surviving the winter.

Coincidentally, the other two national parks in Alberta are excellent sites for observing buffalo, although each provides a markedly different experience. Elk Island Park, a little over 30 kilometres east of Edmonton, is small, as national parks go—less than 200 square kilometres. Trails wend their way through spendid examples of rolling aspen parkland and wetlands, where you can see moose, mule deer, enormous old beaver lodges, and glimpses of shaggy buffalo. Sitting astride

the Yellowhead Highway, this park marks a good spot for a picnic and a leisurely nature walk on a Sunday afternoon. Binoculars and a book on bird-watching make first-rate companions here, where over two hundred species of birds have been spotted.

In contrast, Wood Buffalo National Park, established in 1922, is a huge, wild stretch of land, mostly unapproachable except by canoe and float plane. Although this park covers nearly 45,000 square kilometres in both Alberta and the Northwest Territories, two-thirds of it lie in Alberta. Wood Buffalo Park encloses the largest remaining herd of wood bison in the world, numbering now in the thousands, but you may have to travel a long way to see them. Unlike Elk Island Park, no paved road here conveniently guides you to any comfortable viewing distance.

This park also encompasses the Peace-Athabasca delta, a unique, watery habitat that comes alive with birdlife during the migration season. Ducks, swans, and geese pass through in the thousands. One species that does not travel on is the extremely rare whooping crane. Wood Buffalo Park is the only remaining nesting area for these birds, and every spring 15 to 20 pairs, carefully observed by biologists trying to preserve them from extinction, come here to lay their eggs.

As fine and varied as they are, our national parks are not the only way to get to know outdoor Alberta. There are also dozens of provincial parks, picnic sites, recreation areas, and private campgrounds scattered around the province. With the notable exception of Kananaskis Country, which we will come to in a moment, provincial parks tend to be smaller. They provide either destination sites, where vacationers might like to spend a few days, or en route sites, geared for overnight stopovers. Examples of the former are North Buck Lake and Writing on Stone.

North Buck Lake, south and west of Lac La Biche, is a large recreation area where swimming, boating, and fishing are encouraged by nearly 100 lakeside campsites. There is swimming as well at Writing on Stone Park, which lies on the banks of the Milk River, at the southern edge of the province. It is also the site of prehistoric petroglyphs, and parks staff give guided tours of these enigmatic traces during the summer months.

An example of an en route site is the campground near Big Valley, with room for 10 tents. Although such a site may not supply the curious with enough to explore over an extended stay, it does make for a pleasant stop when touring the by-ways and backroads of the province.

Most of these sites, considered final destinations or not, are associated with water in some form: river, lake, or stream. This of course provides extensive opportunities for every kind of aquatic amusement, from wind surfing to pulling on a pair of gumboots and pottering around the edges of a pond with a dip net and magnifying glass.

Fishing is very popular, and with good reason. There are seven varieties of trout in Alberta waters, from the semi-nocturnal brown trout to the vividly marked cutthroat, as well as perch, walleye, pike, arctic grayling, goldeye, and sturgeon. Sports fishing is regulated, in

▶ *Fishing is very popular in Alberta, although a special license is required for fishing in Jasper Lake, shown here, and other lakes located in national parks. Photo by Dick Dietrich*

▶ *These canoes are lined up and ready for a trip on Cameron Lake in Waterton Lakes National Park. Photo by Wilfried D. Schurig. Courtesy, Hillstrom Stock Photo*

order to conserve stocks, and, with the exception of those under 16 and Alberta residents over 65, everyone needs a licence. You will also need a special licence if you wish to try your luck in the national parks or in one of the seven trophy lakes in the north—one of which is appropriately called God's Lake. And, a word of warning—if you catch a sturgeon under three feet, you have to put it back. It's just a baby. Come back later after it has grown up and you'll get a real fight.

Even if you never put a line in the water, though, you can enjoy a fine canoe trip, and conditions can be as tame or as dangerous as you wish. Glide across just about any pothole at dawn and you're likely to see shorebirds already awake and teetering along the sedges and the bulrushes, looking for breakfast, or perhaps a kingfisher diving for minnows. Or, if you want to take in the sights but don't want to work too hard, a downriver float trip can be the height of straw-hat laziness. All you need to do is pick the right stretch of river, and keep an eye out for gravel bars and sweepers. If, on the other hand, you can't enjoy yourself without the possibility of being drowned, there are excellent stretches of whitewater here for canoes and kayaks, especially in the Sundre region.

Hunting in Alberta is good also, depending on the season and what you hope to bag. There are antelope in the south; elk, sheep, and bear in the foothills; ducks east of Edmonton; and geese in the fields around Coronation, east of Red Deer. Regulations do change from year to year, however, in response to populations, and hunters must have a licence. Thus it is always advisable to check with a regional office of Alberta Fish and Wildlife before setting off. If you want to try unknown territory or plan a serious big-game expedition, the names of licensed guides and outfitters may also be obtained from Fish and Wildlife, but be sure to book well in advance. Finally, to accommodate the stealth and woodcraft of the neo-bronze age hunter, the Canmore corridor portion of Kananaskis Country has been designated a bowhunting zone. Hunting here is by bow and arrow only, and hunters must have a bowhunting licence as well as a regular hunting licence.

As for outdoor recreation areas, several areas deserve special mention. One of these is Kananaskis Country, a 4,000-square-kilometre multi-use recreation region in the Rocky Mountains southwest of Calgary. It is an area the provincial government has developed in the last decade, using money from the Alberta Heritage Savings Trust Fund, and it incorporates facilities for almost every kind of outdoor recreation possible outside the tropics.

For reasons best known to itself, Alberta Parks and Recreation has divided Kananaskis Country into a number of zones, some of which are called Provincial Parks, and some of which are not. It needn't matter. From Bow Valley Provincial Park in the north, and stretching over a hundred kilometres south to Cataract and Wilkinson Creeks, the area is filled with campsites, picnic areas, scenic lookouts, trails of every degree of difficulty, streams, lakes, and ski slopes. Some of the more notable facilities include the Kananaskis Country golf course, with white sand specially trucked in so that a visit to the bunkers won't

▲ *Nakiska at Mount Allan was the
site of the downhill ski events during
the 1988 Winter Olympics. Photo by
Jerg Kroener*

prove too depressing; William Watson Lodge, available for the handicapped and senior citizens, and the Mount Lorette fishing ponds and
picnic site, designed for wheelchair use; the ski slope at Mount Allan,
site of the downhill events in the 1988 Winter Olympics, and the accompanying cluster of luxury hotels and hostels at Nakiska; an extensive network of cross-country ski trails; special areas reserved for snow-
mobiles and off-highway vehicles; and about 2,000 automobile
campsites. For the climber, there are also some challenging peaks, and
for the sedate and the curious, well-marked interpretive trails.

Kananaskis Country makes a valiant attempt at offering something
for everyone; but, of course, the more it offers, the further it departs
from what some hardy souls crave above all else—true wilderness. For
these, three areas along the eastern edge of the national parks have
been set aside by the province. The White Goat, Siffleur, and Ghost
River Wilderness areas are as wild as you can find in Alberta, although
they are certainly not the only wilderness left. Access to such areas
is by foot only; neither is there any hospitable jumping off point to
reach them. The sturdy trekker, however, will rejoice in the solitude.
Bring along all the food you'll need, of course, since no hunting or fishing is allowed here—and don't leave anything behind when you go.

Water the plants; feed the fish. Put the kids in the car.
Catch the dog and put him in the car, too. We're
going on a vacation. Not to the wilderness, not this
time. We want to drive around Alberta and just look—at the sights,
at the towns, at the traces of history.

The truth is, though, that there is too much to see on one trip. Certainly there is too much to write about here, and so what follows is
only a selection of what we could visit.

Let's begin in the south. We've already mentioned Writing on
Stone Park. What we haven't mentioned is the atmosphere compounded of sunbaked hoodoos, blue skies, dry sage, and an ancient
presence represented by the scratched and painted images found
along the base of the cliffs. This is a spot well worth a pilgrimage.

West of Milk River is the Crowsnest Pass, an old coal mining district, and the site of the disastrous Frank Slide of 1903. Early one April
morning, a huge slab of limestone fell off Turtle Mountain and obliter-
ated the town below. It is believed that 70 people died that morning,
though we will never know for certain. The province has now put up
an interpretive centre here, which tells the story of the Slide and re-
creates life in the Pass at the turn of the century.

Also in the south is Lethbridge, which offers the two completely
different experiences of Indian Battle Park and Nikka Yuko Japanese
Gardens. Indian Battle Park, in the river valley near the west edge of
the city, is named for a terrible struggle that took place here in 1870.
Between 200 and 300 warriors died in this last significant Indian battle
in Alberta history. Now the site is marked by the park, where there
are picnic tables, interpretive programs, and a replica of Fort
Whoop-Up, the American-run whiskey trading post. Nikka Yuko

▲ *A September morning dawns in
the prairie country east of Lethbridge.
Photo by Jerg Kroener*

Gardens, on the other hand, is a formal garden in the Japanese style, with carefully sculpted trees and waterways, paths arranged according to a ritual aesthetic, and a tea house built in Japan and reassembled here. At one edge of the garden there is an enormous iron bell, rung in the Japanese fashion by an external clapper. An inscription on the bell suggests that when it is rung, good fortune follows both here and in Japan.

Although not surrounded by postcard kiosks, and at night lacking *son et lumiere,* the Big Rock near Okotoks is worth a look, just the same. It is . . . just that: a big rock, in the middle of a field. What makes it unusual is that it is so big. It is a glacial erratic, one of the largest in North America. It weighs an estimated 18,000 tons, and was carried hundreds of miles on the back of the last ice sheet. When the ice melted, Big Rock came to rest here. We can't be sure where it started out, but it does have the same quartzite composition as Mount Edith Cavell, in Jasper National Park.

And those glass insulators from telephone and power lines—some people collect them. Some people collect a lot of them. At Pincher Creek, there is a 2.5-acre Crystal Village made from 200,000 of the things.

It is possible that some of those insulators were made locally. In Medicine Hat, the Altaglass plant takes advantage of the ready supply of natural gas to run a large glass-making operation, and visitors are welcome during business hours. To watch a glob of red-hot "taffy" blow into a bottle or spin into a plate is like standing in an alchemist's workshop. You may also wish to take a short walking tour through downtown Medicine Hat, where a number of churches, homes, and buildings offer splendid examples of turn-of-the-century architecture.

North and west of Medicine Hat, along the steep banks of the Red Deer Valley, lies Dinosaur Provincial Park. The badlands here are spectacular, but even more important are the extensive bone beds which are gradually being revealed by erosion. In fact, this is one of the most important fossil sites in the world, and is recognized by the United Nations Educational, Scientific, and Cultural Organization (UNESCO) as a World Heritage Site. Although access to much of the park is restricted, during the summer months, interpretive hikes and bus tours give you some idea of the richness of this paleontological treasure chest.

If fossils are of special interest to you, you will want to go on from Dinosaur Park to Drumheller, further up the Red Deer River. There are badlands and hoodoos here as well, and such a profusion of bone beds that the provincial government was prompted to build the recently completed Tyrrell Museum of Paleontology, just west of town. The Tyrrell is a $30-million, world-class facility that includes hands-on displays, film and videos, 800 fossil specimens on view, the skeletons of 40 dinosaurs, and a paleoconservatory growing plants that were contemporary with the dinosaurs here on display. After touring the museum, you can complete your experience into prehistory with a short hike along trails into the badlands themselves, where you may see

▲ *Hoodoos—natural pillars of rock, cemented gravel, or clay caused by erosion—are common in the Alberta badlands. These fantastically-shaped hoodoos are in the Red Deer River Valley. Photo by Jerg Kroener*

▶ *This bison skull was found in the badlands near Drumheller. Photo by Wilfried D. Schurig. Courtesy, Hillstrom Stock Photo*

fossils as they are found in the field.

East of Drumheller, on the way to Hanna, are the Hand Hills. These were important wintering grounds for the Indians, and they have the appearance of a hand from the air. Mother's Mountain is the highest point between the Rockies and eastern Canada, with the exception of a point in the Cypress Hills to the south, which is four and a half feet higher.

On your way to the Hand Hills, you may pass by the little village of Morrin, with a population of 245. In 1980 the citizens of Morrin built a replica of the sod hut which was the first shelter for many settlers on the prairie. It was an ingenious solution in an environment where timber was scarce, though as one veteran of the "soddy" put it, "It leaked when it rained. And you got dirt in the soup."

The central portion of the province was settled in patches by different nationalities. Dickson, west of Innisfail, was a nucleus of Danish settlement, and Markerville, a little north and east, was an Icelandic community. Just outside of Markerville, the home of Stephan G. Stephansson is now a provincially designated historic site. The reason for this honor is that Stephansson was not only a farmer, but also a poet. He was, in fact, one of the greatest poets in the Icelandic language, and much of his work was written in this house. As well as touring his home, and reading translated examples of his work, you can also view traditional Icelandic crafts such as spinning and knitting.

As you wander through the province, you will find that many of the towns and villages boast museums. How carefully you investigate them depends on your dedication to the past. Some are merely dusty, haphazard collections of relics—both odds and ends and treasures—locked away until you ask the town clerk to show them to you. Others, probably with more money at their disposal, take the role of local history depository very seriously, and can be gold mines of information. One of the best regional museums in the province is in Red Deer. The Red Deer and District Museum houses displays of the early growth and development of the area, as well as exhibits of local art and natural history.

A less professional, but every bit as devoted, collection can be found at the Lamp Museum in Donalda, northeast of Red Deer. Mr. and Mrs. Lawson of Donalda started collecting lamps in the 1950s and donated their collection to the village in 1979. Over 500 lamps are on display here, the oldest being a cast-iron whale oil lamp from the 1600s.

And while we are in the area, consider the history of the Canadian Forces Base at Wainwright. We like to think that when part of the landscape has been made a park, it is safe forever, but what about Buffalo National Park? In 1908 about 200 square miles of pastureland was fenced off to hold a herd of buffalo. The herd did well here, but in 1941 the park was closed and much of the area taken over for military training. If you drive by, you can still see buffalo wandering about, but don't bother stopping. The armed forces don't encourage tourists.

Instead, go west to Bawlf, where you will be welcome to visit Alberta's Littlest Airport. In fact, it is a model of a normal airport, with

▶ *The Red Deer and District Museum has exhibits pertaining to the growth and development of the area. This permanent exhibit portrays a turn-of-the-century Christmas. Courtesy, Red Deer and District Museum*

a number of runways, used by radio-controlled model planes. It is open June to October, weather permitting—VFR only.

Another point of ethnic interest is the Ukrainian Cultural Heritage Village, on the Yellowhead Highway east of Edmonton. Buildings have been moved here from surrounding communities, in an attempt to re-create the atmosphere of an early settlement in east-central Alberta, and many traditional crafts are on display.

East of Smoky Lake is the new and very large Pine Ridge Forest Nursery, an important part of the provincial reforestation plan. In 1986 alone, close to 25 million seedlings were shipped from here. It is possible to visit the nursery during the summer, but only for information and the merest hint of millions of tiny trees. The nursery has no seedlings to spare for sale or distribution to the public.

There is also an important historic site south of Smoky Lake. Victoria Settlement, on the banks of the North Saskatchewan, was the location of both a Methodist mission founded by the Reverend George McDougall in 1862 and a Hudson's Bay Company post erected in 1864.

▶ *This hardware store is one of numerous historic buildings brought together in the Ukrainian Cultural Heritage Village. Photo by Jerg Kroener*

By 1870 close to 100 children were attending school here. The company clerk's quarters have been restored to reflect life in the settlement in the 1890s. Victoria Settlement is also the site of the oldest building in Alberta still on its original foundations. Now a secluded spot at the end of a side road, it is difficult to imagine that this was once, relatively speaking, a bustling crossroad of trade and culture.

Perhaps by the time you get to Lac La Biche, you will want to stop and gaze at the scenery for a while. Sir Winston Churchill Provincial Park is an island of tranquility, quite literally. The park is a sandy-beached island in Lac La Biche, accessible only by a causeway two and a half kilometres long. You may want to fish there for pike, or relax and watch the strangely prehistoric pelicans scoop up perch for their dinners.

If everyone in your party is still speaking to one another by the time you get as far north as Fort McMurray, a visit to one of the oil sands plants is essential. The scale of these plants is awesome, as you realize when you witness the enormous bucket wheels and draglines chewing away at the sticky black sand. One casual swipe and your carefully tended yard back home would be a vacant lot. If the tar sands intrigue you, you will also want to visit the Oil Sands Interpretive Centre, which shows the history and technology of oil sands mining.

There are also docks at Fort McMurray, from which barges tow freight downriver to the oldest settlement in Alberta, Fort Chipewyan. Unfortunately, no passenger service is available. If you must see Fort Chip, as it is known, you must travel by air.

Far to the west of Fort McMurray (this is turning into a very long vacation) is the land of the mighty Peace River. If you want to go further north, Grimshaw is mile 0 of the Mackenzie Highway, which leads to Yellowknife and Fort Smith in the Northwest Territories. But if you stop on Judah Hill, near the town of Peace River, and take in the wide, majestic view of the confluence of the Heart, Smoky, and Peace rivers, you may just be persuaded to spend some time on the water. Take an overnight river cruise, then, to Tar Island. If the river is low enough, you will see a startling natural gas flare rising from the water. When you get back to town, stop at the Peace River Centennial Museum, which has displays of Indian clothing, traps, and guns, as well as old Hudson's Bay Company journals and an extensive archive and photo collection.

North of Peace River, just before you get to the village of North Star, the Charles Plavin Homestead is worth a visit. Plavin was a Latvian settler, and this is his original homestead, built in 1918 of hand-hewn logs. There are handmade wooden beds, and, because Plavin was of good Baltic stock, a sauna.

At the southern edge of the Peace River district lies the city of Grande Prairie. The symbol of Grande Prairie is the trumpeter swan, because the lakes around the city are one of the few nesting areas in North America for this splendid but rare bird. Saskatoon Island Provincial Park, about 20 kilometres west of the city, is one such nesting spot. The area is rather marshy, and therefore not inviting for

▲ *The symbol of the city of Grande
Prairie is the trumpeter swan, the majestic, rare bird that nests in nearby
lakes. Photo by Wilfried D. Schurig.
Courtesy, Hillstrom Stock Photo*

swimmers. It is great for bird-watching, though, and of course for berry picking, given the right season.

Did we say during which season your trip is taking place? Perhaps it is winter, and you've been driving around with your trusty snowmobile in the back of the truck, looking for a snowy track. If so, you can stop at Whitecourt and stay until spring. Whitecourt calls itself the Snowmobile Capital of Alberta, and it has a race track sanctioned by the NorthWest Snowmobile Association to back up the claim. Furthermore, the Alberta Forest Service has developed extensive, marked trails throughout the Whitecourt Forest Area.

Father Albert Lacombe was one of the most important figures in the development of Alberta, working tirelessly to bring religion, education—and harmony—to the region. His courage and integrity helped maintain an often-shaky peace between the Cree and Blackfoot. At St. Albert you can tour his original log cabin, built in 1861 and now restored, and view some of his personal effects. Nearby, beside St. Albert Church, stands a remarkable bell tower. The tower itself is new, erected in 1980 to commemorate the 75th anniversary of the province, but the bells are almost as old as the city. And if you sidestep busy St. Albert Trail and cross the Sturgeon River on Perron Street, you will be crossing on the first bridge built west of the Great Lakes.

In this grand, though admittedly arbitrary, tour of the province, we have kept away, so far, from the two major cities of Edmonton and Calgary. Now, intrepidly, we strap ourselves in, and roll at speed down multi-laned St. Albert Trail, where once horses and ox carts toiled along a muddy track. Before we know it, Edmonton has surrounded us. Perhaps our first stop, simply because it is near our point of entry, is the Space Sciences Centre.

Years ago, when Coronation Park was a broad plain full of little twiggy trees resembling broomhandles, Edmonton stepped into the civic vanguard with the first planetarium in western Canada. Appropriately, it looked somewhat like a flying saucer. Now the trees have grown up, and the planetarium has been superseded by the Space Sciences Centre, a bold black and white building on the other side of the park.

The centre is a multi-purpose facility, with an observatory, science shop, interactive displays, and two special theatres. One is the Margaret Zeidler Star Theatre, where you can watch a million years of stellar evolution in air-conditioned comfort. The other is the Devonian Theatre, whose four-storey IMAX screen makes visits to the Grand Canyon or deep space alarmingly real. The next logical step for Coronation Park would probably be to put a launch pad in place, but local residents might object to the noise.

From here you might want to head south to the Valley Zoo, especially if you're travelling with younger children. The zoo has been designed with a storybook and nursery rhyme motif to help youngsters feel comfortable with the animals. If it's a hit with your family, you should know the zoo can be rented for private functions after hours.

Also in the west end is Fort Edmonton Park and the John Janzen Nature Centre. This is the original fort, though not the original location. In fact, there were several "original" locations, since the fort was moved frequently during the fur trade era. What the visitor sees today is a reconstruction of the fort as it stood on the present-day grounds of the Alberta Legislature in 1915. Inside, you can tour 1885 street and 1905 street to get a flavour of early Edmonton, and visit a Farmer's Market.

Just outside the fort gates, the John Janzen Nature Centre is a splendid introduction for children to the ecology of the Edmonton area. Depending on the season, displays may include bees, ants, snakes, and salamanders. Sunday nature walks are of interest to the whole family.

And of course, while in *west* Edmonton, how can we overlook West Edmonton Mall? It is, after all, the largest shopping mall in North America, maybe even in the solar system. Some people love it, others hate it, but how can you ignore a place with over 100 shoe stores and a dolphin theatre? Other features, or at least curiosities, include: a submarine ride; an aviary; exotic tropical fish; a 175,000-square-metre wavepool; an ice rink and a Fantasyland with games, arcades, and 50-odd amusement rides; an indoor car showroom; the squarerigger HMS *Bounty*; stores, stores, and more stores; and the Fantasyland Hotel, which includes such theme suites as the "Truck" room, where you

▼ *The flavour of early Edmonton has been captured at Fort Edmonton Park. Courtesy, Westfile, Inc.*

▲ *At Fort Edmonton Park, you can take a trip back in time by traveling on the Yukon Pacific Railway. Photo by Jerg Kroener*

▶ *This waterpark is only one of dozens of attractions and amusements at the West Edmonton Mall. Photo by Jerg Kroener*

sleep on the back of a pick-up truck. It is, in short, the Versailles of shopping malls. Once you've been here, the mini-mart will never be the same.

Turning in toward the city centre, we soon come upon the Provincial Museum and Archives. The museum takes a broad view, offering displays on everything from paleontology to pre- and post-settlement cultural history. Of special note are the remarkably lifelike dioramas, showing, with scrupulous care, wildlife in its natural habitat. The museum also hosts touring exhibits, so that there is no shortage of things to see here. If you have a specific historical question—about family, for example (Was Grandpa really a rustler? What ever happened to Uncle Frank?)—you may be able to solve it here at the Archives, a large collection, open to anyone, of government, municipal, and church records.

Behind the museum stands stately Government House, once the residence of the lieutenant-governor, and now used for ceremonial occasions. Behind that, across the parking lot, is a fine view of the river valley. To your right, while you stand on the brow of the hill, in a green loop of the North Saskatchewan, is Hawrelak Park, named for a well-remembered mayor of the city. Away to your left, like a webbed iron veil transecting the valley, is the High Level Bridge.

This was this bridge that brought the railway across the river from Strathcona in 1913. It is nearly half a mile in length, contains an estimated 1.4 million rivets, and weighs 8,000 tons—less than half of what the Big Rock at Okotoks weighs, if you've been reading this book carefully.

But what, you might ask, is so amusing about a bridge? The answer, if the timing of your viewing is right, will be revealed shortly—although you can't discover this very well from the museum parking lot. Hurry downstream now, and find a prime spot on the south bank, below the bridge.

The Great Divide Waterfall was a project conceived in 1980 by local artist Peter Lewis. Huge pipes have been laid the length of the bridge, and on special occasions, the water through them is transformed into a beautiful, man-made cascade. The first such event was the celebration of the province's 75th birthday. Since the waterfall is too costly to run all the time, you must plan ahead if you want to see it. The most likely time to catch this sight is the Sunday evening of the holiday weekend at the beginning of August.

From where you are sitting, you also have a fine view of the domed, sandstone Alberta Legislature, completed in 1912. During appropriate times, there are tours every half-hour, which are well worth the effort. Not only does a visit to the Legislature offer a fine education in statecraft and politics, but also in architecture. The building was conceived in a period when "dignity" meant Greek columns, marble stairways, galleries, finely carved stone detail, and of course a dome. We do not build this way any more, and there are few places in Alberta where you can experience the spatial quality of the rotunda in the Legislature. Take the time, as well, to visit the greenhouses, strategically located

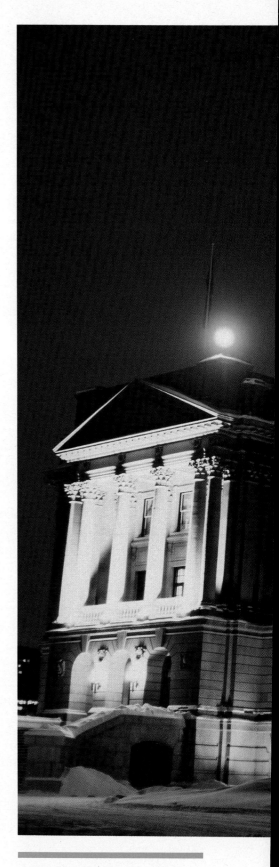

▲ *The magnificently constructed Alberta Legislature Building is studied by architects from all over North America. Photo by Chris Bruun. Courtesy, Westfile, Inc.*

◀ *The Strathcona Hotel is the oldest wooden building in Old Strathcona. Photo by Jerg Kroener*

◀ ◀ *This Calgary skyline features the Saddledome Stadium at the right. Photo by Wes Bergen. Courtesy, Hillstrom Stock Photo*

on the sunny, south-facing slope below the Legislature.

Another, "flashier" greenhouse is the Muttart Conservatory, further downriver. You'll know you're in the neighbourhood if you notice four glass pyramids on the south bank. Inside, you discover that each pyramid houses a different environment—tropical, arid, temperate, or a show pavilion full of blooms no matter what season it is. The full wonder of the conservatory is not really apparent, however, unless you come to Edmonton in winter. Then, when you stamp in, stiff-fingered and slab-footed from the snow-covered parking lot, you suddenly find yourself, miraculously, basking under enormous palms or gaping at magnolia blossoms the size of dinner plates, and you remember that there *is* an end to the cold, after all.

As noted earlier, southside Edmonton started out as the separate and distinct community of Strathcona, and it retains a subtle difference in flavour, even to this day. Efforts have been made to renovate and rehabilitate the main shopping district, along Whyte (82nd) Avenue. This is an interesting place to go exploring—it's full of little shops, bookstores, and cafes, many of them in carefully restored old buildings dating as far back as 1891. If you have no money to spare for frivolities, you can still amuse yourself with a free, self-guided walking tour of Old Strathcona, a brochure for which is available.

Sharing the community's name, but not its location, is the Strathcona Science Park, on the eastern edge of the city. This complex actually contains two entities. One is the Alberta Natural Resources Science Centre, four pavilions devoted to the science and technology we use in our land, and to our forests and energy-based industries. The other part is the Strathcona Archaeological Centre. The Natural

▲ *The glass pyramids of the Muttart Conservatory are pictured with downtown Edmonton in the background on an evening in July. Photo by Jerg Kroener*

◀ The Calgary Tower has an observation terrace and a revolving restaurant at its top. It looms over the sign for the Calgary Olympic Centre. Photo by Jerg Kroener

Resources Centre has a number of hands-on displays, and is open year round. The Archaeological Centre is open from Victoria Day to Labour Day, and features on-site excavations, with a guided tour available.

But now we have left the capital and are heading south. After an uneventful trip on Alberta's major artery, multi-laned Highway 2, we enter Calgary on the Deerfoot Trail, and then swing on to Memorial Drive. This drive is named for the trees which, although not immediately apparent, can be glimpsed further along. The trees themselves are the memorial, really, a living memorial: each tree represents a Calgary soldier who lost his life in the First World War. We have not travelled far, then, when a strange shape looms into view—a strange, prehistoric shape that fills us with unease. Isn't that . . . a tyrannosaur?

It is. Putting curiosity before caution, we pull into the parking lot for the Calgary Zoo and go have a look.

The Calgary Zoo, Botanical Gardens, and Prehistoric Park is located on St. George's Island, in the middle of the Bow River. What we have seen from the road is of course merely a tantalizing fragment of the Prehistoric Park, where life-size models of dinosaurs are displayed in typical habitats. The rock formations throughout the park have been specially sculpted to imply a number of geological processes—there are hoodoos, folded strata, and a young range of mountains struggling to wakefulness. The flora, unfortunately, cannot be quite accurate, since Calgary's climate has changed over the last 200 million years. Nevertheless, the best possible approximations have been planted in the park, so that as you stroll the paths, you get some idea of what it actually may have been like when these prehistoric creatures were alive. Just look at how that tyrannosaur is ogling the triceratops . . . or is he ogling us?

The zoo itself contains over 300 species of (living) animals, and is, in fact, the second largest zoo in Canada. In the large mammal house, there are elephants, rhinos, hippos, and giraffes; in an extensive, securely fenced enclosure, Siberian tigers prowl; and polar bears sprawl in a cool white habitat, looking deceptively like stuffed toys. For nine months of 1988, the zoo will also host a pair of highly prized Chinese pandas. This is a place to explore at leisure.

A visit here is not complete without a stop at the Conservatory, an enormous glass-house reminiscent of the Crystal Palace. The jungle atmosphere therein is enhanced by the numerous small birds that sing and fly at liberty among the branches of the trees.

From the zoo, it is only a short drive to that imposing downtown landmark, the Calgary Tower, immortalized during the Winter Olympics as the largest torch ever lit. You can dine at a revolving restaurant at the top of the tower; but even if you're not hungry, stop at the observation deck anyway, just for the view. The tower itself is 190 metres high, and you can easily see the city mounting over the nearby hills, and the distant Rockies. This is ranching country, and a sense of wide open spaces is part of Calgary. Closer to the tower, just east of the downtown core, is the confluence of the Elbow and the Bow, the green and infinitely charming spot just opposite St. George's Island that was the origin of this metropolis.

That confluence is marked now by a 40-acre park, where the outline of the original fort can be seen. In a way, this stark outline is more impressive than an entire reconstruction or replica could ever be. Although the walls and buildings may not themselves be standing before you, you can't help but be aware that *this* is where it all took place. For an elaboration of the events that took place here, the park also houses an interpretive centre, with displays and audio-visual presentations that detail the history of the city from 1875 to the present.

Reconstructions do have their place, of course, and Heritage Park is one of the best. Located on a small headland in the Glenmore Reservoir, it contains nearly 100 restored exhibits from the early 1900s. Visitors slip into living history the moment they walk through the gates. Here they can ride in original passenger cars pulled by a steam

▲ *At Heritage Park in Calgary you can explore an authentic pre-1915 Alberta town. Photo by Jerg Kroener*

▶ A dancer limbers up for a show at the Calgary Centre for the Performing Arts. Photo by Ray F. Hillstrom, Jr. Courtesy, Hillstrom Stock Photo

▶ A dancer limbers up for a show at the Calgary Centre for the Performing Arts. Photo by Ray F. Hillstrom, Jr. Courtesy, Hillstrom Stock Photo

locomotive, take a cruise on the reservoir in a paddle-wheeler, or stroll by the blacksmith's shop where the smell of hot iron and the ring of hammer on anvil harken back to another age. Spend the entire day here. You can bring a picnic lunch, or buy old-style food made right in the park.

And, if history fascinates you, you will also want to spend a day, or maybe several days, at the Glenbow Museum. The Glenbow is downtown, across the street from the Calgary Tower, and it is a world-class institution. In fact, the multi-storey building houses a number of different collections, including extensive ethnology holdings, everything from fine beadwork to hand-axes; archives with hundreds of thousands of photographs and *three kilometres* of shelves full of documents; a large assortment of military objects, including dozens of suits of armour and a wide range of weapons; and a collection of cultural artifacts that would make your biggest garage sale ever seem like a mere hiccup. The Glenbow also has a large collection of fine arts, and hosts major touring exhibitions as well. Displays are constantly changing, ensuring that this is a place you will keep coming back to.

Next door to the Glenbow Museum is the glittering, still-new Calgary Centre for the Performing Arts (CCPA). The CCPA covers almost a whole city block; situated on the Stephen Avenue Mall across from the Olympic Plaza, and standing just across the street from the ultra-modern city hall, it forms part of the handsome civic centre that has evolved in the last few years. There is no shortage of performances at the CCPA, which is home to the Calgary Philharmonic, Theatre Calgary, and Alberta Theatre Projects. Because it contains three different performance spaces, the Centre can also easily host touring acts of every description. Thus scarcely a night goes by without some event drawing Calgarians here.

◀ *The Glenbow Museum in down-town Calgary contains an impressive collection of artifacts that document the history of western Canada. Courtesy, Westfile, Inc.*

▶ *An LRT train is pictured at the intersection of 1st Street S.E. and 7th Avenue in Calgary. Photo by Jerg Kroener*

While you stroll about downtown Calgary, you may notice that many of the buildings are connected above street level by pedestrian skywalks. These walkways constitute the "Plus 15" system, a boon to office workers and shoppers, who can go for blocks and blocks without having to step outside. That may not mean much to you in July, but what about in January, when you have to run out during your lunch hour to pick up those tickets for the opera, and a blizzard is heading through town at 60 kilometres per hour? The system is not complete yet, but hopefully, in time, new links will be built.

Also scattered throughout Calgary are a number of, quite frankly, spectacular sports facilities. Many of these were built as venues for the 1988 Winter Olympics, and of course they remain now to make life richer for the athletically inclined. Just off the Trans-Canada Highway at the western edge of town is Canada Olympic Park, with 70- and 90-mile ski jumps and the twisting, sprawling luge and bobsled track, looking vaguely intestinal. The track is in fact finely engineered, precision finished, and refrigerated, so as to extend the season somewhat. Across the river at the University of Calgary is another legacy of the games, the Olympic Speed Skating Oval.

Finally, to complete our trip, we must include at least one visit to

▲ *The 70- and 90-metre ski jump towers in the Canada Olympic Park are shown on a cold morning in March. Photo by Jerg Kroener*

a summer fair. Almost every town has one. Some call them fairs; others, emphasizing the agricultural element in which local farmers compare livestock and crops, refer to them as exhibitions. Still other towns call them stampedes or rodeos. The Calgary Stampede is known worldwide, but Edmonton's Klondike Days is every bit as noisy and popular. Depending on which local version you drop in on, you'll get the chance to eat cotton candy, let the children yell their lungs out on the roller coaster, maybe run your eye over some prize Herefords or Charolais, watch a team of big-hearted Percherons in a heavy horse pull, and then take in a slice of rodeo.

Rodeo is one of those oddities: part sport, part professional skill. With the possible exception of bull riding, the standard events are in fact stylized versions of chores a cowboy might have to perform in his day-to-day work. The quickness of eye and hand demanded in calf roping, for example, are needed by working cowboys, too. The only difference is that a good toss on the range may mean getting home before dark, while in the arena it might earn a man $50,000. In the last 10 years, big prize pots have made this sport a popular spectator event; but for ranchers, the activities themselves have always been worthwhile.

Sports certainly are an important part of Alberta life. For example, we have a number of professional teams. In the National Hockey League (NHL), the rivalry between the Calgary Flames and the Edmonton Oilers is long-standing and intense. For years, the Oilers, with such superstars as Mark Messier and Wayne Gretzky, beat Calgary with remarkable consistency. Then the Flames, with first-class players like Lanny MacDonald and Jim Peplinski, began to turn the tide. They learned to beat the Edmonton team, and in 1986 overcame them in

▲ The Calgary Stampede attracts well over one million visitors during its ten-day run every summer. Photo by Wes Bergen. Courtesy, Hillstrom Stock Photo

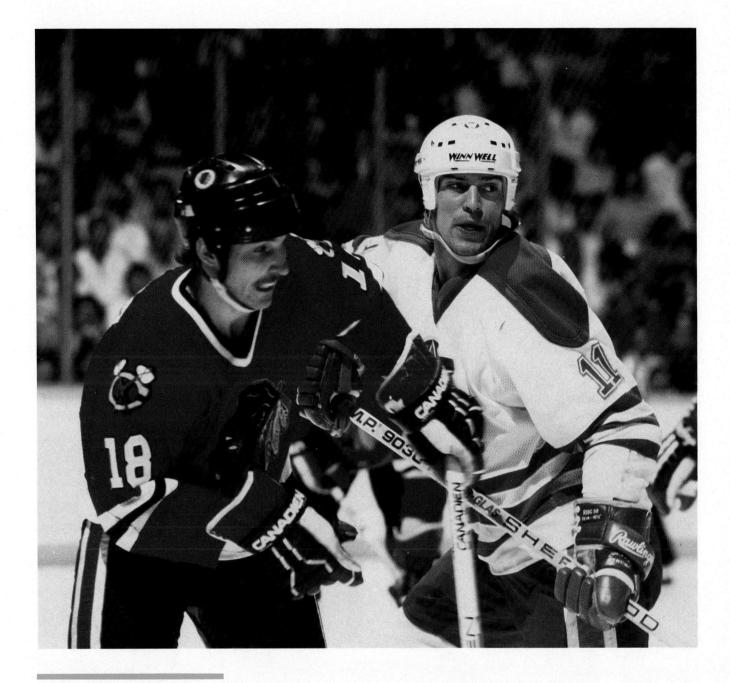

▲ *The Edmonton Oilers, in white,*
and the Chicago Black Hawks, in red, have
an aggressive and longstanding
hockey rivalry. Courtesy, Westfile,
Inc.

the divisional playoffs. The following year, although the Flames still seemed capable of beating the Oilers, they never reached a showdown, and it was Edmonton that went on to win the Stanley Cup.

Edmonton and Calgary also have professional football teams. The home of the Calgary Stampeders is the 34,688-seat McMahon Stadium. The Edmonton Eskimos, winners of the 1987 Grey Cup, play out of the 67,000-seat Commonwealth Stadium. Both are members of the Canadian Football League.

And what about pro baseball? Both Edmonton and Calgary have teams in the Pacific Coast League, a triple-A league just a step below the majors. The Calgary Cannons, farm team to the Seattle Mariners, sell out regularly at Foothills Stadium. The Edmonton Trappers, part of the California Angels' system, play at Renfrew Park.

Even professional soccer can be found here. Worldwide, soccer is probably the most popular sport there is, although it has been slow to catch on in Canada. Nevertheless, during the first year of the Canada Soccer League, the Calgary Kickers astonished everyone—and strengthened their following considerably—by winning the championship.

Just as active in the province as pro sports is the extensive network here of amateur and junior league sports. All winter long, buses shuttle back and forth between such towns as Olds and Fort Saskatchewan and Sherwood Park, ferrying young players to games in the Alberta

▼ Baseball fans in Alberta can enjoy Pacific Coast League teams such as the Edmonton Trappers. Photo by Bill McKeown. Courtesy, Westfile, Inc.

▲ *Rugby is one of a number of sports enjoyed by physically fit Albertans. Photo by Bill McKeown. Courtesy, Westfile, Inc.*

Junior Hockey League. Some of these players will show that extra spark of talent, drive, or luck and graduate to the NHL. Others will remember having a good time, and will continue playing through their thirties and forties in unofficial "old men's leagues," staying up sometimes until one o'clock or two o'clock in the morning to get ice time at the local arena.

Another ice sport that has a strong following in Alberta is curling. Since 1968, Alberta has supplied three Canadian Ladies Championship rinks, and five Canadian Men's. Of the men's rinks, three went on to win world championships, the most recent being Ed Lukowich in 1986. Interest in curling can be expected to grow even stronger in the future, as it was included in the Olympics as a demonstration sport.

And beneath the visible layer of leagues and competitions and races and playoffs, there lies the simple fact that Albertans enjoy being physically active. Every small town has a ball diamond and an ice rink, and maybe a curling rink, too. Bigger towns have swimming pools and athletic fields, and you don't have to go very far to find golf courses and jogging trails and tennis courts. We're on the move, it seems, and we like it.

If we leave the impression, though, that physical activity is our *only* source of amusement, we will be doing a disservice to Albertans.

Since the days of the Indians, there has been a strong tradition here of creative expression in song, dance, and the visual arts, a tradition now augmented by performance, plastic arts, and the written word. Alberta artists in every field play an important part in the national and international scene—but even if we didn't, it wouldn't matter to us. We would still enjoy doing and showing for each other.

As mentioned earlier, there are a number of training grounds in Alberta for artists in various media. Both the University of Alberta, in Edmonton, and the University of Calgary have fine arts programs, encompassing subjects like painting, sculpture, theatre, and dance. There is also the Alberta College of Art (ACA) in Calgary, with nearly 700 students each year. The ACA takes a very broad approach to visual arts, offering courses in a range of media, from painting to textile design, jewelry, and ceramics.

Other colleges around the province offer courses in response to community need, and a large number of these include some form of artistic education. In Edmonton, Grant MacEwan Community College has a division devoted to Performing and Visual Arts. Lakeland College, in Cold Lake, has recently implemented courses in fiction and non-fiction writing. Red Deer College has a Visual and Performing Arts division, and, during a recent Artists-In-Residence program, the campus hosted a musician and a choreographer. In Calgary, Mount Royal College maintains a Conservatory of Music and Speech Arts, with over 7,000 course registrants per year.

Nor could we pass on without mention of the Banff Centre for Continuing Education. The Centre began as an experiment by the University of Alberta's Extension Department during the Depression, when poverty and dislocation had left the province's cultural life in shambles. In 1933, 190 people took advantage of the offer of a three-week drama course in exchange for a $1 registration fee and no tuition. Now the Centre, autonomous and tremendously enlarged, provides training and work space to world-class musicians, artists, dancers, and writers.

Naturally, all of the institutions mentioned here have associated with them galleries and performance spaces. All of the larger centres also have commericial galleries devoted to the visual and decorative arts, and in uncelebrated studios across the province, painters and potters and weavers and printmakers are producing work according to their inner vision. There are many places along our hypothetical tour of the province where we could have stopped and bought a unique glass vase or a one-of-a-kind mug for our morning coffee—produced right on the premises, of course.

Meanwhile, there is the Edmonton Symphony Orchestra, which can be heard on many classical recordings, and the Calgary Philharmonic; there is the Alberta Ballet Company and the Edmonton Opera Association; there is the Citadel Theatre and Workshop West and Stage West and Theatre Calgary and Alberta Theatre Projects and Loose Moose Theatre, the home of improvisational theatresports. Don't forget that each summer, Edmonton is host to the Fringe Theatre Festival, with small and experimental productions scattered all around the city. But then what about the Calgary Folk Festival and the Banff Festival of Mountain Films and the Festival of Films for Television and . . .

Writing and publishing? Well, there is Dandelion and Red Deer College Press and NeWest and TreeFrog and Hurtig, publisher of the prestigious Canadian Encyclopedia. But those publishers don't begin to account for all the writing, from poetry to plays for children to novels to history, that is accomplished by the scores and scores of Alberta writers, some of it read and enjoyed on the other side of the globe.

In short, Albertans make art in every way, just as people everywhere do—and if there is a particular flavour to it, a memory of blue skies and open spaces and optimism, maybe, well, that's just part of who we are, and how we enjoy ourselves.

Today, Albertans with a taste for the lively arts and for sporting events can feast their fill. The world's top performers in music and dance appear regularly in classy venues like the Citadel Theatre in Edmonton and the Calgary Centre for the Performing Arts. Furthermore, Edmontonians have come to expect annual ownership of hockey's premier prize, the Stanley Cup.

Needless to say, Albertans of bygone days did not have it this good. More precisely, they did not have entertainment conveniently served to them, and thus had to become adept at manufacturing their own. Here is a quick look at entertainers and entertainments in Alberta before the age of radio.

Visitors making rare excursions to Alberta fur trading posts during the last century were wont to comment on the boredom they encoun-

Entertainment Before the Radio Age

by Fred Stenson

◀ *John Ware and family. Courtesy, Glenbow Archives, Calgary*

tered. According to one such visitor, the men spent most winter evenings staring glaze-eyed into the fire.

Nevertheless, on special occasions, such as Christmas, New Year's, and whenever a boat brigade arrived, the people of the fur trade kicked up their heels. Each man was given a portion of rum and, to the music of fiddlers, danced until it was all gone. Fur trader Henry Moberly described New Year's at one Alberta fort as "a day given up to hand-shaking, kissing, and sport." The women of the fort did not go in for hand-shaking but instead offered their cheeks, "in the old French fashion," to be kissed. The sport on such occasions was largely fighting. According to Moberly, the damage was limited "to a few black eyes and bloody noses," after which, presumably, everyone went back to dancing.

In the ranching era, the British traditions of the land-holding families found expression at formal "balls." One of the annual events at Fort Macleod was the Bachelors' Ball, when all the region's single gentry repaid those who had hosted them in the previous year. These were stuffy, fancy dress affairs, though the cowboys who worked for the ranches took some of the stiffness out of proceedings. One of their tricks was to switch the clothes on the babies while the mothers were dancing, in hopes that, in the rush to gather up and go home, the mothers wouldn't notice.

A fact of cowboy life was the shortage of single women, so that, in their bunkhouses and on the prairie, cowboys staged "stag dances." In these entertainments, some of the men could be found sporting armbands, which identified them as the missing contingent—female dance partners.

The cowboys also amused themselves with contests testing their skills, the precursers of the modern rodeo. Alberta's all-star cowboy during this era was John Ware, a black man who was born on a South Carolina cotton plantation. At the Calgary Exhibition of 1893, John Ware easily beat two rivals at roping and tying a 1,500-pound steer. Later accounts give Ware's time as 59 seconds, but the report in the *Calgary Tribune* of June 28, 1893, clocked Ware's speed at 5 1/2 seconds—which would have been a world record for the event. It is doubtful that a typographical error is to blame for the discrepancy, as the report in the *Tribune* described Ware's performance as being over almost as soon as it started.

When it came to sports, the gentleman class in ranch-era Alberta preferred polo. E.M. Wilmot of Pincher Creek returned to England in 1891, and brought back polo sticks and balls. Thereafter, an active polo league operated throughout southern Alberta.

In a society with few formal entertainments, the ability to tell or write a funny story was highly prized. The butt of Alberta frontier humour for several decades was the "remittance man." John Sandiland, in his *Western Canadian Dictionary and Phrasebook*, defined a remittance man as "a peer's son who left his country for his country's good and who receives a regular remittance from home conditional on his keeping away from home." An 1895 newspaper article described the remittance men as "too lazy to plow and too shiftless to own cattle. Their only redeeming feature is that they do not marry and are not therefore likely to perpetuate the breed."

"Remitter" jokes were the common coin of the day. One joke told of a remittance man found dying of thirst on the banks of a river. His rescuer asks, "Why don't you drink out of the river?" The remitter answers, "Can't you see I haven't a bally cup?"

Bob Edwards, editor of the satirical Calgary newspaper *The Eye Opener*, dined out regularly on remittance man stories. He created an apocryphal remittance man for his paper, named Albert Buzzard-Cholomondeley, late of Skookingham Hall, Skookingham, Leicestershire. Whenever his parents stopped his remittance, "Bertie" had only to suggest his coming home to start it up again.

Bob Edwards' typical remittance man was sent to Alberta because of a drinking problem or an indiscretion with a parlour maid. He bought a "ranche," went steeply into debt, and wound up giving his land to his capable foreman for back wages. Thenceforward, he lived in town, largely in the hotel's beverage parlour. Between remittances he would be reduced to menial labour, which he would do badly. When his remittance came, he would pay off his debts, and then resume living flamboyantly, entertaining his friends extravagantly—and be broke again within days. All the while he would be sending ingenious letters home, boasting of his prosperity and the wonders he could do with just a little more cash.

Crisis came to the remittance man's life in the form of a visit from his parents. One Bob Edwards story describes a remitter resolving such a fix by borrowing a friend's prosperous ranch for a day. With his family pictures on his friend's walls, he greets his elderly parents. Shortly into the conversation, his mother asks him the meaning of "jaggon." She heard one of the ranch cowboys remark of her son, "It's a wonder he hasn't a jaggon." Thinking quickly, the son informs his mater that a "jaggon" is a white shirt.

Only half the stories told of remitters could possibly be true, of course, but passing them along was an essential part of the local fun.

Bob Edwards was a funny man, but he was not without peers.

Donald Ross, proprietor of a low-rent hotel in the river-bottom flats of Edmonton, was also quick with a line. Once when his rooms were full, he put a late arrival to bed on the pool table. The next morning the man complained about being charged full rate (50 cents) for such a hard bed. Ross offered an alternative: he could pay the pool-room rate of 60 cents per hour.

Ross' counterpart in southern Alberta was Harry "Kamoose" Taylor, who ran the Macleod Hotel. One winter morning, Taylor came upon a man thawing icicles out of his moustache over the hotel stove. "Which room did you stay in?" "Kamoose" wanted to know.

Even a judge could be funny in frontier Alberta, although perhaps inadvertently so. Colonel James Macleod of Mounted Police fame was also the stipendiary magistrate for the town that bears his name. Macleod once sat as judge during a jury trial in which a Mountie was charged with libel. The jury acquitted the man. Judge Macleod, in his closing remarks, instructed the acquitted man not to commit the crime again.

The first time Macleod faced a lawyer for the defence, the man so infuriated him with legal technicalities that Macleod roared, "We want Justice in this country, not law!"

Mrs. Macleod's black servant, "Auntie," was also famous for a witticism. As an old woman, she was fond of saying that, when she and Mrs. Macleod came to Fort Macleod, they were the only white women in the country.

The most serious challenger to Bob Edwards' title as funniest Albertan of his time was another man of the courtroom, the Irish lawyer Paddy Nolan, who worked the courts of Calgary and Fort Macleod from 1889 to 1913. Not surprisingly, Nolan and Edwards were close friends. According to a recent biography of Nolan by Grant MacEwan, many good *Eye Opener* lines origi-

nated in the head of Nolan.

Paddy Nolan was a splendid actor and after-dinner speaker. Even his court appearances drew crowds. He often appeared for the defence opposite future Prime Minister, R.B. Bennett. Bennett had an annoying habit of coming to court armed with several legal tomes which he drew upon extensively. An anecdote related in MacEwan's biography of Nolan describes Bennett sending his assistant out of court repeatedly for yet more books. "Boy, fetch me Lewin on trusts." "Boy, bring me Phipson on evidence." When his turn came, Nolan turned to a clerk and said, "Boy, bring me Bennett on bluff."

The radio age killed neither Albertan sense of humour nor Albertan resourcefulness in finding entertainment, although it was the beginning of a process of sophistication that has put the local storyteller slightly in the shade. Alas, we no longer go to court expecting to be amused, and nowhere amongst us are there human beings so well-bred as to, as Rudyard Kipling put it paraphrasing the Alberta joke, "rather die of thirst than drink out of their hands."

PART **2**

Partners in Progress

ATCO Ltd.

Canadian Utilities Limited

Edmonton Power

Lep International Inc.

Canada Northwest Energy Limited

TransAlta Utilities

Government of Alberta

Time Air

Alberta Energy Company Ltd.

CHAPTER **7**

Networks

Alberta's transportation, communication, and energy firms keep people, information, and power circulating inside and outside the province.

ATCO LTD.

Originally a pioneer in manufacturing transportable industrial housing, ATCO currently operates the world's largest fleet of leasable accommodation in addition to its diversified energy interests.

ATCO Ltd., today a major Canadian corporation diversified in energy, manufacturing and leasing, and property development operations, was founded in 1946 by a Calgary fireman determined to earn extra money to send his son to university.

Don Southern and his son, Ron, scraped together $4,000 to buy 15 unassembled utility trailers and began renting them from a backyard shack. This modest moonlighting venture quickly expanded into retail mobile-home sales, and within five years it was the largest trailer sales and rental firm in Western Canada.

In 1959, the same year Ron Southern completed his university education and joined ATCO as president, the firm landed a multimillion-dollar contract with Boeing that boosted ATCO into the American industrial shelter market. The company then expanded its production capabilities in 1969 to include cabinets and fine woodwork interiors, and four years later new factories were established in California, Idaho, Montreal, and Calgary.

ATCO (the Alberta Trailer Company) is now the world's largest manufacturer of transportable industrial shelters, and also operates the largest fleet of leasable accommodation in the world.

Today ATCO's divisions include electric and natural gas utilities, oil and gas exploration and production, gas marketing and processing, contract drilling and well servicing, and real estate development and management.

The 1978 acquisition of Thomson Industries Ltd., a drilling contractor and oil field service company with operations in Canada and the United States, marked the firm's expansion into the energy business. Renamed ATCO Drilling, the subsidiary became Canada's largest drilling contractor and one of the largest in North America.

The cornerstone of the corporation's present prosperity and its launch into the energy and resource fields was the $350-million acquisition of a controlling interest in Canadian Utilities Limited in June 1980. This holding company has subsidiaries engaged in the operation of electric and natural gas utilities that serve much of Alberta and parts of British Columbia, the Yukon, and the Northwest Territories. Canadian Utilities has provided the stable financial base that has allowed ATCO to expand into new ventures.

In 1988 ATCO was proud to salute its home city by becoming an Official Sponsor of the Olympic Winter Games in Calgary. In addition to elaborate VIP entertainment lounges, the company also provided temporary housing for more than 3,000 people, a 50,000-square-foot television broadcast studio for ABC Television, and 600 buildings from the rental fleet for use at all major Olympic venues.

Although ATCO Ltd. sponsors a variety of community service programs, Ron Southern and his wife, Marg, have contributed greatly to the sport of Canadian horse show jumping with the establishment of Spruce Meadows in southwest Calgary. Since its construction in 1976, the multimillion-dollar equestrian competitive and breeding centre has become the site of the Masters Tournament, the classic of world show jumping. Its facilities, including stables, jumping courses, and practice rings, are second to none, and competitors at its events rank among the best in the world.

ATCO's energy division includes contract drilling and well-servicing operations, oil and gas exploration and production, gas marketing and processing, and electric and natural gas utilities.

CANADIAN UTILITIES LIMITED

Canadian Utilities Limited is one of Alberta's largest investor-owned companies, with in excess of $2.6 billion in assets and more than 4,000 employees.

A holding company since 1972, Canadian Utilities (CU) is best known through its operating companies: Alberta Power Limited, Canadian Western Natural Gas Company Limited, Northwestern Utilities Limited, and its nonutility subsidiary, ATCOR Ltd. These companies, through their own subsidiaries, reach beyond Alberta into Saskatchewan, British Columbia, the Yukon, and the Northwest Territories.

The name Canadian Utilities Limited was originally given to an amalgamation of small electric power systems in east-central Alberta in 1928. This organization expanded into the rural north-central and east-central regions of the province and ultimately into the Yukon and the Northwest Territories. In 1972 the name Canadian Utilities Limited was assigned to the holding company, and the electric utility became known as Alberta

Power Limited.

Controlling interest of the firm was held by IU International of Philadelphia until ATCO Ltd. purchased IU's shares in 1980. Today Canadian Utilities is 100-percent Canadian owned.

Since its formation as a holding company, CU has been responsible for raising the enormous amounts of capital required by its operating companies. Between 1972 and 1988 CU issued well over $2 billion in securities. This capital, along with reinvested earnings, has been used to build power plants, pipelines, electrical transmission systems, and distribution facilities essential to the growth of Alberta and Western Canada. Through taxes, payroll, and other expenditures, the firm contributed another $3 billion to the economy during the same 16-year period, generating thousands of jobs throughout its service areas.

CU's pioneer gas utility, Canadian Western, began its life with a flare-lighting ceremony in Lethbridge, Alberta, on July 12, 1912, just seven years after the province

Canadian Utilities is also involved in oil and gas exploration and production, and natural gas marketing and processing.

joined Confederation. A few days later natural gas was turned on officially in Calgary. Northwestern Utilities, Canadian Western's sister company based in Edmonton, was established in 1923.

Today CU serves 620,000 natural gas customers and 150,000 electric customers in residential, commercial, and industrial markets.

ATCOR Ltd., CU's major nonutility subsidiary headquartered in Calgary, is Alberta's largest independent marketer of natural gas, with interests in natural gas processing, and oil and gas exploration and development. ATCOR has a significant interest in the Gulf-Amauligak discovery in the Beaufort Sea, a world-class find with an estimated 800 million barrels of oil.

CU is also involved in a number of other promising nonutility enterprises. Frontec Logistics Corporation, a joint-venture company owned equally by ATCO and CU, has been awarded a Canadian government contract to operate and maintain the North Warning System, which is to replace the DEW line by 1992.

Another joint CU/ATCO company, CATS Defense Support Systems Inc., has completed development of a mobile targeting system for gunnery training, which is now being marketed internationally.

Canadian Utilities, an ATCO company, provides natural gas and electric utility services to eight out of 10 Alberta households.

EDMONTON POWER

Edmonton Power, the largest municipally owned generating utility in Canada and the second-largest electric utility in Alberta, has provided reliable and economical electricity for Edmontonians since 1902. Historically, Edmonton Power's attention to serving the needs of its customers provided a foundation for its rapid development. Today expansion, system improvements, and progress highlight the success story of Edmonton Power, achieved through the commitment of the utility's employees to serving customers. The municipal utility's mission provides constant direction.

"We provide safe, reliable, cost-effective electric service to enhance the quality of life in the community through excellence in employees and systems," says general man-

to streetcars, not only did the city's electrical services expand, but the network of customers capitalizing on the city's history of economic diversity and opportunity continued to expand as well. In 1970 Edmonton opened its new Clover Bar generating station on the riverbank in the northeast part of the city. Today the utility is looking to the Genesee Power Project, 50 kilometres southwest of Edmonton, to meet future electricity requirements for the city and the province.

Genesee marks a return by Edmonton Power to coal-fired generation—the most economical source today. Construction began in 1982 and now is progressing well toward completion of the first unit in October 1989. The site is a beehive of activity, with as many as

800 Albertans employed on site as work continues inside the mammoth plant and outside on coal-handling structures, switchyard, and transmission towers. As the only current mega project in Alberta, the $1.5-billion project is providing valuable employment and business opportunities for Edmonton and Alberta workers and contractors. Once operating, the Genesee plant will contribute needed electricity to help maintain reliability on the provincewide grid. The two natural gas plants, Rossdale and Clover Bar, will be reserved for peaking and emergency supplies.

The construction and operation of Genesee will provide future benefits to the city and area residents; today Edmonton Power customers continue to receive the reliable service they expect from their utility company.

Customers also enjoy competitive rates—among the lowest in Canada. And they benefit from the added advantage of lower property taxes because of the utility's contributions to the City of Edmonton's general revenues. For example, with-

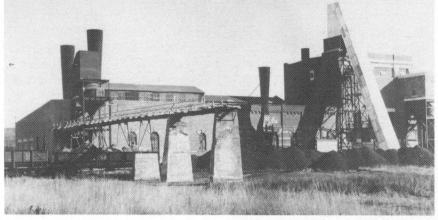

The Rossdale Power Plant in 1902 (left), as an original coal-fired steam operation, and in 1987 the plant of the future under construction at Genesee.

ager Ed Kyte.

Edmonton Power was formed when the Edmonton Electric Light and Power Company's 10-year franchise expired and the town council purchased the firm in 1902. The original power plant, a coal-fired steam operation beside the North Saskatchewan River, was soon replaced with a new station above the reach of floodwaters on the Rossdale Flats. As town became city and demand for power increased with growth, the Edmonton plant expanded and by the early 1950s converted its energy source to natural gas, then abundant and less costly.

The demand for power continued to escalate. From street lighting

Edmonton Power lights up the Edmonton city skyline.

out Edmonton Power's contribution of $41 million in 1987, property taxes could have been 21 percent higher for homeowners and local businesses.

System improvements and new technologies introduced in recent years have had a hand in Edmonton Power's high level of performance. For example, fibre optics now are used for communications in new substations. In 1986 a High-Voltage Test Lab was created, one aspect of Edmonton Power's continuing efforts to ensure safety for its employees and the public. The lab now checks safety equipment in-house, from rubber gloves to aerial buckets, resulting in significant savings in time and expense. And a new Supervisory Control and Data Acquisition (SCADA) system soon will be complete. Providing remote control of the utility's transmission and distribution system, it also will improve information exchanges with the Alberta Interconnected System's main control centre in Calgary.

Remote monitoring of 40 major customers' meters was initiated in 1987, providing a cost-effective system of gathering information for load surveys and billing without on-site visits. Edmonton Power also is contributing to a major project for residents by designing the electrical system for the southward extension of the city's light rail transit system.

But Edmonton Power would be nothing without its greatest resource. Inevitably it is its people who can take credit for Edmonton Power's fine reputation and continued progress. Employee dedication is steadfast. Witness the fact that the utility sells 25 percent more energy with the same number of staff as in 1980.

The utility supports community events and encourages employee participation in city festivals such as the Klondike Days Parade and in charitable endeavors that include the Christmas season's Adopt-A-Family program. Emphasis on on-the-job safety is illustrated by the annual Play Safe Work Safe exhibition, while the Social Club's Family Picnic invites employees and families to get to know one another in a recreational atmosphere.

Edmonton Power will continue to recognize the many contributions its 850 employees have made toward its system's progress. In fact, progress has been a consistent feature in Edmonton Power's 85-year history. Serving more than 230,000 customers within the city, including more than 25,000 commercial and industrial customers, Edmonton Power has a reputation for efficiency, productivity, and reliability. And it is people—the citizens of Edmonton—who enjoy the benefits.

LEP INTERNATIONAL INC.

Lep International Inc. is probably the best known customs broker and international freight forwarder in Calgary. Its local reputation and worldwide coverage secured the appointment as Official Customs Broker and International Freight Forwarder to the XV Olympic Winter Games in Calgary, 1988.

In the old days Canadians depended on sailing ships, canoes, covered wagons, and the railway to transport goods. Today transportation modes have advanced with the advent of container ships, diesel trains, cargo aircraft, and specialized ground vehicles.

Progress was rapid in this field, and 50 years ago Lep International Inc. was there to help. One of the largest international freight forwarders and customs house brokers in the world, Lep arranges transportation by truck, rail, air freight, and ocean freight, and ships goods across Canada and around the world.

Lep has 14 branches and airport offices across Canada, employing 250 staff members in offices located in Montreal, Toronto, London, Vancouver, Calgary, and Edmonton. The company operates air freight

An early morning pickup for Lep long-distance distribution.

Lep Project Services arranges the loading of a 145-foot chamber onto a heavy lift ship.

and sea freight export and import consolidations to and from the United Kingdom, Scandinavia, Continental Europe, Eastern Europe, the Far East, and the Caribbean.

The first key date in Lep's development was 1849, when a partnership known as Langstaff Ehrembert & Company was established in Le Havre, France. Two years later a branch was opened in London. The company expanded between 1851 and 1885, adding a new partner, Pollock. Hence, the name Lep was derived from the initials of all three partners.

Apart from forwarding goods the firm was one of the first motor

car packers, developing a good business in both the importing and exporting markets. When HRH The Duke of Connaught was appointed Governor General of Canada, Lep delivered a fleet of state coaches and motor cars to Canadian shores. In 1910 a separate company, Lep Transport & Depository Limited, was formed to take over the fledgling motor and continental department.

Today the Lep Group of Companies has principal offices in more than 25 countries, and agents in every industrialized country in the world. Headquartered in London, England, the Lep Group now employs 8,000, and annual turnover is in excess of $2 billion. The group is, in essence, a network of offices and companies that work both autonomously within their particular locale or field of operation, and within the framework of a cohesive international organization. This structure provides considerable flexibility, combined with a high degree of personal on-the-spot service.

The first Canadian office was founded in Montreal in 1930. Two years later R.K. Leeper joined the Lep Group as managing director of the United Kingdom companies, and later that year was appointed to the executive staff. The company's name was changed to Lep Transport Limited in 1936. Leeper's son took over the business in the 1940s and served as chairman until 1983. Leeper's grandson is now the president of Lep Canada, a wholly owned subsidiary of the Lep Group.

The first Alberta office was opened in Calgary in 1980 with only one person, and the Edmonton office was established the following year. As of 1987 Lep had 12 employees in Alberta reporting via the Calgary vice-president to the Canadian head office in Toronto.

Lep has expanded its services in response to the rapidly changing modes of transportation and communication during the past two decades. The company has built and leased warehousing facilities and improved the range of its services by directing much of the overseas transportation chain on an in-house basis. Lep's overseas companies and agents provide ocean and air transportation, consolidation, consulting, customs clearance, warehousing, distribution, packing, and insurance, and now communicate with Canada via computer.

The success of Lep is based on the high degree of reliability and coordination between the Canadian offices, sister companies, and agents abroad, all working together to provide complete door-to-door service. The scope of Lep's activities ranges from transportation of thoroughbred livestock to the delivery of the first Candu Reactor to Romania. The company has carried pulp and paper mills to Poland and Malaysia, drilling rigs to the Caribbean, and smaller shipments to every corner of the world.

In addition to providing a full range of import and export services to clients, Lep is also a major customs broker throughout Canada. Some of Lep's services include presenting Canada Customs entries at all major Canadian ports of entry;

negotiating and surrendering all types of transport documentation; and applying to Revenue Canada, Customs & Excise for refunds, claims, drawbacks, import and export permits, remissions, and all other customs formalities.

Lep's special services include air and sea chartering, removal and baggage, insurance for cargo moving in all modes of transport at competitive rates, transportation analysis and customs consulting services, handling trade fairs and exhibitions, and arranging third-party trade between any two overseas countries.

Lep's Projects Services Division plans and coordinates a client's transportation needs, from source to site. Bearing in mind abnormally

ABOVE: Exports are weighed in a Lep air freight warehouse.

LEFT: The Canada II *competing for the America's Cup off Perth, Australia, in 1986.*

heavy loads or outsize pieces, Lep works out the best consolidation point, ports, steamship lines, and routes to the site (even conducting route surveys where needed). Quotations are given, timetables agreed upon, and the whole project movement supervised from beginning to end.

Lep worked very closely with the Olympic Organizing Committee and various government departments to be ready for the XV Olympic Winter Games in 1988. Lep developed a customs regulations handbook, which was distributed to Olympic participants worldwide and during the Games; and they imported and, subsequently, reexported thousands of shipments of athletic gear and media equipment.

CANADA NORTHWEST ENERGY LIMITED

From its beginnings as a land settlement company in England in the 1880s, Canada Northwest Energy Limited has emerged as an international oil and gas exploration firm with interests that range from properties in Alberta to offshore interests in Italy and Spain.

The firm was incorporated as Canada Northwest Land Company Limited in 1893 to acquire 2.5 million acres of land owned by the Canadian Pacific Railway. Although all of this prairie land was subse-

Oil storage tanks at the Hays East battery site in southeastern Alberta.

quently sold, the subsurface mineral rights on approximately 300,000 acres were retained.

During the early 1950s a number of oil discoveries were made on some of this acreage in southeastern Saskatchewan. The royalty income received from these wells provided the foundation for Canada Northwest's evolution into the natural resource exploration and development company it is today. Since 1969, when it was renamed Canada Northwest Energy Limited, the firm has become a

global explorer for hydrocarbons, with interests in oil and gas rights in 10 countries.

These assets are managed by more than 180 employees, a significant increase from six in the early 1970s. The firm operates from its head office in Calgary, with subsidiary offices in Denver, Rome, Madrid, London, and Sydney, and it has major reserves of oil and gas in Canada, Italy, and Spain.

The cornerstone of Canada Northwest's success has been geographic diversification in the search for oil and gas. Emphasis is placed on looking for conventional oil and

gas in areas that provide a market for the company's product and a reasonable profit margin.

Canada Northwest has enjoyed two major turning points since it adopted its focus on energy in 1969. The first was the discovery of the Casablanca Oil Field in the Gulf of Valencia, offshore Spain, in the spring of 1975. This discovery, and subsequent installation of permanent production facilities in 1981, represented a milestone in the company's history. An excellent economic climate for exploration, devel-

Canada Northwest Energy Limited's pumpjack at the Calgary International Airport welcomes visitors to the city in the true Stampede spirit.

opment, and production of oil in Spain has contributed to a solid return on the firm's investments.

Canada Northwest's second milestone, and its most important project to date, is the development of the Vega Oil Field in the Malta Channel, offshore southern Sicily. This giant oil field, one of the largest in the Mediterranean Sea, has recoverable reserves of more than 317 million barrels of oil. The Vega Oil Field, discovered by Canada Northwest in 1981, commenced production in August 1987 and is expected to increase the company's oil production by more than 80 percent.

In addition to its 12-percent working interest in the Casablanca Oil Field and another 20-percent holding in the Vega Oil Field, Canada Northwest has made five gas discoveries onshore Italy since 1986, adding net reserves of more than 25 billion cubic feet of gas.

Although Canada Northwest is generally perceived to be a foreign asset company, it has significant land holdings and oil and gas reserves in Canada. The firm's main oil-producing areas are in Saskatchewan, and in the Morinville area in central Alberta, and in the Hays area of southeastern Alberta. Its main gas-producing areas are Campbell-Namao, Hilda, Tweedie, and Westlock, all in Alberta. Canada Northwest has committed $60 million for an exploration and development program in Canada through 1989. The firm is also an investor in exploration for and production of gold and strategic minerals in North America and Australia.

Canada Northwest continues to actively explore for hydrocarbons and is currently conducting or planning geophysical programs in nine countries, including Colombia, Pakistan, and France. Exploratory drilling is in progress in Italy, Spain, Australia, the United Kingdom, Indonesia, and the United States. The company also has applications for concessions in China and Egypt, and it is looking at a number of other potential areas of exploration throughout the world.

In 1968 Canada Northwest's market capitalization was about $2.8 million, with annual revenues of about $200,000. Today the firm's market capitalization is more than $400 million, and annual revenues exceed $100 million.

Canada Northwest's financial strength, coupled with its reserve and land base, provides shareholders with a high degree of exposure to possible discovery of large reserves of conventional crude oil. The company's high volumes of low-cost production mitigate the nega-

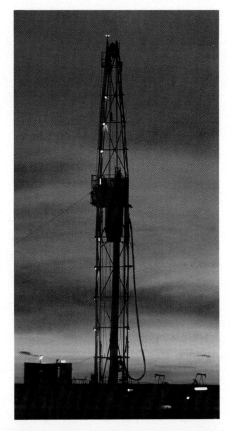

Development drilling in the Hays East area of southeastern Alberta.

tive effect of decreased world oil prices, enabling Canada Northwest to continue at a reasonable level of growth.

The firm's major shareholder is TransAlta Resources, a wholly owned subsidiary of TransAlta Utilities, the largest investor-owned electric utility in Canada.

Canada Northwest Energy Limited also supports a wide range of community organizations in Calgary and Western Canada. Company donations are contributed to more than 80 cultural, educational, medical, athletic, and political groups, including the Banff Centre for Performing Arts, the Glenbow Museum, the Mount Royal Music Endowment Fund, the University of Calgary Future Fund, the YMCA, and the Calgary Philharmonic Orchestra.

The Vega production platform located offshore southern Sicily.

TRANSALTA UTILITIES

TransAlta Utilities supplies low-cost, reliable electric service to satisfy more than two-thirds of Alberta's electric energy needs.

New technologies are emerging that make more efficient use of electricity. Adjustable-speed drives, heat pumps, improved electric arc furnaces, microwaves, and lasers are some industrial applications of electricity used by Alberta businesses.

TransAlta is helping its customers find out how these new technologies can increase efficiency and cut costs. This kind of customer service has been a TransAlta priority since the corporation began operations in 1911 under the name Calgary Power. TransAlta's first hydro plant at Horseshoe Falls, upstream from Calgary on the Bow River, began operations in May of that year.

The City of Calgary, host of the

More than two-thirds of Alberta's electric energy requirements are supplied by TransAlta's coal-fired generating plants, located near Wabamun Lake, 65 kilometres west of Edmonton.

1988 Olympic Winter Games, was one of TransAlta's first major customers—today it is still the corporation's biggest wholesale customer.

TransAlta has maintained a tradition of customer service, excellence, and value. This tradition has kept the corporation strong through good years and lean, enabling it to meet its goal of supplying safe, reliable electric services to Albertans at the lowest-possible cost.

Today TransAlta is the largest investor-owned electric utility in Canada, with assets exceeding $3.7 billion. TransAlta owns and operates three coal-fired generating plants and 13 hydro-electric plants. A fourth coal-fired plant, Sheerness, is jointly owned with Alberta Power Limited. TransAlta's total generating capability was 4,293 megawatts in 1987; total electric energy sales were 18,597 million kilowatt-hours.

The operations of the plants are

TransAlta's Horseshoe Falls hydro-electric generating plant on the Bow River has been providing 13,900 kilowatts of reliable, low-cost power since it started operating in 1911.

combined to achieve minimum overall cost of power: The large coal-fired units supply the base or continuous load, while the hydro-electric plants provide additional electric energy requirements, particularly during peak load periods.

TransAlta's coal has among the lowest sulphur content of any in North America. It is the primary fuel for TransAlta's generating plants, accounting for approximately 93 percent of the corporation's generation.

During the 1950s, when the cost of coal was relatively low, TransAlta's management identified coal as the preferred fuel for the corporation's generating plants. As a result of such foresight, TransAlta's customers today enjoy electrical rates that are among the lowest in the world. Low industrial rates help to attract industries to TransAlta's service area, creating business and employment opportunities for Albertans.

Since 1962 TransAlta has provided most of its own fuel requirements. It owns and operates two large coal mines—Whitewood and Highvale—which together produce more than 14 million tonnes for use in the Wabamun, Sundance, and

Keephills generating plants. Trans-Alta is the largest producer of coal in Canada, in terms of tonnes of coal produced in 1986.

The corporation has been active in reclamation activities since the early 1960s. TransAlta reclaims land over its mines to a state of productivity equal to or greater than that prior to mining. To date TransAlta has reclaimed more than 971 hectares (2,398 acres) of land for agricultural and recreational purposes.

In 1982 TransAlta relocated the hamlet of Keephills as a direct response to residents' concerns about the impact of the Highvale Mine on their community. An 80-acre country-residential development, nestled in a pine forest, was built eight kilometres northeast of the original hamlet. Thirty-one residential lots, a commercial lot, an eight-acre school and community hall, and a 28-acre environmental reserve are part of the new community. The story of Keephills demonstrates the importance of social impact in TransAlta's planning for development.

To ensure reliable, safe electric service to customers throughout its large service area, TransAlta owns more than 65,000 kilometres of transmission and distribution lines. The transmission system is interconnected with all major generating plants in Alberta. The system is also connected with the electric system in British Columbia through a 500-kilovolt transmission line interconnection, further ensuring reliable supplies of electricity.

From the System Control Centre in Calgary, TransAlta monitors and controls the operation of more than 68,000 kilometres of transmission and distribution lines. The centre also provides dispatch of electric energy for the entire Alberta Interconnected System.

Some of the corporation's most important assets are not to be found in the corporate financial reports. They are TransAlta's 2,500 dedicated employees. Their hard work and innovation have helped to more than triple productivity in the past 30 years.

In the pursuit of even higher productivity and improved service to customers, TransAlta encourages employees to participate in several programs. For example, the Action Recommended Program rewards those who develop an idea that improves productivity or reduces costs. The Employee Recognition Program provides recognition for those who excel in productivity, innovation, and customer service.

Training programs to improve employees' effectiveness have been a continuing feature at TransAlta. Programs covering such subjects as customer service, effective management, and the regulatory process are offered throughout the year.

TransAlta is interested in the progress of the communities it serves. Through a variety of volunteer activities, individual TransAlta employees contribute personal time, money, and effort to improve conditions in their home communities. The corporation supports such

individual involvement. TransAlta also sponsors many socially beneficial programs, such as the Alberta Junior Citizens of the Year Awards.

TransAlta Resources Corporation, the principal nonregulated subsidiary of TransAlta Utilities, develops business opportunities that are in keeping with the management and technical strengths of its parent corporation. TransAlta Resources' assets include investments in Canada Northwest Energy Limited, AEC Power Ltd., TransAlta Energy Systems, and Keyword Office Technologies Ltd.

From its beginnings more than 75 years ago, TransAlta Utilities has grown to become one of the largest companies in Canada in terms of assets. The corporation is 99 percent owned by Canadian investors, more than 40 percent of whom are Albertans.

With the continued cooperation of its customers, shareholders, suppliers, and employees, TransAlta Utilities will continue to meet its goal of providing safe, reliable electric service to Albertans at the lowest-possible cost.

LEFT: TransAlta takes great care to reclaim the land after the coal has been removed from the mines. Most of the reclaimed land is returned to agricultural production, while some of it has been turned into a wildlife reserve.

BELOW: Good customer service requires hard work and dedication. TransAlta's 2,500 employees have shown time and again that they have what it takes.

GOVERNMENT OF ALBERTA

AGRICULTURE

The province of Alberta was built on the strength of its vast agricultural resources—resources that today contribute to the overall strength of the Alberta economy. Agriculture is one of the province's most important economic sectors and a major renewable resource industry. The government of Alberta recognizes agriculture as a key force in Alberta's future and remains committed to its maintenance as a strong and viable industry.

The influence of the agriculture sector to both the people of this province and its economy is undeniable. Primary production and agriculture processing sectors directly or indirectly affect more than half the province's economic activity and provide, directly or indirectly, jobs for one of every three working Albertans.

Agriculture and food products account for more than $2 billion in foreign exports annually. Grain and grain products are sold throughout the world, while livestock and livestock products appear on markets across North America, in Europe, and Asia. More than 12.1 million hectares of rich agricultural land are devoted to crop and livestock

Farm families continue to build Alberta's agricultural future.

production. As many as 9 million hectares can be added to farmland inventory in the future.

Because the health of the agriculture sector is largely dependent upon international developments, weather conditions, and other forces beyond the control of producers, the government lends support to agriculture to ensure its continued growth and development.

The government of Alberta has implemented an extensive agricultural program, encompassing both development and assistance programs that provide farmers and ranchers with a viable safety net to maintain and enhance production. Alberta's extensive value added and agri-business sector is also supported by a wide range of programs.

CULTURE AND MULTICULTURALISM

The government of Alberta considers the development of cultural and historical resources to be an essential part of the province's future. A major goal is to ensure Albertans have access to and derive benefits from cultural events, goods, and properties. Recognizing the benefits associated with displaying and promoting Alberta's distinctive cultural environment and products, the Department of Culture and Multiculturalism seeks to expand this distinctiveness by focusing on three broad areas: historical resources, cultural development, and cultural heritage.

Historical resources, be they documents, artifacts, specimens, structures, or sites, contribute to the quality of life and enhance understanding of the distinctive roots of the citizens of this province. They provide a tangible link to the past, and serve to educate and entertain citizens and tourists alike.

From traditional to experimental art forms, visual, performing, film, and literary arts and the encouragement of public library service throughout the province, cul-

tural development is encouraged because of its vital contribution to the social and economic fibre of the province.

Cultural heritage emphasizes the many backgrounds of Alberta's citizens who contribute to a unique cultural mosaic. Culture and Multiculturalism operates under the mandate that sharing this rich inheritance profoundly influences the lives of Albertans and serves to strengthen the identity of its people.

The department further believes that the responsibility for building a lively, participatory cultural sector in Alberta is a cooperative responsibility that must be shared by organizations and institutions; by the professionals, amateurs, and volunteers who comprise the cultural sector; and by all levels of government and the private sector.

ECONOMIC DEVELOPMENT AND TRADE

The province of Alberta boasts one of the most dynamic business regions in North America. With its free enterprise status, vibrant business climate, and strong economy bursting with extensive natural resources, Alberta has earned the international reputation as "the province of opportunity."

Alberta Economic Development and Trade projects this "opportunity image" to the rest of the world and is aggressive in bringing business and investment to the province. The department markets the advantages of Alberta to the world: its superb infrastructure in transportation, communication, education, health care, and world-class facilities in science and technology.

But it is the overall business climate, ripe for investment, that is most attractive to potential international partners. Enhancing Alberta's strength as a promising location for investment are a highly educated and productive work force, a stable social climate, and a cooperative government, not to mention the tremendous potential to develop local industry and expand export markets.

International trade, already a key component of the province's economic profile, offers outstanding opportunity for both Alberta business and international partners. Welcoming international buyers, Economic Development and Trade welcomes international interest in the province by hosting trade delegations, marketing missions, and by participating in international trade expositions.

A cornerstone of Alberta's economic activity, international trade accounts for 21 percent of the province's gross domestic product. In 1986 Alberta exported approximately $11.5 billion worth of goods and services comprising 10 percent of Canada's exports and a substantial contribution to the trade performance of the entire country.

The Department of Economic Development and Trade operates under the mandate that export development must be approached with imagination and innovation. Working with private companies and with entrepreneurs is key to the expansion of trade and the pursuance of development opportunities throughout the world.

ENERGY

Alberta has long been known for the magnitude of its oil and natural gas resources, and for proven technology and innovation in exploration and development. The energy industry has shaped the province's economy.

A major oil discovery in Leduc, Alberta, in 1947 sparked the beginning of the province's modern oil industry. Most of the province overlies the Western Canadian Sedimentary Basin, the source of the oil and gas. Reserves of conventional crude oil, that is oil capable of being pumped to the surface from an underground well, total about 4 billion barrels.

Much of the province's future energy potential lies in the 290 billion barrels of bitumen recoverable from the oil sands deposits located in the northern half of the province. Bitumen is extracted from the oil sands and is converted to synthetic crude oil, which is refined in Alberta and Eastern Canada. Synthetic crude production accounts for about 13 percent of Canada's total crude oil production. Bitumen from deeper oil sands is primarily

An Edmonton refinery.

recovered by injecting steam into the formation. This heats the oil and allows roughly 20 percent of it to be pumped to the surface. This is done at Cold Lake and in the Peace River area.

Natural gas production in Alberta supplies almost 90 percent of Canada's total production, and reserves are approximately 85 percent of Canada's total. Alberta's natural gas is marketed both domestically and in the United States.

While Alberta's reserves of oil, gas, and oil sands are substantial, the magnitude of the province's coal reserves is even larger. Alberta contains two-thirds of Canadian-defined coal reserves that could be developed in the near future. Alberta has other minerals, too, both metallic and quarriable, including

A gas plant in the Rocky Mountain foothills.

sulphur, gypsum, phosphate, and silica sand, as well as gold, platinum, silver, magnesium, rare earth metals, and others.

Alberta's resource base feeds a world scale petrochemical industry. Using natural gas liquids as the feedstock, industry produces a variety of chemical products sold to the United States, Japan, Korea, and Europe.

TECHNOLOGY, RESEARCH AND TELECOMMUNICATIONS

The Department of Technology, Research and Telecommunications was established in 1986 to accelerate the adaptation of technology to Alberta's traditional resource industries and to support the growth of new knowledge-intensive employment opportunities in specific niche sectors.

Specific sectors include those built on the province's research history that have developed expertise in the fields of medical and biological sciences, electronics and microelectronics, advanced materials and processes, computing and software, and telecommunications. These sectors give Alberta entrepreneurs the necessary edge to compete on a global scale.

Working closely with the province's universities, technical institutes, research organizations, and the business community, the department's goal is to encourage the transfer of technology from the laboratory to the marketplace and to help create an environment where inventors and innovators can create new products, new processes, and new methods.

Through a Technology Commercialization program, the department provides financial assistance for the support of technology institutes, the development of new products, the commercialization of research, and feasibility studies.

Technology, Research and Telecommunications is also responsible for the development of Alberta's telecommunications and communications public policy. It works to ensure an awareness and understanding of the economic, social, and environmental benefits of advanced technologies to the lives of present and future generations.

FORESTRY, LANDS, AND WILDLIFE

Alberta has North America's largest unallocated timber resource.

Forests cover approximately 370,000 square kilometres, about half the total area of the province. Tremendous potential exists for further expansion of Alberta's forestry resources. In softwood harvesting, only slightly more than half of the 14.2-million-cubic-metre annual allowable cut is taken, and loggers only take 1.5 million cubic metres of the available 11.4 million cubic metres of hardwood.

The billion dollar mark was topped in 1986 for the value of shipments in Alberta's forest products industry. Together the province's major sawmills produce more than 1.3 billion board feet of lumber a year.

Other large scale operations include two bleached kraft pulp mills, three plywood mills, three oriented-strandboard plants, and Canada's first medium density fibreboard plant.

Alberta's uncommitted timber resource has drawn major forest projects to the province. Several new pulp and paper projects are either on the drawing board or under construction. These represent close to $2 billion of investment and thousands of direct and indirect jobs. These developments are a boon to the province's economic diversification strategy, creating new employment and investment opportunities.

Alberta's Department of Forestry, Lands, and Wildlife is prepared for this explosion in new investment. The department sets the standard for the rest of the country with secure long-term tenure arrangements and progressive forest management policies. Alberta is committed to proper management of its forests so everyone has the opportunity to benefit from this renewable resource.

Timber harvesting in Alberta.

Reforestation policies ensure that Alberta will maintain, throughout the future, a viable forest industry and preserve the natural beauty, wildlife, and recreational potential of its forests.

KANANASKIS COUNTRY

Welcome to Kananaskis Country. Whether you've come for a camping excursion, a day's skiing, or a relaxing drive to get away from it all, Kananaskis Country welcomes you.

A 4,000-square-kilometre, four-season, multiuse recreation area, Ka-

A breathtaking shot of Kananaskis Country.

nanaskis Country is located 90 kilometres west/southwest of Calgary and encompasses some of Canada's most spectacular terrain.

It is described as rich with rolling hills, grazing lands, crystalline rivers, mountain forests teeming with wildlife, the stark timeless beauty of the high alpine's rock and ice, rugged Rocky Mountain peaks soaring up to touch the sky—this is Kananaskis Country, open for enjoyment in 101 different ways. Established in 1978 by the Alberta government and financed by the Alberta Heritage Savings Trust Fund, Kananaskis Country is planned to allow recreational activities to co-exist in harmony with the wildlife sanctuaries, three provincial parks, recreational facilities, and other recreation areas in the forest reserve.

Hike it, ski it, paddle it. Kananaskis Country's unique facilities and year-round recreational opportunities mean there is something here for everyone—fisherman, golfer, camper, skier, hiker. Spring, summer, autumn, or winter, the natural beauty of this area is worthy of a visit.

RECREATION AND PARKS

From the peaks of Kananaskis Country in the Canadian Rockies to the badland valleys of Dinosaur Country—from Notikewin, north of the 57th parallel, to Police Outpost bordering Montana, Alberta's provincial parks truly offer blue skies and golden opportunities for Albertans and visitors alike.

The majestic mountain views, scenic hiking trails, and cool mountain streams lock the vision of breathtaking scenery and exhilarating experiences deep in the mind.

Whether you want to camp, hike, ski, walk, ride, or just lay back and enjoy our mountain majesty —you can do it here in Alberta.

This is Alberta's heritage, a heritage strong in traditions and the key to the very essence of what makes Alberta beautiful. A heritage worth protecting and conserving for generations to come.

Heritage resources in Alberta are more than our mountains. It encompasses the rolling foothills, undulating plains, desert badlands, and lake land regions.

With 61 provincial parks, 44 provincial recreation areas, 10 ecological reserves, and three wilderness sites, Alberta Recreation and Parks presents a wide variety of outdoor experiences. Winter, spring, summer, or fall—Alberta has it all.

Not only are outdoor experiences in the parks offered, but, also participative and competitive opportunities for Albertans. Alberta Recreation and Parks has hosted world class sporting events—the 1988 Olympic Winter Games, the 1983 Universiade Games, and the 1978 Commonwealth Games, all involving countries around the world.

As a result of these games, Alberta has been able to develop recreation facilities second to none. These facilities provide a legacy for generations to come; recreational and sport facilities for all to enjoy.

Alberta Recreation and Parks is people; people helping people, working together to provide excellent lifestyle opportunities for all Albertans. The recreation programs promote community development as well as individual and family enrichment.

Energy, enthusiasm, and commitment have become a trademark. Alberta Recreation and Parks is proud of the blue skies of its past

and the golden promises of its future—a future designed to enhance the quality of life for all Albertans, and an invitation to their neighbors and friends to join in that pursuit.

TOURISM

Tourism is one of Alberta's leading opportunity industries. A strong contributor to the provincial economy, tourism generated $2.25 billion in revenues in 1986 and employed 100,000 Albertans. More than half of the revenue came from out-of-province visitors from the United States, the United Kingdom, continental Europe, Japan, and other Canadian provinces.

Even greater opportunities for the industry lie ahead. According to the United Nations, tourism will be the world's leading industry by the year 2000. Alberta will be in a prime position to capture a large share of this growing market base.

Capitalizing on the lure of the spectacular Rocky Mountains, tourism representatives feel that once here, visitors will take advantage of the many attractions extending beyond the Rockies. With four World Heritage Sites, Canada's largest share of national and provincial park space, and extensive recreational and accommodation facilities, the entire province of Alberta is a natural major tourism destination.

Boasting an all-season tourism appeal, Alberta's attractions extend provincewide. From Drumheller's Tyrrell Museum of Palaeontology to the cosmopolitan centres of Calgary and Edmonton, visitors will be captivated by the diversity of this re-

World class exhibits for avid dinosaur seekers at the Tyrell Museum.

markable province.

The role of the provincial government in Alberta's tourism industry is to stimulate and support the actions of the private sector. The common goal is to develop Alberta into a year-round holiday destination that will be among the most favored in North America and the rest of the world.

Development of tourism resources provides significant economic and social benefits to everyone in Alberta. Investment in tourism opportunities increases economic activity and contributes to the economic growth and development of local communities and, ultimately, to the growth and development of the province itself.

The Banff Springs Hotel.

TIME AIR

With a route system extending across the four western provinces and into the Yukon as well as Montana and Minnesota, Time Air is recognized as Canada's leading regional airline. Though the company now reaches far beyond the provincial boundaries, Time Air will forever be a part of the Alberta heritage, for it was there that one man's dream became a reality.

Stubb Ross loved to fly and had decided at an early age to make flying his lifelong ambition. A man of vision, Ross could see potential in a Lethbridge-Calgary air service, and so he stepped forward to challenge the giant of his day—Air Canada. In 1966 he founded his own

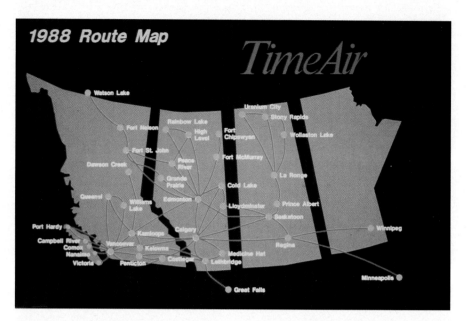

1988 Route Map — TimeAir

A friendly staff makes flying Time Air a rewarding experience.

airline—Lethbridge Air Service, the forerunner of today's Time Air. With just three employees and a single 9-passenger aircraft, the tiny airline began operating a twice-daily service to Calgary.

Increased frequency of flights was a convenience passengers appreciated, especially those who travelled on business, and the fledgling airline quickly garnered community support. Though a mere 2,703 passengers made the journey with Lethbridge Air Service that first year, the route looked promising. On the heels of success came more opportunity, prompting a change of name, but not a change of heart. By matching the equipment and the frequency to the de-

mands of each community, Time Air had discovered the formula for success—a simple formula that remains valid to this day.

Time Air employees are special people. They take pride in the work they do—evidence that true craftsmanship has not disappeared. They enjoy their work, and they reap the rewards when the firm does well. Every employee has a vested interest in providing their best performance because each of them receives a share of company profits.

A similar level of top-rated performance is evident in the airline's record of safe operation. Made possible by the company's thorough maintenance program and its highly skilled maintenance and flight crews, it's an enviable record the company endeavors to maintain. With such a responsibility, it's not surprising that passenger safety is a primary concern at every level of the operation.

For many of the communities it serves, Time Air's presence has positive implications. Distances suddenly become shorter, and even the most remote location becomes more accessible. Business and commerce is attracted to those areas, providing more opportunity for even greater prosperity.

When the economic climate is good, Time Air shares in that

As Canada's leading regional airline, Time Air provides service to 39 communities.

prosperity. In a province where nearly half the economic activity springs from the petroleum sector, many of those same communities have also been faced with adversity. Time Air, too, has been forced to weather times of economic strife. Turning to the very formula that has spelled success for the company from the beginning, Time Air will adjust the equipment and the frequency to match current demand. As long as the infrastructure remains intact, citizens can view Time Air as a permanent member of their community.

As the company continues with its growth, the airline is continually seeking ways to extend improved products and services to its customers. This philosophy is reflected in Time Air's aircraft fleet. New aircraft require large capital commitments, and it isn't practical to replace the entire fleet all at one time. As new, technologically advanced aircraft come on line, the older, less efficient planes are phased out. Modern aircraft boost passenger confidence and provide an air of total professionalism. State-of-the-art technology in new aircraft such as the de Havilland Dash 8, 37-seat Series 100, and the 50-passenger Series 300 allow Time Air to operate a most cost-effective operation.

In partnership with Canadian Airlines International, Time Air is connected to a route network that virtually encompasses the globe. With a single call to the Canadian Airlines reservation office, travellers can book passage to destinations on five continents, and to more domestic points than any other airline. Continued success for Time Air and its larger partner will result in even further expansion of the route network.

With a Charter Division based in Calgary, Time Air is able to open a whole new world of specialized group travel. Fishermen, executives, musicians, and convention-

Richard Barton, president and chief executive officer.

eers have all found Time Air charters to suit their needs perfectly as have sports teams, ballet troupes, political parties, roughnecks, and royalty. People and cargo, in varying combinations, to virtually any location—there's a Time Air charter going where and when the customer says, and with all the in-flight amenities the client requests. With jet and turboprop equipment ranging from as few as eight seats

to as many as 65, Time Air has the right aircraft for a wide variety of groups. Charter consultants will make all the necessary arrangements to ensure that every flight goes without a hitch. Many high-profile people, including her majesty the Queen, have already enjoyed a Time Air charter.

Of Time Air's Alberta destinations, Calgary is very important to air travellers. As one of the province's primary hubs, Calgary is the key connection point for people flying abroad not only with its Canadian partner but with a multitude of other international carriers that serve all points of the globe. Edmonton is another major city in the Time Air route network. This gateway to the North serves as a collection point for passengers and cargo, and is Time Air's second-busiest Alberta port of call.

Grande Prairie, Rainbow Lake, Fort McMurray, and Lloydminster are examples of the many towns and cities that derive much of their livelihood from the petroleum industry. Made more accessible through regularly scheduled Time Air flights, these communities have

A Dash 8, Series 100, wings its way over Alberta's Rockies.

prospered. Forestry, construction, government, and agriculture have supported other communities served by the airline, and Time Air has endeavored to target the needs of each community.

Fort Chipewyan on the western tip of Lake Athabasca is Alberta's oldest settlement. The link provided by Time Air is valued by the 1,800 inhabitants of this isolated community. Goods and supplies are transported in a timely manner, and passengers can travel to the more populated centers of the South.

With its roots in Alberta, Time Air is proud of its heritage and proud of its record of service to the province. Alberta's once-tiny air service has grown to become Canada's leading privately owned regional airline, carrying more than one million passengers each year. Time Air owes its existence to its founder who pursued his dream in this land of opportunity; its success is due to its people who carry on the winning tradition.

ALBERTA ENERGY COMPANY LTD.

Alberta Energy Company Ltd. (AEC) was established to provide Albertans and other Canadians with an opportunity to participate in the development of the province's resources.

Originally a Crown corporation, AEC became a public company in late 1975 with the sale of $75 million in shares, matching the initial investment made by the Alberta government. Provincial residents had the opportunity to apply for the $10 shares during a 15-day Alberta Priority Period, after which the remainder of the 7.5 million shares was to become available to other Canadians.

Shares were offered through chartered banks, participating trust companies, and credit unions, as well as the customary investment dealer offices. At that time, the share issue was one of the largest equity offerings in the history of Canada and possibly the largest issue of common stock for a new Canadian company.

Response to the share offering was overwhelming. When the number of Alberta subscriptions exceeded the number of shares offered, the plan to sell nationally was abandoned, and limits were placed on the number of shares allotted to each buyer. The shares of the company are now traded on all Canadian stock exchanges. The company remains 100-percent Canadian- and dominantly Alberta-owned.

Today, with approximately 47,000 Canadian shareholders, AEC operates in a variety of areas within Alberta's natural resource industries, including oil and natural gas exploration and development, pipelines, forest products, and petrochemicals.

The company's principal investments include petroleum and natural gas rights in Suffield, Primrose, and other areas of Alberta; a 10-percent joint-venture interest in the world's largest oil sands project; oil pipelines; and a joint-venture interest in a major Alberta-based fertilizer business. The firm also owns a forest products complex in central Alberta; half of Pan-Alberta Gas Ltd., which is one of Canada's major natural gas marketers; and 57 percent of Chieftain Development Co. Ltd., which is involved in Canadian and international oil and gas operations. AEC's oil and gas investments make it one of Canada's top 10 oil and gas companies. The firm is the largest intraprovincial transporter of oil.

In 1986 AEC opened Canada's first medium-density fibreboard plant at the site of the corporation's lumber mill near Whitecourt, Alberta. Fibreboard is a premium wood product suitable for use in the manufacture of furniture and cabinets, and the plant serves Canadian, U.S., and offshore markets.

That same year AEC and Cominco Ltd., one of Canada's largest chemical fertilizer producers, formed a joint venture to develop and expand Alberta's nitrogen fertilizer production and marketing business.

With an eye to the future, AEC's research and development team pursues identification of new technology with the potential to enhance AEC's businesses. Recent projects include new technology for the more efficient transportation of heavy oil, direct conversion of natural gas to chemicals, improved methods of heavy oil recovery, and innovations in the field of forest products development.

Alberta Energy Company Ltd. also invests time in developing special training programs to help employees meet the challenges of new technology and productivity. An advocate of community involvement, the firm encourages its employees to volunteer their time to local service activities. The company also supports the United Way, community services, education, arts and culture, and amateur sports.

Courtesy, Westfile, Inc.

Photo by Jerg Kroener

Alberta Wheat Pool

Alberta Cattle Commission

CHAPTER 8

Land and Water

Companies drawing their lifeblood from the earth vitalize the Alberta economy.

Alberta Wheat Pool 264-265;
Alberta Cattle Commission 266

ALBERTA WHEAT POOL

In the early 1920s Alberta's farmers were suffering at the hands of unscrupulous grain merchants. Forced to sell their wheat at cut rates, they were trapped in a marketplace balanced in favor of the buyer.

In response to growing anger and frustration in the farm community, the Calgary *Herald* brought a California political activist to Alberta to raise a stir. Aaron Sapiro, who had been instrumental in organizing community farm commodity pools in the United States, gave an inspiring speech to a group of farmers in Calgary on August 3, 1923. A resolution was passed that night, and the Alberta Wheat Pool was born.

A membership drive began immediately, and the Alberta government loaned the fledgling group $5,000. With an additional $10,000 in

Due to the Alberta Wheat Pool network, more than 60,000 farmers are served by grain storage facilities at 300 locations.

working capital from the United Grain Growers, the organization gained a solid footing. By contracting the services of existing private elevators, the co-operative soon was able to repay its debts and begin building its own grain-handling system across the province.

Since the opening of its first office in Calgary in 1923, the Alberta Wheat Pool has become one of the largest grain-handling co-operatives in Canada. The organization is completely owned and controlled by its members—more than 60,000 farmers. It operates country elevators in 300 locations across Alberta and northeastern British Columbia.

By grouping together, farmers have been able to create stability and fairness in a market once dominated by chaos and greed. Today the pool handles about two-thirds of Alberta's grain exports, with gross revenues exceeding one bil-

Greg Steiger, assistant manager at Beiseker, and Gary Lang inspect a load of grain.

lion dollars annually, and total assets approaching $500 million. Through its grain-handling system, the organization moves from 5 million to 7 million tonnes of grain and oilseeds annually.

In its official mission statement the Alberta Wheat Pool outlines its commitment to members: "Together our mission is to competitively produce, process, and aggressively market diverse world-class agricultural products, and to respond to the changing demands of our customers and our environment with integrity so we share in an enhanced social and economic future."

To further these goals, delegates representing districts throughout the province meet annually to study operating results, set policy, and elect officers. The pool's democratic system of ownership ensures that outsiders cannot gain control of the organization.

The Alberta Wheat Pool is an integral part of Alberta's farming community. Farmers enjoy higher returns for production, improved facilities, greater security, and a

Trains line up to unload grain at the Alberta Wheat Pool Terminal at Vancouver. Through the co-operative's efforts, Alberta farmers' grain competes favorably on the world market.

higher standard of living, thanks to the positive influence of the pool. And by providing the most comprehensive grain-collection system in Alberta, the pool network serves many towns that otherwise would not have a grain elevator.

Although its original mandate was to enable farmers to bargain collectively with grain buyers, the Alberta Wheat Pool has grown in scope to provide its members with much more. More than 1,600 employees provide complete grain services for members, including storage and handling, grain merchandising, fertilizer and seed grain sales, farm equipment, financing, and advanced agricultural research.

The co-operative has also ensured farmers a powerful voice in the formation of national grain-marketing policies, and it has been a key player in the establishment of the Canadian Wheat Board, the re-

tention of fair freight rates on export grain, and the conclusion of several international wheat agreements.

The organization's seed division is Alberta's main seed distributor and one of Canada's largest seed suppliers. The pool successfully competes on the world market, pursuing business for its members as far away as Japan and South Korea. Closer to home, the association has researched and developed its own brand of grain varieties, designed to improve agricultural production for the farmer.

Partially owned subsidiaries of the pool include Western Cooperative Fertilizer Ltd., Prince Rupert Grain Ltd., Pacific Elevators Ltd., XCAN Grain Ltd., Pool Insurance Company, Prairie Pools Inc., Cooperative Energy Corporation, and ABL Engineering Ltd.

The Alberta Wheat Pool also has a hand in many community projects. As a major supporter of the 4-H Club, the co-operative provides leadership training and development to Alberta's rural young-

sters, the farmers of tomorrow. Field staff assist in the education of young people on all facets of agriculture, and the organization offers scholarships and bursary programs to postsecondary students.

The Alberta Wheat Pool is responding to the ever-changing needs of its members by upgrading its elevators at key points and designing new elevator systems. High construction costs and an improved road network have prompted the association to move toward a smaller, more efficient network of elevators and an increased use of truck transportation.

The general public can learn about the history of the Alberta Wheat Pool, as well as current issues in agriculture, by visiting its large agricultural reference library, or by tuning in to daily radio farm programs broadcast on 21 Alberta stations. Visitors to Calgary can take in the displays at the Alberta Wheat Pool Grain Academy, a small museum devoted to Western Canada agriculture. The academy, in the Round-Up Centre at the Calgary Exhibition and Stampede Grounds, has educated thousands of visitors since its inception in 1974.

Tim Brown, assistant manager at Rosebud, sealing a load of grain.

ALBERTA CATTLE COMMISSION

Alberta has developed a reputation for the finest breeding stock in the world.

The Alberta Cattle Commission (ACC) was established as a vehicle to represent the opinions of all sectors of the beef cattle production industry. Headquartered in Calgary, the nonprofit organization acts as a lobbyist and catalyst for the beef industry, promoting and protecting the interests of Alberta's cattle producers.

In 1969 representatives of five farm associations requested that the Government of Alberta establish the ACC to create a unified voice on agricultural policies affecting the cattle industry. The ACC is a democratic organization funded and elected by Alberta's cattle producers.

The ACC provides a wide range of services to the beef industry, including market information, promotional activities, market development, and new product development assistance, as well as funding for research and seminars. Since its inception the Alberta Cattle Commission has gained recognition by governments and industry and has a powerful voice in the direction of agricultural policy both in Alberta and across Canada.

Albertans have been raising beef since the late 1800s. The indus-

try grew as the province's population increased, and today 30,000 farms raise cattle, generating more than one billion dollars in sales each year.

The province's cold winters and warm, dry summers, combined with rigid health standards, excellent breeding, and knowledgeable producers, make Alberta's beef industry one of the world's best. And Alberta's large land base makes it ideally suited to forage production. Cattle are grain fed, resulting in bright red meat and white fat, characteristics that produce a tender, juicy cut.

The province's 3.8 million cattle produce in excess of 40 percent of Canada's beef, only 25 percent of which is consumed by Albertans. The remaining 75 percent is sold to Quebec, British Columbia, Ontario, the United States, and Japan. The United States, Alberta's main competitor in the beef industry, often purchases up to 20 percent of the province's cattle production.

Alberta has also developed a reputation for the finest selection of breeding stock in the world. Nearly

4,000 head of purebred Alberta beef and dairy cattle were sold around the world in 1986, representing $7.8 million. Livestock genetics (semen and embryos) generated more than $10 million in sales in 1985.

Beef packing is the largest food-processing industry in Alberta. The ACC works closely with the manufacturing and retail industries to monitor consumer buying habits and attitudes. This has resulted in new packaging procedures and smaller portion sizes, along with a comprehensive national advertising campaign launched in 1986 to promote the nutritional value of beef.

The ACC unveiled new beef data in 1987 that shows the cholesterol level of Canadian beef to be dramatically lower than indicated in federal nutrition tables. The latest figures from Agriculture Canada prove that the fat content of beef is 49 percent lower than in the old federal nutrition tables, and that beef contains 21 percent less cholesterol.

The Alberta Cattle Commission is also directly involved with the public through its educational and promotional extension, the Beef Education Association. This organization, represented by volunteer beef producers, disseminates consumer information promoting beef at mall displays, trade and county fairs, and schools.

Beef packing is the largest food-processing industry in Alberta.

Photo by Larry Schaefer. Courtesy, Hillstrom Stock Photo

Scepter Manufacturing

Engineered Air

Engineered Profiles Ltd.

ITT Barton Instruments

Dow Chemical Canada Inc.

Labatt's Prairie Region

Standen's Limited

Gilbey Canada Inc.

*General Motors of Canada
Limited*

EDO Canada Ltd.

CHAPTER

Manufacturing

Producing goods for individuals and industry, manufacturing firms provide employment for many Alberta residents.

SCEPTER MANUFACTURING

Scepter Manufacturing, "the pipe dream that became a reality," is a saga of innovation and progress, a chronicle of individual initiative and enterprise. What began as a young immigrant's dream 37 years ago has since evolved into the world's leader in large-diameter PVC pipe extrusion technology. Today Scepter's products are used in the United States, throughout Europe, and across many other transnational borders, bringing Canadian pipe manufacturing expertise to the world.

This "plastic revolution" began with the manufacture of vinyl toys in the Toronto basement of Evold Torokvei in 1949, but Torokvei's fascination for new and improved applications led to an expansion into extruded and injection molded plastic products.. While Torokvei provided the innovative force for the dynamic expansion, it was the continuous hard work of his family and long-term employees that led to Scepter's current status as a vibrant, progressive company with 15 facilities throughout Canada and the United States, employing more than 800 people.

Early Scepter products included hula hoops, garden hoses, and wading pools, but these items gradually gave way to the manufacture of products in rigid polyvinyl chloride, an innovation putting corrosion-proof, waterproof, lightweight plastics to work in many diverse areas. Today plastic products are used almost everywhere, since they are light, easy to handle, and cost effective. Scepter's products range from the virtually indestructible soft drink and dairy case made of high-density polyethylene, to the perfected jerry can, used for safe, easy transport of flammable liquids such as gasoline or kerosene. Plastics have found their way into heavy industry, the military—almost everywhere imaginable.

The true enterprising success of Scepter is PVC pipe and fittings for municipal and industrial use, now considered the traditional pipe, replacing material such as concrete, as-

Scepter's Edmonton plant, recently expanded to 160,000 square feet, is a modern extrusion and injection-molding facility.

bestos cement, and iron. PVC pipe offers the best hydraulic performance with the lowest maintenance cost for an indefinite lifetime. *Scepter's unique extrusion process manufactures pipe diameters from one-half inch to 30 inches for practical transmission of water, sewage, and industrial processing.*

Another well-accepted use of rigid polyvinyl chloride has been in the electrical industry, where Scepter is a leader in designing and setting the standard for conduit, fittings, and fixtures in a wide variety of sizes. Scepter takes great pride in the fact that today electrical wiring can be installed anywhere, and can be left virtually maintenance-free.

The true success of Scepter is evidenced by many factors, notably its highly advanced research and development operation, responsible for design, material selection, production, and extensive testing. Complementing the effective research

and development capabilities lies an efficient distribution system that brings Scepter's broad range of industrial piping systems and electrical conduit systems to customers across Canada and the United States. This commitment to distribution is backed by manufacturing locations in Toronto, Montreal, and Edmonton.

Scepter's Edmonton plant, recently expanded to 160,000 square feet, is a modern extrusion and injection-molding facility, with a production capacity of 75 million pounds annually—the equivalent of running a pipeline from Edmonton to Toronto and back. Scepter is also proud to announce the opening of its newest warehouse and distribution facility in Calgary, built to better serve the needs of southern Alberta.

Scepter Manufacturing is truly a self-contained world of plastics, designed to meet any requirements at any or all stages of the process. Its tool-making facility, manufactur-

Scepter's newest warehouse and distribution facility in Calgary.

ing capabilities, coast-to-coast distribution centres, and strong commitment to research and development all contribute to Scepter's enormous industrial growth and growing list of satisfied customers.

"We are a company of the future, equal to the challenge, ready for tomorrow." From its humble basement beginning to its current status as a North American leader in PVC pipe and plastics, Scepter maintains that its success bears directly on the pride in quality that goes into every product. Scepter Manufacturing will never forget its modest beginnings, and the emphasis placed on care and quality stems from the cooperation among employer and employee—working together to keep the "pipe dream" alive and prospering.

ENGINEERED AIR

From computer rooms in high-rise offices to huge manufacturing plants to the corner fast-food outlet, Engineered Air provides Canada with controlled environments. A manufacturer of heating, air conditioning, ventilation, and refrigeration products for more than 20 years, Engineered Air serves commercial and industrial clients across Canada.

Since its incorporation in 1966 the company has established itself as a national organization with 11 sales offices across Canada. By focusing on custom design and manufacture rather than mass production and catalogue sales, Engineered Air has enjoyed a rate of growth unprecedented in the industry.

From an initial staff of five working in 2,000 square feet of leased space in Calgary, the firm has expanded to three factories with a total of 300 employees and more than 150,000 square feet of space. Sales have increased from $90,000 in the company's first year to $35 million today.

Engineered Air is an organization with a well-established policy of research and product development. From its original direct-fired heaters, manufactured in 1966, to a wide range of heating, ventilating, and air conditioning equipment, the company's products create the working environment for many Canadian industries.

Because of its adaptability to any job, Engineered Air can alter its product menu to suit market

With 300 employees Engineered Air has expanded to three factories encompassing more than 150,000 square feet of floor space.

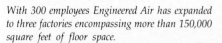

Engineered Air has manufactured quality heating, ventilating, air conditioning, and refrigeration equipment for commercial and industrial clients across Canada for more than 20 years.

trends. This ability to provide cost-effective, custom-made products gives the firm a competitive edge.

Engineered Air has also earned a reputation for producing reliable and durable equipment. Every unit is thoroughly tested before leaving the factory to ensure adherence to code standards, design specifications, and durability.

Attention to client need results in product innovation. Engineered Air has developed and manufactured a number of firsts in the industry, including the first low-pressure natural gas construction heater and the first single-fan, large-capacity, direct-fired makeup air equipment.

Engineered Air products can be found in many downtown office, commercial, and industrial sites in cities across Canada. The firm's involvement with major projects at the site of the 1986 World's Fair,

Vancouver, British Columbia; the 1988 Olympic Winter Games, Calgary, Alberta; and many other prominent Canadian locations, particularly with the supply of $13 million worth of equipment to an automobile manufacturer, has earned it international stature.

Engineered Air is expanding into U.S. and world markets. On an international level, the company's custom products may be found in locations as remote and diverse as the Antarctic, Tunisia, and Afghanistan.

In addition to its two Calgary factories, Engineered Air has a manufacturing plant in Newmarket, Ontario, with its own engineering, accounting, purchasing, production, and service departments. The Newmarket plant increases the firm's penetration of the eastern Canadian markets.

As a progressive company, Engineered Air encourages participation by all levels of management in the activities of industry-related associations. It is active in the field of education, maintaining representation on the Southern Alberta Institute of Technology Advisory Board, as well as working with technical and engineering schools across Canada. This kind of industry involvement, combined with a solid dedication to its employees, ensures Engineered Air of a strong leadership role in Alberta's economy.

ENGINEERED PROFILES LTD.

Incorporated on March 30, 1979, in Calgary, Engineered Profiles Ltd. manufactures custom-made extruded plastic products for the Canadian residential construction industry and has a proprietary product, the "enerpro" all-vinyl window system.

The company supplies moldings, tracks, weather stripping, and other products to Canadian and U.S. companies that manufacture wooden and aluminum window frames according to customer specifications. Engineered Profiles supplies its enerpro fabricators with extrusions that are used to construct finished all-vinyl windows for the housing market.

The two partners in the firm, Warren Hutchings and Glenn Syrowitz, moved to Alberta from Winnipeg in 1979 to take advantage of Calgary's booming economy. They opened a 5,000-square-foot plant in June 1979 and began manufacturing plastics with two extrusion lines. (Extrusion is a method of producing high-density, durable plastic products in which polyvinyl chloride pellets are heated and forced through metal dies.)

The bulk of the business in the early days of the company focused on custom work for fabricators in Alberta, British Columbia, Manitoba, and Saskatchewan. Engineered Profiles built its own dies and delivered extrusions throughout Western Canada on an ongoing basis. However, Hutchings and Syrowitz soon began looking for other products to manufacture during the winter months, when house building and construction in general were slow.

In the early 1980s the firm developed a two-inch-diameter polyvinyl chloride pipe for use in central vacuum systems in the Canadian housing market. The pipe is now produced and sold to more than 20 vacuum manufacturers throughout Canada and the United States.

Hutchings attended an equip-

An Engineered Profiles staff member performing a quality inspection on the plastic extrusion line.

ment and product show in Germany in the fall of 1983, returned to Calgary, and began work on a new window design. Using European equipment and tooling, Engineered Profiles began manufacturing polyvinyl chloride window frames. The company initially marketed this new product to two of its licenced fabricators in March 1985, and by 1987, 15 Canadian fabricators were manufacturing and distributing the new window system. Further expansion into Canada and the U.S. markets is planned.

The enerpro vinyl window system is unexcelled as a window-framing material, outperforming wood, steel, aluminum, and other metal framing products. Made of 100-percent vinyl, enerpro window frames are precision-engineered with hollow-core construction that traps air inside the frame. One of the most effective insulators, this

"dead air" works with the low heat conductivity of vinyl to produce a highly energy-efficient window.

Engineered Profiles originally designed the window system for the retrofit market, but the maintenance-free product is gaining popularity in the new-home market. Indal Building Products Ltd. is the firm's licenced fabricator in Calgary for the enerpro vinyl window system.

Engineered Profiles Ltd. has experienced growth every year since it began, and is now a multimillion-dollar manufacturer with a 30,000-square-foot plant and 35 employees. The firm supports the local economy by purchasing most of its raw materials within Alberta or elsewhere in Western Canada.

ITT BARTON INSTRUMENTS
A DIVISION OF ITT INDUSTRIES OF CANADA LTD.

ITT Barton Instruments, a manufacturing and international sales organization based in Calgary for more than 30 years, can trace its origin to a California inventor tinkering in his garage workshop.

It was in the 1920s that Barton Jones engineered a new flow meter for the local fire department. He soon found himself operating a full-scale manufacturing plant that produced a wide range of precision measurement instruments.

Today ITT Barton provides instrumentation for many industries, including petrochemical, oil and gas production and refining, pipeline transmission, pulp and paper, and nuclear energy.

If the right instrument doesn't exist, Barton engineers can design or enhance instruments to meet a customer's specific needs and standards of accuracy. The company can also call upon a stock of other manufacturers' products chosen for their quality, compatibility with Barton equipment, and ability to augment the Barton line.

A division of ITT Industries of Canada Ltd., the Calgary office manufactures the Barton product line, deriving 80 percent of its materials and components from Canadian sources. The current staff of 66 has more than quadrupled since ITT, a multinational corporation based in New York, acquired Barton Instruments in 1967.

The Calgary facility, which houses administrative offices as well as the manufacturing plant, has grown from 14,000 to 25,000 square feet, and further expansion is planned. Barton also rents an ad-

ITT Barton Instruments, a manufacturer and supplier of precision measurement instruments, has been based in Calgary for more than 30 years.

ditional 2,500 square feet for its nearby Calgary sales office, and runs a sales and service outlet in Edmonton.

As a manufacturer and supplier of process measurement and control technology, Barton employs sales agents worldwide. During an intensive training program Barton sales representatives spend several months in the factory, learning how instruments are built and calibrated. Then each representative spends an additional six months on the inside order desk to ensure a knowledge of the capabilities and applications of each instrument.

Barton also provides customers with a complete field service pro-

Field installation in Alberta of 202A recorders (below). The photo at right shows a 202A recorder enlarged.

An ITT Barton first-rate flow totalizer (above).

Shown here are 6000 series transmitters (left).

gram, assisting clients in instrument installation and start-up, as well as a comprehensive user training program either in the Barton factory or at the job site. And if a problem arises, the firm has the capability to get damaged equipment repaired, calibrated, and back into the client's system with a minimum delay.

The corporation exports 15 percent of its products, primarily to Southeast Asia and the Pacific Rim; smaller shipments are distributed to Europe and the United Kingdom. The need for precision and rugged reliability in process measurement and control makes Barton's Canadian-approved equipment especially desirable in foreign industry, where manufacturing standards are often less stringent.

Since 1979 the annual sales of the company have more than tripled, and, with the introduction of the new products, this growth is expected to continue. This success is due to the dedication of its employees, who ensure a high quality of product and service for Barton clients.

Barton has been particularly successful in identifying current trends in the marketplace, taking full advantage of its expertise in flow measurement and control. The firm has developed a microprocessor-based flow computer that is being marketed worldwide and a low-cost flow totalizer designed to measure gas flow from any frequency device. The company is constantly developing new products to meet client needs. With each technological advance comes a new line of Barton products.

As a Canadian company, Barton understands the needs and expectations of local industry, and product innovation is a sure way of attracting clientele. Just as important is fast turnaround time. A custom microprocessor-based flow computer, designed and marketed within 90 days, was conceived on a napkin over lunch with a potential client.

Barton also maintains a strong profile in the Alberta community. ITT Barton Instruments sponsors a girls' slow-pitch team, helps young entrepreneurs in the Junior Achievement organization, and donates money to the United Way and the handicapped. Management likes to see company funds used to benefit the local community directly. Barton also takes an active role in its industry, belonging to the Canadian Manufacturing Association and the Industrial Instrument Manufacturers' Association.

A Floco installation at Jumping Pound, Alberta.

DOW CHEMICAL CANADA INC.

Dow Chemical Canada Inc.— Western Canada Division—is one of North America's most modern petrochemical complexes. In Fort Saskatchewan, Dow weds its advanced technology with Alberta's vast resources to supply the world with a broad range of chemicals and plastics.

An autonomous, fully integrated, world-scale operation, Dow's Western Canada Division houses six interrelated plants operating around the clock at maximum efficiency to achieve high yields at competitive costs. Three billion pounds of petrochemical products worth $500 million are shipped annually to Canadian and international markets worldwide.

Starting with salt, air, water, electricity, and natural gas, Dow produces basic chemicals used in the manufacture of a wide variety of industrial materials and consumer items, ranging from disposable diapers, plastic raincoats, and aluminum utensils to plastic food containers, automobile upholstery, and residential siding. One well-known Dow product straight from the Fort Saskatchewan plant is StyroFoam* brand foam insulation.

The history of this Dow com-

plex dates back well over two decades, when Dow recognized Western Canada's need for petrochemicals in the agriculture, oil and gas, and lumber industries, and set up in Alberta, taking full advantage of the province's vast salt and petrochemical resources. In the early 1970s Dow made a long-term commitment to Western Canada, launching a $1.2-billion natural gas pro-

While highly autonomous, Dow's Western Canada Division enjoys the benefits of membership in Dow's global family, including the advanced technology and expertise that have made Dow a global leader.

gram and the $350-million Cochin pipeline—with Dow Fort Saskatchewan sitting at the head of this 3,058-kilometre pipeline. In addition, the firm designed and assisted in the start-up of two Alberta Gas plants at Joffre to supply major feedstock, ethylene.

And growth at Dow Fort Saskatchewan continues: A world-scale polyethylene plant opened in 1985, additional research and development facilities in 1986, and major expansions of polyethylene and ethylene oxide in 1987.

Throughout Dow's petrochemical expansion, the company has maintained and strengthened ties with the community, ensuring that Fort Saskatchewan remains a safe, prosperous, and pleasant place to live. Through its community outreach program, neighbors and visitors alike are invited to tour the facilities and to learn the many intricacies of the chemical complex.

Dow emergency resources such as fire equipment, trained personnel, and training programs are available to the City of Fort Saskatchewan and to other industrial companies operating in the vicinity. Further to this, Dow's concern for worker health and safety and environmental protection has led to the implementation of an innovative program. The program represents a major commitment to prevention as a primary factor in minimizing health and safety problems. And Dow's commitment to the environment has resulted in more than $2 million for environmental monitoring—and a dedication to meeting and surpassing legislated environmental standards.

Dow's technology forms the backbone of the firm's success. More than 5,000 of Dow's 50,000 employees worldwide are involved in research and development; Dow Fort Saskatchewan is no exception. Researchers conduct both basic and applied research in a central on-site facility as well as research on behalf of each of the six plants.

Research efforts in Alberta are primarily related to products used in the pulp and paper and oil and gas industries, and are directed toward improving product quality and plant performance. Western Canada's research efforts are further enhanced by the company's worldwide research network, bringing international expertise to Western Canada and, more specifically, to Western Canadian customers.

Customer satisfaction is Dow's guiding principle; commitment to its customers and to the continuing growth of Alberta's petrochemical industry are fundamental aspects of the firm's successful operation. It is Dow's commitment to growth and expansion that contributes to long-term security for its suppliers, which, in turn, assures Dow's long-term feedstock supply at internationally competitive prices. This guaranteed long-term security, coupled with Dow's highly competent, versatile work force, will guarantee both quality products and satisfied customers now and in the future.

*Trademark of The Dow Chemical Company

Basic chemicals produced by Dow at Fort Saskatchewan are used in the manufacture of a wide range of familiar household items and their packaging.

LABATT'S PRAIRIE REGION

John Labatt is a broadly based food and beverage corporation with interest in three major industrial groups: brewing, agri products, and packaged foods. It is, however, Labatt's breweries that are the most widely recognized aspect of this multifaceted company, with 12 breweries operating coast to coast in Canada; a network of 400 distributors in the United States; and, most recently, plans for further sales expansion abroad.

An Irish immigrant, John Labatt began brewing in Canada in 1847, immediately recognizing the potential for expansion across the new country. He could not possibly foresee the tremendous potential for expansion abroad, but luckily his successors did.

Today Labatt Breweries brews and markets 39 brands of beer, including national brands such as the ever-popular Blue, Labatt's 50, Budweiser, John Labatt Classic, and Labatt's Lite, which accounts for most of the firm's sales. Important regional brands include Keith's in the Maritimes, Club in Manitoba and Alberta, Kokanee in British Columbia,

and Blue Light in Ontario. In the United States, Labatt Importers markets a number of Labatt brands in 45 states through its huge distribution network, while its new operating unit, Labatt Breweries of Europe, will increase the focus of international expansion by identifying and developing opportunities in the United Kingdom and in Europe.

Labatt's boasts enormous success in its brewing endeavors. In the very competitive brewing market, Labatt increased its market share for the third consecutive year in 1987 to more than 41 percent—thanks to Blue, Canada's most popular beer. In the United States, Labatt Importers outpaced other Canadian brewers in the imports segment with volume gains of 9 percent over the previous year. The key to this success is a business philosophy that incorporates the principle of divisional autonomy, coupled with the hiring of superior employees.

Since John Labatt's stresses a decentralized management approach, it follows that the company attracts

highly motivated and competitive managers, capable of addressing opportunities in different businesses in different geographic areas. This autonomy in the many and varied branches of Labatt's has given the company a strong business base and has given Labatt's 16,200 employees the initiative, creativity, and spirit to assure continued success.

One shining example of regional initiative is witnessed by the Prairie Region's Olympic Experience Caravan. As a proud sponsor of Calgary's 1988 Winter Olympics, Labatt's sought to bring the spirit of the Olympics to all Albertans in every corner of the province via this majestic travelling caravan.

Believing that the thrill of the Olympics should not be solely restricted to the residents of Calgary, Labatt's Prairie Region conceived the plan of creating a mobile exhi-

This travelling Olympic Experience Caravan treated Albertans to a simulated 125-kilometres-per-hour bobsleigh ride by using a television monitor and motor mechanisms. The ride is similar to the new course at Canada Olympic Park in Calgary.

Labatt's Alberta Brewery is located in Edmonton and will celebrate its 25th year of operation in 1989.

bition to promote the various facets of the Olympic Winter Games. Within the caravan, pictures and displays told the story of various events in the Olympic Winter Games, which created a sense of excitement and anticipation for the XV Games in Calgary in February 1988.

Throughout the summer of 1987 this huge caravan, an 18-wheel tractor-trailer unit with a carrying capacity of 45,000 pounds, ventured all over Western Canada recounting the exciting story of the Olympic Winter Games. One major drawing card to the caravan was the simulated ride on the Labatt's bobsleigh. Through the use of a TV monitor and motor mechanism, visitors thrilled to the first-hand feel of the 125-kilometre-per-hour trip around the twists and turns of the new course at Canada Olympic Park.

Labatt's keen interest in the Olympics is symbolic of its vested interest in sports. Sporting events have always been integral to the operation of Labatt's, perhaps because the two, sports and beer, go hand in hand. In any case, the company's passion for sporting events is evidenced by its outside investments, notably The Sports Network (TSN) and the Toronto Blue Jays baseball team.

TSN, with more than one million Canadian subscribers, is a wholly owned Labatt subsidiary, a 24-hour specialty programming service delivered to viewers via cable-television systems. Featuring coverage of professional baseball, hockey, and football, and many other professional and amateur sports, this service is uniquely complemented by Labatt's 45-percent partnership interest in the Blue Jay's baseball team.

Labatt's sporting affiliations are perhaps more a welcome relief from the intense competition in the brewing industry. But competition, as any true entrepreneur knows, separates the weak from the strong—with only the strong surviving. The Canadian brewing industry is expected to remain intensely compet-

Labatt Breweries brews and markets 39 brands of beer, but it is the ever-popular Blue that is Canada's favorite.

itive in future years, but John Labatt plans to strengthen and increase its position as Canada's leading brewer by maintaining its superior strategies of operation, while at the same time pursuing opportunities for growth in international markets.

STANDEN'S LIMITED

The advent of the automobile in the 1920s created many business opportunities for aspiring Calgary entrepreneurs. Cyril Standen and his father, William, took advantage of this new invention by learning to adapt their blacksmithing and harness-making skills to the automobile maintenance field. That decision resulted in the creation of Standen's Limited in 1924, one of the most successful spring-manufacturing firms in North America today.

A harness maker from England, William Standen came to Calgary in 1912 with his eldest son, Val, and spent the winter in a tent on the banks of the Bow River. The rest of the family joined them a year later, and it was then that son Cyril decided to become a blacksmith.

Cyril Standen obtained much of his early experience in a basement workshop in the Standen home. There, at the age of 15, he worked on a borrowed anvil, forging steel inserts for cowboy boots. His first business was sharpening skates for 15 cents a pair, and he later went to work at a Calgary blacksmith shop.

Standen's Limited began as a partnership in July 1924 with only $600. The first location was a two-stall stable in the backyard of the Standen home in southeast Calgary. Cyril picked up a second-hand forge for two dollars, borrowed an anvil, improvised a blower, and used his skate grinder motor to operate it. Cyril and his father often visited the city dump in search of springs and scraps of iron and steel, and it wasn't long before Cyril made his own set of tools.

Cyril's brother Alec joined the family business in 1929, and within 10 years brothers Sid and Reg were also welcomed aboard. Although a shop addition was completed in 1935, a fire destroyed the roof, and by 1938 Standen's opened a new fac-

The increasing popularity of the automobile in the 1920s inspired the inception of Standen's Limited. Today the Calgary spring-manufacturing firm is one of the most successful in North America.

tory. Expansions were made in 1943 and again 10 years later, and a frame and alignment shop was added in 1959.

In March 1970 a five-alarm fire destroyed the southeast Calgary factory, but within six weeks Standen's was installing new equipment under a temporary roof. In 1974 the company celebrated its 50th birthday by moving into a new 90,000-square-foot plant on a 7.5-acre site at 58th Avenue and 11th Street, Southeast. The number of employees jumped from 85 to 120 almost overnight. By 1987 Standen's had grown to a work force of 260 and a payroll of $6 million, and the plant has since expanded to include a total of 130,000 square feet.

Standen's Limited is today one of the largest leaf spring manufacturers in North America. The firm also leads the industry in the use of computer-assisted design and manufacture, a system that ensures precise specifications are met on each order. A total of 65,000 square feet of the plant space is dedicated to spring manufacture, with an annual consumption of 23,000 tons of spring steel.

Standen's has a dealer network across Canada. Although steel spring products remain the back-

The totally integrated axle division produces an extensive line of axles for recreational and industrial trailers.

One of Standen's skilled technicians performs heavy-duty spring forming.

bone of the business, the company also manufactures and exports an extensive line of products for light agricultural, recreational, and industrial trailers. Standen's industrial balancing department is the largest and most modern in North America, and can balance anything that revolves, from four ounces in weight to 9,000 pounds.

The plant also includes a fully equipped tool and die shop that complements a strong engineering department. This enables Standen's to carry through every type of custom order, from design to finished product. Much of the firm's special machinery and equipment has been engineered and constructed in house. During every production run, state-of-the-art equipment is in constant use, performing tests for such factors as fatigue, impact, hardness, and stress.

And the company's just-in-time delivery method of manufacturing has given it a competitive advantage. The firm will match delivery of its products to a client's production schedule, reducing inventory to days instead of months. Because manufacturing lines at the plant

can be changed or modified to place production strength where it is most needed, Standen's can react quickly to unexpected client demand.

The majority of the firm's employees learn their trade on the job, and many have worked up to positions of responsibility. Mel Svendsen, formerly plant superintendent, has climbed the corporate ladder to become general manager. In the same vein, one of Standen's most

significant management moves came in 1967, when Cyril decided to appoint two younger employees as directors. J.P. Iozzi, who had joined the firm in 1944, was made vice-president/manufacturing, and W.A. Kilbourn, who started in 1959 as frame and alignment service manager, was made vice-president/operations.

In 1967 Sid and Reg Standen retired. Iozzi and Kilbourn bought out the retired brothers' share of the company, and later on also bought out Cyril and Alec Standen, who remain involved as directors. Despite these ownership changes, Standen's is still a family business. Kilbourn married Cyril's daughter, and their son, Douglas, is assistant general manager.

Standen's Limited contributes financially to many worthwhile causes such as youth groups, handicapped children, and the Junior Achievement of Southern Alberta Association. The company is also a member of the Society of Automotive Engineers and the Spring Research Institute of America.

The heat-treating and assembly section of the plant.

GILBEY CANADA INC.

The opening of the $12-million Palliser Distillery in Lethbridge in 1973 marked the beginning of a major industry in southern Alberta, and the biggest investment ever made by parent company Gilbey Canada Inc.

In operation in Canada since 1933, Gilbey had built a solid market for its famous brands such as Smirnoff and Black Velvet. The company wished to establish a second plant to supplement expanding markets in the western United States.

The selection of Lethbridge as the site of the new distillery was related to the fact that the region had all the necessary resources—adequate supplies of energy fuels for power requirements, proximity to both Canadian and U.S. markets, good water sources, a surrounding farming area capable of producing all needed varieties of high-quality grains, and a substantial and readily available labor pool.

One of the most modern distilleries in Canada with more than 60 employees, Palliser sits on 50 acres of land in Lethbridge's northeast industrial park. The name Palliser was chosen for its close ties with Western Canadian history. Its namesake, Captain John Palliser, was instrumental in the establishment of the Canadian Trans-Continental Railway system that exists today. The Palliser Triangle, situated in the Canadian Rockies, was named after this legendary pioneer.

The Palliser plant incorporates the most up-to-date facilities and techniques available to the industry—automated control systems for unloading, storing, milling, and measuring grain, and extremely precise, computer-controlled systems to govern production from a central control room. The integrated plant handles the entire distilling process, from unloading the bulk grain to loading the packaged, labelled, and bottled goods for shipment to the consumer.

The Lethbridge distillery, with a capacity of 10 million litres, produces rums, ryes, vodkas, and gins. Three vast warehouses can accommodate up to 300,000 oak barrels of whisky, which mature for periods ranging from four to 10 years. The plant supplies Palliser and Gilbey brands to markets from Manitoba west, including the Yukon and the Northwest Territories.

Palliser also ships Black Velvet Canadian Rye Whisky to the western United States. Other company brands include Smirnoff Vodka (the best-selling spirit brand in Canada), Popov Vodka, Gilbey's London Dry Gin, Green Island White Rum, J&B Scotch, and John Palliser Liquor.

As the Canadian arm of International Distillers and Vintners (IDV), which in turn is a division of the Grand Metropolitan Group of companies based in London, England, Palliser is also able to market internationally well-known brands such as Cinzano from Italy; Le Piat D'or from France; Almaden, Inglenook, and Beaulieu Vineyards wines from California; and Cuervo Tequila from Mexico.

When the Palliser plant opened in 1973, annual sales of Canadian whisky in Canada were more than 7.5 million cases. Gilbey, with Palliser, was selling 7.8 percent of the total. As the 1970s progressed, however, the whisky market began to slacken. Changing life-styles and consumer tastes were part of this gradual decline. North America was becoming diet and fitness conscious, and as for liquor consumption, moderation was the rage.

Gilbey's eagerly met this challenge by researching and developing new brands to replace the "brown goods" (rye and rum) section of the market. In the late 1970s the company obtained the Canadian rights to the success story of the era—Bailey's Irish Cream. Here was a novel idea from Ireland developed by Gilbey's parent company, IDV. The new cream and whisky combination was a success in Ireland, as well as in all the other countries to which it was introduced, including Canada. From an early sale of just 50 cases on private order from Ireland in the first year, Bai-

The Palliser Distillers sits on a 50-acre site in Lethbridge's northeast industrial park. Three vast warehouses can each accommodate 100,000 barrels.

Gilbey's Smirnoff Vodka is bottled at the Palliser Distillers plant in Lethbridge.

ley's has risen to a commanding 200,000 cases per year in Canada alone.

The company's Malibu Coconut Rum liqueur is another example of a product that took the market by storm. Now familiar in more than 80 countries, there are few brands that have been so successful in such a relatively short period of time. Malibu, produced in the Lethbridge plant, may have initially benefited from the pina colada boom of the late 1970s, but it is now enjoyed with orange, lemonade, grapefruit, lemon, or wild cranberry juices.

In 1982 Gilbey took another major step in a time when many distillers were losing money. The company bought an interest in Canada's oldest winery, Barnes Wines. It was a daring move, but the increasing emphasis on lighter products had given the Canadian wine industry a new vigor. The result was a series of wines that seriously challenged the European imports at a much more competitive price. Once again, Gilbey had made a wise move.

One of the keys to Gilbey's success has been its practice of brand-building. The firm advertises brand names rather than its products. As a result, Smirnoff and Bailey's are known worldwide.

As one of the top three distillers

Gilbey acts as a Canadian agent and distributor for a wide range of products.

in Canada, Gilbey also keeps a close eye on consumer tastes. The industry trend during the past few years has changed from cream liqueurs, to white and fruit-flavored wine spritzers, to Peach Schnapps. Colby's entry into the Schnapps market under the brand name Archer's has been successful in Canada and around the world. Both the Toronto and Lethbridge plants experiment with new tastes and novel packaging ideas to maintain Gilbey's strong hold in the marketplace.

Embarking on its 55th year of operation, Gilbey Canada has grown from a simple gin distiller employing 14 people to one of the most important corporations in Canada. Today 360 people in two modern distilleries produce 1.8 million cases of distilled spirits per year for Canadian customers, as well as 2 million cases of Black Velvet for the United States and the rest of the world.

Gilbey, through Palliser Distillers Limited, is also active within the community, supporting a variety of cultural, educational, and athletic causes. The company contributes to the Southern Alberta Art Gallery and the Lethbridge Symphony Orchestra, and sponsors scholarships at the University of Lethbridge and the Lethbridge Community College. Gilbey Canada Inc. is also the sponsor of the Smirnoff Cup at Spruce Meadows in Calgary, the site of one of the world's premiere horse show jumping competitions.

GENERAL MOTORS OF CANADA LIMITED

In recent years General Motors of Canada has been building for its future, a future that holds both competitive challenges and bright promise.

To meet these ever-increasing competitive challenges from automotive manufacturers around the world, General Motors maintains a cross-Canada emphasis on new people development programs, innovative technological advances, and synchronous manufacturing systems linking production directly with suppliers.

General Motors is the world's

Adopting a dual role in securing customer satisfaction General Motors has established regional marketing offices in Calgary, complemented by the new 250,000-square-foot Western Regional Distribution Centre housed in Edmonton, a city recognized for its strategic location as a warehouse/ distribution centre for Western Canada.

largest automobile manufacturing company with operations extending across North America. General Motors Canada was fostered in 1907, when William Crapo Durant sought to extend American activities at that time by purchasing a 40-percent interest in the newly created McLaughlin Motor Car Company in Oshawa, Ontario. The name McLaughlin refers to R. Samuel McLaughlin, who together with Durant created the basis for the future General Motors of Canada, focusing early on the Buick line of car production.

Today automobile products from General Motors Canada range from the highly reputed Buick, Oldsmobile, and Cadillac lines—to popular models in the lines of Chevrolet, Pontiac, and, as recently as 1986, a joint venture with Suzuki.

To ensure these products are

distributed effectively and efficiently across Canada, and that the needs of all customers are met, General Motors has adopted a new market-driven approach recognizing the very different economic and marketing climates in the various regions of the country.

In response to the varying demands of customers throughout Canada, three regional marketing offices have been established in Toronto, Montreal, and Calgary. Calgary representatives note that their marketing office for the province of Alberta will enhance the effectiveness of their long-term marketing plans through a special emphasis on customer needs.

In Alberta, General Motors has adopted a dual role to secure customer satisfaction. The corporation takes care of its customers with the regional marketing office in Cal-

gary, complemented by a Parts Distribution Centre housed in Edmonton.

The city of Edmonton is well recognized for its strategic location as a warehousing/distribution centre for Western Canada, and General Motors chose the city of Edmonton as the location for its Parts Distribution Centre for this reason. According to economists, northern Alberta presents the greatest opportunity for economic expansion and market development. With more than 60 percent of the parts distribution business conducted from Red Deer north and with excellent highway arteries to northern and central Brit-

ish Columbia and Saskatchewan, Edmonton is the natural choice.

Serving the 225 General Motors dealers and 40 AC/Delco distributors in Alberta and Saskatchewan with their daily parts requirements quickly and efficiently, General Motors' Edmonton centre believes its parts supply service is the best in the industry. Parts not in stock in Edmonton are shipped by Air Canada cargo daily from the National Parts Distribution Centre in Woodstock, Ontario.

Both Calgary's marketing office and Edmonton's distribution centre work cooperatively to service the needs of Western Canadians. This

General Motors' sales department in Calgary is one of three regional marketing offices established in Canada by the company. Along with branches in Toronto and Montreal, the Calgary office will enhance the effectiveness of its long-term marketing plans through a special emphasis on customer needs.

attention to service is all part of GM's commitment to the future and to the success of the company. "GM—A pledge to Canada, and example to the world," is setting standards of quality and service that will guarantee it a prominent position in the international automotive marketplace.

EDO CANADA LTD.

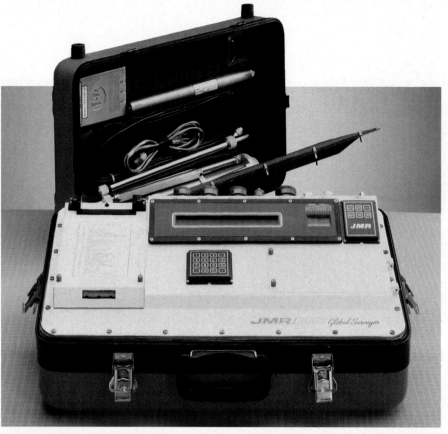

From modest beginnings in Calgary in 1978, EDO Canada Ltd. has grown into a multidivision, high-technology company servicing the international aerospace and defence industries. Jointly owned by EDO Corporation of New York and the Alberta Government, EDO Canada has three divisions specializing in the areas of electronics, fibre composites, and structural ceramics. The Alberta Government purchased an equity interest in the company in 1987 as part of its efforts in nurturing high-technology industries in the province. EDO Canada's involvement in satellite navigation systems dates back to 1979, when it opened its facility in Calgary as JMR Instruments Canada Ltd. Its mandate at that time was to expand the manufacturing and design capabilities of JMR Instruments Inc., a company known for its involvement with the Navy Navigational Satellite System. In July 1983 EDO Corporation of New York acquired JMR Instruments and immediately consolidated all former JMR businesses under the name EDO Canada Ltd. At that time EDO Canada was primarily involved in technology relating to the positioning and navigation of surface ships and vessels using both earth and space sensors.

Keeping pace with new technology, EDO began marketing its first Global Positioning System (GPS) product, SatTrak, in 1985. SatTrak is a fully portable and durable receiver capable of accurately positioning both stationary and moving objects. The system is used for the navigation of land vehicles and surface ships.

Further development in GPS hardware is continuing with Geo-Trak, a product that will address the needs of the geodetic industry. The unit will provide the geodetic survey community with precise, three-dimensional positioning using information it receives by simultaneously tracking up to seven different satellites. GeoTrak will also

be used for general land navigation and offshore positioning.

Caliper II, a software package being developed to support GeoTrak, will load data from field cassettes or receivers and archive the raw data on a storage medium for later processing by the user.

In 1980 EDO became involved in a Canadian Department of National Defence development program known as MINS (Marine Inte-

ABOVE: The JMR-2000 Global Surveyor—a Portable Satellite Doppler Positioning Instrument.

LEFT: Model 6051 MINS (Marine Integrated Navigation System).

grated Navigation System). EDO was contracted to develop a low-cost navigation system to meet the need for increased navigational accuracy of the Canadian Navy. The first version, MINS-A, was successfully tested at sea during the summer of 1982, and as a result of those trials, the MINS program was expanded in scope to add refinements to the system.

In 1984 EDO Canada was awarded the MINS-BII contract. This upgraded MINS, with a number of key features, including reduced package size, increased performance, and built-in self-test and maintenance software, resulted in a Marine Integrated Navigation System that exceeded the original design goals of the Canadian Navy.

In 1987 EDO Canada was awarded a production contract to equip the Navy's surface vessels with the new MINS system. This advanced navigation technology provides estimates of positioning and velocity from a variety of inputs. The MINS technology is being promoted to other NATO countries, including the U.S. Navy.

The Navigation Technology Division is also supplying eight Automatic Position Correlators (APC) to the Land Electronic Warfare Group of the Canadian Army. The APC incorporates EDO Canada's GPS technology and hardware, and will be used for the positioning and navigation of electronic warfare vehicles.

EDO Canada underwent a major expansion of its facilities in 1988, which included the addition of an advanced materials manufacturing

The winding process for filament-wound structures.

A wide variety of sizes and configurations of structural ceramics are offered by EDO Canada Ltd.

facility. The company uses high-performance plastic resins and fibres to produce products for the high-technology market, and manufactures heat- and corrosion-resistant structural ceramic products primarily for use in the aerospace industry.

The research and development initiative of EDO's U.S. counterpart has allowed it to remain at the forefront of composite technology. EDO has pioneered filament-winding techniques to develop new composite products such as commercial aircraft waste tanks, and extremely strong fuel tanks, and fabrication and molding techniques to help expand the use of laminated composites in the transportation and military markets.

EDO's filament-wound parts range from hand-held components to items weighing as much as 8,000 pounds. The firm manufactures products able to withstand temperatures well beyond the capabilities of most alloys, coupled with strength and durability far surpassing that of metals.

One of the most promising and exciting new product develop-

ments at EDO Canada is a class of advanced materials, commonly known as Technical Ceramics. In reality, these materials should be classified as Super Ceramic Alloys because of their phenomenal physical characteristics, extreme hardness, high-strength retention, and resistance to abrasion at higher temperatures than traditional metals.

EDO Canada is assembling a core of technology, through licences gained from inside and outside the EDO Corporation, that can effectively address the requirements of this expanding market. EDO's goal is to apply structural ceramics to the problems of the modern aerospace and military marketplace.

EDO Canada Ltd. has assumed a global mandate with products mainly targeted for export opportunities outside Alberta. With the equity investment by the Alberta Government and the support of the EDO Corporation in the United States, EDO Canada is fast becoming a major supplier to the aerospace industry. The company will substantially increase employment opportunities for Albertans in this high-technology sector.

Alberta Chamber of Commerce

Alberta Blue Cross

First Calgary Financial Savings and Credit Union Ltd.

Bennett Jones

Burnet, Duckworth & Palmer

Alberta Stock Exchange

Herman J. Bell Associates Architects Inc.

McLennan Ross

Graham McCourt

Clarkson Gordon / Woods Gordon

The Cohos Evamy Partnership

Edmonton Economic Development Authority

Thorne Ernst & Whinney

CHAPTER **10**

Business and Professions

Financial institutions, realtors and real-estate developers, architects, engineers, accountants, and attorneys all provide essential services to the province.

THE ALBERTA CHAMBER OF COMMERCE

The Alberta Chamber of Commerce speaks for the business sector as the only viable voice that lobbies to promote and support their interests in the province. The survival of all business, large and small, is dependent upon government thrust and legislation, and it is the Alberta Chamber of Commerce that ensures the interests of business are kept in the forefront of any government initiatives.

As the primary lobby group for business, the Alberta Chamber of Commerce provides a unifying force through its promotion of commercial, industrial, civic, and agricultural interests, while working for effective legislation and adminstration at all government levels.

Primary areas of concern include:

—simplification of tax regulations and minimization of any negative impact tax reform may have on small business and the individual.
—reduction of the federal and provincial government debt to restore confidence in Canada's ability to compete internationally.
—establishment of a national agricultural policy.
—freer trade across the United States border and the expansion of Canadian markets worldwide.

Maintaining close contact with key officials in the legislature, government departments and agencies, advisory boards, and leaders in both labor and management, the Alberta Chamber of Commerce believes that access to information ensures the concerns of business are recognized and acted upon.

The Alberta Chamber of Commerce establishes and maintains a reciprocating relationship with local community chambers and Alberta business in order to lobby effectively on behalf of business at the municipal, provincial, and na-

tional level.

Governments create legislation. The Alberta Chamber of Commerce works on behalf of every business in Alberta, seeking to foster a business climate that minimizes the need for government intervention.

The chamber actively supports and promotes Canada's system of private enterprise by utilizing the full potential of the private enterprise system and enabling chamber members to accomplish collectively

Alberta Chamber of Commerce president Dick Parr (right) meets with the Canadian Chamber of Commerce president Roger Hamel.

what no one could do individually.

Receiving a variety of input ranging from the complex policy of the federal taxation system to requests for assistance with trade shows from local chambers, the Alberta Chamber of Commerce stays abreast of all situations, keeping the businesses of the province informed and aware.

Alberta Chamber of Commerce executives participate in the Annual General Meeting, held in Fort McMurray in 1987.

ALBERTA BLUE CROSS

Blue Cross is both a symbolic emblem and a national health benefit program that is recognized and respected by Canadians as a protection plan from major and minor health care costs. Celebrating its 40th anniversary in 1988, Alberta Blue Cross owes its success to the dedication of its staff and their commitment to excellence.

Today Blue Cross-administered benefit programs are in place in major businesses and among employees across Canada. Through these locally administered but nationally coordinated prepaid programs, employers provide a comprehensive range of health benefits that supplement basic provincial government-sponsored health plans.

In Alberta the idea of a prepaid hospital plan originated with Dr. A.F. Anderson, superintendent of the Royal Alexandra Hospital in Edmonton. He brought the idea back with him from a trip to the United States in 1934 and, as a result, convinced Edmonton hospitals to form the Edmonton Group Hospitalization Board (E.G.H.B.). The board consisted of the Royal Alexandra, University, Misericordia, and Edmonton General hospitals.

Prepaid hospital care was a novel idea for its time. During the Great Depression many people who required medical attention avoided it because they could not pay for it. An experiment undertaken by a group of teachers in the United States dramatically changed this situation when each teacher paid a small fee to the hospital in exchange for 21 days of care for any sick or injured teacher. The experiment worked, and the concept of paying in advance for hospital and medical services spread rapidly. The idea took on a name and sponsor: Blue Cross.

By 1947 the Alberta Hospital Association, or the Associated Hospitals of Alberta as it was known then, decided the plan should be implemented provincewide through the E.G.H.B. In 1948 the provincial government passed the Associated Hospitals of Alberta Act, and the Blue Cross Plan got under way. Today in excess of 5,000 satisfied employer groups participate in the benefits plan. Blue Cross' state-of-the-art claims system ensures customer satisfaction—from the giant corporations to small businesses, labor unions, and associations.

A network of six Alberta branch offices with 275 staff members is the largest Western Canadian provider of prepaid group health, dental, vision care, and travel benefits plans. In addition, individual plans for travel, student accident and travel, hospitals, and prescription drug services are offered. Alberta

Blue Cross Place—home of Alberta Blue Cross and the Alberta Hospital Association.

Blue Cross annually pays out more than $200 million in claims.

Alberta Blue Cross prides itself on its pragmatic and ethical management philosophy. Its reputation for honesty and a straightforward approach to the health business has left in excess of one million Albertans more than satisfied with the plan. Strictly a private business, Blue Cross' strength lies in its positive working relationship with hospitals, pharmacists, optometrists, and dentists—a relationship based on mutual cooperation for the best provision of quality service.

FIRST CALGARY FINANCIAL SAVINGS AND CREDIT UNION LTD.

First Calgary Financial represents a turning point in the history of Alberta's financial institutions. With the amalgamation of seven Calgary credit unions, First Calgary Financial was formed to provide a centralized administration and to increase the range of services available to members.

Credit unions have played an important role in Alberta communities for many years. While the majority of Alberta credit unions are growing and profitable organizations, the economic downturn in the early 1980s slowed the growth of others.

All Alberta credit unions are members of a $41-billion system that includes central organizations at the provincial level and the Canadian Co-operative Credit Society nationally. The provincial centrals and national organization provide liquidity support and other financial services.

Today First Calgary has 18 branches across the city and provides members with comprehensive financial services ranging from everyday banking to personal financial planning. The creation of the new organization has allowed for

improved quality of service, innovation and development, and financial strength to protect against future economic reversals.

Albertans are not strangers to hard times. The province's first credit unions were established during the Great Depression. Commercial banks were reluctant at that

One of a series of billboards that ran in Calgary to create awareness of First Calgary Financial.

time to give credit to working people in need of financial assistance. Albertans responded by grouping together and pooling their own resources, creating a fund that would provide members of the co-operative with loans and mortgages. Thus, the credit union system began.

Wholly owned by their members, Alberta's credit unions have provided a vital service for more than 50 years. And unlike other financial institutions, whose deposits flow to head offices outside the province, the credit unions put members' deposits to work in Alberta's economy. Deposits in First Calgary Financial are protected by the Credit Union Stabilization Corporation of Alberta. All deposits are fully guaranteed.

Every member, regardless of his or her financial standing, is entitled to a voice in the organization's af-

An inside view of the 17th Avenue branch.

Alberta's credit unions have been responsible for a number of firsts in the financial world: the first in Canada to establish deposit guarantees, the first to install automated tellers, the first to develop a daily interest savings account, and the first to accept weekly payments on open mortgages.

First Calgary Financial draws a wide membership from Calgary and the surrounding area. Fifty percent of the company's current membership are between the ages of 25 and 44. The firm plans to concentrate on its existing membership and small businesses, eventually expanding to special packages for young people and seniors.

This First Calgary Financial branch is located in the Kensington area (left).

The Trans Canada branch is on the main floor of this building, while the administration office is located on the second floor (below).

fairs. Through democratic participation in annual meetings and the election of a board of directors, each member has a fair and equal say in how the credit union is run.

First Calgary Financial is one of the largest credit union systems in Canada, with more than 300 employees and combined deposits of more than $400 million. Members benefit from the convenience of citywide branches, automated teller service, and more in-branch services than ever before. First Calgary Financial also offers a variety of new services, including income tax preparation, personal financial planning, RRSPs, and a credit card service.

With expansion on the horizon, First Calgary Financial is exploring the possibilities of establishing even more services, such as direct-mail campaigns offering special merchandise to members and an improved credit card deposit service for business clients. A small-business package, incorporating loans, seminars, and similar services, is also planned.

BENNETT JONES

The origins of the firm date back to the 1890s, before the Province of Alberta came into existence, to the Calgary law practice of Sir James Lougheed and R.B. Bennett.

The business was reorganized in 1922 with R.B. Bennett (late Prime Minister of Canada from 1930 to 1935), Alexander Hannah, and P.L. Sanford as partners. Bennett Jones has since grown to become one of the largest law firms in Canada, with offices in Calgary, Edmonton, and Saskatoon.

The firm is organized into a number of departments, including corporate commercial, litigation, natural resources, taxation, real estate, estate planning, and a legal research group. Each client is the responsibility of a specified partner or partner group, ensuring continuity and coordination of services.

The firm's clients include large financial, natural resource, energy, oil and gas, manufacturing, transportation, and utility corporations, as well as many small and medium-size businesses. Limited partnerships and other joint ventures, together with consortia, both domestic and international, constitute another major client group. In the noncorporate sector, the firm acts for nonprofit foundations and associations, federal and provincial government agencies, and for many individuals with respect to their business, professional, and personal needs.

Bennett Jones is equipped with the latest in office technology, including modern computer, word-processing, printing, and communication systems. This ensures delivery of service to the client in a timely, reliable, and cost-efficient fashion.

The largest department at Bennett Jones is the corporate commercial group, which offers experience and ability to clients ranging from the biggest corporations to small businesses and proprietorships. The firm advises in matters such as banking, securities, mergers, acquisi-

tions, and reorganizations, and provides counsel on international and constitutional aspects of the client's affairs.

Much of the firm's commercial practice involves business forma-

tion, contracts and leases, the enforceability of obligations, and includes the effect of relevant legislation. Bennett Jones acts as counsel to a number of chartered banks and lending institutions. Members of the corporate commercial group specializing in securities law have considerable experience with private financings and public equity and debt offerings. The firm also acts in all aspects of negotiated corporate mergers.

The firm has acted in many corporate reorganizations, and has been called upon to give advice with respect to disposition of assets or subsidiaries, and the consolidation of operations. Increasingly, Bennett Jones is advising both domestic and foreign clients on the provisions and scope of legislation, regulations, and policies to be considered when establishing operations in Canada.

The litigation group forms the second-largest department in Bennett Jones, with an emphasis on litigation of a commercial nature. The firm is also active, however, in virtually all other areas of civil litigation and, to a lesser extent, criminal practice.

In addition, Bennett Jones has experience before energy, transport, conservation, surface rights, and public utility authorities, as well as before councils and planning commissions at the local level.

In cases of corporate reorganization, the firm has provided advice on termination packages for large groups of employees, and has experience representing both employers and employees in the courts and in labor relation matters. Bennett Jones also acts for clients in civil and criminal cases, defamation, immigration, and product liability matters.

The firm's natural resources department represents a broad base of clients involved in the exploration, production, and marketing of oil, natural gas, sulphur, coal, uranium, and other minerals. Clients include several major Canadian and foreign corporations with international operations, utilities, and many small and medium-size independent producers and marketers.

The tax group provides advice directly to clients and to all other departments within the firm, primarily in the area of income taxation, and to some extent in the area of customs and excise taxation. The practitioners in this group have experience in corporate, natural resource, international, and personal taxation.

Bennett Jones has a substantial real estate practice, acting on behalf of corporations, real estate developers, banks, institutional lenders, as well as smaller businesses and individuals involved in property transactions.

The firm's estate planning group advises clients as to their personal family concerns and acts for trustees charged with managing the assets and affairs of others. Services include probate and estate administration, income tax planning, the administration of charitable foundations and institutions, and the creation of family and business trusts.

Since its inception Bennett Jones has supported its surrounding community. Members of the firm are actively involved in a wide range of community interests, including many business, cultural, sporting, and educational activities. In addition, members of the firm, on a continuing basis, participate in the activities of the legal profession, including involvement in the Canadian and Alberta bar associations, as well as the Law Society of Alberta.

BURNET, DUCKWORTH & PALMER

Burnet, Duckworth & Palmer (BD&P) can trace its beginnings back to the 1920s with the formation of the two-member law firm of Ballachey and Burnet. Since that time BD&P has become a full-service firm with more than 65 lawyers at its principal office in Calgary.

A full range of legal services are provided to meet the domestic and international needs of a growing and diversified clientele. The firm is organized into nine broad areas of practice: corporate and securities, energy, finance, real estate, business law, commercial and general litigation, insurance and risk management, realizations, and administrative law. Clients have access to a comprehensive library as well as information provided through the firm's data base subscriptions. Word processing is available 24 hours per day.

BD&P has extensive experience in legal transactions involving Calgary's business community. Members of the firm have been prominent in many of the more innovative takeovers and corporate reorganizations in Alberta. BD&P has been involved with financing through the use of many types of securities, including common and preferred shares, debentures, limited partnerships, joint-venture interests, real estate ventures, and other enterprises. The firm has also been retained to advise a major foreign stock exchange on aspects of Canada's energy policies.

BD&P has gained national recognition for its activities in the area of Canadian taxation of resource properties. A senior partner is the immediate past chairman of the Canadian Tax Foundation, and another has delivered papers at various meetings of the foundation and the Canadian Petroleum Tax Society. The firm has pioneered the

holding of resource properties by mutual fund trusts to permit investment by RRSPs in producing oil and gas properties.

As a Western Canadian firm situated at the centre of Canada's energy industry, BD&P is heavily involved in the operational, financial, and governmental aspects of the oil and gas industry. The firm is often called upon to represent clients before administrative tribunals and regulatory agencies. On occasion BD&P has also provided input on drafting and implementing energy legislation. In recent years, as corporations look farther afield for untapped energy reserves, the firm's oil and gas practice has become increasingly international in scope.

The firm also represents Canadian-chartered banks and their borrower customers in the

One of the reception areas that greet BD&P clients and visitors on three floors of Calgary's Esso Plaza office complex.

area of secured and unsecured lending, including the preparation and placing of securities for the financing of energy, energy-related, and real estate projects.

BD&P's real estate department offers financial institutions, corporations, builders, developers, and individuals full-service commercial and residential real estate and mortgage capabilities, including land-use planning, condominium development, regulations governing foreign ownership of land, and tax shelters.

BD&P has experience before all levels of Alberta courts, the federal courts, and the Supreme Court of Canada. In addition, members of the firm have appeared before nu-

A meeting of several partners in the firm's main board room, which provides a panoramic view of Calgary and the Rocky Mountains.

merous provincial and federal administrative and regulatory tribunals. The litigation section of BD&P handles trial and appellate commercial litigation in disputes involving contract performance and interpretation, and a wide range of controversies involving energy, corporate reorganizations, tax, and real estate.

The firm counsels national and multinational insurance companies on insurance contracts and litigates claims ranging the broad spectrum of insurance-related claims. BD&P also counsels insurers who provide professional liability coverage. The firm emphasizes advice on internal assessment of liability expense and risk management.

Members of the firm's realization group work in close contact with partners and associates involved in commercial litigation practice to advise creditors and debtors on all aspects of insolvency.

The firm also has substantial experience in advising municipal, provincial, and federal governments and agencies on a wide variety of topics.

The firm is proud of its tradition of service and participation in com-

Word Processing on the 33rd floor, overlooking the Calgary Tower of Olympic flame fame.

munity activities. Many partners and associates have made important contributions to the political, social, economic, and cultural life of Calgary. Senior partner James S. Palmer, Q.C., was named chancellor of the University of Calgary in 1986 for a four-year term. BD&P has also established a scholarship at the University of Calgary Law School in honor of its founder, the late Frank L. Burnet, Q.C.

Burnet, Duckworth & Palmer also has close links with several cul-

Elevator lobby accessing one of ten BD&P meeting rooms situated throughout the spacious premises.

tural organizations, including the Calgary Philharmonic Society, Theatre Calgary, Alberta Theatre Projects, and the Alberta Ballet.

REPRESENTATIVE CLIENTS: Royal Bank of Canada; Canada Trust Company; Canada Trustco Mortgage Company; Renaissance Energy Ltd.; Canada Deposit Insurance Corporation; Coopers & Lybrand.

ALBERTA STOCK EXCHANGE

The Alberta Stock Exchange (ASE) was established in 1914 as the Calgary Stock Exchange in response to the Turner Valley oil boom. The founding of the Exchange can be traced back to a group of independent Calgary brokers who wanted to provide a marketplace to facilitate trading among the local brokerage community.

Since its inception the Exchange has experienced a boom/bust cycle that reflects the resource-based economy of Western Canada. In 1929, just before the Great Depression, 19 million shares, which represented a total value of $37 million, traded on the Calgary Stock Exchange.

In 1974 the Calgary Stock Exchange became the Alberta Stock Exchange to coincide with the proclamation of the Alberta Securities Act, which updated provincial security regulations.

Taking inflation into account, activity in 1929 was nearly matched in 1976, when approximately 26 million shares worth a total of $46 million crossed the ASE. The average share price in 1976 was $1.74. Since 1976 the volume of business has grown dramatically at the Exchange. Each year since 1976, which saw double the activity of 1975, trading activity on the ASE has leaped by at least 50 percent of the preceding year. Trading in 1987 exceeded even the frantic buying and selling at the height of the energy boom that occurred during the early 1980s. In March 1987 an all-time record of $117 million worth of shares were traded on the Calgary-based exchange, roughly three times the average value of shares traded monthly in 1986. The trading volume for 1987 was 740 million shares, with an unprecedented worth of $971 million. That compares with a trading value of $476 million for all of 1986, which placed the ASE 11th among major North American stock exchanges. The Exchange currently holds less than 3 percent of the Canadian

The imposing modern, glass Alberta Stock Exchange Tower in downtown Calgary.

market—its goal is to reach 5 percent.

Until the 1980s the ASE remained predominantly an oil exchange. Today listings on the ASE—like the Alberta economy in general—are more diversified. Junior oil and gas stocks now represent less than 50 percent of the Exchange's listings. The combination of the National Energy Program and the 1982 recession hit Canada's fourth-largest stock market hard, and prompted a diversification into mining, industrial, and high-technology companies, and, most re-

cently, junior capital pools.

The rebound in oil prices, coupled with an improved economic environment and the junior capital pool program led to an unprecedented 268 new listings in 1987, compared with 118 new listings in 1986, which was the previous record. Also noteworthy was the introduction of the Alberta Stock Savings Plan (ASSP) in the fall of 1986. The ASSP program produced 20 new listings during 1987, which enabled initial investors the benefit of a provincial tax credit.

It is anticipated that the ASE will continue to grow at a significant pace and will experience an estimated 160 to 180 new listings in 1988. It is anticipated that by early 1989 the ASE will have more than 1,000 listed companies.

Its small size has enabled the ASE to attract junior companies and offer them a higher profile than they would receive on a major stock exchange. The ASE has continually provided an environment for start-up companies, many of which graduate to a more senior exchange. As a result, the ASE provides more personalized service to listed companies and member firms. Some 60 percent of the Ex-

The floor of the Alberta Stock Exchange in 1914 (above), when it was established as the Calgary Stock Exchange, and today (left).

change's 740 listed companies are Alberta based. Almost all the rest are from Ontario, the United States, Australia, or offshore, with a handful rooted in Manitoba or Saskatchewan.

Record trading and listing activity were not the only highlights of 1987. In November 1987 the ASE completed its three-year project of computerizing the trading floor.

Along with a fully computerized data base, the Exchange has an automated trade execution system for low-volume issues; as of December 1987 approximately 500 issues traded on the automated system. Future development plans include a data base of listed company information accessible by the public and remote trading terminals in brokerage offices. The ASE is now well po-

sitioned to take part in the eventual globalization of the industry through electronics. The total project was completed and implemented for slightly more than one million dollars.

The ASE is owned and directed by 47 member firms; during 1987 the Exchange admitted seven new firms to its membership role, however, there was one deletion. The Exchange is confident that the 1988 growth in membership will at least match that of 1987. Currently the entire membership is comprised of Canadian-owned brokerage firms. However, during 1988 the Exchange is anticipating several applications from foreign firms and financial institutions. There are 12 member governors and two public governors elected annually to provide operating direction to the Exchange.

In addition to maintaining a regulated secondary market for securities listed on the Exchange, part of the Alberta Stock Exchange's mandate is to inform and educate the public.

HERMAN J. BELL ASSOCIATES ARCHITECTS INC.

Calgary architect Herman Bell started his own practice in 1984 in the midst of a downturn in the building industry with only an empty office and a phone to his name. Within three months the young company had 12 employees, and today Herman J. Bell Associates Architects Inc. has a staff of 28 professionals, including architects, senior technologists, and skilled support staff. The firm serves a wide cross section of clients in commercial, retail, residential, institutional, and industrial settings.

Within two weeks of making the decision to start his own firm, Bell had secured office space, a telephone, and listings in the Calgary white and yellow pages, as well as five drafting tables for his new venture. While he was making phone calls to drum up business, his wife, Carol, was designing business cards and letterhead in addition to providing clerical and administrative help for the new company, originally named Herman J. Bell Architect.

Bell says the time wasn't particularly propitious for starting a new business, but his belief in a vibrant Alberta economy and the free enter-

The 1988 XV Winter Olympics International Broadcast Centre.

prise system contributed to his perseverance. "It certainly was a downtime in the economy," Bell says. "In terms of setting up a practice it wasn't the logical time to choose, but if you believed in the strength of the province and the city, it was a good time to start.

Herman J. Bell Architect was officially open for business on June 4, 1984. Thanks to the support he received from many business acquaintances with whom he had worked for some eight years previously, his move to full time employees demonstrated the vitality of the new company.

"To promote consistent quality and reliable services I had to hire senior design and technical people," Bell recalls. The firm has continued to be successful and those individuals who started wth him are still actively involved in the firm today.

Perhaps the key to Bell's success is his unwavering confidence in the Alberta economy. The firm was launched with a wide array of small projects, from parking lot layouts and interior design commissions to house additions. Bell's mandate is to make a client's expectations or dreams become a reality

ATCO Office Building

through the technical and creative expertise of his staff. His client list is composed of many satisfied, repeat customers, who often refer the firm to potential new clients.

"Our philosophy has not changed even though we have undergone considerable growth," Bell says.

"We offer to our clients an experienced team of outstanding professionals with special skills, and a spirit of dedication that shapes and gives focus to our work."

The company keeps pace with design and technological advances, and strives to maintain personal and responsible service. Bell and his staff can accommodate clients with projects of any size.

A turning point for the company was the securing of a major contract with CTV Host Broadcaster to design the International Broadcast Centre for the 1988 Olympic Winter Games in Calgary. Other key projects include the Canmore Recreational Centre, an athletes' village that housed 600 competitors and support staff during the Olympics, the International Press Centre for OCO'88, a nine-storey office building for ATCO Development,

Raymond Home Psychiatric Centre

and a Psychiatric Centre in Raymond, Alberta, for Alberta Public Works.

The Raymond project, the firm's first major job for the Alberta government, marks a significant milestone for Bell. The design of the centre is based on an innovative philosophy of care that makes it a unique addition to Alberta's health care system.

Bell is proud of the innovation

Canmore Recreation Centre

his company has attained in terms of products, creativity, and ability to solve clients' problems in a contemporary fashion. Herman J. Bell Associates Architects Inc.'s willingness to custom-tailor each project to meet a client's specifications has earned it success in a particularly challenging time in Alberta's history.

McLENNAN ROSS

Founded in 1910, McLennan Ross is one of the oldest law firms in Edmonton. The firm has enjoyed steady growth and currently operates with 26 lawyers and an efficient support staff of more than 25, working collectively to serve the legal needs of a wide range of clients.

The premiere reputation of

Some McLennan Ross partners in consultation.

McLennan Ross is maintained as a result of three carefully preserved guiding principles: quality work, timely service, and cost efficiency. Its basic philosophy: "Through our people, our facilities, and our expertise, we combine efficiency with excellence to provide clients with superior yet cost-effective legal services." The firm is well regarded by its clients, the courts, the community, and its contemporaries.

McLennan Ross provides expertise to clients in almost every area of the law, including litigation, labor, administrative, corporate, commercial, real estate, wills, estates, and family. The lawyers of McLennan Ross are highly motivated and well trained; the firm boasts three members who have obtained their master's degree in law from highly respected Canadian universities, and five partners who have been honored with Queen's Council appointments.

The litigation department is second to none in Alberta. Of special interest is the firm's expertise and experience relating to the Canadian Charter of Rights and Freedoms, particularly before the Supreme Court of Canada.

As well, the litigation department deals with a wide range of problems experienced by individuals and businesses, including insurance claims, personal injury matters, commercial contracts, debt collection, wrongful dismissal, and family disputes. McLennan Ross represents its clients at all levels of courts, from the lower courts to the Alberta Court of Appeal and the Supreme Court of Canada.

The firm's respected labor department has represented management in labor relations for more than 35 years; it dedicates more lawyers to labor law than any other firm on the prairies. The cumulative experience of the labor lawyers at McLennan Ross covers the complete spectrum of labor, employment, and administrative law. The firm's lawyers assist management clients in negotiations, arbitrations, unfair labor practice complaints, certifications, and any other issue that may arise in the management of human resources.

McLennan Ross' commercial members provide a full range of service for the corporate client. The cor-

McLennan Ross lawyers meet in one of the boardrooms to discuss a case.

porate commercial department has extensive experience in the purchase and sale of major corporations operating nationally and internationally. Advice is given on workout and refinancing arrangements to large and small financial institutions as well as to borrowers and developers. From the purchase of a home to the disposition of a major international corporation, the corporate commercial department has the resources to meet the needs of its clients.

In keeping with its reputation as a full-service law firm, McLennan Ross provides expertise in the areas of wills, estates, and family law. The firm provides all estate services—from the drafting of wills to providing advice regarding disposition of property, tax consequences, probate, and administration of estates. As well, McLennan Ross provides family law services, including advice in matrimonial disputes, assistance in the course of custody-related litigation, and re-

lated areas. The firm's lawyers appear regularly on behalf of young persons in both Youth Court and Family Court.

Beyond establishing reputations as leaders of the profession in their respective areas of practice, the lawyers of McLennan Ross share their experience with others through teaching, both at the University of Alberta and through the medium of Continuing Legal Education. Many of the lawyers are consulted regularly by other firms on complex matters. As well, the lawyers of McLennan Ross are actively involved in the community through service clubs, community leagues, and charitable organizations. The firm believes its obligations to the public extend beyond providing expertise in the practice of law to all areas of community and social life.

The senior partners have established reputations as leaders of the profession in their respective areas of expertise. Roderick A. McLennan,

Q.C., is widely respected for his courtroom skills and has properly earned a reputation as one of the finest barristers in the province. David J. Ross, Q.C., leads the labor department in providing indispensable and valuable advice to governments and corporations in Alberta and is regularly consulted by other law firms in labor relations matters. John Sterk, Q.C., provides practical as well as academic leadership to a dynamic and growing corporate commercial department.

McLennan Ross' detailed record of accomplishment in all aspects of the law has given the firm a reputation for excellence. The combination of complete legal services, sensitivity to the needs of the client, community involvement, and experience acquired throughout the years ensures that it will continue as one of Alberta's distinguished law firms.

GRAHAM McCOURT

provides professional services in the areas of architecture, interior design, and urban planning, and believes that success is the product of the energy, the commitment and the brain power of a design team made up of the project owner, the architects, and the various engineering disciplines. This ensures that a project has addressed the client's needs in an innovative, economical, and rational manner. Over the years the firm has built a reputation for handling unique challenges efficiently and economically.

Graham McCourt designed two of the world-class facilities, the Olympic Saddledome (left) and the Olympic Oval (below), for the 1988 Olympic Winter Games. Photos by James Richard Hall

Creating world-class facilities for the 1988 Olympic Winter Games in Calgary was a challenge that led to the selection of Graham McCourt to design two of the major venues—the Olympic Saddledome and the Olympic Oval.

These two projects illustrate the firm's commitment to producing functional, technically sound, and innovative buildings. Both facilities have been recognized for excellence as recipients of awards for design, construction techniques, and engineering originality. Success creates opportunity, and this work has led to invitation to submit proposals for major recreation facilities around the world.

Since the Saddledome opened in 1983, 5 million visitors have enjoyed events ranging from hockey games and rodeo to rock and symphony concerts. The success of the facility is in the manner in which it can respond to the demands of the performances.

The Olympic Oval is the world's first building designed for speed skating and is located on the University of Calgary campus. The building was opened in 1987 and since then has been acclaimed by international athletes.

Other recreational projects designed by Graham McCourt include the Village Square Leisure Centre for the City of Calgary, a complex that contains North America's first indoor wave pool, and the Eau Claire YMCA in downtown Calgary, a facility that will provide athletic and recreation facilities for the total community.

Since its formation in 1966 Graham McCourt has developed from a group with an initial focus on institutional projects to one that specializes in the development of a variety of "one-of-a-kind" projects for a wide spectrum of clients. The firm

Three active partners lead a team of approximately 30 associates and employees, supported by skilled personnel in the allied fields of building science technology, code analysis, specification writing, interior design, and project management. The partners demand highly technical and competent solutions for major recreational, health care, school, laboratory, and manufacturing facilities. Graham McCourt has designed buildings throughout Western Canada, and has acted as special consultant for building technology problems and the design of

The Alberta Research Council administration offices and laboratories in Edmonton. Design was provided by a Graham McCourt architectural team.

major recreational facilities throughout North America.

The philosophy of the firm is one of design process rather than style. The design team, including various special consultants, work with the client from the initial stages to develop the concept of the project. Many factors are considered in arriving at the initial design, including scale, proportion, color, material, light, and historical influences. According to Graham McCourt, a successful building is one that fulfills all aspects of the client's needs— functional planning, budget, maintenance, and life costs, and has an aesthetically appropriate appearance.

Another area of extensive involvement is that of health care and research facilities. Graham McCourt provided the architectural team for the new laboratories and administration offices for the Alberta Research Council in Edmonton. This $40-million facility includes laboratories for oil and gas testing, heavy engineering, and research into the frontier sciences.

Health care facilities include the $72-million Peter Lougheed Hospital in Calgary, the $46-million Special Services Building and Cancer

Another award-winning building project by Graham McCourt—the Medicine Hat City Hall. The firm received the 1986 Royal Architectural Institute of Canada Governor General's Medal for outstanding achievement in architectural design.

Clinic at the Foothills Hospital in Calgary, and the Activity and Treatment Facility for the Alberta Hospital Ponoka.

A number of office buildings and commercial projects, as well as administrative facilities for government and institutions, have been completed by Graham McCourt. One such facility, the Medicine Hat City Hall, received a 1986 Royal Architectural Institute of Canada Governor General's Medal, which recognizes outstanding achievement in architectural design and the contribution architecture makes to the quality of life in Canada.

Graham McCourt is one of the few architectural firms in Canada that is involved in the aesthetic design control of bridges and highways, and has received a number of international awards over the years for work in this area.

During 1988 the firm will be working on the development of a new high school designed to accommodate the educational delivery systems of the twenty-first century for the Calgary Board of Education, as well as a centre for the treatment of the brain-injured patients for the Alberta Hospital Ponoka. A medical/dental office building, student housing for a community college, sewage treatment plant, and a number of other varied projects are now under development.

The active participation of members of the firm in community professional and political activities, on a local and national level, is ongoing and includes the Housing Design Council, the Calgary Planning Commission, the Economic Development Authority, the boards of a community college, and the Alberta Ballet Company.

CLARKSON GORDON WOODS GORDON

When Thomas Clarkson founded the firm in 1864, his purpose was to help businesses succeed. He made a commitment to provide every client with personal service. Today, as a national firm with more than 400 partners in 25 offices across Canada, the company proudly carries on the tradition. Internationally, the firm is a major partner in the Arthur Young International network, which allows it to provide local expertise and resources in more than 380 cities worldwide.

Clarkson Gordon/Woods Gordon is committed to providing unsurpassed personal service, and the highest standards of competence, independence and objectivity to all its clients. The firm accomplishes

Gordon invests millions of dollars in researching and developing new tools, and its state-of-the-art technology allows the company to offer clients a premium professional service efficiently and cost effectively.

Along with its accounting and auditing practice, the firm provides a broad range of tax services. With more than 300 full-time tax professionals across Canada, the company can offer highly specialized services, such as federal and provincial income taxes, commodity taxes, executive income tax planning, international taxation, and owner-manager remuneration. At a national level, it constantly monitors developments at federal and provincial levels, such as tax reform and

management, financial planning and control, executive recruiting, and systems development in various industries is well known. The size of the firm and the depth of its resources allow it to constantly develop new and innovative services and techniques. The firm believes its responsibility is to offer clients leading-edge services to meet all their needs in the rapidly changing business environment.

Clarkson Gordon/Woods Gordon in Alberta

The firm's Calgary and Edmonton offices provide a full range of professional accounting and management consulting services. Every client, from the smallest entrepreneur to

this by attracting leading talent, providing its people with the highest level of training, and helping its people develop their superb technical skills and intellectual disciplines.

Accounting, Auditing, and Tax

Accounting and auditing remain the foundation of the firm's professional practice. Every year it examines and reports on the financial statements of many thousands of companies, partnerships, and other organizations. The firm's national auditing and accounting groups are at the forefront of financial information technology, pioneering developments in automated audit techniques. Clarkson Gordon/Woods

business transfer tax, to help its clients plan for the effects of changing legislation.

Management Consulting

Clarkson Gordon/Woods Gordon provides the widest range of management consulting services of any consulting firm in Canada. Its people come from varied academic and business disciplines; they are very carefully selected. They are recognized leaders in their fields, and many have held senior positions in government or business before joining the firm.

The firm's experience in providing traditional consulting services—marketing, operations and strategic

ABOVE LEFT: Clarkson Gordon's team approach to accounting and auditing ensures clients receive the best-possible service.

ABOVE: State-of-the-art technology allows the firm to serve its clients efficiently.

the largest multinational organization, receives intensely personal service for which the firm is well known.

Clarkson Gordon/Woods Gordon has a strong national network. This provides the ability to work together, share new technologies and ideas, and combine resources to provide the best-possible team approach. The firm's Calgary and Edmonton offices often exchange ideas and resources to serve clients most effectively.

The Calgary Office

The firm's first office in Calgary opened in 1949 with eight people. It has since grown to 28 partners and more than 170 professional staff members who serve a wide variety of clients in southern Alberta.

With Alberta's oil and gas industry centered in Calgary, the firm has established a special team of professionals highly experienced in the industry. "The unique nature of this industry requires special expertise in many disciplines," says Dave Finlay, Calgary's managing partner. "This team approach ensures that our clients receive the best-possible solutions to their problems."

helping entrepreneurs succeed. Our firm's entrepreneurial clients not only receive our personal commitment to their businesses, they also get immediate access to our firm-wide resources. As they grow and prosper, all the resources they need are at their fingertips."

The Edmonton Office

Established in 1956, Clarkson Gordon/Woods Gordon's Edmonton office has 11 partners and 65 professionals, providing a full range of services to a wide variety of clients. In particular, the firm has a strong client base among owner-managed businesses, construction, manufacturing, mining, communications, and public-sector agencies.

provides a full range of services to clients in northern Alberta and the Northwest Territories."

Commitment to the Community

Not only is Clarkson Gordon/ Woods Gordon committed to providing the Alberta business community with its professional services, it is also committed to supporting the local communities. The firm's Alberta partners and staff are involved on a volunteer basis with more than 60 different charitable and philanthropic organizations, including the United Way, UNICEF, the Calgary Philharmonic, Junior Achievement, the Alberta Ballet Company, Big Brothers, the Canadian Diabetes Association, and the

ABOVE: Dave Finlay, a member of the firm's national management committee, is Calgary's managing partner.

ABOVE RIGHT: As managing partner, Les Tutty directs the operations of the Edmonton office.

The firm also has a wide variety of other clients, particularly owner-managed businesses. It has found that entrepreneurs depend on Clarkson Gordon/Woods Gordon for personal service and sound financial advice. "Not only are we independent auditors, we are also business advisers, confidants, and sounding boards for new ideas," comments Dave Finlay.

"We thrive on the challenges of

The firm offers its clients a full service approach by bringing to its engagement teams professionals with a wide range of skills, including accounting, auditing, taxation, computers and general business advice.

In keeping with the firm's tradition, our people are committed to providing the intensely personal service for which we are well known. We feel we can understand our clients' businesses better if we stand where they stand, says Les Tutty, Edmonton's managing partner.

In addition to servicing clients in the Edmonton area, "Our office

Edmonton Symphony.

"Our professionals take pride in all aspects of life in Alberta. We are dedicated to providing intensely personal service to all our Alberta clients, and we look forward to fulfilling this commitment to new clients," say Dave Finlay and Les Tutty.

309

THE COHOS EVAMY PARTNERSHIP

Some of the most prestigious design projects in Canada provide testimony to the innovative solutions and unique designs emanating from The Cohos Evamy Partnership, the largest integrated architecture, interior design, and engineering firm in Alberta.

The integration of form and function is a great challenge. The ability of The Partnership to design effective and pragmatic solutions has marked a strength that began with the firm's inception in 1960. The creative talent, mature management skills of the firm's partners, and technical expertise of the more than 120 architects, engineers, interior designers, and project managers have led to The Partnership's success in winning hundreds of assignments throughout Canada and the United States. With offices in Calgary and Edmonton, The Partnership has been responsible for projects from British Columbia to the shores of Cape Breton and from the High Arctic to the 49th parallel.

The firm is built on the concept of partnership. In fact, it forms the cornerstone of the corporate philosophy. That philosophy is evident throughout the firm's client relationships, in the interdisciplinary coordination within the firm, and in the way the form of its projects reflect the required function.

The professional activities of The Partnership are marked by creative design, close attention to detail, and experienced management. This design philosophy contributes to a significant list of ongoing clients. It consists of respecting efficiency and function, but also understanding the importance of a work space that creates an attractive and comfortable environment for employees and visitors.

The Cohos Evamy Partnership also ensures that new projects will be in harmony with the surround-

RIGHT: Bankers Hall, Calgary

BELOW: Canmore Municipal Hospital

ing environment. The design must become symbolic of the project's owners, and yet must not overpower the building site or surrounding buildings.

A critical aspect of this team approach to projects has been The Partnership's commitment to listening—listening to the client and listening to other members of the team, to ensure that all needs and all innovations are thoroughly examined. This plays a major role in achieving the objectives of the project.

The firm's pioneering role in the use of computer-assisted design in architectural, interior design, and engineering projects is well known. Through the use of three-dimensional computer modelling, clients are actually able to see design alternatives on the computer screen. Computer-assisted drafting (CADD) creates excellent, coordinated drawings. The use of these computers provides the architects and the client with great flexibility

in space planning, material, furniture, and equipment selection.

The highly disciplined team approach to all projects typifies the attitudes found throughout the firm's various departments. For example, The Partnership's interior design capabilities are well known throughout the marketplace and call for a close consultative relationship between designers and architects to develop designs, color schemes, and furnishings for new projects.

The mechanical, electrical, and structural services that make up a key portion of the integrated partnership give Cohos Evamy an advantage in the marketplace. While the primary function of these specialties is to act as components of the overall team, they also actively compete with other engineering

RIGHT: Heritage Medical Research Building, Calgary

BELOW: Market Mall, Calgary

consultants to provide purely engineering services to the firm's clients. This flexible, collective approach to projects is unique in Alberta's architectural industry and provides clients with significant savings in time, as well as providing a solid base for decision making.

An examination of the project lists of The Cohos Evamy Partnership reads like the who's who of architectural projects in Western Canada. Often these projects provide a unique view of the various capabilities of the firm.

An excellent example of the firm's expertise in structural engineering technology is Western Canadian Place, a 42-storey office building that is one of the highest post-tensioned concrete structures in North America. The rounded corners and innovative design of this Calgary building are benchmarks in structural engineering textbooks.

The Animal Diseases Research Institute in Lethbridge demon-

strates the firm's abilities in mechanical engineering, with air-purification systems and energy conservation methods in the $20-million Federal Government project setting new technological frontiers.

Unique, functional designs are evident in many of The Partnership's corporate projects, each of which must achieve a sense of permanence, elegance, and drama within its environment. No better examples of this can be found than Trimac House, Western Canadian Place, or Bankers Hall in Calgary.

The Partnership has earned an outstanding reputation for the design of health care facilities through its work on more than 40 hospitals, auxiliary hospitals, and nursing homes across Canada. In Alberta, the firm has completed more than 25 health care facilities during the past few years, ranging from large general hospitals to expandable prototypes and small-town nursing homes. These projects include The Lethbridge Regional Hospital, the Alberta Children's Hospital, the Canmore Hospital, and the refur-

ABOVE: Western Canadian Place, Calgary

LEFT: Sally Borden Centre (at the Banff Centre), Banff

bishing of the Edmonton General Hospital.

The learning environment is critical in influencing one's attitude toward life, and it is that philosophy that is the framework for The Partnership's use of natural light and spatial variety in its school and college designs. The Alberta College of Art in Calgary, Pond Inlet School in the High Arctic, and the Strathmore High School are outstanding examples of this philosophy in built form.

Perhaps recreational buildings demand some of the most unique solutions in architecture, engineering, and interior design. Excellent examples can be found of exceptional resolutions of these challenges in The Partnership's projects at Nakiska on Mount Allan and the Sally Borden Centre at the Banff Centre. Both illustrate an imaginative use of structural and architectural elements to affirm the partnership required of a building and its environment.

This dedication to the highest standard of design and function, combined with a fastidious commitment to budget and schedule, are key factors in the success and growth of this award-winning architectural, interior design, and engineering partnership.

EDMONTON ECONOMIC DEVELOPMENT AUTHORITY

The Edmonton Economic Development Authority is a progressive, one-stop shop in the city for provincial, national, and international businesses, clients, or travellers seeking economic and market information on Edmonton's trading area.

Established to promote and develop the Edmonton economy through growth and diversification, the Authority is designed to be both responsive to local business needs and active in the promotion and development of new business for Edmonton.

Programs initiated by the Authority are set up to assist the private sector, and to stimulate and enhance additional local business development. These economic programs range from the Advanced Technology Project—stimulating high-technology investment for the advanced technology industry—to sponsoring promotional opportunities such as the World Trade Centre Edmonton. The World Trade Centre operates in 49 countries, building and identifying international trade opportunities for its members.

Additional current programs include the Edmonton Motion Picture and Television Bureau, dedicated to increasing Edmonton's status as a major motion picture and television production centre, and the Business Innovation Centre, a private-sector, nonprofit organization. The Authority served as the catalyst in the formation of the Business Innovation Centre, whose purpose is to facilitate the growth of new Edmonton businesses in an incubative environment, thereby adding to further diversification of Edmonton's economy.

This much-needed diversification is fostered by a number of quality Authority publications that summarize both the structure of Edmonton's economy and the nature of its people and accompanying quality of life. The publications range from the Authority's Annual Economic Report, through detailed construction activity in the city, to a demographic breakdown of Edmonton residents.

The Authority also publishes the "Edmonton New Business Guide" for companies wishing to establish a business in Edmonton, and the "Welcome to Edmonton" list of contacts and services for the newly arrived Edmontonian. All publications are distributed on a regular basis; all are designed to inform and entice investment and development in this city.

Of course, service is available to anyone in the form of counselling from professional Economic Development personnel as well. This counselling service provides industrial and commercial site selection, acts as a liaison with commercial real estate companies, and provides details on provincial and federal government business assistance programs. Authority staff also provides general business, financial, and marketing counselling; locates sources of products and services; and assists with liaison among other businesses.

The Edmonton Economic Development Authority has the facts and figures at its fingertips. For potential investors evaluating Edmonton's economic environment, the Authority is the natural one-stop shop for information, assistance, and advice.

The Edmonton skyline with the new Canada Place in the upper right and the Muttart Conservatory in the right foreground.

THORNE ERNST & WHINNEY

Serving more than 40,000 clients from 54 offices across Canada, Thorne Ernst & Whinney is the country's largest integrated accounting firm. The organization has a total professional staff of 3,500, including more than 400 partners.

Thorne Ernst & Whinney Chartered Accountants provides a full range of services to both large and small clients. The services include auditing and accounting, financial and business advice, income and commodity taxation, valuations, mergers and acquisitions, receivership and insolvency, and computer services.

The origins of the firm in Canada date back to the 1860s. Today the firm offers Canadian clients an unparalleled depth of professional resources nationwide plus a wealth of international expertise

When Roxby Hughes, president of Enderco Systems, Inc. (seated), decided to take his engineering company into the software development business, he relied on Thorne Ernst & Whinney partner Bill Corbett to guide him through the financial complexities of the business conversion.

through Ernst & Whinney International, one of the largest accounting and consulting firms in the world. Through the nearly 400 offices in 76 countries, Ernst & Whinney International ensures Alberta clients will receive professional service and quality control anywhere in the world.

Thorne Ernst & Whinney has been growing with Alberta since the 1920s. The Calgary office now consists of 22 partners and more than 180 staff members. As Calgary grew to become the heart of the oil and gas industry, so did the office's involvement in that industry. Today in excess of 65 percent of the firm's audit practice in Calgary is related to the oil and gas sector. In those early development years many of the young entrepreneurs exploring for and discovering new sources of oil were Thorne Ernst & Whinney's clients. From these small enterprises grew the companies that are now the backbone of the Canadian oil industry: Okalta Oils became Oakwood Petroleums;

West Magill Gas & Oil became the multinational Ranger Oil; and Canadian Industrial Gas & Oil Ltd. (CIGOL) grew into Norcen Energy Resources. All are still major clients of the firm.

Thorne Ernst & Whinney is committed to meeting the needs of its clients. An example of this commitment is the firm's development of Petroman, a computer-based petroleum management information system encompassing all the land management, production, and financial accounting functions specific to the oil and gas industry. Because information is entered and validated through the use of on-line terminals, Petroman streamlines the flow of data and eliminates redundant coding and data entry.

Another example of the firm's commitment to client needs was the recent commissioning of a study that was designed to address the oil and gas industry's unique accounting issues. The project's research team consisted of representatives from the University of

Thorne Ernst & Whinney takes the team approach to meeting clients' needs. Each client service partner is responsible for the co-ordination of all professional services and has the authority to commit any of the firm's service resources whenever they are required to meet client needs.

Western Ontario, the oil and gas industry, the investment sector, and Thorne Ernst & Whinney oil and gas specialists. The study examined the industry's effectiveness in communicating key economic data to investors, and made recommendations to improve this process. The published study, released in 1985, was an instant success throughout the industry.

The primary emphasis of Thorne Ernst & Whinney's Edmonton office has always been to service the needs of owner/managers in Edmonton and north-central Alberta. Its success is exhibited by its growth from a one-man proprietorship, established in the 1930s, to the largest accounting office in the city with a total staff of 185, including 21 partners. Today more than 80 percent of the Edmonton office clients are owner/managers who call on Thorne Ernst & Whinney regularly for professional advice.

The office serves a broad spectrum of clients, ranging in size from independent businesses to large multinational corporations. The accounting professionals are involved with hundreds of organizations—from government and large corporations in a variety of industries to small businesses and individuals.

The Edmonton office has a specialized, full-time Corporate Advisory Service (CAS) practice that was formed to encourage entrepreneurial activity across Western Canada. The CAS merger and acquisition professionals provide a full range of services, including establishing acquisition strategies, candidate identification and screening, valuation, negotiation, and closing. In addition, Edmonton CAS has assisted clients in the evaluation of alternative financing methods and sources.

Providing computer-related services to Alberta's public and private sectors for more than 20 years, Thorne Ernst & Whinney's Edmon-

ton office has the largest information systems practice of any Canadian chartered accountancy. This division provides services ranging from advisory to processing in mainframe, mini- and micro-computers environments. Mainframe services include system design and specifications, programming, and implementation support.

The Lethbridge office of Thorne Ernst & Whinney traces its origin back to a proprietorship founded in 1945. Over the course of its history, the office has maintained a reputation as a leader, with a strong and continuing commitment to serve the growing needs of the southern Alberta business community.

With seven partners and a staff of 53, the Lethbridge office provides a variety of services, including tax, accounting, auditing, receivership and insolvency, business advisory, and computer analysis, to a wide cross section of clients. The office's client base ranges from small and medium-

Thorne Ernst & Whinney's approach to service is based on a thorough, up-to-date understanding of a client's specific environment and the nature of their operations. Thorne Ernst & Whinney partners Lyle Harrison (left) and Ed Nedza (center) meet regularly with their client Time Air president Richard Barton to ensure the company's wide-ranging requirements continue to be met.

size businesses to large corporations involved in agriculture, construction, real estate, manufacturing, hospitality, retailing, wholesaling, and government.

Situated in the heart of Alberta's agricultural industry, the Lethbridge office has developed accounting systems to meet the unique needs of farmers and ranchers. Satellite offices in rural communities and seminars specifically designed for the agricultural sector have contributed to the office's growth.

Thorne Ernst & Whinney is part of the fabric of Alberta. The firm has enlarged and evolved and it has continued to uphold a strong commitment to provide fast, efficient, business-oriented solutions for its clients.

Photo by Chris Bruun, Courtesy, Westfile, Inc.

Foothills Medical Centre

Calgary Exhibition and Stampede

DeVry Institute of Technology

Alberta College

Southern Alberta Institute of Technology

First Medical Management Ltd. / Med+Stop

Alberta Cancer Foundation

Calgary Convention Centre

Photo by Wes Bergen. Courtesy, Hillstrom Stock Photo

CHAPTER

Quality of Life

Medical, educational, and religious institutions, and recreation and leisure-oriented companies all contribute to the quality of life enjoyed by Alberta residents and visitors to the region.

Foothills Medical Centre 320-323; Calgary Exhibition and Stampede 324; DeVry Institute of Technology 325; Alberta College 326; Southern Alberta Institute of Technology 327; First Medical Management Ltd./Med+Stop 328; Alberta Cancer Foundation 329; Calgary Convention Centre 330

FOOTHILLS MEDICAL CENTRE

Located on a panoramic 98-acre site in northwest Calgary, the Foothills Medical Centre integrates three autonomous institutions: the Foothills Provincial General Hospital, the University of Calgary's Faculty of Medicine, and the Alberta Cancer Board's Tom Baker Cancer Centre. These three bodies work cooperatively, combining clinical service, education, and research to provide southern Alberta with world-class health care.

Although the programs and services provided are diverse and complex, the idea behind the Foothills Medical Centre is simple: Patient needs are best served when educators and researchers can participate directly in the health care process. Everyone benefits—patients get the most up-to-date, professional care available; medical students receive a more relevant and direct education; and researchers keep in close contact with the ultimate beneficiaries of their work. And, with all participants sharing in the provision of services, costs to the taxpayer are significantly reduced.

The core of the centre is the

A legacy of the 1988 Olympic Winter Games in Calgary, the state-of-the-art medical control laboratory at Foothills Hospital is contributing to therapeutic drug monitoring and research in Canadian sports. Robotics arms (pictured) are one component of the highly sophisticated equipment.

Foothills Hospital, which opened its doors on June 10, 1966. Built in response to a burgeoning Alberta population and an increased government emphasis on health care, the hospital helps meet the needs of patients not only in southern Alberta, but also in southeastern British Columbia and southwestern Saskatchewan.

A 1,000-bed facility, Foothills serves nearly a half-million patients per year, either as inpatients (30,000) or on an outpatient basis (430,000). The hospital employs 5,000 full- and part-time staff members and has about 500 doctors on its medical staff.

As a major health care referral, research, and teaching centre, the Foothills Hospital has many pro-

The emergency helicopter, S.T.A.R.S., helps Foothills Hospital fulfill its role as the main health care referral centre in southern Alberta. S.T.A.R.S. works in concert with the Neonatal Intensive Care Unit to offer life-saving care for premature newborns.

grams unique to southern Alberta, Alberta, and Western Canada. Premature newborns facing possible death or disability are given a chance at life through a neonatal intensive care program. The hospital is also the centre for dialysis and transplants for kidney patients in southern Alberta, and offers a mobile life-support service to a growing number of outpatients.

Foothills houses a major burn unit, and provides delicate reconstructive surgery not only for patients with severe burns, but also for individuals with damaged limbs and facial areas.

Patients throughout Alberta are referred to the hospital's cardiac electrophysiology program, which manages various types of heart problems, including sudden cardiac death, a disorder that accounts for 3,000 adult deaths per year in Alberta. Foothills keeps track of many southern Albertans who have pacemakers by monitoring their heartbeats by telephone.

Alberta's elderly receive special care, with a 180-bed auxiliary hospital on site. Alzheimer's disease sufferers are treated through the

Foothills Medical Centre

outpatient Dementia Clinic, while other neurological disorders such as Parkinson's disease and Huntington's Chorea are diagnosed and managed with the assistance of the Movement Disorders Clinic.

Other special programs include a province-wide Poison and Drug Information Service that responds to more than 40 public inquiries per day, 85 percent of which are successfully managed at home; a Human Organ Procurement and Exchange Program that responds to an increasing need for organs and tissues in Alberta, Canada, and the United States; and 107 outpatient and emergency clinics that serve southern Alberta.

As a teaching hospital, the Foothills is closely connected to the University of Calgary's Faculty of Med-

A generous gift from Rosalie Bacs, matched by the Alberta government, enabled the University of Calgary to create the Bacs Medical Learning Resource Centre, an audiovisual study centre that supports the self-learning concept. The centre brings together videotape, slide-tape, and computer equipment, as well as anatomy and pathology specimens and other teaching materials.

icine. Most of the hospital's 500 physicians also hold joint appointments with the faculty, and, through these doctor/educators, patients benefit from the most advanced medical knowledge and technology.

Training new doctors at a rate of 72 graduates per year, the faculty takes a direct, human approach to teaching. Students have contact with hospital patients right at the beginning of the program. They learn early that caring skills, the ability to solve problems quickly and effectively, and the connection between science and health care are very important parts of the medical profession. Because the medical school was born in the late 1960s, its philosophy reflects a humanistic approach to education and medicine, with an emphasis on interpersonal skills, a dedication to self-learning, and a focus on the most vital factor in the medical equation: the patient.

When the school admitted its first class in 1970, this patient-oriented approach was revolutionary. Today the faculty retains a style of medical education unique in North America. The performance of students in national exams is excellent; the school is rated as having one of the top medical faculties in Canada; and residency directors at other hospitals report positively on students' practical abilities.

Thanks to funding from granting agencies such as the Medical Research Council and the Alberta Heritage Foundation for Medical Research, the Faculty of Medicine is able to attract many scientists and scholars from around the world. Being part of such an advanced and comprehensive medical facility also attracts many national and international specialists to the university, adding to the depth and breadth of the teaching offered students and the service provided to patients.

As well as talented scientists and educators, the medical school also has one of the most modern re-

Research is a very important element of teaching and learning at the University of Calgary Faculty of Medicine. Investigation laboratories comprise a large area of building capacity, sharing space not only with university personnel, but also the physicians and researchers from the Tom Baker Cancer Centre, Foothills Hospital, and other institutions in the City of Calgary.

search facilities in North America, the Alberta Heritage Research Building, completed in 1987.

The school makes significant contributions to both patient-based and basic research. Research is conducted in many areas, including academic investigation into the problems of the aged, arthritis and joint disorders, immunology, genetic and infectious diseases, gastrointestinal disorders, growth and development, endocrinology and metabolism, cell regulation, and respiratory problems.

The faculty has gained worldwide attention for its research in the field of electrophysiology, which looks at the causes of heart attack deaths, and the school's diabetic research group is in the forefront of the search for a cure for the disease, which affects one million Canadians.

In co-operation with the Foothills Hospital, the Alberta Cancer Board, and the Tom Baker Cancer Centre, the Faculty of Medicine also offers teaching programs for students of health care administration, laboratory technology, medical radiation technology, social work, pastoral care, dietetics, respiratory therapy, and rehabilitation disciplines. In addition, the hospital has a School of Nursing that offers a three-year program that attracts 150 new students annually.

Cancer remains the greatest challenge for health care, and the Tom Baker Cancer Centre (TBCC) helps put the Foothills Medical Cen-

The equipment and facilities at the Tom Baker Cancer Centre are some of the most advanced available for cancer treatment programs. This machine, part of the simulator suite, helps the medical team design the appropriate program for a patient to ensure the best care.

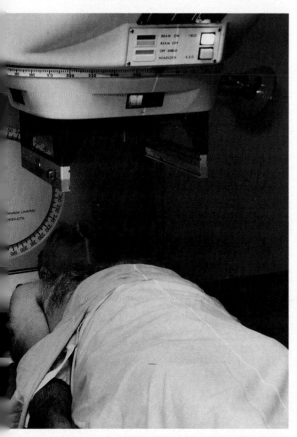

tre at the forefront of cancer research and treatment in North America. Operated by the Alberta Cancer Board, the TBCC is built on a World Health Organization model for comprehensive cancer care. Multidisciplinary care is delivered by many medical and surgical subspecialties that combine to provide the patient with comprehensive cancer treatment.

Diagnostic, radiology, nuclear medicine, laboratory, anesthesia, and housekeeping services are "purchased" from the Foothills Hospital, which in turn uses the TBCC's staff for treatment of its cancer patients. Here again, the concept of the Foothills Medical Centre as an integrated health care facility allows the TBCC to operate effectively and economically, drawing on the resources of the other key players of the centre.

The TBCC is directly involved in the treatment of 70 percent of southern Alberta's cancer patients, and collaborates with other medical facilities through 115 community physicians and surgeons.

Founded in 1982, the TBCC is named in honor of Dr. Tom Baker, who chaired the Alberta Cancer Board for the first decade of its existence and played an essential role in the establishment of cancer services for southern Alberta. The TBCC has a full-time staff of 200, including 25 physicians.

Joint offerings with the Foothills Hospital include programs in bone marrow transplantation and gynecologic oncology. Affiliation agreements with the Faculties of Medicine and Nursing enable staff of the TBCC to participate in undergraduate and graduate educational activities that relate to the teaching of cancer treatment, and to engage in cancer-related research. Through these activities, modern advances in prevention, treatment, and diagnosis of cancer are transferred to the community.

The TBCC has, at any given time, about 20,000 patients across

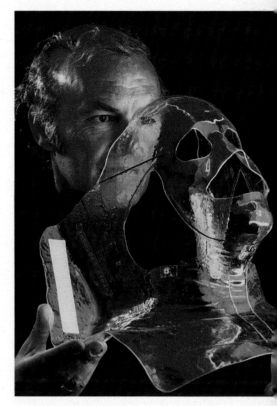

Sophisticated technological developments allow the medical team at the Tom Baker Cancer Centre to provide advanced cancer treatment to patients in southern Alberta. The mold shown here is custom made for the patient and is used in the radiotherapeutic treatment program.

southern Alberta, with 3,500 to 4,000 new cancer patients annually. One in four men and one in five women in Alberta develop cancer, and the disease remains a major health care priority in the province.

The unique, multidisciplinary coordination of many organizations at the Foothills Medical Centre includes community health programs such as the Southern Alberta Provincial Laboratory of Public Health and the Tuberculosis Clinic.

From helping premature babies enter the world safely to ensuring a higher quality of life for the elderly, the Foothills Medical Centre has a profound influence on thousands of lives each day. This multi-institutional, patient-centered approach sets the highest standards for quality of care, education, and research: an integrated program of excellence.

CALGARY EXHIBITION AND STAMPEDE

The Calgary Exhibition and Stampede has been an integral part of Alberta's history for more than a century. Since its inception in the fall of 1886, "The Greatest Outdoor Show on Earth" has continued to draw record crowds with the variety of entertainment it offers to Calgarians and Canadian and international tourists.

A nonprofit organization, the Calgary Exhibition and Stampede focuses on preserving and enhancing the agricultural and historical legacy of Alberta, as well as providing services for agricultural, entertainment, and sports organizations.

The Stampede is the cultural heart of Calgary, a 10-day celebration with a worldwide reputation. With its huge parade, nightly grandstand shows, midway rides, and renowned chuckwagon races and rodeo, the Stampede rivals such festivals as New Orleans' Mardi Gras and Munich's Oktoberfest.

The Stampede tradition began with a modest agricultural fair in October 1886. The success of the first fair, which offered prize money in the neighborhood of $900 and drew an attendance of about 500 people, led to the establishment of an annual event. In July 1889, 94 acres of the land that would eventually become Stampede Park was purchased from the Canadian government.

"The Greatest Outdoor Show on Earth" has been a Calgary tradition for more than a century.

The stage was now set, and in 1912 Guy Weadick, a trick roper who had performed in many Wild West shows, vaudeville, and travelling rodeos, arrived in Calgary. A dreamer, Weadick envisioned Calgary as the birthplace of the biggest "frontier days show the world has ever seen . . . hundreds of cowboys and cowgirls, thousands of Indians. We'll have Mexican ropers and riders . . . we'll make Buffalo Bill's Wild West Extravaganza look like a sideshow . . ."

To make his dream a reality, Weadick managed to gain the financial backing of four prominent Calgarians: George Lane, A.E. Cross, A.J. MacLean, and Patrick Burns. These men, who later became known as The Big Four, agreed to invest a total of $100,000 in Weadick's project, called The Stampede.

Although 14,000-plus Calgarians attended the first Stampede in September 1912, organizers just broke even, and Weadick left Calgary to accept work with other shows in North America. His return in the spring of 1919 fueled high hopes for a second Stampede, which was a resounding success.

In 1923 the Calgary Exhibition and Stampede became one and the same—a winning combination of great rodeo excitement, southern Alberta agriculture, and the first chuckwagon races in history under competitive rules. The Stampede expanded from a six- to a nine-day show in 1967, and since 1968 fair-

In 1982 the Stampede introduced the Half-Million-Dollar Rodeo, and today the event boasts the richest purse ever offered in the history of the sport.

goers have had 10 days per year to enjoy the flavor of the Old West.

In 1982 the Stampede introduced the Half-Million-Dollar Rodeo, and today the event boasts the richest purse ever offered in the history of the sport. More than $250,000 is paid out to the winning professional cowboys in a grand finale infield competition.

A self-supporting organization, the Calgary Exhibition and Stampede attracts more than one million visitors each year, and in 1986 it enjoyed a gross revenue of $46 million. Revenues generated by Stampede Park's operations are spent on improvements and additions to the park and its facilities.

The Calgary Exhibition and Stampede has more than 300 permanent employees and a volunteer staff of more than 2,000 dedicated individuals who serve on more than 50 committees established to run the organization's many operations. Stampede Park has seven major facilities open year round, with more than 500,000 square feet of space available for trade shows, expositions, conventions, banquets, concerts, business seminars, meetings, and agricultural and sporting events, as well as many other activities.

DEVRY INSTITUTE OF TECHNOLOGY

Since its inception in Calgary in 1981, DeVry Institute of Technology has offered educational programs adaptable to the rapid changes in high technology. DeVry's primary mission is to provide students with career-oriented programs in areas consistent with the most current needs of business and industry.

DeVry Institute of Technology was established in 1931 in Chicago, Illinois, by Dr. Herman A. DeVry, an inventor and motion picture projector manufacturer. In 1956 DeVry established a Canadian subsidiary with the opening of an institute in Toronto. Bell & Howell Co. acquired the DeVry schools in 1967. By 1983 the system had grown to 11 campuses—two located in Canada and nine in the United States. The DeVRY INC. network, which was purchased by Keller Graduate School of Management, Inc., in August 1987, is one of the largest organizations of proprietary post-secondary institutions in North America.

An advisory board of representatives from major North American corporations and educational institutions meets three times a year, updating DeVry's curricula to match current trends in the marketplace.

Although DeVry's technology-based programs emphasize the practical aspect of learning, students also have the opportunity to supplement their hands-on knowledge with theory courses. The combination of these two learning methods not only provides a well-rounded education, but also enables students to gain the problem-solving skills necessary for application in the real world.

DeVry offers courses within four diploma programs that can either lead to a baccalaureate degree, after transferring to a U.S. DeVry In-

DeVry instructors are chosen for their broad background in business and industry, and the curricula is constantly changing to match the current trends in the marketplace. Photo to right shows a DeVry instructor working with students in the electronics lab.

stitute, or directly to a job.

The Electronics Engineering Technology Program is designed to produce technical specialists in areas such as space communication systems, local area networks, and artificial intelligence.

For more technically oriented careers, the Electronics Engineering Technician Program is structured to train students to analyze sophisticated technical hardware and electronic systems for work in field service and sales.

DeVry's Computer Information Systems Program is designed for students who wish to enter the fast-growing world of business computers. This program educates students in current business languages and application tools, with instruction in database management, computer security, and advanced business applications.

The Business Operations Program develops managers who can use computers to tie diverse business functions together and to streamline operations for greater efficiency. Students will be taught to effectively analyze, plan, communicate, and manage.

Combined day and evening enrolments in all 11 DeVry Institutes was nearly 25,000 students in the fall of 1987. DeVry in Calgary has more than 1,000 students and about 60 employees, including 25 instructors with a broad background in business and industry. About 65 per-

DeVry's Computer Information Systems Program and Business Operations Program are designed for students who wish to enter the fast-growing world of business computers.

cent of DeVry's students come directly from high school, while the remaining 35 percent are working adults who wish to gain training for a new career.

DeVry maintains a Career Counselling and Placement Office to assist graduates of all programs in attaining positions in their chosen fields. This placement office is equipped with an on-line computerized communication system linking all Canadian and U.S. DeVry Institutes, making countless employment opportunities available to graduates. DeVry consistently places more than 80 percent of those students who actively pursue employment into jobs related to their training within four months of graduation. About 300 students graduate from the DeVry Institute of Technology in Calgary each year.

ALBERTA COLLEGE

The philosophy of Alberta College is straightforward: Without an ideological base, educational planning takes place in a vacuum. Thus, ideally, education should stress the quality, excellence, and appropriateness of its offerings with the paramount aim of education for living and not simply training for work.

There is nothing vacuous about this Edmonton-based educational institution. Alberta College typifies an institution that has and can adapt quickly to the changing demands of students, employees, and society, offering well-rounded programs and courses in business education, music, office automation training, accounting, and management, to name a few.

The college offers flexibility and quality instruction in a positive learning environment for young and not-so-young adults in a convenient downtown location. The flexibility of the college is evidenced by its educational program, which offers serious students the opportu-

Ideally situated at a convenient downtown location, Alberta College offers part- and full-time programs and courses to students of all ages in the Edmonton area.

nity to take a partial course load so as to maximize their learning and marks, or for academically talented students, a heavier-than-normal course load to meet diploma requirements in a shorter period of time.

Recognizing that the educational process is an overpowering experience for many returning students, the college provides a number of services and appeal processes to ensure that studies are enjoyable and that the results will benefit all individuals, both socially and economically.

Alberta College offers special programs for deaf and hearing-impaired adults and special training programs for people working with the handicapped. It also continues a long tradition as Edmonton's second-chance institution for those who are seeking another opportunity to achieve self-fulfillment and a measure of success. From its English as a Second Language course to its Conservatory of Music, the largest music facility of its kind in the city, Alberta College offers something for everyone.

Alberta College was established in 1903, predating both the City of Edmonton and the province. It was

Dr. R.H. Pridham, president of Alberta College.

founded by concerned citizens as the first postsecondary school in the area, on land bequeathed by pioneer George McDougall for educational purposes.

The institution has always striven to be innovative and resourceful with its programming. The history of the college's continuing adaptation to the demands of society is illustrated by its many milestones: It offered the first university-transfer courses in the province, introduced secondary business education for women, was the first local school to adopt the semester system, and was the first school to commence night classes.

The college's mission statement is concise and practical, especially given today's demand for specialized training to fit the ever-changing labor market. The institution purports to "effectively and efficiently provide to its communities, educational programs and opportunities and be capable of adapting to meet ever-changing societal, technological, and educational needs."

The future for Alberta College is bright with plans for expansion of programs and the development and construction of new campus facilities.

SOUTHERN ALBERTA INSTITUTE OF TECHNOLOGY

Established in 1916 to meet the needs of a growing industrial economy, the Southern Alberta Institute of Technology (SAIT) has progressed from the technologies of telegraphy and steam-powered farm machinery to the latest in robotics and fibre optics.

One of the oldest and largest institutes of its kind in Canada, SAIT offers more than 60 diploma programs in the applied arts, trades, engineering technologies, and medical sciences to approximately 5,200 students each year. In addition, continuing education courses are delivered by various instructional methods including audio-graphic teleconferencing to more than 25,000 students annually throughout Alberta. SAIT has graduated more than 130,000 individuals over the past 70 years, and today graduates about 2,000 students per year.

The first permanent facility constructed on SAIT's campus on Calgary's North Hill in 1922 was Heritage Hall. Designated a provincial historic resource in 1985, Heritage Hall was home to two schools of higher learning in SAIT's early years—the Provincial Institute of Technology and Art, and the Calgary Normal School, later to become a founding faculty of the University of Calgary. The Alberta

Heritage Hall, an outstanding example of Collegiate Gothic architecture. Building upon its traditional strengths, SAIT is developing new educational markets in research, customized employee training, and international education.

College of Art, now an autonomous school, originally evolved from SAIT's art department, which also operated in Heritage Hall for a number of years.

The society SAIT serves has changed dramatically in 70 years, and the institute has created a new mission as "an innovative organization equipping people to compete successfully in the changing world of work by providing relevant, skill-oriented education."

SAIT is an active partner with industry and government in applied research and technology. The institute's electronics department and Northern Telecom Canada have established a unique telecommunications training facility, using the latest in digital telephone switching systems. The lab not only serves SAIT students, but also is Northern Telecom's western regional training centre.

SAIT is also a partner in two joint international education projects. One involves a partnership with Basic Manpower Training International to develop and deliver pe-

troleum technology courses and related administrative services to the Daqing Petroleum Institute in China. The other is a five-year project in which SAIT acts as an adviser to Alberta Advanced Education and various companies to design and establish a petroleum technology institute in northeast Pakistan.

SAIT also delivers a sophisticated selection of correspondence courses to 6,000 students annually in 10 countries worldwide. Studies are generally of a technical nature and include medical sciences, library and information technology, and power engineering technology. In addition, approximately 10,000 courses are sold to other institutions and organizations annually.

The Southern Alberta Institute of Technology also contributed its services to the 1988 Olympic Winter Games in Calgary. Student residences housed Olympic athletes and media for a three-month period, and catering services for on-campus guests and various city venues were provided by the institute's Hospitality Careers and Food Services departments. SAIT's cinema, television, stage, and radio arts students and faculty assisted in the operation of CTV's two international studios during the games.

A student working in the computer-aided design and drafting laboratory. One of Canada's best-equipped CADD labs, it is used for regular day programs and customized employee training.

FIRST MEDICAL MANAGEMENT LTD./MED+STOP

Established in 1984, First Medical operates a chain of family practice and convenient care medical centres that provide quality, non-emergency medical care on a "no-appointment necessary" basis. The facilities offer extended hours of operation, convenient and accessible locations, attractive design, and state-of-the-art equipment.

Founded in Calgary by a group of doctors and a medical administrator, First Medical owns and operates 10 medical centres in Western Canada in which patients receive quality service from family doctors, dentists, physiotherapists, medical laboratories, and X-ray facilities. The first "Med+Stop" convenient care centre was opened in Calgary in 1984 with a staff of eight. Since then the company has added more than 100 employees, and opened three more medical centres in Calgary, four in Edmonton, one in Winnipeg, and one in Regina.

First Medical designs, builds, and manages the centres, while qualified doctors and dentists run the clinic's medical/dental practices, contracting with First Medical to provide them with a turnkey lease of the premises, as well as complete medical/dental centre management. The firm also attracts physicians who want to convert their existing joint practices into "Med+Stop" centres. In 1987 "Med+Stop" converted two existing medical centres—a 16-year practice in Edmonton and a 10-year practice in Sherwood Park—into the "Med+Stop" concept.

The company opened its first Superstore convenient care medical/dental centre in Edmonton in August 1987, and two more have since been established in Winnipeg and Regina. First Medical has an exclusive agreement to operate medical/dental facilities within the chain's "megastore" complexes in Western Canada.

All "Med+Stop" centres include professionally designed exterior signs and interior layouts with wait-ing, examining, treatment, laboratory, storage, and administrative facilities. Located in high-traffic areas, the medical centres employ professionally trained medical support staff and proven management systems, resulting in efficient clinic administration.

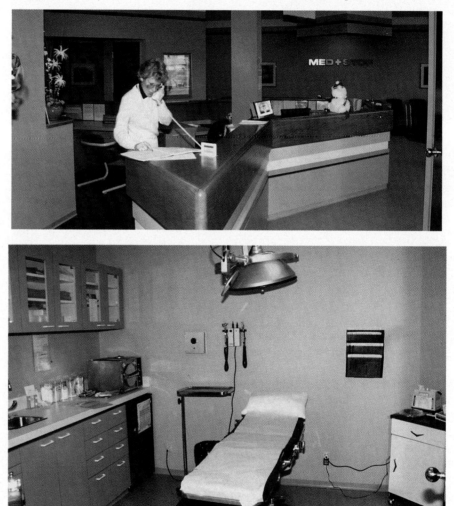

The firm has developed systems to effectively handle centralized billings and patient records; operational policies and procedures; employee recruitment, training, and incentives; centralized cash management and financial control; purchasing; clinic innovation; and marketing.

These management services allow physicians the freedom to practice medicine without the worry of mundane administrative duties. In "Med+Stop" centres, physicians can also accommodate higher patient volume, earn extra income, work defined hours, and remain free from capital commitments. These features are attractive to physicians who are now faced with government regulations, escalating costs, and increased competition.

Both "Med+Stop" and First Med-

First Medical's convenient care centres are staffed by doctors, dentists, and physiotherapists, and have medical laboratories and X-ray facilities.

ical offer equity and management positions to medical professionals. The centres are run by doctor-owned and -operated clinic organizations that make all medical decisions and policies. More than 75 physicians in Western Canada's 10 "Med+Stop" medical centres accommodate approximately 15,000 patients per month.

ALBERTA CANCER FOUNDATION

The Cross Cancer Institute in Edmonton is one of several provincial facilities operated by the Alberta Cancer Board under its mandate: "To establish and operate cancer hospitals and outpatient facilities; to conduct programs for the prevention, detection, and diagnosis of cancer; to treat and care for cancer patients; and to further cancer research."

Located on the southwest corner of the university campus, the institute is closely affiliated with the University of Alberta's Faculty of Medicine and the University of Alberta Hospitals. This affiliation permits joint appointments of professional staff, collaborative research and education opportunities, and multidisciplinary interaction and care.

The Cross Cancer Institute offers the citizens of northern Alberta the combined expertise of 44 full-time specialists and is recog-

The Cross Cancer Institute is closely affiliated with the University of Alberta Faculty of Medicine and the University of Alberta Hospitals. It is located on the university campus in Edmonton.

nized worldwide as being at the forefront in cancer diagnosis, treatment, care, and research. In addition to the 76-bed, inpatient unit at the Cross Cancer Institute, the outpatient clinics and day care serve thousands of patients each year.

Still very much a misunderstood disease, cancer patients demand specialized health care resources to combat this disruptive, debilitating disease. In recognizing the unique need for specialized care for cancer patients, the Government of Alberta created the Alberta Cancer Board to coordinate cancer care services and provide the necessary means for quality care.

The Alberta Cancer Foundation is the vehicle through which Albertans contribute to the well-being of cancer patients and to the support of cancer research. The foundation is responsible for accepting and managing funds, allocating them fairly to the clinics (Cross Cancer Institute, Edmonton; Tom Baker Cancer Centre, Calgary; Central Alberta Cancer Centre, Red Deer; Lethbridge Cancer Clinic; and numerous outreach programs throughout

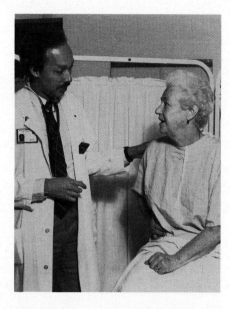

Dr. Anthony Fields, director of the Cross Cancer Institute, provides valuable outpatient care to one of the institute's patients.

the province), and raising funds for major capital expenditures.

The Alberta Cancer Foundation continues to work very closely with the Canadian Cancer Society to identify and maximize the strengths of their respective organizations, and to enhance and expand voluntary contributions to cancer programs, and inevitably, to cancer patients.

CALGARY CONVENTION CENTRE

ABOVE: The Calgary Convention Centre is at the heart of downtown Calgary.

LEFT: The Garden Terrace is a popular spot for a variety of special events..

Located in the heart of downtown, the Calgary Convention Centre is an innovative, three-level building, encompassing more than 184,000 square feet of banquet, exhibition, conference, and display areas.

Perfect for conventions of up to 2,000 delegates, the Convention Centre offers space for a variety of conferences and events. The convention level alone features 50,000 square feet of meeting and/or exhibition space. In total there are 14 meeting and banquet rooms, the largest of which seats 2,200 theatre-style and 1,680 for a banquet.

The centre's 23,740-square-foot Exhibition Hall is equipped with every up-to-date convenience for trade shows, including full communications facilities, a terrazzo floor with no weight restrictions, and gas, water, and electricity. A five-bay loading dock leads to three freight elevators, the largest of which has a 30,000-pound load capability.

Macleod Hall comprises 20,000 square feet of convention space, specifically designed for banquets, receptions, and meetings. This richly decorated hall can be sectioned into four soundproof areas, each independently equipped with temperature, lighting, and audiovisual control. A permanent stage, an extension, and supplemental portable staging is also available.

Exhibition and Macleod halls are linked by Macleod Foyer, which offers an additional 5,100 square feet of floor space. All three areas can accommodate trade shows of 260 booths, each measuring 8 feet by 10 feet.

A beautiful indoor terraced garden on the third level is the perfect setting for fashion shows, luncheons, receptions, or for a quiet interlude between hectic meetings.

Since opening in 1974, the Convention Centre has accommodated more than 250,000 out-of-town delegates and brought in excess of $80 million to the city. A proposal to build a convention complex as part of an urban-renewal project was conceived during the 1960s and presented to the City of Calgary in the early 1970s.

The proposal included a provision for on-site accommodation. Consequently, a partnership was established with Four Seasons Hotels Limited of Toronto, a Canadian company with a reputation for quality and service.

A short time later the Glenbow Museum was incorporated into the convention complex. The project thus consisted of three major elements: a 400-room hotel built by Calgary Convention Centre Limited on land leased from the city, an $8.8-million convention centre complex built and owned by the city, and the Glenbow Museum, constructed and owned by the Alberta Government. The total cost of the complex was $32 million.

The ground-breaking ceremony on September 5, 1972, was attended by more than 80 civic leaders, dignitaries, and businessmen. The official opening ceremony took place two years later on November 14, 1974. The hotel underwent an ownership change in 1985 and is now called the Skyline Hotel.

Convention services include a special centre to handle any last-minute requirements, trained audiovisual technicians and operators, in-house show services for drapery and furnishing needs, customs services, on-site nursing services, and 24-hour security.

The Calgary Convention Centre is also active in the Alberta community. The centre provides rooms for the kickoff ceremonies of the annual United Way and Cancer Society campaigns in Calgary, donates Christmas gifts to the Calgary Indian Friendship Centre, and gives gifts and food hampers to needy families supported by the Salvation Army.

United Farmers of Alberta Co-operative Limited

Ramada Renaissance Hotel

Homestead Antiques

Sinclair Supplies Inc.

Mark's Work Wearhouse

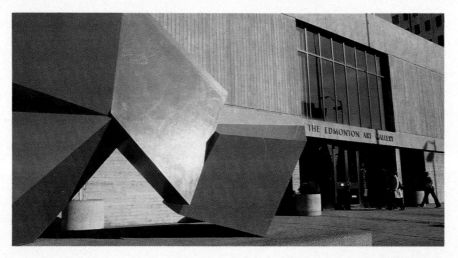

Courtesy, Westfile, Inc.

CHAPTER

The Marketplace

Alberta's retail establishments, service industries, and restaurants are essential to the region's economy.

United Farmers of Alberta Co-operative Limited 334-335; Ramada Renaissance Hotel 336-337; Homestead Antiques 338; Sinclair Supplies Inc. 339; Mark's Work Wearhouse 340-341

UNITED FARMERS OF ALBERTA CO-OPERATIVE LIMITED

United Farmers of Alberta Co-operative Limited (UFA) is the largest marketer of petroleum products and farm supply merchandise to Alberta's agricultural industry. Headquartered in Calgary, UFA has 125 petroleum agencies and 30 farm supply stores throughout the province.

As the oldest farm organization in Alberta, UFA has a rich and colorful history. In 1909, just four years after Alberta became a province, the Canadian Society of Equity and the Alberta Farmers' Association amalgamated to form the UFA. Branches of the organization were established in nearly every part of Alberta, and the UFA soon became the hub of educational and recreational activities in towns and villages.

UFA amended its charter in 1918 to permit business transactions with organization members. This was UFA's first entry into commerce, and a limited farm supply business was conducted through the locals.

In 1921 dissatisfaction with existing political parties convinced farmers to form their own political organization. During the provincial election held that same year, the

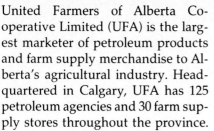

UFA Party won two-thirds of the seats in the Provincial Legislature and gained representation at the federal level as well.

The UFA Central Co-operative was established in 1932 to consolidate the buying power of UFA locals. Basic bulk items, such as coal, wood, apples, honey, and flour, were purchased in carload quantities. In 1935 UFA entered the petroleum distribution field, and a supply contract was negotiated with Imperial Oil Limited. Imperial cre-

ated a subsidiary, Maple Leaf Petroleum, to serve UFA exclusively.

UFA withdrew from political action in 1939; it amended its constitution and requested the resignations of any directors or officials holding political positions. In 1948 Alberta Farmers' Union and UFA amalgamated in order to create a strong, unified voice on government issues.

UFA's first farm supply store was opened in Calgary in 1954. Two years later the association purchased the assets of Maple Leaf Petroleum Limited for one million dollars. Despite a 12-year repayment program, the bank was reimbursed

The United Farmers of Alberta farm supply store in High River, Alberta.

The UFA petroleum outlet in Carstairs.

within three years.

As of 1987 more than 65,000 Alberta farmers and ranchers cooperatively own UFA. The organization's main objective is to reduce farm input costs and provide quality service to its member/customers. UFA has four active divisions: administration, communications, petroleum, and farm supplies.

UFA is the only major petroleum marketing company that is wholly owned by Alberta's agricul-

In 1987 UFA installed a state-of-the-art, farm-oriented computer system that provides staff with detailed information, improved customer service, and inventory records. This system is in use in the majority of UFA's farm stores and in the future may be installed in the petroleum outlets.

UFA is a major supporter of Alberta's rural youth, sponsoring annual scholarships to Fairview College, Lakeland College, Olds College, and Lethbridge Community College. UFA is also heavily involved with the 4-H organization in Alberta, purchasing steer calves annually from rural youth.

UFA further supports Alberta's youth by donating trophies, sponsoring athletic teams, and holding seminars for various organizations, including the Rural Educational and Development Association. UFA has been a major financial contributor to such agricultural organizations as Unifarm, Goldeye Foundation, Co-op College, and the Co-op Union of Canada. UFA's elected officers, management, and staff also contribute their skills and time to the agricultural community.

tural producers. Of the 125 bulk petroleum outlets serving the agricultural and commercial industries, more than 90 now offer retail gas service. A limited line of automotive accessories is also stocked at most petroleum outlets.

UFA has 30 modern farm supply stores throughout Alberta that stock a selection exceeding 10,000 different products. UFA Building Services can assist farmers in the planning, design, and construction of a simple garage or cattle barn, a storage shed, or a complete riding arena. The organization can offer the materials and equipment, as well as construction techniques, for archrib, conventional stud wall, square pole, round pole, and steel-frame buildings.

Because UFA is wholly owned by the farmers and ranchers of Alberta and supplies the area's agricultural community with the materials it needs, the organization proudly regards itself as "an Alberta company serving Albertans."

UFA prides itself on providing one-stop farm stores that carry everything from lumber, building supplies, and fencing materials, to machinery, hand and power tools,

One of the many husband-and-wife teams working together at a UFA Petroleum outlet.

herbicides and other crop supplies, livestock equipment and feed, and animal husbandry needs.

Product quality and customer service and satisfaction are, as they have always been, number-one priorities at UFA, and all merchandise is sold with a one-year guarantee.

State-of-the-art computer equipment aids a UFA employee in the preparation of an invoice.

RAMADA RENAISSANCE HOTEL

The Ramada Renaissance Hotel in Edmonton combines cost-effective luxury with intimate surroundings by setting hospitality standards found only in a world-class hotel.

A new addition to the downtown core, Edmonton's Ramada features 300 well-appointed and comfortable guest rooms, including 14 deluxe suites and the exclusive Renaissance Club, located on the top floor of the hotel.

On the Renaissance Club level, accommodation and extra services are provided in the tradition of top-rated hotels. Services in the form of fresh cut flowers, current magazines, and prestige toiletries all add to the convenience and comfort of the guest. Convenience and comfort are classic Ramada Renaissance traditions.

Within the hotel itself patrons enjoy dining at Le Gueridon, a critically acclaimed gourmet dining room featuring the fine art of classic French cuisine. Or, for lighter fare, there is the Boulevard Cafe, a friendly family restaurant open seven days a week for breakfast, lunch, dinner, and Sunday brunch.

The health spa, located on the second floor, includes an indoor swimming pool, whirlpool, steam room, and extensive exercise facilities. All patrons are welcome to unwind with the first-class equipment—to relax after a long trip or after a long series of meetings.

The Edmonton Ramada Renaissance has all the meeting and banquet amenities available, with all facilities especially noted for their plush atmosphere and up-to-date conference aids and furnishings. Banquet facilities include the elegant Renaissance Ballroom, featuring French service for banquet functions and catering to receptions of 650 people.

Centrally located in the heart of the vibrant business centre and government sector, the hotel offers quick access to fine shopping, excellent restaurants, and a modern light

rail transit system to commute to all major sporting events.

Although the Ramada Renaissance Hotel in Edmonton is relatively new, it conforms to the standards of excellence established by every hotel bearing the Ramada Renaissance label. In fact, the Ramada Renaissance Hotel network extends throughout the world, with hotels gracing major cities such as Hong Kong, Zurich, and Hamburg. Since 1981, 33 Renaissance properties have opened worldwide and 13

Conveniently located in downtown Edmonton, the Ramada Renaissance has all the amenities to ensure guests' continued return to the hotel's first-class facilities.

more are under construction or development.

The Ramada Renaissance network recognizes that success in the travel market today rests to a great extent on the hotel's ability to deliver a top-notch product at a highly competitive price. With today's traveller demanding a high

ABOVE: The Ramada Renaissance Hotel has a variety of suites and rooms to suit every occasion.

RIGHT: The lobby of Edmonton's Ramada Renaissance—where the friendly, helpful staff and management go out of their way to ensure a pleasant stay.

level of amenities, ambience, and personalized service, Ramada Renaissance Hotels have the answer.

Although no two Ramada Renaissance properties are alike, they all adhere to strict standards of excellence. All offer between 200 to 500 rooms, the optimum number for providing the necessary personalized service.

Other necessary amenities include a fine restaurant serving food comparable to the best restaurants in the market; extensive meeting space; a health club, sauna, exercise room, pool, and whirlpool; a Renaissance Club level; and, of course, suites, including two presidential suites, executive suites, and hospitality suites. Edmonton's Ramada Renaissance Hotel has all of these amenities.

Ramada Renaissance Hotels are being patronized by travellers, many of whom have been loyal customers to Ramada for years. Experienced travellers to Edmonton who are seeking an upscale hotel with value, standards, service, and amenities consistent with the price/value relationship will recognize that these services are cornerstones of the Ramada name—in Edmonton and around the world.

HOMESTEAD ANTIQUES

A love for Alberta history and an interest in collecting early pioneer artifacts have evolved into a thriving business for a family in Bragg Creek, Alberta, a small community nestled in the foothills west of Calgary.

In 1977 Bob and Jackie McLennan began selling early homestead items from two rooms in their log home, which also served as the local post office. As the business prospered, Jackie resigned after 18 years as postmaster. Bob, a log builder by trade, moved the family to a new home and the original homestead became a full-fledged antique business, aptly named Homestead Antiques.

Homestead's business started with a focus on pioneer items pertaining to life on the prairies at the turn of the century, but the McLennans soon developed an interest in the beautiful oak furniture of that era. The strong, sturdy furniture of the Golden Oak Era of North America, circa 1880 to 1920, now dominates Homestead Antiques—the round oak tables with their many leaves that can seat 10 to 20 at a family gathering, press-back chairs, the old iceboxes now used for stereo units or liquor cabinets, rolltop desks, china cabinets to hold today's collections, player pianos, parlor tables, beds, dressers, and washstands. This furniture was designed to appeal to people of average means and was built with a certain degree of standardization to enable easy packing and shipping. In the early days on the Canadian prairies, it was distributed to a large extent by the T. Eaton and Hudson's Bay Co. catalogues.

Albertans have a strong desire to own these beautiful, historic oak pieces, and the McLennans search the continent for premium examples. There is tremendous investment potential for oak furniture of this calibre, especially as it nears the significant 100-year mark, which denotes a genuine antique, along with the ever-increasing demand and depleting supply. The leading Canadian manufacturer of premium-quality oak was the George McLagan Furniture Company of Stratford, Ontario.

Round oak table and pressed-back chairs, circa 1905.

The pieces most desired are those in excellent original condition; however, some repair or refinishing is usually required, and Bob, a professional woodworker, has become skilled in the art of restoration for the store as well as for private individuals. "We deal with customers on a personal basis, like good friends," says Bob. "You have to put your heart into your work."

Each piece sold through Homestead Antiques is guaranteed indefinitely, given reasonable care, and customers are encouraged to upgrade their furniture as their family and financial situations change. They are given full credit for their original purchase. Although Homestead's specialty is quality oak, the company also handles pieces in pine, ash, elm, and maple, as well as early Canadian artifacts.

Bob and Jackie McLennan have been residents of Bragg Creek since 1956 and have a long history of involvement in community activities including several youth projects. They look forward to more leisure time to spend with family and friends, and hope that some family members will become interested in the business. To date their youngest daughter, Bonnie Lee, who lives in an apartment above the store, has been learning the trade and seems destined to carry on the tradition of Homestead Antiques.

SINCLAIR SUPPLIES INC.

Sinclair Supplies Inc. is an Edmonton-based company that has made growth and expansion its trademark, taking great pride in its evolution from a one-man, two-car garage operation to a massive office, warehouse, distribution and manufacturing complex with separate warehouses located in Edmonton and Calgary.

Sinclair Supplies is primarily a wholesale and distribution company for all products pertaining to the heating, ventilating, and mechanical trades. Founded by Walter Sinclair in 1946, the firm soon moved from his two-car garage to a 3,600-square-foot warehouse and never looked back.

Growth is the key word here, and Sinclair Supplies matched the growth of the Alberta economy, with its tremendous growth in sales and service, to Alberta's burgeoning construction industry during Alberta's "boom" cycles. The real success lies in the firm's ability to keep up with product technology and to remain cognizant of the many new products hitting the market. Customers receive the fin-

est products from more than 200 suppliers, thanks to Sinclair's dedication to keeping up with new technology and product advancement.

According to Sinclair president Dan Sorochan, pure market acceptance dictates whether the product is valuable and "through the conscientious approach by our employees, we stay alert to what the market offers and to what the market requires—making sure our customers receive the best. We are always ready and willing to warehouse and distribute new products for the Alberta market." The aim, says Sorochan, is to provide a 90- to 95-percent service level on all products Sinclair represents to the heating, ventilating, and mechanical trades.

With more and more products coming on-stream and with its client base expanding annually, it was inevitable that Sinclair would also expand its office, showroom, and warehouse space to better serve customers with larger inventories.

The first expansion took place in 1956, when the 3,600-square-foot warehouse space doubled. In 1967 a combination 3,000-square-foot office/9,000-square-foot warehouse building was purchased, home to

Sinclair Supplies for the next 20 years, although the company kept outgrowing the building. It was expanded by 6,000 square feet in 1968 and another 10,000 square feet in 1975.

By 1986 it was becoming increasingly obvious that a new, larger facility was needed for the head office and main sales area. In celebration of the company's 40 years of operation, a new facility was opened with 10,000 square feet of office space, 57,000 square feet of warehouse space, and 10,000 square feet of manufacturing space.

Service will now be increased, thanks to the larger warehouse space, suitable for the display and demonstration of equipment, as well as allowing for rapid introduction of new product lines. Larger warehouse space means larger inventories on hand to service the needs of clients immediately.

A Red Deer branch was acquired on October 1, 1987, and will provide the central Alberta mechanical trades and local industry with supplies and inventory.

Larger warehouse space means better service, since new equipment and product lines can be displayed and easily demonstrated for potential customers.

Sinclair Supplies houses office, warehouse, and manufacturing space in this new facility. In keeping with Sinclair's reputation, expansion is an ongoing process.

MARK'S WORK WEARHOUSE

In 1977 Mark Blumes left a management position at The Bay. Today he is the founder and president of an innovative and successful national retail chain—Mark's Work Wearhouse.

Mark's Work Wearhouse opened its first store in Calgary in 1977, catering to the working men and women of the Alberta oil patch. Within four years that single store

in the retail industry. Blue-collar workers found it difficult to shop for their clothes. Department stores had turned into fashion centres and downplayed heavy-duty workwear by putting it in the basement. Blumes wanted to create a store where men could feel comfortable stopping in after a day on the job to pick up needed workwear.

He developed his idea during

less cost control are passed on to customers. Mark's also designs and manufactures several exclusive lines, including Mark's Work Wearhouse jeans, WorkPro, GadAbouts children's wear, Denver Hayes, and Gila safety clothing. The company has also underwritten the development of freestanding specialty clothiers such as the Wind River Outfitting Company.

had grown to a 36-store chain operating in five provinces. Blumes has never looked back, and today Mark's Work Wearhouse is a leading retailer not just of workwear, but also of jeans, casual wear, and sports clothing. Mark's operates more than 120 stores located in every Canadian province, as well as a successful mail order business in Canada's remote regions.

The son of a Calgary doctor, Blumes graduated from the Southern Alberta Institute of Technology's business administration program and went to work for The Bay in Winnipeg in 1964. Given the breadth of his vision and ambition, his tenure was predictably stormy.

By the time he left The Bay, Blumes had discovered a large void

several months of recuperation in a hospital from two corneal transplants, and by the time he departed from The Bay, he had a 65-page concept and a network of wholesale contacts willing to give him inventory on credit. The Mark's Work Wearhouse concept was born with the Calgary store, generating sales of $1.2 million the first year. This store and those to follow were specifically designed to cater to the working man, creating an informal, durable atmosphere with sturdy display counters piled high with goods and staff wearing blue jeans to make the blue-collar man feel at ease.

The majority of merchandise Mark's Work Wearhouse carries is made in Canada. The fruits of relent-

Mark's Work Wearhouse stores are bright, modern, and specifically designed for ease of shopping.

The firm experienced dramatic expansion during the late 1970s, but the recession created havoc for Mark's Work Wearhouse and put a stop to new store openings. Mark's twin brother, Moe, joined the organization in 1981 as chief financial officer, and the two set out to reduce the impact of the economic downturn. By 1983 operations were streamlined, stores were closed, overhead costs were cut, and inventories were reduced to more manageable levels.

New capital was injected into Mark's Work Wearhouse with the acquisition of four profitable car dealerships from Financial Trustco Capital Ltd. of Calgary. The acquisition provided diversification, a larger capital base, and increased cash flow to support renewed expansion of the retail business.

Mark's Work Wearhouse opened four new stores in Winnipeg in 1987, recognizing that major metropolitan area as a significant source of revenue with a relatively stable economy. The company also instituted a franchise program in 1986 that will play an increasingly important role in the overall growth of Mark's Work Wearhouse; up to 30 franchise stores are to be in operation by 1989.

As Mark's product mix has evolved to include more casual clothing for men, women, and children, stores have become bigger, brighter, and more colorful.

A customer service department was introduced in 1986 to assist sales staff in locating merchandise from any of the vast resources available to satisfy the individual needs of Mark's Work Wearhouse customers. "How did we do?" cards are handed out to customers and returned, at the rate of 7,000 per year, to be answered personally by Mark himself. Customer service became such a motto that one request for closing tabs on both back pockets of a pair of jeans prompted the firm to produce them on the entire line.

The company's retail sales and support staffs number 1,200. Sales staff members are holders of Professional Selling Skills diplomas from the Mark's Work Wearhouse Training Department. The diploma course helps to ensure customer satisfaction by providing employees with a full knowledge of Work Wearhouse's return and guarantee policies, improving product knowledge, and helping staff ask customers the right questions.

As employees gather experience, they are encouraged to become in-store product managers. They not only become experts on the items in question but also handle the ordering, stocking, and even planning for their own area. By keeping the corporate decision structure as close to the grass roots as possible, Blumes ensures his stores can respond to his customers' immediate regional and seasonal needs. Thus, this commitment to staff training reflects a commitment to meet the needs of customers, which has helped Mark's Work Wearhouse to become the only major national retailer based in Alberta.

A look at one of the departments within a Mark's Work Wearhouse store.

Gulf Canada Resources Limited

Husky Oil Ltd.

Domtar Energy Inc.

Shell Canada Limited

Nova Corporation of Alberta

Bow Valley Resource Services Ltd.

Fekete Associates Inc.

Alberta Research Council

Pancontinental Oil Ltd.

CEDA-Reactor Ltd.

Alberta Oil Sands Technology and Research Authority

BP Canada Inc.

Amoco Canada Petroleum Company Ltd.

ProGas Limited

Total Petroleum Canada Ltd.

Badger Drilling Ltd.

Western Atlas Canada Ltd.

Esso Resources Canada Limited

Pan-Alberta Gas Ltd.

Erskine Resources Corporation

Interprovincial Pipe Line Limited

Resources and Technology

Alberta's vast natural resources and technology-related industries play a significant role in the province's economy.

GULF CANADA RESOURCES LIMITED

Gulf Canada Resources Limited, a Canadian-owned natural-resource company based in Calgary, is engaged in worldwide oil and gas exploration and production.

Gulf was founded as the British American Oil Company (B-A) in Toronto, Ontario, in 1906. By 1955 B-A had become a fully integrated oil company, with marketing operations from coast to coast, and was an active oil and gas explorer and producer in Western Canada.

In a 1956 amalgamation B-A acquired the assets of a Calgary-based exploration and production operation, Canadian Gulf Oil Company. In 1966 B-A sold its wholly owned U.S. producing subsidiary, The British American Oil Producing Company, to concentrate its exploration and production efforts in Canada. B-A and two other Canadian firms, Shawinigan Chemicals Limited and Royalite Oil Company Lim-

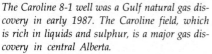

ited, formed Gulf Oil Canada Limited in 1969. The firm was renamed Gulf Canada Limited in 1978 to reflect a broader involvement in other forms of energy and minerals.

In 1985 Olympia & York of Toronto purchased majority interest in Gulf Canada Limited from its U.S. owner, Chevron Corporation. Gulf subsequently sold its downstream refining and marketing

The Caroline 8-1 well was a Gulf natural gas discovery in early 1987. The Caroline field, which is rich in liquids and sulphur, is a major gas discovery in central Alberta.

assets, and reorganized as Gulf Canada Corporation. Today the company is known as Gulf Canada Resources Limited and employs approximately 1,700 people.

Gulf is one of Canada's leading producers of crude oil and natural gas. In 1987 oil production stabilized at about 90,000 barrels per day, and natural gas sales increased to approximately 280 million cubic feet per day.

Enhanced oil-recovery projects accounted for about 9 percent of Gulf's total crude oil production. The company has production from four enhanced oil-recovery projects: a miscible flood project (a process in which a hydrocarbon solvent is injected into the reservoir, moving otherwise unrecoverable oil to producing wells) at Fenn-Big Valley, a new project at Goose River, and partner-operated projects at South Swan Hills and Swan Hills in Alberta.

The firm also owns or has substantial interests in 10 major Alberta gas-processing plants, which process raw gas to produce market-

Senex-Trout, in northern Alberta, is a key area of current oil exploration, development, and production activity for Gulf. Production from the area had increased to 2,600 barrels per day by the end of the third quarter of 1987.

able gas and recover natural gas liquids and sulphur.

Gulf has a 9-percent interest in the Syncrude project in northern Alberta, a joint venture created for mining shallow deposits of oil sands and extracting and upgrading the crude bitumen into synthetic crude oil. The firm is also involved in planned expansion at Syncrude, and has a 20-percent interest in the OSLO lands for which a 75,000-barrel-per-day project is being considered.

Gulf has extensive land holdings in Western Canada and the frontiers, providing a base for its petroleum and natural gas exploration and development programs. Gulf participated in the drilling of 454 gross wells in Western Canada in 1986, which resulted in 277 successful oil and 23 successful gas wells. While many of these wells were extensions to known accumulations, significant discoveries were made at Senex-Trout, Erskine, Westerose, and Groat-Haddock, all in Alberta. Noteworthy discoveries in 1987 include oil in the Senex-Trout region, and at Enchant and Weir Hill, plus gas at Caroline and Chedderville.

Gulf is a major participant in the two largest oil discoveries in the frontier areas of Canada. The company holds a 51-percent interest in the Amauligak structure in the Beaufort Sea and a 25-percent interest in the Hibernia oilfield off the coast of Newfoundland.

In 1987 Gulf announced plans to pursue opportunities internationally in the search for oil and gas. Al-

Amauligak, in the Beaufort Sea, is a world-class oil discovery with reserves estimated at up to 700 million barrels. In 1986 the mobile arctic caisson Molikpaq conducted extended flow tests at the Amauligak I-65B well.

though its major focus will continue to be Canada, Gulf is pursuing international opportunities to add reserves and production. The company is currently involved in exploration programs in the Gulf of Suez and in Southeast Asia. Gulf also has one of the world's largest deposits of high-quality, surface-mineable anthracite at Mount Klappan, British Columbia.

Gulf has also been active within the community, donating about $1.9 million to a variety of regional and national causes and programs in 1987. Gulf supports local United Way campaigns, hospitals and other medical institutions, community service groups, and civic organizations. A large portion of the company's donation budget is allocated to education, the arts, and amateur sports.

Gulf Canada Resources Limited has sponsored a set of concerts called the Gulf Collector's Classics Series, performed by the Calgary Philharmonic Orchestra. The company has donated funds to the Canadian Hostel Association for a hostel in Kananaskis Country, and has sponsored a lecture hall at the University of Calgary. The firm has also sponsored a backstage rehearsal studio for the Calgary City Ballet Company. In addition, Gulf supports science fairs and Junior Achievement both nationally and in areas where it operates.

Gulf is involved in heavy oil production, primarily from Saskatchewan, and in oil sands development in Alberta. Gulf is a founding partner in Syncrude, and is also involved in the OSLO project.

HUSKY OIL LTD.

Husky Oil Ltd., an integrated Canadian oil and gas company with head offices in Calgary, is engaged in the exploration, development, production, and transportation of crude oil and natural gas. Husky is also involved in the refining of crude oil and the wholesale and retail marketing of refined petroleum products.

The company's upstream operations are in Western Canada, off the country's East Coast, and in the Beaufort Sea. Downstream operations extend from Western Canada through to the Ontario/Quebec border, and the firm has international interests in Southeast Asia.

In April 1987 Husky shareholders approved the complete reorganization of the ownership of the corporation. Husky Oil Ltd. is now a privately held company controlled jointly by two principal shareholders, NOVA Corporation of Alberta and Hong Kong-based Hutchinson Whampoa Limited. Remaining shares are held by VHHC Holdings Inc. and the Canadian Imperial Bank of Commerce.

The Husky Refining Company, founded by Canadian Glenn E. Neilson, got its start in the heavy oil business in 1938 in Cody, Wyoming. The firm expanded into retail marketing in 1939, and by 1946 had

Husky is an active player in exploration and production of conventional and heavy crude oil and natural gas.

established a wholly owned Canadian subsidiary in Calgary known as Husky Oil and Refining Ltd. In 1953 the Canadian and U.S. organizations split into two separate companies, and by 1960 Husky Oil Canada Ltd. had become the parent of the U.S. subsidiary. In 1978 NOVA acquired shares on the open market and the following year acquired additional shares held by the founding Neilson family, thus gaining majority ownership of Husky. Husky sold its U.S. subsidiary in 1984.

Husky now has a substantial asset base in heavy oil properties in the Lloydminster region of Saskatchewan and Alberta, and during 1986 and 1987 the company made several conventional oil discoveries in the Peace River Arch in northwestern Alberta. Husky is also involved in a significant gas discovery made in the Caroline area of southwestern Alberta. Indications are that when this field is developed, it will be one of the largest in Western Canada. The company's East Coast discoveries and participation in the Amauligak project in the Beaufort Sea also look promising.

Husky's infrastructure—pipelines, production batteries, treating facilities, gas compressor stations, and gas-processing plants—supports the production of about 41,000 barrels of oil and natural gas liquids and about 60 million cubic feet of natural gas each day. Husky has working interests in about 5,000 oil and gas wells, one-half of which are operated by the company. Husky's heavy oil production is approximately 27,000 barrels per day,

Husky's corporate headquarters is located in Calgary's twin-tower Western Canadian Place complex, 50 percent of which is owned by the company.

or two-thirds of its total production. Heavy oil represents about 60 percent of the firm's proven oil reserves.

Engaged in all aspects of downstream petroleum operations, Husky Oil Ltd. owns and operates two refineries located at Lloydminster, Alberta, and Prince George, British Columbia. The firm distributes, stores, and markets a wide variety of light petroleum products in Western Canada, Ontario, and the Yukon. Product distribution and marketing are carried out through an established network of wholesale and retail outlets extending from Vancouver Island to the Ontario/Quebec border.

An example of one of Husky's modern retail marketing outlets, incorporating a convenience store.

DOMTAR ENERGY INC.

In 1979 Domtar Inc., a resource-based multibusiness Canadian corporation, invested $44 million in oil and gas projects and created a wholly owned subsidiary to manage these interests.

From small interests in a few joint ventures in Western Canada and the United States, Domtar Energy has grown to become a significant junior operator in the Alberta oil patch, assuming direct responsibility for management of its purchased joint-interest lands and engaging in extensive programs in Alberta to explore and develop oil and natural gas reserves. The firm currently invests about $8.5 million annually, most of it in new prospects.

As of January 1, 1983, Domtar assumed management responsibility for all of its Canadian properties. A large portion of the company's acreage is located in the Deep Basin area of northwestern Alberta and northeastern British Columbia. Since 1979 Domtar has shared in the development of the Elmworth-Wapiti gas field in west-central Alberta, from which about half of its energy revenues are currently generated. The firm is a working-interest owner of two gas plants near Grande Prairie, Alberta, which remove ethanes, propanes, and butanes from the gas stream, increasing the value of the product. For 1987 Domtar's production of gas, oil, and condensates was about 1.95 billion cubic feet and 210 MSTB, respectively.

Virtually all of Domtar's gas reserves are in areas in which gas is contracted for sale to pipeline companies. the firm's competitiveness as a junior producer rests on its quality product, dependably supplied, and its low finding and production costs. As of December 31, 1987, the company held interest in 96,500 net unexplored acres, mostly in Alberta. At that time the proven plus probable reserves of the business comprising 84 BCF as gas had a pre-tax present value, discounted at 15 percent, of $68 million.

Drilling Domtar Niton Gaswell 80 miles west of Edmonton, Alberta.

Domtar geologists review well logs from a discovery in southern Alberta.

In 1987 Domtar Energy commenced an exploration program to find 35 BCF of gas reserves. A successful start has been made on the project in an area 80 miles west of Edmonton, where the firm controls 12,000 net acres. Domtar is also involved in joint-venture exploration projects on a number of other properties, including Neutral Hills and Leedale, southwest of Edmonton. During 1987 the company participated in drilling about 69 wells.

Although Domtar Energy Inc. has a permanent staff of only 14, the company contracts a variety of specialized services, including geophysicists, engineers, and field operators.

Directly and through its parent company, Domtar's corporate donations support health, welfare, educational, and community programs—nationally, regionally, and particularly in the areas where the firm has operations. Employees in the energy company also contribute their own time, skills, and personal funds to a wide range of community and philanthropic causes.

347

SHELL CANADA LIMITED

Shell Canada Limited, with assets of more than $5 billion, is one of the largest integrated petroleum companies in Canada and the largest investor-owned petroleum company headquartered in Calgary.

In recent years Shell has ranked as the largest natural gas and sulphur producer in Canada, and is a major producer of crude oil and natural gas liquids, and an important producer of coal. The company is a leading manufacturer, distributor, and marketer of refined petroleum products and petrochemicals, and operates refineries in four provinces.

In 1984 Shell Canada moved its head office from Toronto to Calgary, underlining the company's confidence in Alberta's petroleum sector and its future. About one-half of Shell's 7,000 Canadian employees is now located in Alberta.

The firm traces its origins to 1911, when the Royal Dutch/Shell Group of Companies established a bunkering plant in Montreal to serve the ocean shipping trade. From this beginning Shell expanded operations into marketing, refining, and, later, oil and gas exploration and development.

Over the years Shell developed and implemented a wide range of innovative production and market-

Most of the styrene produced in the Scotford complex at Fort Saskatchewan, northwest of Edmonton, is for export.

ing techniques. It was the first to market propane from a Canadian refinery and the first to manufacture chemicals from petroleum in Canada. It became a leader in developing natural gas processing technology and is recognized for its technological advances in the drilling and production of gas with a high sulphur content.

Dramatic expansion marked the 1960s, when Shell acquired North Star Oil and Canadian Oil Companies. In that same period it became a public company, and today 21-percent ownership is held by public shareholders.

Shareholders saw, as result of improved productivity and chemical markets, 1987 earnings for the company that were almost double those of 1986. The company's exploration team has also had notable recent successes, making several oil and gas discoveries in Western Canada. The highlight was Shell's gas discovery at Caroline, near Sundre, Alberta. With a potential of some 2 trillion cubic feet of raw gas, the new Caroline field ranks as one of the most significant discoveries

made in the Western Canadian Basin in the past 20 years. Shell has acquired the rights to roughly 50 percent of the field, which is likely to commence production in the early 1990s.

The first phase of expansion of the Peace River oil sands complex in northern Alberta was completed in September 1986, on schedule and under budget. The project, started in 1985, involved the construction of a 10,000-barrel-per-day processing plant and related facilities, and the drilling of more than 200 wells.

In step with a new marketing slogan, The Move Is On, the corporation also launched new gasolines in 1986: Formula Shell and Super Formula Shell. The result of eight years of research and development at Shell laboratories around the world, Formula Shell contains a unique potassium-based spark-enhancer compound to stimulate faster and smoother engine performance, as well as improved detergent additives to clean the carburetor and fuel systems.

Shell is also undertaking an intensified gas-marketing program in the U.S. Pacific Northwest and California, and will soon begin

A production oil well reflected in the waters of northern Alberta.

delivering gas to the New England area.

In refining and petrochemicals, Shell has launched one of its most technologically advanced projects—the $1.4-billion Scotford complex near Edmonton. The new refinery is the first in the world designed to process synthetic crude oil produced from oil sands. The nearby world-scale petrochemical plant is the largest of its kind in Canada.

A distinct feature of Shell's participation in the petroleum industry has been its commitment to technology and innovation. Its Research and Technology Department team provides the company with a competitive edge. At the Calgary Research Centre the emphasis is on improving technology for exploration and production of hydrocarbons, developing techniques for enhanced oil recovery, and conducting research in materials corrosion and production chemistry.

Shell has more than 7,000 dedicated employees stationed across Canada, applying their expertise to one of the firm's five major departments: Resources, Products, Business Services, Research and Technology, and Corporate. The company is distinguished by its broad, ongo-

A drilling rig explores for natural gas in the foothills of Alberta.

Shell products on their way to service customers in the important industrial sector of the Alberta economy.

ing community support programs in Canada. Through Shell's Community Service Fund, active and retired employees, dealers, and agents receive grants in support of community projects to which they volunteer their time.

Complementing Shell Canada's technical leadership is its commitment to environmental protection. The company's positive environmental record is widely recognized. Shell Canada's Health, Safety, and Environment department works closely with company operating departments and project groups to ensure environmental considerations are integrated into project design. In 1986 Shell received an Alberta government environmental award to recognize its exemplary contribution to environmental protection.

Shell Canada Limited also supports Alberta's educational and cultural institutions. For example, an official sponsor of the 1988 Olympic Winter Games in Calgary, Shell supported "The Spirit Sings," the flagship event of the Olympic Arts Festival. This exhibition brought together from around the world 650 rare Canadian Indian and Inuit art objects. Organized by Calgary's Glenbow Museum, the exhibit later moved to Ottawa under the auspices of the Canadian Museum of Civilization. As a sponsor of this unique project, Shell believes it has contributed to a better understanding of Canadian native heritage.

NOVA CORPORATION OF ALBERTA

In the 35 years since it was formed as a natural gas pipeline company, NOVA Corporation of Alberta has become one of the largest corporations in Canada, with assets of close to $5 billion invested in energy-related industries throughout the province and around the world.

NOVA, headquartered in Calgary, has a unique position in the economic development of Alberta. NOVA was incorporated in 1954 by a special act of the Alberta government, which granted the company rights to build, own, and operate a provincewide natural gas-gathering

Headquartered in Calgary, NOVA has expanded its scope of operations dramatically since its incorporation in 1954 as a pipeline company.

and transportation system. Today NOVA has five main business sectors—gas transportation and marketing, petroleum, petrochemicals, manufacturing, and consulting and research—which successfully compete in the international marketplace.

In the spring of 1957 NOVA issued its original 2.5 million common shares. The *Financial Post* referred to the offering as "the biggest stock bonanza ever to hit the Prairies." Available only to Alberta residents, the shares were so popular that a rationing system was required. NOVA shares today are widely held, with more than 90 percent registered in Canada. The corporation has retained a strong Al-

berta ownership, and the shares trade actively on Canadian stock exchanges.

Throughout the 1960s NOVA continued to expand in line with the growing demand for Alberta natural gas. Today the 9,000-mile NOVA pipeline system is a sophisticated pipeline network and a key element in North America's energy infrastructure. The system carries more than 75 percent of Canada's marketed natural gas production and employs more than 1,700 people. Operations of the Alberta Gas Transmission Division, extend from the extreme northwest corner of the province to the southern, eastern, and western boundaries, forming one of the main components of Alberta's vital natural gas industry.

NOVA has earned international recognition for its innovative pipe-

With facilities in Alberta and Ontario, NOVA is the largest producer of polyethylene in Canada. Products are marketed around the world.

line technologies and practices. These innovations include the first large-diameter pipeline-installation project undertaken during winter months, and an automation program that allows the entire system to be monitored and controlled from a single control centre.

NOVA was also the first company in Canada to practise topsoil conservation, and one of the first to restore forested areas in pipeline rights-of-way. In addition, the NOVA system uses the world's first oil-free gas compressors, in which mechanical gas-sealing systems and magnetic bearings have replaced traditional equipment.

In the mid-1970s NOVA began a 10-year period of rapid growth, evolving from a pipeline utility company to the diversified energy corporation that exists today. At the end of 1987 assets totalled \$4.7 billion, and the NOVA group of companies employed some 7,000 people, with more than half located in Alberta.

Through sponsorship and joint ownership of the Canadian sections of the Alaska Highway Gas Pipeline and the Trans Quebec & Maritimes Pipeline, NOVA serves major new markets for Alberta gas in the

United States and Eastern Canada. Foothills Pipe Lines (Yukon) Ltd. was established in 1976 to design, build, and operate the Canadian segment of the Alaska Highway pipeline. The first phase of the pipeline project delivers Alberta gas to several U.S. markets, including Califor-

NOVA experts use their technical skills and specialized equipment at Airdrie, Alberta, to maintain high standards of safety and reliability for pipeline operations.

NOVA's petrochemical complex at Joffre, Alberta, boosts the Alberta economy by producing value-added products that are marketed worldwide.

nia and the midwestern states. Trans Quebec & Maritimes delivers Alberta gas to markets in Quebec.

NOVA's gas-marketing activities are conducted by Pan-Alberta Gas, one of the largest gas-marketing companies in Canada, with contracts to market gas for more than 400 Alberta producers. About 85 percent of its sales are made to U.S. customers in the midwestern states, California, and the Pacific Northwest.

Through investments in Husky Oil and Novalta Resources, NOVA is involved in oil and gas exploration in Alberta, the Canadian frontiers, and internationally. Husky also develops, produces, refines, markets, and distributes energy products. Novalta Resources is a natural gas producer serving diverse markets. Among its commitments is providing a secure supply of fuel gas to NOVA's petrochemical operations, near Red Deer at Joffre, Alberta.

NOVA played a pioneering role in the development of the Alberta

petrochemical industry, which is based on the use of Alberta's extensive natural gas reserves as a petrochemical feedstock. Since the early 1970s this industry, with NOVA a leading participant, has been one of the province's largest capital investors. More than 75 percent of NOVA's petrochemical production is exported from Canada to markets throughout the United States and the Pacific Rim.

NOVA operates facilities for the production of ethylene and polyethylene at a world-scale petrochemical complex at Joffre. Methanol production takes place at Medicine Hat. With plants in Alberta and On-

NOVA's investments in oil and gas exploration, production, refining, and marketing spur economic activity throughout Alberta.

tario, NOVA has about 45 percent of the total Canadian polyethylene production capability and a full range of products to market in Canada and around the world.

NOVA also has investments in

Novacorp International Consulting markets specialized products and engineering, project management, and operations expertise to clients worldwide.

telecommunications, international consulting, manufacturing, and research and development.

NovAtel Communications designs, manufactures, and markets a wide range of cellular systems and telephones in Canada, the United States, China, Australia, New Zealand, and the United Kingdom from its headquarters in Calgary. Owned 50 percent by NOVA, this company has grown rapidly since it was formed in 1983.

An industry leader in the research, development, and manufacture of cellular technology in Canada, NovAtel also installed Canada's first cellular telephone system, the 400 MHz Aurora. NovAtel's manufacturing facilities are in Lethbridge, Alberta.

Novacorp International Consulting markets the engineering, project management, and operations expertise of the NOVA group of companies to clients worldwide. Novacorp provides state-of-the-art engineering, technical, and operating expertise—particularly in pipeline transmission systems for hydrocarbons, industrial gases, and other commodities. The company's consulting skills are based on NOVA's

commitment to improving the quality of life in Alberta through successful business ventures, the corporation manages and maintains an active corporate contributions program by assisting local nonprofit voluntary organizations, provincial and national. The firm contributes financially to five major areas: health and welfare, arts and culture, education, civic, and recreational activities. NOVA also served as an official corporate sponsor of the XV Olympic Winter Games held in Calgary in February 1988.

Through diversified operations and through contributions as a responsible corporate citizen, NOVA Corporation has established itself as an integral part of the continuing development and success of the Province of Alberta.

Research and development of new products by Nova Husky Research Corporation focus on petroleum, petrochemical, and pipeline technology for the NOVA group of companies.

Computer-aided technology helps NovAtel Communications maintain its position on the leading edge of excellence in design, manufacture, and installation of cellular telephone systems and products.

involvement in a wide range of major Canadian energy projects over the past 25 years. Novacorp is actively involved with major projects in countries throughout the world, including Malaysia, Turkey, and China.

Business activities of NOVA and Husky are supported by a joint commitment to ongoing research and development through Nova Husky Research Corporation, which was formed in 1981 to pursue research and development for both companies and their affiliates. Research focuses on petroleum, petrochemical, and pipeline technology. Close liaison with Alberta's universities adds strength to the firm's ability to discover and develop new products and technologies.

In addition to NOVA's ongoing

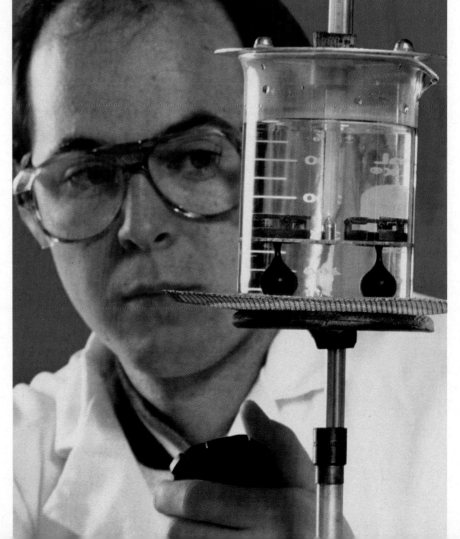

BOW VALLEY RESOURCE SERVICES LTD.

Bow Valley Resource Services Ltd. (BVRS) and its subsidiaries provide environmental and waste-management services, and onshore and offshore oil and gas drilling to industries worldwide. In addition, the company manufactures and markets machinery, equipment, and supplies to the energy, forest products, trucking, and mining industries in North America, Europe, Asia, South America, and Australia.

BVRS, based in Calgary, was formed in 1977 to integrate the service and manufacturing operations of Bow Valley Industries Ltd. BVRS, a public company since 1981, runs one of the largest drilling operations in Canada and employs more than 1,400 people.

BVRS is divided into four seg-

ments: Offshore Drilling and Marine Services, Land Drilling, Environmental, and Manufacturing and Distribution. Each segment operates through subsidiary companies and joint ventures.

Bow Valley Offshore Drilling provides contract drilling and marine services to the international petroleum industry. Expanding upon the company's North Sea drilling experience of the mid-1970s, BVRS became a major Canadian offshore contractor with the acquisition of three semisubmersible offshore drilling rigs in the early 1980s designed to operate in harsh weather conditions. These units are capable of operation in waters to depths of between 1,200 and 1,500 feet anywhere in the world.

The Land Drilling segment of BVRS comprises three subsidiaries, each serving a specific market. From its Calgary office, Hi-Tower Drilling operates 17 rigs in Western Canada with depth capabilities ranging from 6,500 to 25,000 feet. Sedco Drilling, also based in Calgary, operates 24 rigs with depth capability to 6,500 feet. The shallow-capacity rigs drill primarily for crude oil of varying qualities, including the heavy grades of Alberta and Saskatchewan. Apollo Drilling operates nine rigs with depth capabilities ranging from 9,500 to 16,000 feet. Apollo's operations are headquartered in Denver, Colorado, and focus on the Rocky Mountain area of the United States, primarily in the Powder River Basin of Wyoming and areas

Alberta Special Waste Treatment Centre, Swan Hills, Alberta.

ical and treatment services to customers in Western Canada.

The division's consulting and technical services include meteorology, air-quality monitoring, lab and field precision testing, environmental and acoustical engineering, socioeconomic research, occupational and public health, and environmental management.

VerTech Treatment Systems Inc., based in Denver, is an innovative and environmentally effective system for destroying municipal sludges and hazardous industrial wastes. The system uses principles of wet-oxidation to destroy wastes continuously in a subsurface unit suspended down to 5,000 feet underground. The subsurface system is constructed using conventional oil field drilling equipment and services available from BVRS. A mobile surface unit meets the needs of smaller-volume industrial-waste generators, and the requirements for hazardous waste site cleanups.

VerTech constructs, sells, and operates waste-disposal systems in domestic and international markets. VerTech has a joint-venture agreement with Van Wijnen Holdings N.V., a Netherlands-based international corporation involved in the development of complete town sites and other major civil construction projects. The joint venture markets, sells, and operates VerTech systems in the Netherlands and selected Western European countries.

Chem-Security provides hazardous-waste-management services in Canada and worldwide. This service includes waste categorization, collection, transportation, treatment, and disposal. In addition, the division provides customized technical services to clients with specific needs regarding site decontamination and reclamation, laboratory-chemical packaging, and other

of Montana.

"Foothills" and "overthrust" drilling are highly specialized types of drilling for which Bow Valley's Hi-Tower and Apollo operations are known. The firm's Sedco division also has extensive experience in the high-performance requirements of shallow drilling for heavy oil. Bow Valley engineers have developed a new Pad Drilling Rig package that allows multiple-hole drilling over a wide acreage from a central pad.

Recognizing the enormous potential of geothermal energy for many countries worldwide, BVRS has conducted considerable research and testing to adapt conventional drilling techniques and equipment to this specific energy source.

Bow Valley also pioneered Arctic island drilling. In 1968 it became the first Canadian drilling contractor to drill on artificial islands in the Arctic. The company has gained invaluable experience in difficult drilling situations such as directional drilling and harsh-sea drilling off Canada's East Coast.

BVRS' environmental segment consists of three operations, including Western Research, VerTech Treatment Systems Inc., Chem-Security Ltd., and their respective subsidiaries.

Calgary-based Western Research provides process-control instrumentation and testing services to the international gas-processing and sulphur-recovery industry. Further, this division offers environmental and hazardous-waste analyt-

specialized services. Chem-Security is based in Calgary and is considered a leader in North America in the development of integrated facilities for management of hazardous waste.

In 1986 a joint-venture agreement between BVRS (60 percent) and Alberta Special Waste Management Corporation (40 percent) was concluded for the design, construction, and operation of North America's first comprehensive and fully integrated waste-treatment facility, at Swan Hills. Chem-Security was responsible for the facility's design and construction, and now handles the operation of the facility and management of the related waste-transportation and collection operations throughout the province. Limited amounts of waste were first received in November 1986, and the plant was fully operational in late 1987.

One of Mainland Manufacturing's sophisticated numerically controlled machine tools machining a very close tolerance thruster swivel to meet rigid specifications.

Bow Valley Manufacturing and Distribution consists of several subsidiary and affiliate companies that manufacture and provide a complete range of equipment and services to the forestry, mining, and petroleum industries.

Mainland Manufacturing, headquartered near Vancouver (Richmond), British Columbia, offers an integrated custom-manufacturing service to resource-based industries. Facilities include a foundry, a comprehensive machine shop, assembly and fabrication facilities, a saw-manufacturing shop, and belting service centres. The division has the ability to design and manufacture a diversified range of products for the petroleum, mining, forestry, metal-reduction, and construction industries.

The Mainland Manufacturing foundry has electric arc furnaces with a capacity to process 12,000 pounds of raw material per hour. A computerized spectograph provides Mainland's metallurgists with highly accurate analyses of each heat level. The foundry is capable of producing most grades of iron

and low-alloy steels, as well as specialty metals such as heat- and abrasion-resistant iron and chrome-moly steel.

Mainland's machine shop contains some of the largest machine tools in Western Canada, and the fabrication shop is armed with state-of-the-art equipment for cutting, rolling, bending, and sawing steel.

The Mainland Oilfield Supply division, headquartered in Calgary, markets general oil field supplies, tubular products, and oil field service rigs to the oil and gas industry in Alberta, Saskatchewan, and British Columbia.

Bow Valley Resource Services Ltd.'s business strategy includes a commitment to remain a major player in North America oil and gas drilling activities. The company will continue to diversify through expansion of its role in waste-management services and other selected areas of business. Included in its plans for profitable growth is the recognition of the necessity to develop its employees' skills and ensure their commitment to BVRS's goals.

HiTower Rig No.14 drilling by Fort St. John, British Columbia.

FEKETE ASSOCIATES INC.

Fekete Associates Inc., one of Canada's leading petroleum consulting firms, specializes in reservoir engineering and geology, economic evaluations of oil and gas properties, well test interpretations, and computer software development and marketing.

FEKETE employs 30 people in its Calgary office, and the company is owned 100 percent by three partners: Gurmeet Brar, president; Glen Ambrose, vice-president; and Louis Mattar, vice-president/engineering. The consulting experience of the three principals dates from 1973, giving FEKETE a strong resource base of technical expertise.

The firm emphasizes a multidisciplinary team approach to reservoir management projects. In this way FEKETE is able to integrate geology, engineering, and economics into a comprehensive analysis of oil and gas reservoirs. The firm advocates a practical approach to the industry and seeks the simplest-possible solution. The scope of projects completed ranges from a detailed single well study to an engineering geological study involving more than 5,000 wells.

FEKETE promotes a comprehensive technical approach in the evaluation of reserves and economics of oil and gas properties. The staff initially treats each evaluation as a reservoir engineering problem. Engineers and geologists jointly analyze the available data and map the reserves, which are designated as proven, probable, or potential. Once the technical phase is concluded, economic considerations such as pricing, royalties, and taxes are applied to generate cash-flow forecasts.

Throughout the production life of a well, a knowledge of the reservoir's flow characteristics is essential to reach higher production rates. The Well Test Analysis Group applies a wide variety of pressure transient analysis techniques to define, improve, and forecast well performance. FEKETE's comprehen-

Partners in the petroleum consulting firm of Fekete Associates Inc. include (from left) Gurmeet S. Brar, P.Eng., president; Louis Mattar, P.Eng., vice-president/engineering; and Glen G. Ambrose, C.E.T., vice-president.

sive set of computer programs greatly enhances the speed and quality of well test interpretations.

FEKETE is at the forefront of technical knowledge and is a worldwide leader in the technology of well test interpretation. By using measurements of pressure, rate, and time, the firm can detect properties of rock hundreds of feet into the reservoir. And FEKETE has an advantage—the theoretical aspects of well test analysis are mastered by the firm's specialized staff. Two of the principals, Brar and Mattar, prepared the Energy Resources Conservation Board publication, "Theory and Practice of the Testing of Gas Wells," in 1975. The firm has analyzed more than 15,000 well tests, and can therefore claim unparalleled experience in the practical aspects of testing and analysis.

The Computer Software Development Group was initially formed to supplement FEKETE's consulting services, but has since expanded into an industrywide sales and support team. As clients became aware of the user-friendly nature and the technical sophistication of the computer programs, a demand was created, and the group expanded rapidly. A large number of oil and gas companies now utilize computer packages from FEKETE. The firm also provides training, upgrading, maintenance, and support to its software clients.

Although calculations and graphics are all performed by computer, FEKETE believes the actual interpretation must be done by experienced analysts. The firm is exploring fifth-generation computer systems that will ultimately model the decision-making process of an experienced engineer in interpreting well tests.

ALBERTA RESEARCH COUNCIL

The story of the Alberta Research Council symbolizes individual determination, innovation, and the fundamental belief that Alberta's natural resources demand enhanced development for the benefit of all Albertans.

The Alberta Research Council's history patterns the prosperity of Alberta's economy, documenting the many developments in the province's energy and agriculture sectors. Complementing provincial advances in transportation and environmental protection, the Research Council reflects a blend of industrial and scientific resources that today makes Alberta an internationally recognized centre of high technology.

Established by the Government of Alberta in 1921 as the Scientific and Industrial Research Council (later to become the Alberta Research Council) with a mandate to document Alberta's resources for industry, the Research Council has evolved to the pinnacle of technology development.

Today the mandate of the Alberta Research Council is best exemplified by its Mission Statement: "to advance the economy of the province by promoting technology development, performing applied research, and providing expert advice, technical information, and scientific infrastructure that is responsive to the needs of the private sector and supports activities of the public sector."

With its major research programs the Research Council success-fully fulfills this mandate, offering a diversified range of scientific, engineering, and technological research and testing capabilities. One of the Research Council's more prominent programs is Oil Sands and Hydrocarbon Recovery; many of this department's endeavors are jointly funded with Alberta Oil Sands Technology and Research Authority (AOSTRA). There research into the use of steam-based processes for in situ recovery of heavy oil and oil sands deposits in Alberta takes place to support major oil companies operating in Alberta.

The remaining major research programs are Coal and Hydrocarbon Processing, Natural Resources, Biotechnology, Industrial Technologies including Forest Products, Advanced Technologies, and Service to Industry, a provision of short-term advisory and technical service to Alberta companies. In 1986 assistance was provided to more than 2,000 Alberta businesses and government agencies.

In addition, the Alberta Research Council operates five specialized information centres in industrial information, electronic industry information, oil sands geology, and waste materials exchange. Finally, there is the Electronics Test

Designed to foster a biotechnology industry in Alberta, the Alberta Research Council offers scale-up services to biotechnology companies developing new products. The $6-million plant has a range of fermenters from bench scale to 15,000 litres for developing fermentation processes for traditional or genetically engineered organisms. Here technologist Indira Draper takes samples from a small fermenter.

Sophisticated X-ray computed tomography is used by the Alberta Research Council scientists to unravel the mysteries associated with enhanced oil recovery techniques. In the CT laboratory, Dr. George Sedgwick sits at the console to view the images while technologist John Woolley aligns an oil sands core in the scanner.

Centre, providing testing and evaluation services for electronic and telecommunications products that require product certification. The Test Centre also provides companies with engineering assistance in planning and developing new products.

The opening of new Alberta Research Council headquarters and facilities in 1986 confirms the Alberta government's support for an enduring scientific community, an industry that has now placed this province in a world leadership position in many areas of adaptive research.

With the current worldwide explosion in technology, the Alberta Research Council is proud of its ability to respond to the needs of Alberta as the province moves into this diversified high-tech arena.

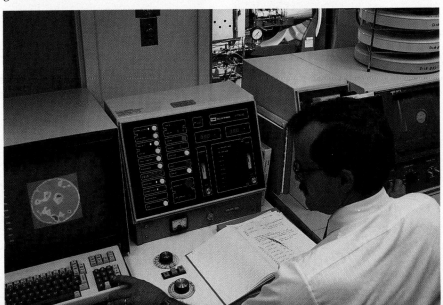

PANCONTINENTAL OIL LTD.

Pancontinental Oil Ltd. is an active, publicly traded (T.S.E.), independent energy company with headquarters in Calgary. The firm acquires petroleum and natural gas rights and explores for, develops, produces, and markets crude oil, natural gas, and natural gas liquids in Western Canada.

The company began operations in early 1980 as a subsidiary of Pancontinental Mining Limited of Australia. At that time Pancontinental Mining was a junior mining company whose major asset was a 65-percent interest in Jabiluka, one of the largest high-grade uranium deposits in the world. Today Pancontinental Mining is a large and profitable Australian gold and coal producer and a diversified minerals explorer.

Pancontinental Oil evolved in a fashion similar to that of many other emerging oil and gas companies in the early 1980s. During 1980 and 1981 Pancontinental raised $20.2 million in risk capital through various limited partnerships and joint ventures to be spent on exploration in Western Canada. But in mid-1981, as a result of changing Canadian government policies and a downturn in the economy, oil and gas capital markets deteriorated, and by mid-1982 the general economy was in a recession with the oil industry suffering even further. Pancontinental reduced its level of activity accordingly, and in late 1982 and early 1983 broadened the equity base of the company by raising new capital in Europe and acquiring the assets of some of its limited partnerships and joint ventures. In 1984 the firm successfully negotiated a significant discounted gas sales contract with Stelco Inc. and immediately acquired, drilled, and developed what is now Pancontinental's major producing property in the Rimbey area of central Alberta. Gas sales from this area commenced within five months of first drilling and resulted in substantial production and revenue increases

for 1985.

Pancontinental has retained an average 68.2-percent working interest in six company-operated gas wells at Rimbey, and in 1987 two new gas wells were prepared for continuous production. The company's share of daily production from the Rimbey area during 1987 was 6.9 million cubic feet per day of natural gas and 573 barrels per day of natural gas liquids compared to total production, net to the company, of 7.4 million cubic feet per day of natural gas and 672 barrels per day of crude oil and natural gas liquids over the same period.

The firm's brief history is similar to that of other junior oil companies, with the exception of two important differences. Pancontinental survived, refinancing, and restructuring during the recession of 1982, and it prospered during the 1984-1987 period. This was a time when many other North American companies were unable to function in a complex, changing oil and gas environment because of high debt loads and declining cash flow.

On June 30, 1987, Pancontinental's oil and natural gas liquids reserves stood at 3.5 million barrels and natural gas reserves of 63.3 billion cubic feet. The value of the company's reserve base has soared

from $19.6 million in 1983 to $60.7 million in 1987, a threefold increase in four years. For the three months that ended June 30, 1987, gross revenue was $6.9 million, cash flow was $3.8 million, and Pancontinental had 17 employees.

During 1987 Pancontinental focused its exploration efforts in Alberta, the firm's traditional area of expertise. Despite the general downturn in industry activity, the company drilled or participated in a total of 19 wells, increasing its average working interest in all projects.

Pancontinental has developed new reserves in addition to those stated, at Hays, Gilwood, Holburn, Gilby, Peco, and Mitsue, Alberta, as a result of its ongoing exploration program.

The company participated in an excellent Nisku gas discovery in July 1987 in the Hays area. Prior to running casing, the well tested gas at rates of up to 1,850 million cubic feet per day. Pancontinental's exploration program revealed numerous untested geophysical anomalies,

and the firm has implemented plans for an active land acquisition and drilling program in the Hays area.

Pancontinental has interests varying between 8.1 percent and 100 percent in 3,695 acres in the Holburn area of Alberta, and has recently participated in the drilling of a second successful gas well on the property. The company has also participated for a 30-percent working interest in a significant multizone gas and oil discovery at Peco East, Alberta, and holds a 40-percent interest in two new gas wells at Gull Lake, Alberta. Pancontinental owns an average 28-percent interest in 9,920 acres in the Gull Lake area. Since 1983 the company has historically spent between $4 million and $6 million annually on exploration and development but has budgeted a threefold increase for 1987-1988.

Pancontinental's management philosophy has evolved over the years, during two dramatic and diametrically opposed boom-bust cycles. The firm's goal has been, and continues to be, to provide above-

average short- and long-term value to shareholders. This has been achieved by adhering to strict operating guidelines: Pancontinental internally generates 80 to 90 percent of exploration and development prospects, acts as operator whenever possible, secures large working interests, develops internal marketing strategies, and maintains a competitive position within the industry.

Pancontinental Oil Ltd. believes strongly in the long-term advantage of investing in the oil and gas industry in Canada because of low finding costs, access to the large U.S. market, and the potential for significant new discoveries. Pancontinental Oil Ltd. is a company that learned the hard lessons of the early 1980s and has prospered in the past three years. It is debt free and has $20 million in the treasury for exploration and development. By placing existing reserves on stream, production will increase by a minimum of 50 percent during the next six to nine months.

CEDA-REACTOR LTD.

Whether it's a refinery, gas plant, processing plant, or oil and gas production field, present-day industrial cleaning and maintenance is a highly technical undertaking. CEDA is a company that specializes in developing chemicals, equipment, and procedures that reduce the costs of production and maintenance.

Chemical research and development take place in CEDA's main laboratory in Calgary. Chemists and technicians formulate compounds for cleaning and descaling production equipment, stimulating oil wells, treating oil, and improving the environment. CEDA researchers have developed a product line of more than 200 proprietary chemicals.

CEDA engineers and service technicians design and fabricate special equipment for specific industrial cleaning services. High-pressure water-blasting units, truck-mounted vacuum systems, chemical-circulating units, and waste-handling equipment are matched to the specific job at hand. In the industrial cleaning industry, CEDA's ongoing technical development is keeping production equipment from fouling, maintenance costs low, and production efficiency high.

Safety during inert entry into plant reactors and vessels is of utmost importance. CEDA's Reactor Services Division routinely enters these alien atmospheres using the Reactor Life-Support System to perform complicated tasks. The most outstanding feature of this Life-Support System is that the respirator is "locked on" the wearer to ensure maximum protection.

Technical innovation in the

Chemists monitor the customer's production system for trends in corrosion, scaling, and the effectiveness of the chemical-treatment program.

CEDA scientists analyze petroleum and scale samples to custom design specialty treating and cleaning chemicals.

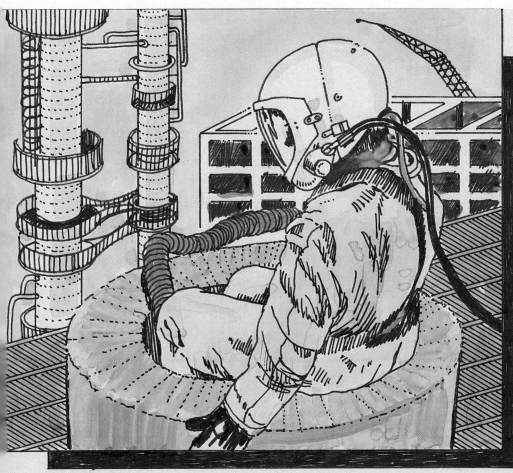

High-pressure water is used to remove scale buildup. This helps to optimize the efficiency of plant production equipment.

cleaning and maintenance industry requires that the right people are matched to the job. The employees of CEDA are committed to customer satisfaction. CEDA is majority owned by active employees, and the beneficial results of this are experienced daily by customers.

What does it take to maintain a plant and keep production costs down? It takes a service company with the right people, the right equipment and products, and an ongoing investment into research and development. CEDA is an Alberta-based company—a company that is proud to be making this contribution to Alberta's international reputation for technical and service excellence.

Worker safety is crucial in performing maintenance such as catalyst handling inside plant vessels. Here CEDA's Reactor Services worker enters a vessel wearing a lock-on life-support system to minimize safety hazards.

ALBERTA OIL SANDS TECHNOLOGY AND RESEARCH AUTHORITY

Alberta is Canada's energy province. Blessed with enormous quantities of conventional oil, natural gas, coal, hydroelectric power, and heavy oil and oil sands, Alberta provides approximately 80 percent of Canada's total oil production. The Alberta Energy Resources Conservation Board estimates there are at least 270 million cubic metres (1.69 trillion barrels) of conventional oil and heavy oil and bitumen located in Alberta.

Alberta's Minister of Energy, the Honorable Dr. Neil Webber.

Canadians consume nearly 2 million barrels of oil per day. Because of its cold climate, immense distances, and high industrialization, Canada is the largest per capita user of oil in the world. One-quarter of the nation's needs is imported; the remainder is supplied domestically from Alberta's 4.5 billion barrels of conventional crude oil reserves. Current projections suggest that by the year 2010, production from these reserves will have decreased to one-third of its present level. Consequently, Alberta's resources assume new significance as Canada's rate of energy consumption grows and production of crude oil declines—none perhaps so much as the massive reserves of

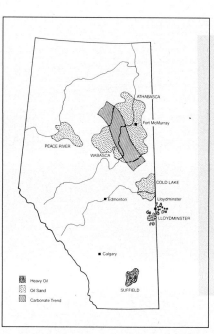

A map of Alberta showing the major oil deposits.

heavy oil and oil sands.

Heavy oils are thicker, heavier, and slower to pour than medium and light oils because they lack the more fluid components of petroleum. Heavy oil is composed mostly of high-density materials such as gas oil, lube oil, and asphaltenes, and a high content of sulfur. A small portion (5 percent) of the lighter of the heavy oils can be brought to the surface by pumping. However, the denser, more viscous oils must first be thinned to create a greater mobility before they can be produced. The majority of the heavy oil deposits are located in the eastern portion of Alberta near the city of Lloydminster.

There are four major oil sands deposits in Alberta. The largest and best known is Athabasca, located in the northeastern part of the province, and containing an estimated 114 billion cubic metres or 712 billion barrels of low-grade bitumen-in-place. Near the Athabasca River the oil sands are close to the surface and can actually be seen along the river escarpment.

The three other oil sands deposits are more deeply buried, lying from 150 to 800 metres below the

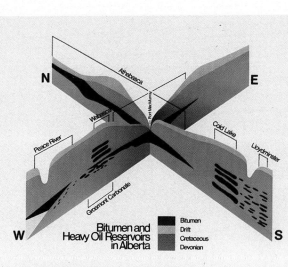

A cross section of the bitumen and heavy oil reservoirs in the province of Alberta.

surface. The amount of bitumen-in-place is estimated to be 6 billion cubic metres (38 million barrels) at Wabasca; 25 billion cubic metres (156 billion barrels) at Cold Lake; and 10 billion cubic metres (63 billion barrels) at Peace River. All of these oil sands deposits are composed of sand (mostly quartz with traces of mica, rutile, zircon, tourmaline, and pyrite) along with clay, water, and bitumen. There is considerable variation in the amount and percentage of these components, not only among deposits but also within each individual reservoir.

It is this deeply buried bitumen that provides an enormous technical challenge for industry and government alike. The Alberta government has always been sympathetic to the need for a substantial program of research and technology development to make these resources available commercially, and has established the Alberta Oil Sands Technology and Research Authority (AOSTRA) to ensure that the technology will be there when needed.

When the Scientific and Industrial Research Council (Alberta Research Council) began in 1921, it initiated an energetic program of coal and oil sands research. Dr. Karl Clark's farsighted research program on oil sands resulted in the development of the hot-water process for the extraction of bitumen from the mined oil sands. This process is still used today by the two commercial mining operations in the Fort McMurray area. It was the initiative of the Alberta government 40 years ago to build and operate a demonstration plant at Bitumount, specifically to demonstrate Dr. Clark's process, that gave the oil industry the confidence to build the Suncor and Syncrude plants that now contribute $29,000m^3/d$ (180,000 barrels per day) of synthetic crude oil to the organization's productive capacity.

The AOSTRA members.

William J. Yurko, chairman and chief executive officer, Alberta Oil Sands Technology and Research Authority.

This long tradition of Alberta government leadership in oil sands research is being continued by the Alberta Oil Sands Technology and Research Authority. AOSTRA, a provincial crown corporation formed in 1974 by an Act of Legislature, is guided by the following mandate: —to promote research and development into the technological methods required for the efficient and economic recovery and processing of crude bitumen and other oil sands products from the oil sands deposits, and the effective and economic recovery of crude oil through the use of enhanced recovery methods; —to promote re-

search into the technological methods required to ensure an acceptable quality of the environment during and after such recovery and processing operations; and —to promote and implement solutions to technological problems impeding the development of production capacity to meet the demand of crude oil, synthetic crude oil, and products derived from crude oil.

An appointed board of seven part-time and two full-time members review applications submitted from a wide range of individual inventors, from academics to small companies and large corporations. AOSTRA has received more than 900 applications for funding, and its interest in a project can range from 50 to 100 percent.

Today much of the petroleum-related research in the province is being conducted jointly by government and industry, and several of the projects undertaken by AOSTRA and its industry partners have progressed from the pilot-testing phase to the early stages of commercialization.

One example of a successful project is the steam pilot at Marguerite Lake in the Cold Lake deposit. It laid the foundation for the $1600m^3/d$ Wolf Lake commercial facility of Petro-Canada Inc. and BP Exploration Canada Ltd. Similarly the

AOSTRA In Situ Pilot in the Peace River deposit has been expanded from $320m^3/d$ to $1600m^3/d$ by Shell Canada Resources Limited and Shell Explorer Limited.

Other AOSTRA in Situ Pilot projects are currently in the early stages of development, and it is confidently expected that some of these will result in new and improved technologies for the heavy oil and oil sands industry in the future. Two of these are particularly significant. The first pilot project to be located in the Carbonate Trend, 100 kilometres west of Fort McMurray, was conducted by AOSTRA, Union Oil Company of Canada Ltd., and Canadian Superior Oil Ltd. It was designed to examine the suitability of steam stimulation,

An aerial view of the ASTRA/BP pilot at Marguerite Lake.

steam drive, and wet combustion processes for bitumen recovery. In the Athabasca deposit, AOSTRA is operating an Underground Test Facility (UTF) 60 kilometres northwest of Fort McMurray in an attempt to learn more about the value of horizontal wells as a thermal in situ recovery mechanism for oil sands.

Canada's federal department of Energy, Mines, and Resources joined the project in early 1987 as a technical participant. Other participants include Chevron Canada Resources Ltd., which will be testing its HASDrive Process at the facility, and several other companies.

The development of technology for enhanced recovery from conventional light oil reservoirs was added to AOSTRA's mandate in 1980. Since that time AOSTRA, together with industry partners, has devel-

The Taciuk Processor.

The Underground Test Facility (UTF) located 60 kilometres northwest of Fort McMurray.

oped technology that has prompted two operators to increase production. The same technology has good potential application for other similarly depleted Alberta oil fields.

The Hot Water Extraction Process, the pioneering method of recovering bitumen from mined oil sands, suffers from two major problems—a difficulty in processing low-grade ore and the formation of large tailings ponds. Since 1977 AOSTRA has pursued the development of a unique retorting process that combines extraction, coking, and heat exchange in one vessel. The AOSTRA-owned Taciuk Process has the potential to solve the low-grade recovery problem as well as eliminate tailings sludge formation. A downturn in the Alberta economy has postponed the construction of a large demonstration-

scale processor. In the meantime, two specific non-oil sands applications have been tested in the Taciuk Processor and have generated a substantial degree of interest. These are the processing of oil shales and the treatment of hydrocarbon-bearing waste materials, such as oil-contaminated soils at abandoned refinery sites.

The bitumen produced from an in situ oil sand operation or from a mining extraction plant is too viscous to be pipelined and contains too many heavy ends to be handled by conventional refineries. Existing upgrading processes utilize carbon rejection, resulting in substantial coke production and limited yields of usable upgraded crude. AOSTRA has sponsored a number of studies, tests, and research projects in an attempt to find improved recovery processes that will yield more refinery feedstock from each cubic metre of bitumen produced. Since 1983 AOSTRA has worked with owners of four processes that add hydrogen and give substantially higher yields of synthetic crude.

Since its inception AOSTRA has devoted a substantial portion of its research dollars to a comprehensive institutional program and a number of these projects are at the Alberta Research Council (ARC). In 1975 AOSTRA joined with ARC to conduct fundamental and applied re-

The Alberta Research Council facilities.

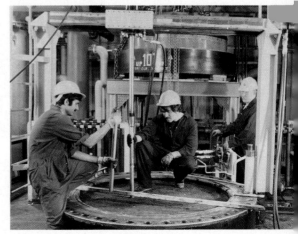

AOSTRA regularly sponsors research at Canadian universities and shares the results with industry.

search toward the development of new methods for the recovery of heavy oil and oil sands buried too deeply for mining. A major portion of this research effort has been devoted to investigating recovery processes using steam with additives. A recent technical review deemed the unique experimental facilities and expertise to be of world-class stature. One process developed by this group is now ready for field testing.

Also at the Alberta Research Council, AOSTRA has established a sample bank that obtains oil sands and bitumen samples from Alberta deposits, stores them under refrigerated conditions, and then distributes them to researchers on request. This group is also working toward developing accepted standardized analytical procedures.

In recent years AOSTRA has also sponsored a small upgrading research program at ARC. This program is just getting under way and will concentrate on co-processing of bitumen and coal, improved catalysts, and utilization of the residues that are left from existing up-grading projects.

AOSTRA and ARC have recognized the need to expand and improve an information data base for oil sands and heavy oils. Together they established a publications index, which is housed in AOSTRA's offices in both Edmonton and Calgary. This index has developed into one of the best sources of published oil sands information in the world. This service is known as the AOSTRA Library and Information Service (ALIS), and provides comprehensive services on publicly available information on oil sands, heavy oil, and enhanced oil recovery requested from all over North America and abroad.

To encourage universities to get involved in solving the problems associated with getting oil out of Alberta's immense oil sands resources and improving recovery from depleted conventional reservoirs, AOSTRA has for 10 years sponsored research at Canadian universities and shared the results with industry. This highly successful program has not only inspired university professors to put their minds to solving these problems, but also has encouraged them to interact directly with their counterparts in industry and has provided a pool of highly trained students who can take their ideas with them when they move into the private sector.

Successful technical achievements are those that can be repeated in various locations under various sets of circumstances. Technology developed from AOSTRA-funded projects and programs is available to all interested parties. AOSTRA believes that maintaining an international awareness and a knowledge of the nature of the petroleum resource industry throughout the world is a vital element in the development of viable technology.

AOSTRA has endeavored to keep abreast of all the variations in the occurrence and nature of the resources and to assist others to understand and apply the technologies it has developed. Numerous technology exchange agreements have been signed with interested foreign organizations, and they are often the forerunners of trade between Alberta and other countries in the petroleum equipment, engineering, and service industries.

AOSTRA is proud to continue with the Alberta government's long-time tradition of oil sands technology development leadership. The organization's funding has resulted in a constant level of research in the province. Its encouragement of cooperative efforts has allowed companies that may not otherwise be able to conduct research to be privy to important new developments. Its technology marketing program has made Alberta technology accessible to organizations and governments worldwide.

What does AOSTRA plan for the future? The organization will continue to assist large and small corporations in their development of pilot projects throughout Alberta, and to assist further expansions toward commercialization. AOSTRA will also continue to assist smaller groups and individuals in their quest to advance oil sands technology. University researchers and students, both at the undergraduate and graduate levels, will continue to play an active and important role in AOSTRA's overall program.

In essence, AOSTRA plans to continue technology development on many fronts. As the economy and world oil situation fluctuate, its emphasis may be redirected, but AOSTRA will essentially continue to pursue its mandate. It will combine its research expertise with the resources of institutes, universities, and government to generate new or improved technology for solving existing oil sand problems and to develop more efficient production from Alberta's massive low-grade hydrocarbon resources.

BP CANADA INC.

BP Canada Inc., a natural resources company based in Calgary, produces and explores for crude oil and natural gas in the Western Canada Basin. It also has exploration interests in Vancouver Island, the Northwest Territories, Ontario, and the Arctic Islands.

The company is a leader in the development of thermal recovery technology, which it is applying on a commercial scale to bitumen at Wolf Lake in northeastern Alberta.

As well, BP is engaged in major mining and minerals exploration projects. It operates both an underground and open-pit mine in northwestern Quebec, producing copper, zinc, silver, and gold. Through a subsidiary company, Hope Brook Gold Inc., BP is developing a gold mine in southwestern Newfoundland. The firm also has a limestone and lime products operation in British Columbia, and explores extensively for minerals across Canada.

BP Canada is a public company whose shares are quoted on the Toronto, Montreal, and Vancouver stock exchanges. Following the issue of 3 million common shares early in 1987, the interest of the majority shareholder, BP Canadian Holdings Limited (a wholly owned subsidiary of The British Petroleum Company, p.l.c.), was reduced from 64.7 percent to 56.9 percent.

BP acquired its first interest in

Pipeline construction near Chauvin in southeastern Alberta.

Canada in December 1953 when it purchased a 23-percent share of a Calgary-based explorer and producer, Triad Oil Co. Ltd.

From that small beginning, BP Canada grew over the next 30 years into a major integrated oil company. It had refineries in Ontario and Quebec, where it marketed a full range of petroleum products, and produced and explored for crude oil and natural gas in the three western provinces.

In 1983 the firm's downstream operations were sold and the head office relocated to Calgary. That same year BP Canada acquired

The central plant at Wolf Lake 1.

Selco Inc., a mining company, from its majority shareholder.

In 1985, after 20 years of trials and pilot operations, a commercial heavy oil operation came into production at Wolf Lake in northeastern Alberta. This is a joint undertaking between BP and Petro-Canada, with BP as operator. Located 50 kilometres north of Bonnyville, Alberta, and covering an area of 30,000 hectares, the Wolf Lake leases contain an estimated 3.8 billion barrels of bitumen.

The first three wells were drilled in 1964, and the first pilot project was started later that year. Through a series of pilots over the ensuing 18 years, BP demonstrated that bitumen could be recovered from the oil sands by injecting high-pressure steam into the formation.

The culmination of this effort was the construction and operation of Wolf Lake 1, with a design production capacity of 1,100 cubic metres of bitumen per day, which was one of the first commercial in situ oil sands projects in Canada.

Wolf Lake 2, launched in mid-1987, is a 2,400-cubic-metre-per-day integral expansion of the initial facility that will bring total bitumen production capacity to 3,860 cubic

Underground exploration at Les Mines Selbaie.

metres per day.

The pre-start-up cost of the project is estimated at $200 million for the construction of the central plant and field facilities, which include the drilling and completion of 248 wells. Over the life of the project another 975 wells will be added. Commissioning is scheduled for late 1989.

The project will incorporate strong environmental safeguards. To minimize water requirements, a $35-million plant will be built to recycle water for both Wolf Lake 1 and 2. Vent gases will be gathered and incinerated at each satellite.

Ongoing research at BP's pilot plant has advanced the development of in situ combustion technology—a process that uses heat generated by combustion inside a formation to increase production—to the point where commercial application is being considered. This technology has the potential to almost double ultimate bitumen recovery.

After the oil recoverable through cyclic steam stimulation has been produced, the wells are converted to combustion by injecting oxygen into the formation. A demonstration satellite is scheduled to begin operation in 1988, using one of the existing Wolf Lake 1 pads.

At Wolf Lake BP is also testing new technology to overcome an emerging problem in the pipeline transportation of heavy oil.

At present the highly viscous heavy oil can be shipped by pipeline only if it is mixed with natural gas condensate to make it flow.

There are already industry concerns that by the early 1990s the supply of condensate will be inadequate to move the growing volumes of heavy oil expected to be produced from Alberta's oil sands.

BP Canada, BP Canadian Holdings, and Alberta Energy Company Ltd. are participating in a joint venture to demonstrate and develop TRANSOIL oil-in-water emulsion technology as an alternative to condensate.

TRANSOIL technology was discovered in 1983 at the BP Research Centre in the United Kingdom as part of a collaborative research and development program with IN-TEVEP of Venezuela. It produces oil-in-water emulsions using a controlled mixing and low concentration of commercially available surfactants.

BP's production of conventional oil and natural gas liquids in 1987 was 3,140 cubic metres per day. Bitumen production was 555 cubic meters per day. Production of natural gas was 3.7 million cubic metres per day.

In 1986 BP Canada made a public offering of shares in Hope Brook Gold Inc., a company established to develop a gold deposit in southwest Newfoundland. BP Canada holds 75.7 percent of Hope Brook Gold.

The property is being developed in two stages. An open-pit, heap-leaching operation came into production in the fall of 1987. An underground mine and mill will be commissioned in the fourth quarter of 1988.

BP also operates Les Mines Selbaie, a joint venture in northwestern Quebec (BP holds 55 percent, Esso Resources Canada Limited 35 percent, and TCPL Resources Ltd. 10 percent). Les Mines Selbaie has two mines in operation—one underground and one open-pit. A second underground mine will come into production late in 1988. The mines produce copper, zinc, silver, and gold.

BP Canada Inc. supports a wide range of organizations and causes, particularly those devoted to health and welfare, but also including educational, cultural, and civic causes in areas where the company operates.

Construction work at the Hope Brook Gold Mine in southwestern Newfoundland.

AMOCO CANADA PETROLEUM COMPANY LTD.

Amoco Canada Petroleum Company Ltd. is a major participant in the exploration and development of Canada's oil and gas resources. With a head office in Calgary, the firm is also engaged in the marketing of crude oil, natural gas liquids, natural gas, and sulphur.

A wholly owned subsidiary of Amoco Corporation of Chicago, Illinois, Amoco has been active in Canada since 1948. Most of the company's exploration and production operations are focused on Alberta, with some additional activity in British Columbia, the Northwest Territories, the East Coast, and the Beaufort Sea. Amoco's marketing activity serves both Canadian and export markets worldwide.

In its 40 years of operation Amoco's participation in conventional oil and gas drilling, and the development and application of enhanced oil-recovery technology, have added in excess of 990 million barrels of crude oil and natural gas liquids, as well as more than 6 trillion cubic feet of natural gas, to Canada's petroleum reserves. Since 1948, $4.1 billion has been invested in exploration and development in Western Canada and the frontier regions.

Amoco Canada is now the

eighth-largest producer of crude oil and natural gas liquids in Canada and the fifth-largest producer of natural gas. Net production of crude oil and natural gas liquids totalled 53,000 barrels per day in 1986; daily net production of natural gas was 257 million cubic feet.

During the 1950s and 1960s Amoco developed the large Pembina, South Swan Hills, and Nipisi oil fields in central and northwestern Alberta, and several notable gas fields that required the application of advanced technology. In 1966 Amoco drilled the first two wells offshore Canada's East Coast, and as of 1987 the company held more than one million acres in that area.

T. Don Stacy, Amoco Canada president, and J. Howard MacDonald, Dome Petroleum chairman, sign the historic Amoco-Dome deal.

Amoco continued an active exploration and development program during the 1970s, and major gas fields were developed throughout Alberta. Amoco's Pointed Mountain gas field came on stream in 1972, resulting in the first exportable natural gas production from the Canada lands.

In the early 1960s Amoco pioneered an enhanced oil-recovery technique known as hydrocarbon miscible flooding. During this process a solvent is pumped into the reservoir and acts like a dry-

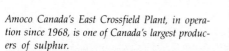

Amoco Canada's East Crossfield Plant, in operation since 1968, is one of Canada's largest producers of sulphur.

In the early 1950s Amoco Canada's geological expeditions in the western sedimentary basin were conducted on horseback.

cleaning agent to strip the rock of much of its remaining oil. In 1973 world-scale miscible flood projects were initiated at South Swan Hills and in Nipisi in 1984.

Since 1980 Amoco has been developing its heavy oil reserves at Elk Point in northeastern Alberta, and the firm also has participated in the discovery and development of the Panny oil field. The $80-million Elk Point development produces 5,000 barrels of heavy oil per day. In 1985 Amoco participated in a major oil discovery offshore the Beaufort Sea and now owns 600,000 acres.

Amoco Canada is one of the country's leaders in the research and development of technology for the exploration and development of oil and gas. In 1955 the firm initiated research to develop a process for in situ extraction of oil from the Athabasca oil sands, and it has since been involved in extensive field pilots. In 1976 Amoco began working on a joint research project with the Alberta Oil Sands Technology and Research Authority to recover a portion of the 740 billion barrels of oil, which is not amenable to surface-mining methods.

Amoco is recognized worldwide for its expertise in processing natural gas containing hydrogen sulphide. The company was responsible for developing and applying the "cold bed absorption process," capable of extracting more than 99 percent of the hydrogen sulphide from natural gas. The firm has been a leader in the development of sour-gas technology since the late 1950s.

Amoco has played a leading role in the marketing of Canadian crude oil for many years, suggesting and implementing innovative solutions to marketing problems. These include developing opportunities for sales out of Canada, imports of both onshore and offshore crude to Canada, and trades that do both. The organization has been particularly active in developing new export markets for Canadian heavy crude.

Amoco Canada has more than 1,500 employees in Calgary, nearly all of whom are Canadian. Another 150 Canadians hold key positions in Amoco's offices in the United States and around the world. This corporate relationship provides reciprocal benefits to Amoco Canada and offers opportunities for Canadians to obtain international experience through postings in parent and affiliate offices.

While Amoco Canada is a Western Canadian company, its sister organization employs more than 685 people at four fabric and fibre plants in Quebec and Ontario, in addition to a staff of 23 at a petrochemical-manufacturing plant in Alberta.

Amoco Canada proudly conducts its affairs in accordance with the highest levels of civic responsibility by offering financial support to institutions that advance educational progress and improve the communities in which we live. In 1987 it assisted more than 150 worthwhile nonprofit organizations.

Amoco Canada Petroleum Company Ltd. now faces its biggest challenge since its inception in 1948—the acquisition of Dome Petroleum, a large, financially ailing oil company. Upon successful completion of the acquisition, Amoco will be Canada's largest producer of natural gas and the second-largest producer of petroleum liquids. By acquiring Dome, Amoco is purchasing the opportunity to expand its exploration and development efforts, and to secure its position in the future as Canada's premier petroleum company.

Technology and innovation have made Amoco a leader in Canada's petroleum industry. Pictured is the advanced drilling technology used in the Nipisi miscible flood project.

PROGAS LIMITED

In the late 1970s Vernon Horte saw an urgent need for an alternative means of marketing natural gas for Alberta's producers. A longtime member of the province's natural gas transmission and marketing community, Horte gained the support of 12 energy companies that needed a cost-effective, consistent way of bringing their natural gas to consumers. The businesses joined forces in 1978 to form the Alberta Producers Gas Marketing Group, which later became ProGas Limited.

Rather than limiting sales to within the consortium, ProGas offered to purchase gas from all producers in Alberta. Today 216 producers are bound by more than 600 contracts to supply gas to the company, which in turn markets the gas to customers in the United States and Canada. In 1986 ProGas reported more than $147 million in gross sales revenue, selling gas at 102 million cubic feet per day from a remaining reserve gas supply of 3.8 trillion cubic feet.

The shareholders' original objective was to market additional gas in Canada on a long-term basis. Initially gas was exported to the United States under long-term contracts with provisions for transferring a portion of those volumes to the Canadian market if required. Over the years ProGas has shifted its focus to adapt to changing market conditions, and the company now works toward continuing its existing export sales while establishing new long-term contracts with U.S. customers.

As a gas marketer, ProGas acts as a middleman for the industry. The firm locates markets for natural gas, obtains the supply, enters into purchase agreements with wholesale buyers, and arranges for transportation of the product to the marketplace.

A key to the company's success was the closing of contracts in 1979 to supply four major U.S. interstate pipelines with long-term supplies of gas. Upon approval from Canadian regulatory bodies, ProGas commenced exporting gas in 1981.

The following year, with a staff of eight, the company moved into its present downtown Calgary location. By 1987 ProGas had expanded its staff to 19, consolidated new regulatory and marketing departments, and expanded its accounting division. The firm has long-term export contracts with a wide range of customers, including a consortium of distributors in the U.S. northeast market and an electric power-generating company in Rhode Island.

In addition to developing markets and negotiating gas sales and supply contracts, ProGas secures removal permits from the Alberta Energy Resources Conservation Board, obtains export authorizations from the National Energy Board, and administers all operational aspects of its gas contracts.

ProGas takes an active role in the Calgary community by contributing to the arts, culture, health care, and the United Way.

The following ProGas Limited shareholders have an equal voice in the affairs of the company, with a common share ownership of 8.33 percent each: Amoco Canada Petroleum Company Ltd., BP Resources Canada Limited, Dome Petroleum Limited, Home Oil Company Limited, ICG Resources Ltd., Luscar Ltd., Mobil Oil Canada, Ltd., Norcen Energy Resources Limited, Numac Oil and Gas Ltd., PanCanadian Petroleum Limited, Shell Canada Limited, and Texaco Canada Resources.

The Empress Gas Liquids Joint Venture Plant processes ProGas shipments at Empress, Alberta.

ProGas contracted gas supply areas.

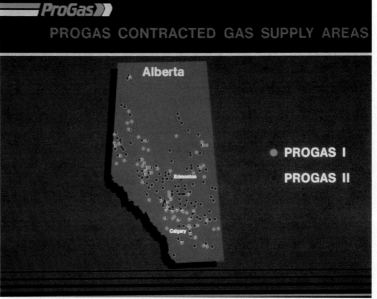

TOTAL PETROLEUM CANADA LTD.

Total Petroleum (North America) Ltd. is an integrated petroleum company 50 percent owned by the French energy company Compagnie Francaise des Petroles, and 50 percent publicly owned. With oil and gas operations in the United States and Canada, and petroleum products operations in the central United States, the firm's head office is located in Calgary, and its principal executive office is in Denver, Colorado.

Total Petroleum Canada Ltd., a wholly owned subsidiary of Total Petroleum (North America) Ltd., was established in Calgary in 1953 by Henri de Cizancourt. Transferred to Canada by Compagnie Francaise des Petroles to open a branch office, de Cizancourt began operating with one employee and an accountant. By the end of 1954 the Calgary office had 21 employees, the majority of whom were Canadians. Originally known as the French Petroleum Company of Canada, the name was changed in 1971 to Total Petroleum Company of Canada Limited, and later to its current name.

Total's operations in Canada are upstream, focussing strictly on the development, production, and exploration of oil and gas. With the 1970 purchase of a refining company in Michigan, Total expanded into refining and marketing operations in the United States.

Total's first major oil and gas discovery was made in 1957 at the Bonnie Glen Field, 50 miles south of Edmonton. This field has produced a major share of Total's cash flow over the past 30 years. Although it has declined sharply, it is still in production.

Also in the late 1950s Total drilled and discovered producing wells in the Swan Hills and Sundrie areas of Alberta. This was followed by exploration in Ontario, and then along the Mackenzie River in the Northwest Territories in 1962.

Engineers meet to decide on a well program.

Development of the Wembley oil field, located in northwestern Alberta, was completed in 1985, six years after the Total discovery. Total, as operator, has 50 to 100 percent interest in 51 producing wells and a share of net production of approximately 2,400 barrels per day.

The Wembley gas plant, operated by Dome Petroleum and 21 percent owned by Total, came on stream in 1986 and added 20 percent to Total's annual gas and liquids production.

The Valhalla water flood project was completed in 1985 at a cost of $3.2 million. This project increased recoverable reserves in the field from 1.5 to 5 million barrels, and increased the cash flow per barrel due to royalty reductions on enhanced recovery oil.

The Wembley oil field, gas plant, and Valhalla project are located in the Elmworth area in central Alberta, which has been the main and most successful focus of Total's activities in Canada for the past 10 years.

Today Total Petroleum Canada Ltd. has gross sales of $80 million. The company produces 9,000 barrels per day of crude oil, condensate, and natural gas liquids, and 30 million cubic feet per day of natural gas. Total conducts capital spend-

A geological technician utilizes computer techniques to analyze well logs.

ing programs worth $35 million to $45 million annually. These programs have enabled the firm to attain a reserve base of 21 million barrels of oil, 14 million barrels of natural gas liquids, and 320 billion cubic feet of natural gas. These reserves have shown an increase, net of production, for each of the past five years.

Total currently employs 70 people in the city of Calgary and 20 people in various field operations throughout Alberta. Despite the current volatility of the oil industry, Total is optimistic about its future in Alberta and intends to maintain its position within the Canadian oil industry.

BADGER DRILLING LTD.

CALGARY OFFICE

Badger Drilling Ltd. is a Calgary-based drilling company serving the Canadian oil industry. From its modest beginnings in makeshift office space in a downtown Calgary high-rise apartment, Badger has grown to become an important player in the Canadian oil- and gas-drilling industry.

It all started in 1977, when John Niedermaier decided that it was time to leave his position as manager of drilling operations for a joint venture in the High Arctic and start his own drilling company. With financial backing from a contact he had developed as a manager and engineer, Niedermaier joined forces with former colleague Al Barker, and on December 16, 1977, Badger Drilling was in business.

The two men had reputations for innovation in the drilling industry. Niedermaier had a degree in engineering from the University of Saskatchewan and a career studded with accomplishment—from designing a support system for drilling on permafrost to engineering special equipment for drilling in the harsh desert environment of the Middle East. Barker worked his way up in the oil patch from a roughneck and floor hand to rig manager for the first diesel electric drilling rig in Canada, and he eventually became High Arctic operations manager for a major Canadian drilling contractor.

With Niedermaier as president in Calgary and Barker as manager of operations in Edmonton, Badger Drilling immediately began to purchase and assemble equipment for its first rig, which went into service on March 17, 1978. By June of that year the firm had another rig operating. The two rigs were designed for fast moving and easy on-site assembly, and had drilling capacities ranging from 850 to 2,100 metres. A third, larger rig was added in February 1979, giving Badger a competitive position in a wide range of drilling situations. By

John Niedermaier

Lyle Schultz

Jim Hill

Connie Fischer

this time the company had added two employees and was growing quickly.

The National Energy Program of 1980 brought profound changes to the economic environment in Alberta, and in 1981 Badger found itself in a crisis, with no Canadian work available for its largest rig. The firm moved the rig into the United States, where the drilling industry was still relatively healthy, and over the next two years added another two rigs to its U.S. division. But cracking the U.S. market proved difficult, and, with the price of drilling rigs steadily decreasing, the company had to absorb much

Lucy Tomie

NISKU OFFICE

Al Barker

Mary Ann Winiarki

Charles "Chuck" Therian

Roy Killaly

Dave Johnson

hole to the operator of the well. In this situation, rare in today's oil industry, the drilling contractor provides the services and takes all the financial risks. Less than 5 percent of modern wells are drilled in this way.

"Day work" is where the drilling contractor provides complete drilling equipment, with trained people, and is obliged to keep the rig mechanically sound. The operator is responsible for drilling the hole, and there is very little risk involved for the drilling company. About 40 percent of current drilling is conducted in this way.

"Meterage," the most common method of drilling, involves drilling a well at a certain rate per metre for an operator, who takes over the well when the required depth is achieved.

Badger is a mid-size drilling company, one of more than 80 drilling contractors operating in Canada. The firm's philosophy has always been to maintain a competitive, fast-moving, efficient operation. Badger's innovative rig designs make it a leader in the industry, and the company has been closely involved in the development of safety standards for the drilling industry.

Through industry committees, John Niedermaier has been involved in the formulation of safety regulations for preventing blow-outs in sour gas wells, and Alberta is recognized as a world leader in this area. Badger is an active member in the Canadian Association of Drilling Contractors, which, in conjunction with The Canadian Association of Drilling Engineers, holds technical conferences and sponsors seminars for the training of engineers and technicians in the drilling industry. Niedermaier is a member of the association, and has served both as vice-president and president. Niedermaier was a founding executive of the Canadian Association of Drilling Engineers.

of its debt. Finally, in 1983, the U.S. rigs were sold, and Badger's American operations were shut down.

In Canada, business continued to grow despite the downturn in the oil industry. Badger added rigs to its fleet each year, and today the company operates a total of 11 rigs with a capacity to drill depth ranges from 850 to 3,100 metres. When all the rigs are operating, Badger employs up to 165 people.

There are several ways the Canadian drilling industry operates.

A "turnkey" job is one where a drilling company is contracted for a certain price to provide a finished

RIG MANAGERS

As of December 31, 1987, Badger had drilled 901 holes, totalling in excess of 1.46 million metres. The firm has a responsible safety record, and operates a program that rewards employees who operate safely over long periods.

As well as safety, the company concentrates on looking for ways of improving the efficiency of drilling wells. Thanks to innovation in design, new drilling technology, and sound project management, Badger has been able to cut the average drilling time for a well.

Badger's corporate objectives are to build and maintain a company that is very competitive in the industry, and to encourage employees to take a proud, sales-oriented approach to the business. The firm actively seeks projects that enhance the training and experience gained by personnel in previous undertakings, and prides itself in its ability to adapt to a wide range of environmental and climatic conditions.

In 1978, through a holding company, Badger and its investors formed a well service organization, Petro Well Servicing, a division of 119201 Alberta Ltd. Petro Well began with the purchase of Hectors Well Servicing Ltd., a company with two service rigs. The operation grew to a fleet of five rigs working throughout eastern and southern Alberta.

Under the supervision of part owner and vice-president/operations Larry Gross, Petro Well sold two of its rigs working in southern Alberta to an employee, and focussed its operations in the Drumheller and Vegreville areas of eastern Alberta.

Petro Well works closely with Voyager Petroleums, Poco Petroleums, and Renaissance Resources. The company has also done work for Tintagel Energy Corporation, Norcen Energy Resources Limited, Canterra Energy Ltd., Legacy Petroleum Ltd., and many others.

Petro Well places an emphasis

Jack Weigel

Bernie McLaughlin

Walter Hopf

Lyle McIntosh

Wade Barker

Chris Herman

on safety in its operations, and from 1985 to 1987 has been able to operate without a lost time accident and with nothing but positive inspections from regulatory bodies. Thanks to this focus on safety, training, and adherence to government standards, Petro Well has won many Canadian Association of Oil Well Drilling Contractors servicing rig division safety awards, including one for best overall performance.

PETRO WELL SERVICING

(Back row, from left) Kevin Kryzanowski, Darcy Waggoner, and Larry Gross.

(Front row, from left) Shelley Rae Bilyk, Sharon Niedermaier, John Niedermaier, Debbie Gross, and Debbie Waggoner.

WESTERN ATLAS CANADA LTD.

Today evolution in energy exploration and development is rapidly erasing the old lines between geology, geophysics, petrophysics, and petroleum engineering. Western Atlas Canada Ltd., incorporated in May 1987, is poised for this new era. By combining forces, Atlas Wireline Services, Core Laboratories, and Western Geophysical have created Western Atlas Canada Ltd.—the industry's first single source for exploration, development, and production services.

Together the three companies represent a proven source for geophysical surveys, well logging, core and fluid analysis, and enhanced oil recovery technologies. Whether services are required from one company or the whole group, the consolidation provides a direct link to the technical resources and experience of all.

Geophysical technology is beginning to provide data not only as to the shape and location of the subsurface rock layers, but also data about the materials from which those layers are formed, and even data as to their fluid content. These types of information are used in making critical geologic and petroleum engineering decisions on how to find and develop new oil and gas fields.

Western Geophysical, the world's leading exploration contractor, provides geophysical expertise to map the structure of underground formations. Core Laboratories is the world's largest independent company for analysis of rock and reservoir fluids sampled from underground formations. And Atlas Wireline Services, a leader in wireline services, provides the latest technology in digital data acquisition and analysis for every stage in the life of a well.

Supporting Western Geophysical's exploration capabilities in the United States is Aero Service, the leading airborne surveying company, and Litton Resources Systems, which manufactures a full line of energy sources, cables, sensors, and electronic systems used in seismic exploration. With the addition of Downhole Seismic Service, Western Geophysical has extended seismic exploration to the well site by offering seismic bore hole surveying techniques such as Vertical Seismic Profiling (VSP).

Cooperation between Core Laboratories' analytical, engineering, and consulting services, and the core-testing instrumentation developed by Core Research, a sister company, will expand oil-well monitoring technology. Reservoir simulation software from J.S. Nolen & Associates will allow an oil company to make full use of exploration and lab data to develop oil and gas reservoirs to their maximum potential.

Members of the Litton/Dresser Group have already established cross-links to reach common goals and share resources and skills. Western Geophysical's instrumentation and data-processing staff members are helping Downhole Seismic Ser-

This artist's concept represents the combined services of three companies—Western Geophysical, the world's largest geophysical contractor and a leader in seismic data acquisition, processing, interpretation, and reservoir geophysics; Atlas Wireline Services, a leader in wireline services, providing the latest technology in digital data acquisition and analysis for every stage in the life of a well; and Core Laboratories, the world's largest supplier of core and reservoir fluid analyses. It offers petrophysical services, interpretive software, petroleum engineering, and mineral and environmental services.

vice enhance the VSP acquisition and processing sequence. Core Laboratories and J.S. Nolen & Associates are working together to produce integrated well-log, core-analysis, and reservoir simulation software. Litton Resources Systems is evaluating the production of new products developed by Aero Service and Core Research. And Atlas Wireline Services, in conjunction with Core Laboratories, is providing more precise parameters for well log analysis.

Western Geophysical of Calgary is a leader in seismic data acquisition, processing, interpretation, and reservoir geophysics. Founded in the United States in 1933 by Henry

One of Western Geophysical's modern seismic vessels.

Western vibrator units working on Canadian prairies.

One of Western Geophysical's "CRYSTAL" interactive interpretation work stations.

Salvatori, Western's crews first operated in Alberta in the spring of 1948.

The initial Canadian headquarters consisted of 4,400 square feet of space in downtown Calgary. More

than 200 people are currently employed at the new site in northeast Calgary, which now encompasses 11 acres and 90,000 square feet of office and warehouse space.

Western maintains a computer processing facility, instrumentation labs, shops, and a fleet of 350 vehicles. A field office is also run year-round at Norman Wells in the Northwest Territories, and a marine office in Halifax serves the offshore industry.

The firm has earned a reputation in the industry as a "bread ™n butter" contractor. For large prospects involving hundreds and thousands of kilometres of data acquisition and processing, Western delivers top-quality work at a fast turn-around time, and at a competitive price.

Western also offers specialized acquisition and processing services that are unique in the industry. In the fall of 1985 the company demonstrated a digital telemetry approach to successfully gather high-quality reflection data under several Alberta lakes.

The Calgary office is prominent in the seismic monitoring of enhanced oil recovery projects. Western uses more multiline recording systems than any other contractor in Canada to maintain its position as the leader in high-resolution three-dimensional imaging.

In order to evaluate the vast volumes of data gathered by these large field systems, Western has developed "CRYSTAL" interactive graphics work stations to use the power of computers for interpretation and mapping.

In 1987 the company entered into a joint-venture agreement with the Research Council of Alberta to improve the economic viability of miscible flood oil recovery processes. The 18-month project involves the use of advanced geophysical, geological, and engineering techniques to produce an accurate method of tracking the course of fluids pumped into older petroleum

reservoirs during enhanced recovery projects.

Several large Devonian reefs in Alberta are in the last stages of secondary production, and tertiary processes are required to extract significant amounts of unrecovered oil. Preliminary work included laboratory acoustic measurements on selected reservoir cores under subsurface conditions and in the presence of miscible fluids.

The project, which began in 1987, is under operation at Western's Calgary facility in association with the Research Council's "CATSCAN" laboratory in Edmonton. Subsequent portions of the venture will involve synthetic modelling of seismic data compiled from the flooding process and actual field testing. The completion of this project will enable Western to offer the service worldwide.

Core Laboratories, the world's largest supplier of core and reservoir fluid services, offers laboratory analyses, field services, interpretive software, and petroleum engineering consulting. Core established a district office in Calgary in 1949, and an Edmonton laboratory was added that same year.

Core analysis is the laboratory measurement of petrophysical properties of core samples recovered from geologic formations. This is a technique that allows visual examination of a portion of the formation and direct measurements of several important characteristics of the rock. Core data play a vital role in exploration programs, well completion, and well and reservoir evaluations.

Core soon became involved with tar sands analysis for the Fort McMurray area, determining the bitumen and water content of oil through extraction processes. As exploration expanded into southern Alberta, oil and gas exploration companies established Calgary as their headquarters. Core then opened a gas, oil, and water laboratory in Calgary in the late 1950s. Gas analysis

Core Laboratories Canada, Ltd.'s, headquarters in South Airways Industrial Park in Calgary.

The CMS-200, a fully automated and computerized core analysis measurement system for prepared samples.

services were later added to the bottom hole sampling services in the company's Edmonton laboratory.

In the boom years of the late 1970s Core was located in southeast Calgary in eight separate buildings. Confident in the long-range potential of Canada's energy industry, Core moved into larger facilities to combine all services. The new lab and office complex in South Airways Industrial Park was built to provide more expedient laboratory response, to make special core analysis and enhanced oil recovery services available locally, and to offer more comprehensive petrology and reservoir description services.

In addition, tar sands and heavy oil services have been expanded, and a broader range of gas, oil, geochemical, and environmental services are now available. The new facility allows Core the flexibility to accommodate specialized laboratory studies and add new, technically compatible services.

Core's gas-driven solvent extraction system is one of the largest of its kind in the world. In a specially designed, explosion-proof room, core samples are cleaned for analysis by an extraction method that employs the pressurization of a hydrocarbon solvent with carbon dioxide. This procedure significantly re-duces the time required to remove oil and water from the pore spaces, prior to porosity, grain density, and permeability measurements.

Core also maintains 7,500 square feet of freezer space at temperatures from -18 degrees Celsius to -30 degrees Celsius. Core freezing is primarily used to consolidate loosely aggregated tar sands material and to minimize fluid loss. These walk-in freezers are housed indoors in Core's 125,000-square-foot building in Calgary.

Core has established laboratories in Edmonton and Estevan, Saskatchewan, and maintains bases for field operations in Red Deer, Grande Prairie, and Halifax, Nova Scotia.

A recent addition to Core's services are fluoroscopy and CT Scan devices similar to those used in hospitals. Integrated with a computer to provide image enhancement, this equipment provides Core with the capability to monitor and evaluate displacement fluids used in enhanced oil recovery processes.

Core's newest service, Mineralog™, directly measures mineral percentages in rock samples. This tool has wide applications to wireline log analysis and reservoir characterization.

Atlas Wireline Services provides a broad range of technical wireline services throughout Western Canada, including open- and cased-hole well logging, perforating, com-pletion, and production logging. Technical wireline services are used by oil and gas companies in the exploration, drilling, and production of hydrocarbon energy.

The firm, originally called Lane Wells Company, got its start in Canada in the spring of 1949. A small office, storage trailer, and sales centre were opened in Edmonton, and by 1951 radiation technology was introduced in Canada. Several service centres were established throughout British Columbia, Saskatchewan, and Alberta during the 1950s.

The organization changed its name in 1955 from Lane Wells Company, a division of Dresser Industries, Inc., and open-hole logging services became available in Canada in 1962. Six years later a merger between Pan Geo Atlas and the Lane Wells Division of Dresser Industries, Inc., formed a new division called Dresser Atlas. Dresser Atlas merged with the U.S.-based Litton Resource Group on May 1, 1987, forming Western Atlas International. Atlas Wireline Services is now a division of Western Atlas Canada Ltd.

Atlas Wireline maintains service centres in all active oil and gas areas in Alberta, including Medicine Hat, Calgary, Red Deer, Edmonton, Slave Lake, Grande Prairie,

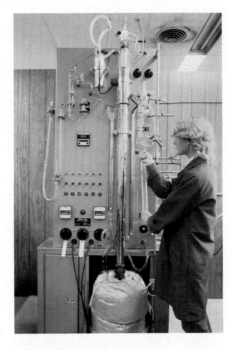

True boiling point apparatus in the gas analysis laboratory allows for precise distillation of hydrocarbon component by boiling range.

An Atlas Wireline Services logging unit on a drilling rig location in Alberta prepares to run electric logs.

High Level, and two other important locations: Estevan, Saskatchewan, and Sarnia, Ontario.

Atlas Wireline's field technical operations are located in Edmonton, where maintenance and repair of mobile "field laboratories" takes place. Administration and sales are centred in the Calgary regional office.

Hoist units containing all necessary equipment and electronic apparatus are dispatched to customer wells on a 24-hour basis from the company's various service centres. The hoist units are truck-mounted for land operations and skid-mounted for offshore or remote locations. These field laboratories are operated by crews of specialists under the supervision of a field engineer.

Atlas Wireline's services vary from the most complex downhole, microprocessor-controlled instrument, to something as basic as a mechanical "junk catcher." The major components of a logging unit (truck) include downhole instruments, a surface computer, and the wireline containing electrical con-

ductors. The conductors provide power to the downhole instruments and transmit information to the surface computer.

The computerized logging system serves two purposes—data acquisition and digital analysis. Data is generally received in two formats: digital data recorded on nine-track tapes or floppy disks, and depth-oriented paper plots. Atlas Wireline's logging units have both voice and data transmission capabilities, giving clients immediate access to information gathered in the field.

Open-hole logging (new oil and gas wells that have not yet been fit with steel casing) involves the evaluation of petrophysical properties to identify potential hydrocarbon reservoirs. Many techniques are employed to measure certain characteristics of the borehole, such as porosity, permeability, reservoir thickness, fluid content, pressure, and lithology.

After the initial open-hole data

An Atlas Wireline Services logging engineer calibrating equipment prior to the logging operation. A computer, located inside the logging truck, calibrates equipment and obtains and stores the data. The final hard copy produced is referred to as a "log."

evaluation and formation tests have been completed, the well is lined with steel casing to prevent the wall of the hole from caving in, to stop vertical migration of fluids, and to provide a means of extracting hydrocarbon from the well.

Atlas Wireline conducts pulsed-neutron surveys on cased holes. This is a special logging method that uses radioactivity decay time to obtain measurements of water saturation, residual oil saturation, and fluid contacts in the formation outside the casing of an oil or gas well. With advances in technology, an increasing number of complex microprocessor-controlled instruments such as this will provide more accurate and reliable measurements.

ESSO RESOURCES CANADA LIMITED

Esso Plaza, in twin 35-storey towers, is the home of Esso Resources Canada Limited in Calgary.

Esso Resources Canada Limited, a wholly owned subsidiary of Imperial Oil Limited, is involved in the exploration, development, and production of conventional crude oil, bitumen, natural gas, liquids, and coal and mineral deposits. Incorporated in Canada in 1978, the firm has its head office in Calgary. Its operations span Canada.

Esso Resources plays a key role in the activities of its parent company. Imperial Oil, founded in Canada in 1880, is one of the country's largest integrated oil companies. Its Leduc No. 1 discovery well southwest of Edmonton in 1947 was one of the most significant events in Canadian oil history and is recognized as the birth of the modern oil industry in Alberta.

In Canada, Imperial is the largest producer of hydrocarbon liquids, one of the largest refiners and marketers of petroleum products, and a significant supplier of natural gas. It is also engaged in the manufacture and sale of chemicals and fertilizers. Esso Resources owns and manages Imperial's natural re-

sources operations and assets.

Esso Resources' natural gas production in Western Canada supplies long-term contracts to gas-transmission companies and a portion of Imperial Oil's internal market in Alberta. The firm also has large gas resources in the North, including the Taglu field on the Beaufort Coast. Taglu is regarded as the largest undeveloped gas field in Canada.

A three-year expansion project

to develop the Norman Wells oil field in the Northwest Territories was completed in 1985. The project included construction of a 12-inch pipeline from Norman Wells to existing pipeline systems in Alberta. The expansion increased total field production of crude oil and natural gas liquids from about 3,000 barrels per day to 25,000 per day in 1986 and more than 30,000 barrels per day in 1987.

Esso Resources has major interests in the Judy Creek, Rainbow, Redwater, and Mitsue oil fields in northern Alberta. These fields currently account for approximately 40 percent of the company's gross production of conventional crude oil.

Esso Resources began work on an enhanced oil-recovery program at the Judy Creek field northwest of Edmonton in 1984. The project uses a miscible flood process in which a hydrocarbon solvent is injected into the reservoir, sweeping otherwise unrecoverable oil to producing wells. By mid-1987 daily production from Judy Creek had increased 26 percent, and the firm expects that an additional 50 million barrels of oil will be recovered as a result of

A noon-hour band concert, sponsored by Esso Resources, illustrates the firm's commitment to community involvement.

ABOVE LEFT: The Syncrude bucket reclaimer has a capacity of 6,000 tons per hour.

ABOVE RIGHT: A typical Alberta scene of a horsehead pumpjack at Boundary Lake.

this project.

Esso Resources has an 83-percent interest in the Leduc oil field, now 37 years old and nearly depleted. After oil recovery is discontinued, associated natural gas will be recovered. The reservoir still contains 320 billion cubic feet of natural gas, and its development has been approved by the Alberta Energy Resources Conservation Board.

Esso Resources is Canada's leading developer of oil sands resources. The company holds a 25-percent participating interest in Syncrude, a consortium formed to mine shallow deposits in the Athabasca oil sands near Fort McMurray. The Syncrude plant extracts very heavy crude oil (bitumen), and produces synthetic crude oil. Syncrude leases 97,000 gross acres from the Province of Alberta for its operation.

Esso Resources holds 197,000 leased acres of oil sands near Cold Lake. This deposit contains high-grade bitumen, which is too deeply buried for conventional surface mining. Since 1964 the company has had an ongoing commitment to developing the technology necessary to produce this oil commercially. Experimental pilot operations provided a cyclic steam stimulation pro-

cess in which hot steam is injected into the reservoir, driving the sluggish oil to hundreds of production wells. A large commercial development currently is being built in phases, and expenditures are approaching one billion dollars. Full commercial production began in 1985, and by early 1988 bitumen production at Cold Lake was in the range of 75,000 to 80,000 barrels per day. Additional phases are under construction, and Cold Lake production soon will represent 10 percent of Canadian oil production.

Esso Resources also is involved in the exploration and development of conventional crude oil and natural gas in the western provinces and in the so-called Canada Lands, which include the Northwest Territories, the Yukon, and the Atlantic offshore.

In 1987 Esso Resources was the leading driller in Canada, accounting for a total of 446 wells. The firm operated 376 completions in Alberta (14 of which were exploratory), 31 in Saskatchewan, and 39 in Northern Canada.

The firm has drilled exploration wells in the Beaufort Sea/Mackenzie Delta since 1964. Substantial quantities of natural gas have been found, and while significant oil reserves also have been confirmed, their size doesn't yet warrant commercial development by the company. In 1984 Esso Resources and the Government of Canada entered into several agree-

ments authorizing an exploration program for 7.9 million gross acres in the Atlantic offshore. The firm drilled five offshore wells and conducted 2,500 kilometres of seismic operations in the area.

The coal division of Esso Resources is responsible for the generation and management of profitable investment opportunities in the coal industry. The division is active in Alberta and British Columbia. Esso Resources has been exploring for coal deposits since 1971 and has been involved in coal mining since 1981, when it purchased Byron

Aerial view of a nonconventional well configuration used in the Cold Lake area for bitumen production. The process, called cyclic steam stimulation (huff and puff), requires closely placed wells linked to central steam generation plants as well as processing facilities.

LEFT: *Esso Petroleum's Strathcona refinery, where crude oil is refined into a wide range of petroleum products.*

ABOVE: *Loader with product at Esso Chemical's fertilizer complex at Redwater.*

BELOW: *A modern Esso Petroleum service station.*

Creek Collieries Limited in southeastern British Columbia. Most of the Collieries' current output is sold as thermal coal for electrical power production.

A $49-million coal wash plant was completed at the Collieries in 1986. This installation increases the recovery of marketable coal, extends the life of the mine, and will allow higher production when markets increase.

Esso Petroleum Canada, a division of Imperial Oil, operates five refineries nationwide and has a major share of the Canadian market for petroleum products. This division is responsible for providing and servicing customer requirements for petroleum fuels, asphalts, petrochemical feedstocks, lubricants, and specialty products.

Although Esso Petroleum's head office is in Toronto, its largest refinery is in Edmonton, serving the three prairie provinces and eastern British Columbia. With major sales offices in Edmonton and Calgary and a network of service stations and agency operations across Canada, Esso Petroleum also provides petroleum products and services to industrial, commercial, and agricultural businesses.

One of the petroleum division's highlights in 1986 was the introduction of its No Trouble Gasoline,

which was launched following an extensive research program. The gasoline contains new detergent additives that can clean fuel injectors and carburetors, thus improving engine performance, summer and winter.

Esso Chemical Canada, Imperial's second division, was formed in 1955 in response to signs of a promising future for petrochemical opportunities in Canada. The widespread use of chemical fertilizer in Western Canada grain production had its first significant impact in 1962, when farmers recorded marked crop increases. Consequently, fertilizer sales began to in-

crease dramatically.

The chemical division's activities are international in scope. Agricultural chemicals are supplied to Canada, the northwestern United States, and overseas. An agricultural-chemicals complex near Redwater covers 370 hectares and employs more than 500 people. The head office is in Toronto, and the Edmonton office operates as the supply, distribution, and marketing centre.

PAN-ALBERTA GAS LTD.

Pan-Alberta Gas Ltd., headquartered in Calgary, was incorporated in 1972. Its major function was to buy and sell natural gas at a time when a shortage of natural gas was being experienced. Initial sales were to domestic markets, and while the company continues to sell gas in every gas-consuming province in Canada, the majority of its sales today are destined for U.S. markets. Now Canada's largest independent exporter of natural gas, Pan-Alberta markets gas in most of the continental United States, from California to Florida and New England.

In addition to long-term sales made directly by Pan-Alberta, the company also has two subsidiaries—NATGAS Canada Inc., which contracts for short-term gas sales in Canada, and NATGAS U.S. Inc., which imports Canadian natural gas into the United States to serve short-, medium-, and long-term market needs.

The sole business of Pan-Alberta and its affiliates is to provide complete gas-marketing services through management of an automated infrastructure of gas supply and transportation contracts. This, coupled with the unique expertise of its employee group, provides a strong, reliable, and secure base of operations and ensures accurate delivery of gas on any day in any season.

Pan-Alberta's home base is Alberta, the primary gas-producing province in Canada. More than 85 percent of Canada's remaining marketable reserves are located in the province of Alberta.

Gas supply for Pan-Alberta and its affiliated gas-marketing companies is provided from long-term gas purchase contracts held with a diversified group of more than 420 Alberta producers. The firm's gas supply is secured through more than 1,200 individual purchase contracts, representing a total in excess of 8 trillion cubic feet of reserves.

Natural gas for Pan-Alberta's markets, and those of its subsidiaries, is transported through various pipelines. Within Alberta, Pan-Alberta's gas is gathered and transported by NOVA Corporation of Alberta. NOVA is the largest gas-transmission company in Canada and is capable of transporting in excess of 9 billion cubic feet of gas daily.

From the Alberta border, gas is moved for Pan-Alberta through every major pipeline system in Canada and many of the major systems in the United States.

Pan-Alberta is a longtime participant in the U.S. marketplace through its involvement in the prebuild portions of the Alaska Natural Gas Transmission System (ANGTS). Pan-Alberta was an influential participant in bringing the ANGTS prebuild into operation and has been exporting gas through its facilities since 1981.

Pan-Alberta places a high priority on maintaining a solid understanding and involvement in the regulatory scenes in Canada and the United States. Beginning with its involvement with the prebuild, Pan-Alberta has a history of success in dealing with regulatory matters in both countries and in responding to changing industry and market requirements. The company moved quickly to accommodate changes resulting from deregulation in the industry on both sides of the border, and has remained competitive in both the marketplace and in its contractual arrangements with its producers in this changing environment.

In 1987 Pan-Alberta and its California customer, Pacific Interstate Transmission Company, set an unprecedented record in Canada/U.S. natural gas trade when, for the third consecutive year, Pacific Interstate purchased 100 percent of its contracted volumes of gas from Pan-Alberta. This unprecedented record was accomplished despite a period of change and uncertainty that affected the industry as a whole and led to a decline in Canadian natural gas exports to the United States.

Pan-Alberta Gas is a people-oriented company—one that encourages its employees to participate in organizations and groups at the local, regional, and national levels. It is also a corporation that shows it cares about the community by sponsoring and supporting cultural, charitable, environmental, and athletic organizations.

This kind of personal and professional involvement is a reflection of Pan-Alberta Gas Ltd.'s belief in a better future—and of its corporate commitment to providing a continuous and reliable supply of gas to fuel that future.

BELOW LEFT: Pan-Alberta markets natural gas throughout Canada and the United States.

BELOW: The 49th Parallel separates pipeline installations at Monchy, Saskatchewan, and Morgan, Montana, which form part of the complex network of pipelines carrying gas to export markets.

ERSKINE RESOURCES CORPORATION

Erskine Resources Corporation is a public, Canadian-owned energy company engaged in oil and gas exploration and development. Based in Calgary, the company also is involved in purchasing producing oil and gas properties in Western Canada.

Operations commenced in May 1981, when Erskine's principal shareholders, Murray J. Berg and Tibor Fekete, acquired their first oil well in the Erskine, Alberta, region. In late 1981 they assembled and operated a successful joint venture program in association with several Canadian corporations not directly engaged in the petroleum industry.

The company, and its joint venture partners in the 1981-1982 program, invested more than $50 million in exploration, development, and the acquisition of oil and gas properties. Erskine has since initiated and operated several additional programs. Oil production (including natural gas liquids) has increased sharply from 30 barrels per day in 1981 to approximately 1,300 barrels per day in late 1987, while natural gas production has risen from 271,000 cubic feet per day in 1981 to more than 10 million cubic feet per day in late 1987.

On the basis of energy content, reserves and production during the five-year period of 1982 to 1986 increased at compound annual growth rates of 63 percent and 85 percent, respectively. Erskine's finding and developing cost for these reserves averaged approximately $3.50 per barrel of oil equivalent, which is significantly below the industry average.

Erskine's investment strategy is to continue to concentrate on acquiring producing properties with upside potential and on drilling low-risk oil and gas prospects. Impressive for a young company with some 50 employees, Erskine already has three significant discoveries to its credit.

In addition to the Erskine oil field, located 80 miles east of Red Deer, Alberta, the company has a 3.72 percent participating interest in the Crystal Viking Unit No. 1 in west-central Alberta. During 1986 Erskine's share of production from this field averaged 166 barrels of oil and natural gas liquids, and 140,000 cubic feet of natural gas per day.

Erskine owns a 12.7685 percent participating interest in, and acts as operator of, the Gleneath Unit in west-central Saskatchewan. In 1988 Erskine's share of production from this unit will be about 130 barrels of oil per day.

Erskine holds a 9.1 percent working interest in the Pembina (Buck Lake) field, which is located in west-central Alberta. In 1986 the company's interest in production from this field totalled 74 barrels of oil and natural gas liquids, and 700,000 cubic feet of natural gas per day.

In addition to these properties, Erskine has significant interests in a number of other oil and gas fields in Western Canada.

Erskine diversified its interests with the acquisition of 90 percent of the outstanding shares of Limeco Products Limited in May 1985. Limeco has quarriable mineral leases covering 484 acres and processing facilities in Rocky Mountain House, Alberta. Limeco's processing plant, which has a design capacity of 300,000 tonnes per year, commenced production in July 1986 and produces crushed and pelletized limestone and gypsum products. Erskine's investment in Limeco amounts to approximately $4 million.

Limestone is used to neutralize acidic soils on farmland and around natural gas processing plants, while gypsum is used to restore alkaline soils and to clean up saltwater spills associated with oil production. Processed limestone is also used for cattle and chicken feed, and in many industrial applica-

The Board of Directors of Erskine Resources Corporation (standing, left to right): Dr. David H.A. Sellers, Tibor Fekete, William H. Bonney, Murray J. Berg, and (seated, from left) Sol Schwartz and John D. Skelton.

TOP: *An Erskine pump jack.*

BOTTOM: *Limeco Products Limited, a recent Erskine Resources acquisition, has quarriable mineral leases covering 484 acres and processing facilities in Rocky Mountain House, Alberta.*

projcts.

One of the prospects is in the Marten Hills, Alberta, gas area, where Erskine has a 20 to 40 percent working interest in 15 undeveloped sections of leasehold rights. This low-risk exploratory play should allow the company to significantly increase its marketable gas reserves. Erskine also holds a 20 percent interest in 1,760 acres of land in Brazeau, Alberta. Recent drilling in this area has resulted in several oil wells, which are producing an average of 70 barrels of oil per day.

Erskine has a total of 604,440 gross acres and 364,400 net acres in its land inventory. The majority of land is located in Alberta and Saskatchewan, with minor holdings in Colorado, New Mexico, and North Dakota.

A large portion of the company's undeveloped net acreage (279,000) relates to a shale oil project in the Pasquia Hills of Saskatchewan, where Erskine has a 70 percent working interest. This unique project is conducive to both in situ production and open surface mining, and has considerable commercial potential. Research indicates recoverable reserves of several billion barrels are possible.

Erskine's prime objective is to add reserves, at relatively low cost, that will generate cash flow in the near future. In order to achieve this objective, the company will continue to emphasize the acquisition of producing properties and low-risk drilling, while at all times being aware of cash flow requirements. The company is actively seeking mergers with similar-size oil and gas companies that will complement and strengthen its position in the industry.

tions. In addition to the oil and gas and animal feed industries, limestone and gypsum products are sold to the mushroom industry. Limestone is also marketed to the fertilizer and farm chemical industry and to asphalt product plants.

Effective May 1, 1987, Erskine Resources Limited and Canadian Bashaw Leduc Oil and Gas Limited (CBL) merged to form Erskine Resources Corporation. CBL was a public Canadian independent oil and gas company engaged in the acquisition, exploration, development, and production of oil and natural gas in Canada and the United States. The merger significantly increased Erskine's asset base with virtually no change in overhead costs, and resulted in its common shares being listed on The Alberta Stock Exchange.

Erskine has a number of untapped exploration and development opportunities in Alberta and Saskatchewan. A 15 to 18 well development and exploratory drilling program will be undertaken on company lands in 1988. Prospects vary from single-well oil potential to multi-well gas development

INTERPROVINCIAL PIPE LINE LIMITED
Name changed to Interhome Energy Inc. May 4, 1988

Interprovincial Pipe Line Limited (IPL), which commenced operations in 1950, is engaged in the transportation of crude oil and other liquid hydrocarbons through a common carrier pipeline system. The company is also involved in the exploration for and production of crude oil, natural gas, and gas liquids. IPL's pipeline operations are headquartered in Edmonton, while the oil and gas operations are based in Calgary.

The need for a transcontinental oil pipeline grew out of the discovery of crude oil at Leduc, Alberta, in 1947, and at other new oil fields discovered during the three subsequent years. The original plans called for construction of a large-diameter pipeline between Edmonton and Regina. As additional oil fields were discovered, the line was extended to the head of the Great Lakes at Superior, Wisconsin.

In 1957 Alberta was linked by pipeline to markets in southwestern Ontario, a distance of 1,900 miles. Throughout the 1960s IPL greatly extended the capacity of the pipeline system and built several branch lines to serve strong new markets for Western Canadian crude oil. The system was entirely computerized in 1968, providing IPL with one of the most advanced pipeline control and communications facilities in the world.

The 1970s witnessed further expansion of the firm's pipeline system. Today the system extends from Edmonton across the Canadian Prairies through the Great Lakes region of the United States to Toronto and Montreal. By 1985 IPL had completed a 540-mile, 12-inch pipeline to transport crude oil from Norman Wells in the Northwest Territories to Zama in northern Alberta. The historic Norman Wells pipeline, the first significant underground line to be constructed through permafrost in Canada's North, represented a major step toward development of the country's vast northern frontier resources.

IPL's pipeline system is now the longest in North America. The main line system consists of some 6,600 miles of pipeline in diameters ranging from 12 to 48 inches, 89 pumping stations with an installed available power of approximately 786,000 kilowatts, and tankage facilities with a capacity of roughly 18 million barrels. In total, 31 refineries receive shipments from the system: 12 in Canada and 19 in the United States.

IPL owns and operates the portions of the main pipeline system located in Western Canada, Ontario, and Quebec. A wholly owned subsidiary, Lakehead Pipeline Company, Inc., owns and operates the portion of the main line system situated in the United States. Another wholly owned subsidiary, Interprovincial Pipe Line (NW) Ltd., owns and operates the pipeline between Norman Wells and Zama. IPL's pipeline deliveries of crude oil and

RIGHT: The control room in IPL's pipeline terminal at Griffith, Indiana.

BELOW: A three-phase expansion program, completed in 1987, increased IPL's pipeline capacity by 327,000 barrels per day.

ABOVE: Two of Home Oil's geologists examining logs from an exploratory well in northern Alberta.

LEFT: A drilling rig operating on a Home Oil property in central Alberta.

other liquid hydrocarbons in 1987 averaged 1.422 million barrels per day.

In December 1986 IPL diversified into the upstream oil and gas sector with the acquisition of all the shares of Home Oil Company Limited. Home Oil's major Canadian oil and gas properties are in Alberta, northeastern British Columbia, southern Saskatchewan, southwestern Manitoba, the Beaufort Sea, and the Mackenzie River Delta.

The company owns various interests in and operates eight natural gas processing plants in Alberta, and markets crude oil, natural gas, natural gas liquids, liquefied petroleum gas, and sulphur. Home Oil also owns interests in and operates three feeder pipeline systems, which transport crude oil and natural gas liquids in Alberta. Internationally, the firm holds direct interests in Australia, Indonesia, Colombia, offshore Italy, and the United Kingdom. During 1987

Home Oil's production of crude oil and natural gas liquids averaged 30,200 barrels per day. Average natural gas sales were 114 million cubic feet per day.

Home Oil was founded in 1925 by Major James Lowery and actively participated in the early development of the Turner Valley oil field in southern Alberta. With a number of other successful finds under its belt, Home Oil was the largest independent oil company in Canada by the end of World War II. In 1957 the firm was the operator of a significant oil discovery at Swan Hills, which was destined to become Home Oil's largest single source of oil production and revenue. In terms of cumulative production, Swan Hills now ranks as the third-largest producing oil field in Canada.

In all respects 1986 was a pivotal year in the history of IPL. The acquisition of Home Oil and a substantial expansion of the company's pipeline facilities in Western Canada greatly increased the size and complexity of IPL. These two developments raised IPL's total assets to close to $3 billion, divided equally between the pipeline and the oil and gas operations, and more than doubled the number of employees to approximately 2,000.

Interhome will continue to expand the pipeline system to meet future requirements, focus on new business opportunities in the transportation of heavy crude oil and in water pipelines, and maintain a leadership position with respect to a pipeline from the Beaufort Sea. Home Oil will continue to place priority on Western Canada, pursue frontier opportunities in Canada as economic conditions merit, and expand international operations.

Interhome emphasizes community involvement and support. The firm contributes to national and local charitable organizations, institutions of higher learning, and agencies in the fields of art and culture, welfare, research, and medical care.

Jager Industries Inc.

Cano Structures Inc.

*Alpine Management Corpora-
tion Ltd.*

Banister Continental Ltd.

CANA Limited

United Management Ltd.

Nicks Flooring Service Ltd.

*W.A. Stephenson Construc-
tion (Western) Limited*

Courtesy, Westfile, Inc.

CHAPTER 14

Building Greater Alberta

From concept to completion, Alberta's building industry shapes tomorrow's skyline.

Jager Industries Inc. 392-395; Cano Structures Inc. 396-398; Alpine Management Corporation Ltd. 399; Banister Continental Ltd. 400-401; CANA Limited 402; United Management Ltd. 403; Nicks Flooring Service Ltd. 404-405; W.A. Stephenson Construction (Western) Limited. 406-409

JAGER INDUSTRIES INC.

If one were to ask the average Calgarian, "Quick, what comes after Jager?" the reply is most likely to be, "Homes, as in Jager Homes, of course!"

William "Bill" Jager, the founder and chairman of the board of Jager Industries Inc., has spent more than 40 years earning this enviable reputation for building quality homes in Calgary. What he has also built is a large, multifaceted international corporation on the solid foundation he established with his first small construction company.

Always a keen and accurate predictor of market trends, Bill Jager's first foray into the construction industry was based on Calgary's growing postwar need for innovatively designed and solidly built homes. Today, more than 10,000 homes later, Jager Industries' Homes Division, the city's largest custom home builder, is still giving Calgarians the kind of new homes they want and has an impressive array of awards to prove it.

From its corporate headquarters on Macleod Trail Southwest, with its distinctive Jager sign shaded by the towering 56-foot rooftop sunflower, Jager Industries directs the business undertakings of its eight divisions operating from seven offices in five Canadian cities.

Family owned and operated from its inception, Jager Industries, despite its size, has retained the integrity only the personal touch of Bill Jager could impart. With his wife, Donna, as vice-chairman; his oldest son, Harvey, as president; and his seven other sons and daughters holding key company positions, Bill Jager continues to actively foster a family feeling in his organization.

Yet, there can be no doubt that Jager Industries Inc. has become a large and vital corporation with local, national, and international markets for its many products and services.

For instance, its Land Division's Calgary history dates back 35 years

William "Bill" Jager, the driving force behind Jager Industries Inc., is a dynamic and single-minded entrepreneur who has parlayed his gifts for organization and invention into a multimillion-dollar corporation.
Born into a poor farming family in Saskatchewan and schooled by the hard knocks of the Depression, Bill Jager is a familiar figure to his employees as he makes his regular tours of his company's construction sites and manufacturing plants.

A young 67, Bill Jager thrives on work and takes great pleasure in overseeing his personal empire from his command post in the Jager corporate headquarters on Macleod Trail. With windows that overlook his TTS Systems Division storage yard and a floor that often shakes from the rumblings of the TTS Connector Plate presses two floors below, this self-made chairman of the board is as much a part of the company as the company is a part of him.

It is this dedication that has ensured Bill Jager a special place in the annals of the city as one of that rare breed of men whose vision has helped make Calgary what it is today. His story and the story of Jager Industries Inc. is an integral element in the phenomenal progress the city has made in the past 40 years.

to the days when builders such as Bill Jager had the foresight to begin to establish their own land banks for future residential construction. It has an excellent reputation for designing and developing desirable neighborhoods throughout the city. Notable among its creatively planned subdivisions are its current endeavors in Signal Ridge in the southwest and Sandstone Valley in the northwest.

Al Bell, the Jager vice-president who directs the operations of the Land Division, also carries the company's colors into the civic arena. A member of the Calgary Hospital Board, he has also served as chairman of the Construction Committee for the Performing Arts Centre and as campaign manager for Mayor Ralph Klein during his last successful election campaign.

Closely allied with Jager's Land Division, the recently revitalized Earthmoving Division provides the heavy equipment necessary for Jager subdivision landscaping as well as undertaking other contract work in southern Alberta.

While the Jager Homes and Land divisions are consolidating

The sweeping curve of rail and stairs combine in pleasing architectural accord to highlight the vaulted hall of this custom-designed Jager home—a recent nominee for Calgary's best custom home award.

the Jager reputation in Calgary, on the national scene it is the manufacturing divisions of the Jager corporation that are making the greatest impact. Vertically integrated to provide the Canadian construction industry with patented truss connector plates, truss engineering, truss machinery, and patented Wood I beams, these divisions, under the leadership of the TTS Systems Divi-

The tranquil view from their lakeside location enhances the value of these beautiful estate-size residences designed and built by Jager in Calgary's Lake Sundance subdivision.

sion, developed out of Bill Jager's continuing concern with building efficiency.

In the early 1960s he reasoned that if roof construction utilizing prebuilt trusses was more efficient

than the traditional board-by-board method other less progressive builders were still employing, then trusses that could be built without nails had to be even better. Hence, Jager's TTS System of truss connector plates was developed.

Soon the local market was convinced and it was not long before Jager's TTS Systems Division was introducing this new and highly competitive product across Canada into the burgeoning truss fabricator industry—a lucrative market in which the firm now enjoys a more than 40-percent market share.

Today, coupled with its connector plates, Jager also offers a comprehensive engineering service backed by innovative computer software developed by its own engineers and computer programmers.

But, back in the early 1970s, Bill Jager was still looking for ways to streamline truss construction. He was concerned that trusses, though improved by the connector plates, still had to be built by hand. Truss-

The western motif in this custom kitchen with its wagon wheel-shaped illuminated ceiling is just one of the special design requests the Jager staff pride themselves on fulfilling for their customers.

building machinery had to be the answer. Thus, Jager's Steel Products Division, with its full line of truss plant equipment, was born.

Again Jager's marketing horizons expanded. This time not only the Canadian truss fabricators but also those in the United States and Australia were interested in these new Jager machines.

Jager, the small Calgary home

Showcasing the best of Jager homes, this professionally decorated model is one of the company's many show homes that help to draw Calgarians to the city's new subdivisions.

builder of the 1940s, had catapulted into the world marketplace just in time for the boom years of the 1970s.

A TTS branch in Switzerland with dealings across Europe, condo-

minium developments and Jager-built residential neighborhoods in the Sunbelt of the United States, and an interest in a winery in Argentina soon rounded out Bill Jager's international portfolio. Tool and die capabilities, a time-sharing computer company, and an award-winning town house complex in Calgary added to his local holdings as he prepared to meet the challenges of the 1980s.

And meet them he did. Unlike those of many of his contemporaries, Bill Jager's company emerged from the recent recession as strong as ever. Always the pragmatist, this hands-on administrator made the changes he had to make to keep his organization going. Under his guidance, the firm re-aligned divisions and reviewed and revamped marketing programs. Today innovation and aggressive marketing techniques are keeping this "leaner and meaner" Jager Industries Inc. at the forefront of the industries its serves.

As case in point is the company's exciting new building component, the patented Wood I beam, which is produced on Jager's prototype machinery in the firm's automated plant in Foothills Industrial Park. Developed in answer to stress and clear-span problems for floor and slant-roof applications in both

residential and commercial construction, the Wood I is quickly gaining popularity across Canada due to the efforts of sales personnel working out of the Jager offices in Ontario, Quebec, New Brunswick, and British Columbia.

Jager Industries has also entered the heady world of high technology with the pioneering software being developed by the computer programmers in its Computer Services Division, the newest member of the Jager family. Orders for this software are arriving in Calgary from as far away as the United States, Europe, Australia, and the

Jager's new and patented Wood I beams form the strong and easily installed roof of this recently constructed Western Canada hotel.

Orient.

Moreover, two of these programs, in keeping with a long-established Jager tradition, have been nominated for computer industry awards. It would come as no surprise if Bill Jager's trophy shelf needed rearranging again in· the very near future.

The chairman of the board would welcome the challenge.

Impressive 100-foot clear span trusses, manufactured by Jager Industries using its patented TTS truss plates, are lowered into position at the Jager plant site in Calgary's Foothills Industrial Park (below).

Bill Jager checks his firm's Wood I beams at a local construction site where they are being installed as floor joists (right).

CANO STRUCTURES INC.

In 1984 Cano Structures Inc. of Calgary introduced a highly energy-efficient exterior wall system to the Canadian residential-construction market. Called NASCOR, the innovative product spelled success for the company, and today Cano is the largest supplier of its kind in North America.

Cano president Richard Dettbarn acquired the patent for the system's original design in 1983 from an Eastern Canadian manufacturer and developed improvements to make the product more commercially viable. The two basic components of the present system are its unique wood-and-polystyrene columns and its solid, expanded polystyrene infill panels. The combination of these parts creates a structurally sound, easily assembled wall system.

Expanded polystyrene (EPS) is a polymer impregnated with a foaming agent that when exposed to heat creates a uniform, closed-cell structure highly resistant to heat flow and moisture penetration (the most popular type of disposable cof-

fee cups are made of similar material). EPS, in use since 1951, is tough, resists vibration, absorbs strains due to building movement, and is much less combustible than wood. These factors make it an excellent insulating material for use in building construction and one of the most economical insulation materials in the construction industry today.

Development and testing of the product were financially supported by Vencap Equities, a venture-capital corporation owned by the Government of Alberta. Vencap invested $1.5 million in the company in 1985, contributing significantly to Cano's successful growth and expansion. Vencap retains a major interest in the firm.

Cano's NASCOR walls are revolutionizing the North American housing industry. Made of high-grade, kiln-dried lumber and polystyrene insulation, the walls are fabricated according to the blueprints of the particular job and can be built to suit any design. Detailed walls with bay windows and

A 29-unit condominium project built in Banff for the 1988 Olympic Winter Games.

turrets are installed almost as quickly as straight walls.

Prefabrication of wall units allows for better quality control on the job site. While builders marvel at the ease of construction, home owners are impressed with the superior structural strength, heat insulation, and soundproofing.

NASCOR walls provide a thermal break by sandwiching polystyrene between the wood studs, eliminating the problem of thermal bridging that occurs at the studs in conventional wall construction. Solid NASCOR walls also eliminate air infiltration, whereas glass-fibre insulation allows air and wind to pass through the batts.

Polystyrene does not sag or settle within the walls like glass-fibre batts. Insulation in conventional walls tends to settle and may leave gaps at the top of the wall where significant heat loss can occur.

NASCOR walls also have no

condensation buildup. The closed cell beads in the expanded polystyrene walls ensure isolated air pockets; no condensation is possible. This superior energy efficiency is combined with superior cost effectiveness. Independent tests on homes with NASCOR walls report up to 50-percent reduction in energy costs. The system, which would cost an additional $800 in an 1,800-square-foot house, usually pays for itself within 18 months.

Cano embarked on commercial production of the NASCOR system in 1984 in a small Calgary manufacture facility with three employees, and it has since expanded to two large plants—one for the manufacturing of polystyrene and the other for wall assembly. The company also has assembly plants in Vancouver, Toronto, and Phoenix, and a network of 24 licensed dealers across Canada who manufacture and sell the system. The privately held firm has 100 employees, 90 in Canada and 10 in the United States.

Although the bulk of Cano's business includes the production of custom-made wall systems for residential construction, the firm also designs and builds foundations, roofs, and floors with the NASCOR system. The roof system is particularly valuable when with the open-beam construction method is used for vaulted or cathedral ceilings. It combines the well-documented energy efficiencies of the NASCOR panels with the structural superiority of Wood I beams. The floor system allows longer, clearer spans, provides an insulated floor, and eliminates the need for cross-bridging.

Utilizing the NASCOR system, a builder can erect an enclosed structure on a completed foundation in just two days, compared to a minimum of two weeks for a conventional wood-frame structure.

NASCOR virtually eliminates insulation as a separate trade. Once the frame is up, the builder can go straight to mechanical, electrical, and dry-wall installations.

Cano has worked hard to keep the system as simple as possible in order to gain acceptance by contractors, dealers, and the public. Now in its fourth year of production, the company anticipates that the NASCOR system will become a recognized method of construction within the next three years. Cano expects NASCOR to parallel products such as dry wall and prefabricated-truss systems in its growth and acceptance by the building industry.

Cano opened a new manufacturing facility and sales department in Phoenix, Arizona, in October 1987.

This 84-unit co-operative town house project is in Willowdale, Ontario.

The NASCOR system can also be utilized in commercial projects such as this Chrysler dealership in Elk Point, Alberta.

home was completed in 1987 in Vancouver, featuring Cano's NASCOR wall system. A four-man construction crew erected all of the exterior walls of the 1,800-square-foot bungalow within two hours. Between January 1985 and January 1987 the NASCOR system was used in more than 3,000 Canadian homes.

In Calgary, the NASCOR system is now used in about 15 percent of new homes. NASCOR walls were installed in a condominium complex in Banff for the 1988 Olympic Winter Games. The product has also been used in apartment blocks, vacation homes, mushroom barns, refrigeration-storage warehouses, agricultural facilities, car dealerships, service stations, churches, hotels and motels, schools, and light industry buildings.

Cano Structures Inc. has also received national recognition for its patented NASCOR system. The company was the recipient of the Most Innovative Product Award 1987, presented by the Sales and Marketing Council of the Toronto Home Builders' Association.

Through this move the firm hopes to increase its market share in both Canada and the United States. The company's sales in 1987 reached more than $6 million, a substantial increase from $758,000 in its first year of production.

In 1986, 90 percent of Cano's business was in the construction of single-family housing, but the company has since expanded into multifamily dwelling projects. Canada's first computer-controlled R-2000

The controlled environment of Cano's assembly plants ensures superior quality control.

ALPINE MANAGEMENT CORPORATION LTD.

Founded in 1952 by Austin Henry Ford, Alpine Management Corporation Ltd. has kept pace with Calgary's growth for more than 35 years. The company owns and manages three high-rise buildings in the city's downtown core, and it has been involved in the acquisition, development, and management of downtown commercial property for three generations.

Austin Ford moved to Calgary from the small town of Bassano in the early years of the Great Depression and began his working life as an in-house accountant for a hardware store in 1932. After serving as a naval officer in World War II, Ford and his father, Henry, bought their own company.

Hayford Ltd. was a manufacturer of pool hall tables and equipment that later expanded into the manufacture of bowling alleys and office furnishings. After a few years of postwar business the firm sold its billiard and bowling operations in East Calgary. The company purchased a property on Ninth Avenue Southwest in 1957 where it continued manufacturing specialty office furniture for another year.

Following the sale of the cabinet business, the Ninth Avenue Southwest warehouse location formed the home for a new venture called Derrick Building Ltd. Ford's dream was to construct an office building on the company's downtown property to accommodate the fledgling petroleum industry. After wearing out several pairs of shoes negotiating between lending institutions and tenants, the young developer finally gained the financial backing he needed, and, with the added help of his father, the dream became a reality.

In 1953 Dome Petroleum became the first tenant of Alpine Management Limited, leasing 2,000 square feet of space in the new 10,000-square-foot Derrick Building. The structure was eventually sold in 1958.

The firm's next project included the development of the Alpine Building on the corner of Sixth Avenue and Sixth Street Southwest in 1959. Three houses were demolished to build this five-storey development, one of the first air-conditioned structures in the downtown core. In 1962 three stories were added to the Alpine, which had been a two-storey structure, making it one of the largest office buildings in the city at the time.

Austin Ford's son, Harry, joined the corporation in 1971. Five years later the 20-storey Ford Tower was erected adjacent to the Alpine Building. Construction of Monenco Place, a 28-storey office and retail complex, followed in 1981. This project represented the reunion of Alpine Management Corporation Ltd. and Monenco Consultants Limited, one of the company's earliest tenants.

Alpine has come a long way since 1952, and plans to continue to expand its real estate operations in Calgary as a locally owned progressive organization that incorporates the latest technology in real estate development and management.

Prior to his death in 1981, Austin Ford turned over the reins of the company to Harry, who has been Alpine Management Corporation Ltd.'s president and chief executive officer since 1978. Austin Ford's wife, Phyllis, still serves as chairman of the board.

Monenco Place, completed in 1983, was chosen in 1987 by Building Owners and Managers Association as building of the year.

BANISTER CONTINENTAL LTD.

Banister Continental Ltd. is an Edmonton-based international construction company with expertise in civil, marine, utility, industrial, building and pipeline construction.

In the exacting world of construction, clients want a company with demonstrated experience. The Banister Construction Group has experience in virtually every aspect of construction. The success of the Group is based on a sense of pride and a resolve to give every client the best value for each construction dollar.

Founded in 1948 as Ditching Contractors by Ronald K. Banister, the predecessor of today's Banister Continental Ltd. began as a subcontractor for ditching work during the Leduc oil boom. As the company improved its pipeline construction capabilities, it expanded across Canada, and in 1966 went international when it constructed a pipeline in Alaska.

Following the incorporation of Banister Continental in 1969, operations were extended to the Middle

East in 1975—and now, in its 40th year of operation, the organization has built an international reputation for reliability.

The Banister Construction Group has nine operating units: Banister Pipelines Ltd.; The Foundation Company of Canada Limited; The Jackson-Lewis Company, Limited; Cunningham-Limp (1983) Inc.; Frontier Construction Company Inc.; Cliffside Utility Contractors Ltd.; Nicholls-Radtke Ltd.; Pitts International Inc.; and Bantrel Group Engineers Ltd.

With the Canadian construction industry facing unprecedented competition, Banister Continental is confident that its widely based operations and diversification capabilities will enable it to compete successfully.

But competing successfully takes the right kind of people. And the Banister Construction Group realizes that people are its most important asset and an integral part of its strategy to achieve corporate excellence. Part of the firm's mandate attests to its philosophy: "Only through constant improvement of our skills and abilities can we offer

Ronald K. Banister, chairman, chief executive officer, and founder of Banister Continental Ltd.

the highest quality services to our clients and provide maximum benefits for our shareholders." Training is carried out in every division and at many levels, and employees are given the opportunity of advancement through achievement. Many employees have furthered their ed-

A bending crew at work on a natural gas pipeline project in Ontario for TransCanada PipeLines.

The Foundation Company of Canada built the bobsleigh and luge track in Calgary, Alberta, for the 1988 Olympic Winter Games (above).

Building superstructures is a trademark of the Banister Construction Group. The CN Tower in Toronto is a prime example (left).

ucations with the encouragement of Banister Continental management.

Complementing Banister's fair and equitable treatment of its employees lies a steadfast commitment to education. Recognizing the role the business sector can play in the success of an educational institution, Banister Continental has contributed in many ways to academic and education facilities.

One of Banister Continental's contributions to the academic sector in Edmonton was a 75th-anniversary contribution toward the faculty conference room in the new Faculty of Business building at the University of Alberta. Banister Continental believes the university is worthy of a first-class business faculty. The corporation also believes the support of the business community is essential to the development of the Faculty of Business. In 1987 the Ronald K. Banister Chair in Business was endowed jointly by Banister Continental Ltd. and the Banister family.

The history of achievements at both the University of Alberta and businesses such as Banister have been cornerstones in the growth of a city like Edmonton. And whether contributing to the growth of a city, or to the expansion of construction throughout the world, Banister Continental Ltd. will take the lead role, setting standards of perfection that will keep it at the forefront of construction and management excellence.

BANISTER

CANA LIMITED

CANA Limited, a privately owned company based in Calgary, is active in all sectors of the construction industry. Since it began in the 1940s as Burns and Dutton Concrete and Construction Company Ltd., CANA has developed into one of Canada's largest diversified construction companies, with branches in Edmonton, Vancouver, Saskatoon, and Toronto.

The firm is active in four major sectors of the construction industry: commercial construction, industrial construction, civil construction, and construction management. Commercial projects include the construction of offices, hotels, shopping centres, and institutional and recreational facilities. CANA's industrial construction jobs include plants for the mining, manufacturing, and forest products industries, as well as facilities for power generation, hydrocarbon processing, transportation, pipelines, and utilities. The firm is involved in civil construction, including roads, bridges, dams, canals, railroads, urban transit systems, water- and sewage-treatment plants, and site preparation for all sectors of the industry. Offering project management and

Canadian Occidental Petroleum Ltd.'s Mazeppa Gas Plant, High River.

construction services, CANA can guide a project from initial conception to its final completion.

A young and aggressive company, CANA is one of the industry's leaders in the field of high technology. Fully equipped computer centres and sophisticated networking make current on-line cost and scheduling information available to all projects, even in remote locations. The firm's data base is easily accessible, enabling reports and graphics to be uniquely tailored to meet a client's specifications. A wide complement of construction equipment, valued in excess of $25 million, enhances CANA's ability to move quickly and complete projects on schedule.

For more than 40 years CANA has worked to create a truly Canadian construction company capable of handling every kind and size of project, from the unique to the commonplace. Approximately 80 percent of its contract volume is achieved by competitive tender. The firm strives to maintain an even flow of construction volume from year to year, which is essential in attracting and retaining the best available tradesmen in the industry.

The company has secured numerous major contracts in Alberta. One of CANA's most challenging

The Petro-Canada Centre, Calgary.

projects was the Calgary Olympic Saddledome. Its largest was the $250-million head office building for Petro-Canada. Other recent CANA projects include the renovations to the Market Mall and Northland Mall shopping centres, the Mazeppa Gas Plant, the Western Co-Op Fertilizer Plant, the Calgary Centre for the Performing Arts, the Edmonton Convention Centre, and the Edmonton Law Courts Building.

UNITED MANAGEMENT LTD.

United Management Ltd. acquires and develops shopping centres, small and medium-size office buildings, multifamily rental projects, and subdivisions from its head office in Calgary.

Incorporated in Alberta in 1954 to consolidate the holdings of two Alberta businessmen, Jack Singer and Abraham Belzberg, United Management was established to purchase, develop, hold, and sell properties in Calgary and Edmonton. In 1969 United Management became a holding company, remaining relatively inactive in the areas of property acquisition and land development until the mid-1970s.

After a number of ownership changes, the firm assumed responsibility for the management of its own assets in 1976.

The primary objectives of this new management group were to develop a team of professional property administrators, to review the value of existing properties, to determine methods of optimizing cash flow, and to begin a program of acquisition and development of income-producing properties.

In June 1977 Alsten Holdings, owned by Jack Singer, acquired 100-percent interest of United Management. During the next few years substantial acquisitions of income properties were made, and the firm decided to diversify its real es-

tate investments into the United States.

At the same time United Management's Development Division began analyzing company-owned lands to determine their suitability for various types of development projects. By 1987 six office buildings, with a combined total of 800,000 square feet and construction costs of more than $70 million, had been completed.

United Management has a strong presence on the Alberta commercial real estate scene. The company enhanced Calgary's skyline with First Alberta Place in 1983. At a cost of $40 million, the office tower is one of the firm's most prestigious projects. Located in the heart of the city's downtown core, this 332,000-square-foot, 23-storey building is clad with imported Vetter stone and has an interior that features solid oak trim with brass inlay.

The company's properties also include Southland Court, a unique three-storey office building in a 25-acre south Calgary commercial park. As part of the same development the firm also completed a 230,000-square-foot, 13-storey office tower in 1982. This structure exemplifies United Management's commitment to quality and innovation with its sky-lit lobby area, red tile floors, tropical vegetation, and wa-

First Alberta Place

ter fountains.

United Management's residential land development projects include Edgemont and Sandstone in northwest Calgary, Christie Park in west Calgary, and the Fairways in southwest Calgary. McLeod Meadows is the company's residential land development in Edmonton.

In the retail division, United Management developed three shopping centre sites totalling 90,000 square feet of net leaseable area during 1985. In 1987 the company commenced development on six more retail sites in Calgary, Edmonton, and Vancouver totalling more than 20,000 square feet.

The firm completed construction of The Village in time for the 1988 Calgary Olympics. A 266-unit, high-profile multifamily development, The Village will be used during the Olympics to house the world's television media and will then become a luxury apartment complex.

The Village

403

NICKS FLOORING SERVICE LTD.

Nicks Flooring Service Ltd. started out as a man and wife operation in the basement of the family's northeast Calgary home. From its meagre beginnings in 1968, the company has grown to be the largest flooring contractor in Alberta with more than 100 employees.

Hardwood flooring was the main thrust of the business in the early years. When carpeting became the rage in the 1970s, Nicks became and still is a major force in the carpet industry "both commercially and residentially." The trend

tradesmen, and by supplying and installing top-quality hardwood.

Although Nicks Flooring primarily serves the Western Canadian market, the company often receives orders for its innovative multi-colored hardwood stains from as far away as New York and California. The firm site finishes oak flooring in a variety of colors and designs, including green, purple, white, and grey.

Nicks Flooring, through its subsidiary, Hardwood Flooring Importers Ltd., is also the supplier of

ceramic tile in large, custom-made homes, or in smaller dwellings that are undergoing remodification. Nicks Flooring can also incorporate a company logo or design directly into special floor or wall carpet manufactured in sections. Carpet and lino remnants and hardwood specials are also available to do-it-yourself home owners.

Nicks Flooring has participated in the development of many innovative products. In addition to multi-colored hardwood stains, the company is partially responsible for

in the residential marketplace has shifted back to wood flooring. One of the secrets to the success of the company has been an ability to adapt quickly to fluctuations in the local economy. And Nicks Flooring works hard at keeping ahead of changes in consumer taste and demand.

Calgary is known across North America as having the highest standards of hardwood flooring. Nicks Flooring has helped earn this reputation by training its own staff and

wholesale hardwood flooring materials throughout Western Canada. Flooring contractors can order hardwood materials, floor finishings, machines, sandpapers, adhesives, and other floor specialty products from Nicks.

In addition to hardwood, commercial, and retail flooring, Nicks Flooring has experience in contract housing and ceramic tile projects. The company serves the growing residential market, installing carpet, hardwood, linoleum flooring, and

Nicks Flooring serves its Western Canadian market from its offices, showroom, and warehouse facilities in Calgary.

introducing noise reducing matting to the flooring industry. Designed in conjunction with a company in North Carolina, this pliable, strong matting insulates floors, thereby obstructing the passage of sound.

Nicks sound matting is ideal for floor systems that must meet new sound rating requirements. The matting reduces noise in multiple-unit dwellings, in both wood frame and concrete slab constructions that have installed ceramic or vinyl tile, marble, wood, native stone, or carpet and pad flooring.

Nick Kulhawy also had a hand in developing a split-floor socket system, now employed in many gymnasiums and athletic facilities throughout North America. The system, ideal for floors designed to accommodate basketball, volleyball, badminton, and indoor tennis, allows the pole socket to move as the floor expands and contracts with changes in the weather.

Lindsay Park Aquatic Centre in Calgary, one of Canada's premiere indoor sporting facilities, is an example of a highly technological floor system installed by Nicks Flooring. The special floor was designed using principles of "biomechanics" to enhance athletic performance and reduce the risk of injury. The University of Calgary's extensive research into biomechanics was employed to construct the centre's floor.

Nicks Flooring has also completed flooring projects in Western Canadian shopping malls, hospitals, schools, and highrises. Local projects include the Performing Arts Centre, La Caille Restaurant, City Hall, Southcentre Leisure Centre, and Canada Place in Edmonton. The latter project called for the largest single carpet order in Alberta—12 feet by 12.6 lineal miles. The company has completed approximately 40,000 projects since its inception ranging in size from service or repair work to the largest highrises.

Nicks Flooring will continue to be a family-owned and -run business. Nick's son, Robert, is in the process of taking over the business. As a boy Robert started out emptying garbage, cleaning floors, cutting carpet, and sorting lumber and is now the vice-president of Nicks Flooring and president of Hardwood Flooring Importers. The family has ventured into the manufacturing and property rental businesses in recent years.

Nicks Flooring Service Ltd. is also involved within the community, supporting minor league baseball, church activities, hearing impaired research, and various programs designed to employ minorities.

Nicks Flooring's spacious showroom.

W.A. STEPHENSON CONSTRUCTION (WESTERN) LIMITED

W.A. Stephenson Construction (Western) Limited, an Alberta-based general contractor, was established at the peak of the Western Canadian construction boom.

Entrepreneur Paul Giannelia established Stephenson in 1977, and, together with two other principals, Dennis Semeniuk and Peter Franklin, formed a winning team. The company is owned and controlled by its key management staff.

Stephenson's first job in 1977 was a $574,000 Alberta Government Telephone Equipment Exchange building in southeast Calgary, and since that start the company has executed in excess of 100 projects. During 1987 annual sales exceeded $200 million, placing Stephenson within the top 20 general contractors in Canada. The firm is divided into several divisions, including civil engineering, institutional, industrial, and commercial construction.

The company employs in excess of 100 people, including clerical staff, engineers, project managers and superintendents, and estimators. Stephenson has worked on projects throughout Alberta and in the cities of Calgary, Edmonton,

LOWER LEFT: The Cambie Street Bridge next to the Expo 86 site in Vancouver, British Columbia.

LOWER RIGHT: The Olympic Speed Skating Oval at the University of Calgary.

Vancouver, and Seattle, and has tendered bids on jobs throughout the rest of Western Canada.

Stephenson's expertise is in civil engineering construction projects such as post-tensioned reservoirs, transit systems bridge and grade separation structures, as well as industrial plants and commercial buildings.

As a young company in pursuit of excellence and available opportunities, Stephenson has always sought young, aggressive, and innovative people. By bringing recent graduates on staff and giving them a chance to apply the new ideas they learned at school, Stephenson has been able to create an environment in which challenges become opportunities instead of stumbling blocks. This emphasis on youth and innovation has helped the firm to gain a competitive edge in recessionary times.

While Stephenson believes that the bid price on a project is extremely important, it is not enough to ensure the success of the company. The firm's most important asset is a stable pool of qualified, dedicated people who can meet the needs of a wide range of clients. As a company, Stephenson takes an innovative approach to projects and has learned to adapt quickly to ever-changing economic conditions.

In 1984 the firm won a contract

to build the Cambie Street Bridge in Vancouver on the basis of a bid package that included a contractor-proposed redesign of the bridge's superstructure. The six-lane bridge, which spanned False Creek and the Expo '86 site, was finished six months ahead of schedule, and this $52-million project was the company's most challenging at the time.

Stephenson's redesign called for a unique two-stage construction procedure of the superstructure. While each side of the bridge was being constructed, the marine spans were built on a barge. Putting the bridge together in this way allowed for marine traffic to flow through False Creek during critical Expo '86 construction. When completed, the 650-tonne, precast marine spans were hoisted into place and connected to the north and south approaches.

Canada's top construction award, the prestigious 1985 Montgomery Medal, was given to Stephenson for construction innovation on the Cambie Street Bridge. The City of Vancouver also presented the company with a Resolution of City Council commending Stephenson for applying innovative construction practices, for reducing overall costs and impacts, and for completing the project well ahead of schedule. This project recon-

Olympic Plaza—the medal presentation facility for the 1988 Olympic Winter Games in Calgary.

roof (6,000 tonnes) above the building, enabling tradesmen to work on the rest of the project at the same time. By supporting the roof system on 31 temporary towers ranging in height from 18 to 24 metres, Stephenson was able to position and connect all precast structural segments of the 90-metre by 200-metre roof prior to lowering the entire roof system into permanent position.

The $39-million project has a 400-metre speed skating track, plus two 30-metre by 60-metre Olympic skating rinks in the centre. In the summer artificial turf can be laid on the surface, creating a football field, six tennis courts, and a jogging track.

Stephenson also constructed the Olympic Plaza in downtown Calgary, the refrigeration complex, and the ski jump superstructure and ancillary buildings at Canada Olympic Park, as well as other auxiliary complexes for the 1988 Olympic Winter Games.

In addition to the various recreational projects for the 1988 Olympics, Stephenson constructed the clubhouse at Bearspaw Golf and Country Club, handicapped facilities in Kananaskis Park, the new Calgary YMCA complex, and a number of skating arenas. The company also built the entrance to the Calgary Zoo and the Australian and Nocturnal World complex.

firmed that it pays for an owner to consider and adopt a bid from a contractor who submits an alternative design guaranteed to reduce construction time, even where such bid is not necessarily the lowest bid price tendered.

In 1986 Stephenson completed a contractor-proposed alternative design/construct crossing of the Bow River in Calgary for the city's light rail transit line. This project was completed ahead of schedule

LOWER LEFT: The Refrigeration Building—Canada Olympic Park, Calgary.

LOWER RIGHT: The Young Men's Christian Association (YMCA) Building—athletic, office, and meeting facility, Calgary.

and also resulted in a 20-percent cost saving to the City of Calgary.

Stephenson specializes in constructing nontraditional projects such as the Olympic Speed Skating Oval for the 1988 Olympic Winter Games in Calgary. The firm won its second consecutive Montgomery Medal in 1986 for its construction innovations on this project. The Olympic Oval is the largest indoor, clear-span speed skating arena in the world. This represented the first time a contractor has won this award twice, let alone two years in succession.

For this award-winning project the company developed a false work system to support the entire

ABOVE LEFT: The expansion of Canada Lafarge Plant at Exshaw, Alberta.

ABOVE RIGHT: The Shell Grease Plant in Calgary.

BELOW: A section of the Advanced Light Rail Transit System (Skytrain) in Vancouver, British Columbia.

Stephenson participated in the expansion of the Canada Lafarge Plant in Exshaw, Alberta, one of the largest cement plants in Western Canada. The firm has also completed numerous contracts in the petrochemical industry.

The company has also worked on underground and ground-level transit system stations, bridges, and tunnels in Edmonton, Vancouver, and Calgary. Other Calgary transportation projects include the widening of Macleod Trail, the Glenmore Trail and 14th Street Southwest interchange, and the construction of the Carburn Park pedestrian bridge.

Commercial projects include a multistorey parkade at the University of Calgary, three- and four-story office buildings in northeast Calgary, and work for the retail industry.

Stephenson has gained experience in residential development. In 1987 the company began construction of a luxury, 141-unit senior housing facility in the Glenmore area of southwest Calgary.

Although this philosophy of looking for innovative approaches to construction projects has some built-in risks, Stephenson has the confidence in its personnel to take these risks. With technological

TOP LEFT: *The Northeast Light Rail Transit Bridge in Calgary.*

LOWER LEFT: *The Deerfoot Office Building in Calgary.*

couver and successfully executed in excess of $45 million in new contracts over the next three years. Again during 1986 the company began to penetrate the Pacific Northwest market of the United States to overcome the general downturn in construction activity in Western Canada. In the spring of 1987 Stephenson won a contract valued at roughly $70 million U.S. ($90 million Canadian) for work on a transit system in Seattle, Washington.

Stephenson has designed and initiated effective management control systems that accurately monitor all sections of the company's business on a weekly basis. The firm has completed the process of outfitting each substantial project with a complete on-site computer facility that is used for both cost control, project management, and scheduling functions.

The company is also working with the University of British Columbia on a combined research program to increase the productivity of the construction industry with the increased use of computers. The program, funded in part by the Federal Government National Science and Research Council, will keep Stephenson up to date on state-of-the-art construction management systems.

Senior management of the company has also delivered guest lectures at engineering schools in universities in Western Canada and on an ongoing basis update university professors on recent changes in the construction industry.

W.A. Stephenson Construction (Western) Limited contributes annually to various charitable agencies, and the management staff belongs to and actively participates in national, provincial, and municipal construction and engineering associations.

advances in building materials and methods, and with the entry of contractors from other cultures, the status quo of the industry is being challenged. The company believes it can stay on top of the marketplace by letting new, young people apply their knowledge without being overwhelmed by traditional ideas. This approach creates a stimulating work environment for staff, and encourages them to build a career with Stephenson.

Another key to the company's success has been its willingness to pursue alternative markets. In 1983 the construction industry in Alberta was depressed. In response to this market condition, the firm established a branch office in Van-

PATRONS

The following individuals, companies, and organizations have made a valuable commitment to the quality of this publication. Windsor Publications and the Alberta Chamber of Commerce gratefully acknowledge their participation in "Alberta: Blue Skies and Golden Opportunities."

Alberta Blue Cross*
Alberta Cancer Foundation*
Alberta Cattle Commission*
Alberta College*
Alberta Energy Company Ltd.*
Alberta Oil Sands Technology and Research Authority*
Alberta Research Council*
Alberta Stock Exchange*
Alberta Wheat Pool*
Alpine Management Corporation Ltd.*
Amoco Canada Petroleum Company Ltd.*
ATCO Ltd.*
Badger Drilling Ltd.*
Banister Continental Ltd.*
Herman J. Bell Associates Architects Inc.*
Bennett Jones*
Bow Valley Resource Services Ltd.*
BP Canada Inc.*
Burnet, Duckworth & Palmer*
Calgary Convention Centre*
Calgary Exhibition and Stampede*

Canada Northwest Energy Limited*
Canadian Utilities Limited*
CANA Limited*
Cano Structures Inc.*
CEDA-Reactor Ltd.*
Clarkson Gordon Woods Gordon*
The Cohos Evamy Partnership*
DeVry Institute of Technology*
Domtar Energy Inc.*
Dow Chemical Canada Inc.*
Edmonton Economic Development Authority*
Edmonton Power*
EDO Canada Ltd.*
Engineered Air*
Engineered Profiles Ltd.*
Erskine Resources Corporation*
Esso Resources Canada Limited*
Fekete Associates Inc.*
First Calgary Financial Savings and Credit Union Ltd.*
First Medical Management Ltd./Med+Stop*
Foothills Medical Centre*
General Motors of Canada Limited*
Gilbey Canada Inc.*
Government of Alberta*
Graham McCourt*
Gulf Canada Resources Limited*
Homestead Antiques*
Husky Oil Ltd.*
Interprovincial Pipe Line Limited*
ITT Barton Instruments A Division of ITT Industries

of Canada Ltd.*
Jager Industries Inc.*
Ken & Ardis Kary
Labatt's Prairie Region*
Lep International Inc.*
McLennan Ross*
Mark's Work Wearhouse*
Nicks Flooring Service Ltd.*
NOVA Corporation of Alberta*
Mrs. Jennie F.E. Oakey
Pan-Alberta Gas Ltd.*
Pancontinental Oil Ltd.*
Ponoko & District Chamber of Commerce
ProGas Limited*
Ramada Renaissance Hotel*
Scepter Manufacturing*
Shell Canada Limited*
Short Grass Ranches, Ltd.
Sinclair Supplies Inc.*
Southern Alberta Institute of Technology*
Speedy Gunsolley's Hot Shot Service Ltd.
Standen's Limited*
W.A. Stephenson Construction (Western) Limited*
Thorne Ernst & Whinney*
Time Air*
Total Petroleum Canada Ltd.*
TransAlta Utilities*
United Farmers of Alberta Co-operative Limited*
United Management Ltd.*
Gerard Violette
Western Atlas Canada Ltd.*

*Partners in Progress of "Alberta: Blue Skies and Golden Opportunities." The stories of these companies and organizations appear in chapters 7 through 14.

SELECT BIBLIOGRAPHY

Alberta. Advanced Education. *Annual Report,* 1985-86. Culture. Ethno-Cultural Groups in Alberta. *Profiles,* n.d. Economic Development and Trade. *Alberta Electronics Directory,* n.d. Economic Development and Trade. *Alberta Industry and Resources 1986 Data Base,* 1987. Economic Development and Trade. *International Trade: Alberta Export Performance 1985,* 1986. Education. *Annual Report,* 1985-86. Hospitals and Medical Care. *Alberta Health Care Insurance Plan Statistical Supplement,* 1985-86. *Annual Report,* 1985-86. Municipal Affairs. *Annual Report,* 1985-86. Office of the Ombudsman. *Annual Report to the Legislative Assembly,* 1986. Treasury, Bureau of Statistics. *Alberta Statistical Review,* 2nd quarter, 1987.

Alberta Heritage Savings Trust Fund. *Annual Report,* 1986-87.

Alberta Office of Coal Research & Technology. *Annual Review,* 1985-86.

Alberta Oil Sands Technology and Research Authority. *Annual Report,* 1986. *Ten Year Review,* n.d.

Alberta Research Council. *Annual Report,* 1986.

Canada. Labour Canada. *Collective Bargaining Review,* September, 1987. Statistics Canada. *1981 Census, 1986 Census,* various bulletins.

Conway, J.F. *The West: The History of a Region in Confederation.* Toronto: J. Lorimer, 1983.

Hardy, W G., ed. *Alberta: A Natural History.* Edmonton: Hurtig, 1967.

Hocking, Anthony. *Alberta.* Toronto: McGraw-Hill Ryerson, 1979.

Lower, J. Arthur. *Western Canada: An Outline History.* Vancouver: Douglas & McIntyre, 1983.

MacGregor, James G. *A History of Alberta.* Rev. Ed. Edmonton: Hurtig, 1981.

Marsh, James H., ed. *The Canadian Encyclopedia.* Edmonton: Hurtig, 1985.

INDEX

GENERAL INDEX
Italicized numbers indicate
illustrations